SCHAUM'S OUTLINE OF

THEORY AND PROBLEMS

of

PROGRAMMING
WITH
C++

•

JOHN R. HUBBARD, Ph.D.

Professor of Mathematics and Computer Science
University of Richmond

•

SCHAUM'S OUTLINE SERIES

McGRAW-HILL

New York   St. Louis   San Francisco   Auckland   Bogota'   Caracas
Lisbon   London   Madrid   Mexico City   Milan   Montreal
New Delhi   San Juan   Singapore   Sydney   Tokyo   Toronto

JOHN R. HUBBARD is Professor of Mathematics and Computer Science at the University of Richmond. He received his Ph.D. from The University of Michigan (1973) and has been a member of the Richmond faculty since 1983. His primary interests are in numerical algorithms and database systems. Dr. Hubbard is the author of several other books, including *A Gentle Introduction to the VAX System* and *The VAX Book*.

Schaum's Outline of Theory and Problems of

PROGRAMMING WITH C++

2 3 4 5 6 7 8 9 10 11 12 13 14 15 16 17 18 19 20   PRS   PRS   9 0 1 0 9 8 7 6

ISBN 0-07-030837-3

Sponsoring Editors: John Aliano and Arthur Biderman
Production Supervisor: Donald F. Schmidt
Editing Supervisor: Maureen Walker

Library of Congress Cataloging-in-Publication Data

Hubbard, J. R. (John Rast), date
   Schaum's outline of theory and problems of programming with C++ /
John Hubbard.
      p.   cm. − − (Schaum's outline series)
   Includes index.
   ISBN 0-07-030837-3
   1. C++ (Computer program language)   I. Title.
QA76.76.C15H835 1996
005.13'3 − − dc20   96-13964
                                                CIP

McGraw-Hill

A Division of The **McGraw·Hill** *Companies*

Preface

Like all Schaum's Outline Series books, this is intended to be used primarily for self study, preferably in conjunction with a regular course in C++ Programming. The book covers nearly all aspects of ANSI/ISO Standard C++. It includes over 200 examples and solved problems. The author firmly believes that programming is best learned by practice, following a well-constructed collection of examples with complete explanations. This book is designed to provide that support.

C++ was created by Bjarne Stroustrup in the 1980s. Based upon C and Simula, it has become the most popular language for object-oriented programming. The final ANSI/ISO Standard was just recently completed, so some of the standard features described in this book may not yet be available on all compilers. In particular, the powerful Standard Template Library is just now becoming available from some vendors.

Although most people who undertake to learn C++ have already had some previous programming experience, this book assumes none. It approaches C++ as one's first programming language. Therefore, those who have had previous experience may need only skim the first few chapters.

C++ is a difficult language for at least two reasons. It inherits from the C language an economy of expression that novices often find cryptic. And as an object-oriented language, its widespread use of classes and templates presents a formidable challenge to those who have not thought in those terms before. It is the intent of this book to provide the assistance necessary for first-time programmers to overcome these obstacles.

Readers may download the source code for the examples and solved problems in this book from the author's World Wide Web home page: `http://www.richmond.edu/~hubbard/`

I wish to thank all my friends, colleagues, students, and McGraw-Hill staff who have helped me with the critical review of this manuscript, including John Aliano, Arthur Biderman, Peter Dailey, Chris Hanes, Walker Holt, John B. Hubbard, Arni Sigurjonsson, Andrew Somers, Maureen Walker, and Nat Withers. Their debugging skills are gratefully appreciated.

Finally I wish to express my gratitude to my wife and colleague, Anita Hubbard, who reviewed the complete manuscript and worked through most of the problems, including many that she contributed herself. I am greatly in her debt.

JOHN R. HUBBARD
Richmond, Virginia

Dedicated to
Anita H. Hubbard

Contents

Chapter 1

Introduction to Programming in C++

A *program* is a sequence of instructions for a computer to execute. Every program is written in some programming language. The C++ (pronounced "see-plus-plus") language is one of the newest and most powerful programming languages available. It allows the programmer to write efficient, structured, object-oriented programs.

This chapter introduces some of the basic features of C++. You should compile and run each example in this chapter.

1.1 SIMPLE PROGRAMS

Our first example illustrates the main parts of a C++ program.

EXAMPLE 1.1 The Hello World Program

```cpp
#include <iostream.h>
// This program prints "Hello, World."
main()
{
    cout << "Hello, World.\n";
    return 0;
}
```

The `#include` directive on the first line is necessary for the program to have output. It refers to an external file named `iostream.h` where information about the `cout` object is provided. Note that the angle brackets `<` and `>` are not part of the file name; they are used to indicate that this is a Standard C++ Library file.

The second line is a *comment*, identified by the double slashes `//`. Comments are included in programs to provide explanations for human readers. They are ignored by the compiler.

The third line contains the function header `main()`. This is required for every C++ program. It tells the compiler where the program begins. The parentheses `()` following `main` are also required.

The fourth and seventh lines contain only the braces `{` and `}`. These enclose the body of the `main()` function and are also required for every C++ program.

The fifth line contains the statement

```cpp
    cout << "Hello, World.\n";
```

This tells the system to send the message `"Hello, World.\n"` to the `cout` ("see-out") object. That object is the *standard output stream* which usually represents the computer display screen. The name `cout` stands for "console output." The output should look like this:

```
Hello, World.
```

1

The $\backslash$n symbol is the *newline* symbol. Note that this single symbol is formed from the two characters '$\backslash$' and 'n'. Putting this symbol at the end of the quoted string tells the system to begin a new line after printing the preceding characters, thus ending the current line.

The sixth line contains the statement return 0. That terminates the execution of the program and returns control to the computer's operating system. The number 0 is used to signal that the program has ended successfully.

The output statement on the fifth line includes several common C++ symbols. The symbol << is called the *output operator* or the *insertion operator*. It inserts the message into the output stream. The symbol $\backslash$n included at the end of the message stands for the *newline character*. Whenever it appears in an output message, it causes the current line of output to be terminated, thereby starting a new line. Note that both of these symbols (<< and $\backslash$n) require two characters, side-by-side, with no space between them.

Note the semicolon ; at the ends of the fifth and sixth lines. C++ requires every statement to end with a semicolon. It need not be at the end of a line. We may put several statements on the same line, and we may have one statement extend over several lines. But no matter how it is positioned on one or more lines, every statement must end with a semicolon.

We can imagine the relationship of the cout object to the program and the display screen like this:

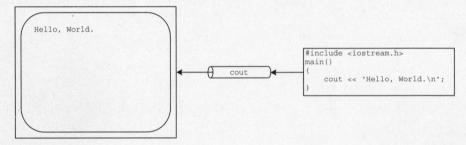

The output stream cout acts as a conduit, piping the output from the program to the display screen (or printer or other output device), byte by byte.

The program in Example 1.1 is not minimal. Only some of its parts are required for every program. In fact, a C++ program need not have any statements. Of course, such an "empty program" will not do anything. The next example shows the shortest possible C++ program.

EXAMPLE 1.2 The Shortest C++ Program

```
main() {}
```

This "empty program" does nothing. It simply reveals the required skeleton for every C++ program.

The return 0; statement is not required by most compilers. Some compilers will issue a warning if it is omitted. We include it in each example in this first chapter.

It is also recommended that you include at the beginning of every program a brief comment that describes what the program does.

1.2 THE OUTPUT OPERATOR

The symbol `<<` is called the *insertion operator* or the *output operator*. It inserts objects into the output stream named on its left. We usually use the `cout` output stream, which ordinarily refers to the computer screen. So `cout << 66` would display the number 66 on the screen.

An *operator* is something that performs an action on one or more objects. The output operator `<<` performs the action of sending the value of the expression listed on its right to the output stream listed on its left. Since the direction of this action appears to be from right to left, the symbol `<<` was chosen to represent it. It should remind you of an arrow pointing to the left.

The reason `cout` is called a *stream* is that output sent to it flows like a stream. If several things are sent to `cout`, they fall in line, one after the other as they are dropped into the stream. Then they are displayed on the screen in that order.

EXAMPLE 1.3 The Hello World Program Again

This version of our Hello World program has the same output as the other:

```
#include <iostream.h>
// This program illustrates the sequential ouput of several strings.
main()
{
    cout << "Hello, " << "Wor" << "ld.\n";
    return 0;
}
```
```
Hello, World.
```

Here the message has been split into three pieces. As the line is executed from left to right, each piece is dropped into the output stream: first `"Hello, "`, then `"Wor"`, and finally `"ld.\n"`. Since there are no newline characters or other symbols added to the stream between these three pieces, they all come out concatenated into a single line, just as before.

The output stream `cout` is usually used with the insertion operator `<<` in this general form:

```
cout << expression << expression << . . . << expression;
```

This syntax statement says that `cout` is followed by one or more pairs, where each pair consists of the insertion operator `<<` followed by some *expression*. In Example 1.3, there are three such pairs.

1.3 CHARACTERS AND STRING LITERALS

The symbol `"Hello, "` is called a *string literal*. It consists of a sequence of characters delimited by quotation marks.

A *character* is any member of a predefined character set or alphabet. Most computers these days use the ASCII (American Standard Code for Information Interchange) character set. See Appendix A for the complete code. This set includes the 52 uppercase and lowercase letters of the alphabet, the 10 digits, all the punctuation symbols found on your keyboard, and some nonprinting characters.

The *newline character* '\n' is one of the nonprinting characters. It is formed using the backslash \ and the letter n. There are several other characters formed this way, including the *horizontal tab* character '\t' that moves to the next tab stop on the line the *alert character* '\a' that produces the system beep when printed. The backslash is also used to denote the two printing characters that could not otherwise be used within a string literal: the *quote character* \" and the *backslash character* itself \\.

Characters can be used in a program statement as part of a string literal, or as individual objects. When used individually, they must appear as character constants. A *character constant* is a character enclosed in single quotes. As individual objects, character constants can be output the same way string literals are.

EXAMPLE 1.4 Another Version of the Hello World Program

This version of our Hello World program has the same output as the other versions:

```
#include <iostream.h>
// This program illustrates the ouput of strings and characters:
main()
{
    cout << "Hello, " << 'W' << 'o' << "r" << "ld" << '.' << '\n';
    return 0;
}
```

```
Hello, World.
```

The single statement in this program sends seven objects to cout: the 2 string literals "Hello and "ld", and the 5 character constants 'W', 'o', 'r', '.', and '\n'.

Of course, an individual character can also be used to form a string. The single statement above could be replaced by

```
cout << "Hello, " << "W" << "o" << "r" << "ld" << "." << "\n";
```

This statement sends 7 string literals to cout. But when dealing with individual characters as separate objects, it is more efficient to use character constants. String literals are stored differently and require some overhead.

The string that contains zero characters is called the *empty string* and is denoted by "". We could print our message using the empty string, like this:

```
cout << "Hello, Wo" << "" << "rl" << "" << "" << "d.\n";
```

But there's not much point in using the empty string this way.

1.4 STRING LENGTH

The *length* of a string literal is the number of characters it contain. The string literal "ABCDE" has length 5.

C++ provides a special predefined function named strlen() that you can use to obtain the length of any string. This is illustrated by the next example.

EXAMPLE 1.5

This program prints the lengths of several string literals:

```
#include <iostream.h>
#include <string.h>
// This program tests the strlen() function:
main()
{
    cout << strlen("Hello, World.\n") << '\n';
    cout << strlen("Hello, World.") << '\n';
    cout << strlen("Hello, ") << '\n';
    cout << strlen("H") << '\n';
    cout << strlen("") << '\n';
    return 0;
}
```

```
14
13
7
1
0
```

The `strlen()` function simply counts the number of characters in the specified string. The first two outputs, 14 and 13, reveal that the *newline character* `\n` counts as a single character. The string `"Hello, "` has length 7, the string `"H"` has length 1, and the *empty string* `""` has length 0.

The `strlen()` function (pronounced "stir-len") is declared in the separate file `string.h` which comes with the C++ programming environment. So when your program needs to use the `strlen()` function it should include the `#include` directive

```
#include <string.h>
```

on a line somewhere above the `main()` program block.

1.5 COMMENTS

You can include messages in your program that will be ignored by the compiler. Such a message, intended only to be read by humans, is called a *comment*.

There are two kinds of comments in C++. The *Standard C comment* begins with the combination slash-star symbol `/*` and ends with the star-slash symbol `*/`. Anything written between these two symbols will be ignored by the compiler. For example, this is a comment:

```
/* This is a C style comment */
```

The *Standard C++ comment* begins with a double-slash `//` and extends to the end of the line. For example, this is a comment:

```
// This is a C++ style comment
```

Most C++ programmers prefer to use the double-slash form because it is easier to write and easier to notice in a program. The C style comment is necessary if you need to imbed a comment within an executable line of code, but that practice that is not recommended.

EXAMPLE 1.6 Using The Two Types of Comments

Here is our Hello World program with six comments added:

```
/*****************************************************************\
 *  Program to demonstrate comments                              *
 *  Written by J. R. Hubbard                                     *
 *  June 10, 1996                                                *
 *  Version 1.5                                                  *
\*****************************************************************/
#include <iostream.h>        // This directive is needed to use cout
//  This prints message: "Hello, World.":
main()
{
    cout <<  /* now printing */  "Hello, World.\n";  /* change? */
    return 0;  // Some compilers will complain if you omit this line
}   /* end of program */
```

Hello, World.

This is a good example of an "overly documented" program. But it does illustrate some of the main uses of comments.

The first comment is a 6-line header that identifies the program and programmer. Notice that the first two characters (at the beginning of line 1) are the slash-star /* and the last two characters on line 6 are the star-slash */. The second comment begins with the double-slash on line 7. It illustrates a standard in-line comment, positioned to the right of the statement that it describes. The third comment occupies all of line 8. It precedes the main() block and briefly describes what the program does. The fourth comment is imbedded inside the output statement. This is <u>not</u> recommended. The fifth comment is at the end of the output statement. It illustrates a common technique of software maintenance: the programmer leaves a message to himself to suggest a possible modification at a later date. The sixth comment, at the end of the program, has little value.

The next example shows our "Hello, World." program with only C++-style comments:

EXAMPLE 1.7 Using Only Double-Slash Comments

This version shows how all the important comments are easily written using the double-slash:

```
//-----------------------------------------------------------------
//  Program to demonstrate comments
//  Written by J. R. Hubbard
//  June 11, 1996
//  Version 1.6
//-----------------------------------------------------------------
#include <iostream.h>        // This directive is needed to use cout
//  Prints message: "Hello, World.":
main()
{
    cout << "Hello, World.\n";  // change?
    return 0;  // Some compilers will complain if you omit this line
}
```

Note that comments delimited by the double-slash extend only to the end of the line; they cannot span several lines unless each line begins with another double-slash.

1.6 VARIABLES, OBJECTS, AND THEIR DECLARATIONS

A *variable* is a symbol that represents a storage location in the computer's memory. The information that is stored in that location is called the *value* of the variable. The most common way that a variable obtains a value is by means of an assignment. This has the syntax

```
variable = expression;
```

The `expression` is first evaluated, and then its resulting value is assigned to the `variable`. The equals sign "`=`" is the *assignment operator* in C++.

EXAMPLE 1.8

Here is a simple C++ program with an integer variable named `n`:

```
#include <iostream.h>
//  A simple example to illustrate assignment:
main()
{
    int n;
    n = 66;
    cout << n << endl;
    return 0;
}
```

```
66
```

The first line between the braces `{ }` declares `n` to be a variable of type `int`. The statement in the second line assigns the value 66 to `n`. The statement on the third line prints the value of `n`.

Note the use of the symbolic constant `endl`. This is a predefined iostream manipulator. Sending this to `cout` is equivalent to the *endline character* `'\n'` and then "flushing" the output buffer.

In the previous example, the variable `n` has the value 66. That value is actually stored in the computer's memory as a sequence of *bits* (0s and 1s). The computer interprets that sequence of bits as an integer because the variable was declared to be an integer.

A *declaration* of a variable is a statement that gives information about the variable to the C++ compiler. Its syntax is

```
type variable;
```

where `type` is the name of some C++ type. For example, the declaration

```
int n;
```

tells the compiler two things: (1) the name of the variable is `n`, and (2) the variable has type `int`. Every variable must have a type. Its *type* tells the compiler how the variable's values are to be stored and used. We can characterize a type by the set of all possible values that could be assigned to a variable of that type. On some computers, the `int` type set consists of all the integers in the range from −32,768 to 32,767.

C++ is an *object-oriented programming language*. Among other things, this means that the language is good at simulating systems that consist of interacting objects such as an airport control system. In such a simulation, the objects in the system (airplanes, people, luggage, *etc.*)

are represented by variables in the computer program. So variables are often referred to as objects themselves and are visualized as self-contained entities endowed with certain capabilities. In this context we say that the declaration *creates the object*. The variable being declared then is the name of the object.

We can visualize the effect of the declaration `int n` like this:

$$n \boxed{\text{??}}$$
$$\text{int}$$

The declaration creates the object shown here. Its name is `n` and its type is `int`. The shaded box represents that area of memory that has been allocated to the object to store its value. The question marks indicate that no value has been given to the object yet.

An assignment is one way that an object's value can be changed. For example,

```
    n = 66;
```

changes the value of `n` to 66. We can visualize the effect of this assignment as

$$n \boxed{66}$$
$$\text{int}$$

In C++, a declaration may appear anywhere within the program, as the next example shows.

EXAMPLE 1.9

This example shows that a variable may be declared anywhere in a C++ program:

```
#include <iostream.h>
// This program illustrates variable declarations:
main()
{
    int x, y1;    // declares the variables x and y1
    x = 77;
    y1 = 88;
    int y2 = 55;  // declares the variable y2, initializing it to 55
    cout << x << ", " << y1 << ", " << y2 << endl;
    return 0;
}
```

```
77, 88, 55
```

The variable `y2` is declared and initialized after the assignment for `y1`. We can visualize these three objects like this:

$$x \boxed{77} \qquad y1 \boxed{88} \qquad y2 \boxed{55}$$
$$\text{int} \qquad\qquad \text{int} \qquad\qquad \text{int}$$

Note that a variable cannot be used before it is declared.

In this book, we use **boldface** in a program to emphasize the part(s) of the program that are being illustrated by the example. When you copy the program to run it, ignore the boldface.

The last example also shows how more than one variable may be declared within the same declaration statement. The statement

```
    int x, y1;
```

declares both x and y1 to be integer variables. In general, any number of variables may be declared within the same declaration statement, if they are all declared to have the same type. The more general syntax is

```
type var1, var2, …, varN;
```

The variables are simply listed after their type. Commas separate the variables in the list.

1.7 KEYWORDS AND IDENTIFIERS

In any programming language, a program is made up of individual syntactic elements, called *tokens*. These include variable names, constants, keywords, operators, and punctuation marks.

EXAMPLE 1.10

```
#include <iostream.h>
// A simple program to illustrate tokens:
main()
{
    int n = 66;
    cout << n << endl;
    return 0;
}
```

```
66
```

This program shows 15 tokens: main, (,), {, int, n, =, 66, ;, cout, <<, endl, return, 0, and }. The token n is a variable; the tokens 66, 0, and endl are constants; the tokens int and return are keywords; tokens = and << are operators; the tokens (,), {, ;, and } are punctuation marks. The first two lines, containing a preprocesser directive and a comment, are not really part of the program.

Keywords are also called *reserved words* because they are words that are reserved by the language for special purposes and cannot be redefined for use as variables or for any other purpose.

An *identifier* is a string of alphanumeric characters that begins with an alphabetic character. There are 53 alphabetic characters: the 52 letters and the underscore character _. There are 63 alphanumeric characters: the 53 alphabetic characters and the 10 digits (0, 1, 2, ... , 9). So main(), int, n, count, and endl are identifiers. So are Stack, x1, y4, LastName, and the_day_after_tomorrow. Note that C++ is *case-sensitive*: it distinguishes uppercase letters from lowercase letters, so Stack and stack are different identifiers.

Identifiers are used to name things, like variables and functions. In the program above, main is the name of a function, int is the name of a type, n and cout are names of variables, and endl is the name of a constant. Some identifiers like int are called keywords because they are an intrinsic part of the programming language itself. (The 48 keywords that define the C++ programming language are shown in Appendix B.) Other identifiers like n are defined in the program itself.

1.8 INITIALIZING IN THE DECLARATION

A variable is *initialized* by assigning it a value when it is declared.

EXAMPLE 1.11 Initializing Variables

This simple program illustrates two ways that a variable can be initialized within its declaration:

```
#include <iostream.h>
// This shows how to initialize variable as they are declared:
main()
{
    int george = 44;
    int martha = 33;
    int sum = george + martha;
    cout << george << " + " << martha << " = " << sum << endl;
    return 0;
}
```
```
44 + 33 = 77
```

The variables `george` and `martha` are initialized to 44 and 33 within their declarations. Then within the declaration of the variable `sum`, the expression `george + martha` is evaluated as 44 + 33, and the resulting value 77 is assigned to `sum`.

An initialization is nearly the same as an assignment. Both use the equal sign "=" followed by an expression. The expression is first evaluated, and then its value is assigned to the object on the left of the assignment operator.

In general, it is better to initialize variables when they are declared.

Initialization may also be used in compound declarations, as the next example shows.

EXAMPLE 1.12   Initializing Variables

```
#include <iostream.h>
// This shows how to initialize variables as they are declared:
main()
{
    int n1, n2 = 55, n3, n4, n5 = 44, n6;
    cout << n2 << ", " << n5 << endl;
    return 0;
}
```
```
55, 44
```

The six variables `n1` through `n6` are all declared to have type `int`, but only the two variables `n2` and `n5` are initialized.

Some compilers (Borland C++, for example) will issue a warning if any variables are not initialized.

1.9 CHAINED ASSIGNMENTS

An assignment itself is an expression with a value. The value of the expression

```
x = 22
```

is 22. And like any other value, the value of an assignment can be used in another assignment:

```
y = (x = 22);
```

This is a *chained assignment*. First it assigns 22 to x, and then it assigns 22 to y. Compound assignments are usually written without the parentheses:

```
y = x = 22;
```

In general, the value of an assignment is the last value that it assigned.

EXAMPLE 1.13 Embedded Assignments

This shows how an assignment can be used within an expression:

```
#include <iostream.h>
// This shows that an assignment can be part of a larger expression:
main()
{
    int m, n;
    m = (n = 66) + 9;  // (n = 66) is an assignment expression
    cout << m << ", " << n << endl;
    return 0;
}
```

```
75, 66
```

The compound assignment first assigns the value 66 to n. Then it evaluates the expression (n = 66) + 9 obtaining the value 75. Then it assigns that value to m.

Embedded assignments can usually be avoided. For example, the first two lines in the program above would be better written as

```
int n = 66;
int m = n + 9;
```

This also illustrates the preferred practice of initializing variables as they are declared.

There are some situations in which embedded assignments do make a program more readable. For example, this single statement is better than 8 separate statements:

```
n1 = n2 = n3 = n4 = n5 = n6 = n7 = n8 = 65535;
```

We will see other common examples of embedded assignments in Chapter 3.

A chained assignment cannot be used as an initialization in a declaration:

```
int x = y = 22; // ERROR
```

The reason this is wrong is that initializations are not assignments. They are similar, but the compiler handles them differently. The correct way to do what was attempted above is

```
int x = 22, y = 22; // OK
```

1.10 THE SEMICOLON

In C++, the semicolon is used as a *statement terminator*. Every statement must end with a semicolon. This is different from other languages, notably Pascal, which use the semicolon as a statement separator. Note that lines that begin with the pound symbol # such as

```
#include <iostream.h>
```

do not end with a semicolon because they are not statements; they are preprocessing directives.

We saw in the previous section that C++ statements can be interpreted as expressions. The converse is also true: expressions can be used as stand-alone statements. For example, here are two perfectly valid C++ statements:

```
x + y;
22;
```

These statements perform no actions, so they are completely useless. Nevertheless they are valid statements in C++. We shall see some useful expression statements later.

The semicolon acts like an operator on an expression. It transforms an expression into a statement. It is not a true operator because its result is a statement, not a value. But this transformational point of view helps explain the difference between an expression and a statement.

1.11 PROGRAM STYLE

The C++ programming language is a *free form* language: it has no requirements about where program elements must be placed on the line or on the page. Consequently the programmer has complete freedom of program style. But experienced programmers know that the tasks of writing, debugging, and maintaining successful software are greatly facilitated by using a consistent, readable programming style. Moreover, others will find your programs easier to read if you conform to standard style conventions. Here are some simple rules that most C++ programmers follow:

- Put all your `#include` directives at the beginning of your file.
- Put each statement on a new line.
- Indent all statements within a block.
- Leave a space on either side of an operator, like this: `n = 4`.

These rules are followed nearly everywhere in this book.

Another worthwhile convention to follow is to choose your variable names carefully. Use short names to minimize the chances for typographical errors. But also pick names that describe what the variable represents. This is called *self-documenting code*. Nearly all C++ programmers follow the convention of using exclusively lowercase letters in variable names, except when a name is composed of several words where the first letter of each appended word is capitalized. For example:

```
char middleInitial;
unsigned maxUnsignedInt;
```

These names are easier to read than `middleinitial` and `maxunsignedint`. As an alternative, some programmers use a underscore to simulate blanks, like this:

```
char middle_initial;
unsigned max_unsigned_int;
```

1.12 INTEGER TYPES

An *integer* is a whole number: 0, 1, –1, 2, –2, 3, –3, *etc.* An *unsigned integer* is an integer that is not negative: 0, 1, 2, 3, *etc.* C++ has the following nine integer types:

```
char                short int           unsigned short int
signed char         int                 unsigned int
unsigned char       long int            unsigned long int
```

The differences between these nine types is the range of values that they allow. These ranges depend, to some extent, upon the computer system being used. For example on most DOS PCs, `int` ranges between the values –32,768 and 32,767, while on most UNIX workstations it ranges between the values –2,147,483,648 and 2,147,483,647. The "int" part may be omitted from the type names `short int`, `long int`, `unsigned short int`, `unsigned int`, and `unsigned long int`.

The program in the example below prints the ranges of all the integer types on your machine. These limits, named `SCHAR_MIN`, `LONG_MAX`, *etc.*, are constants stored in the header file `<limits.h>`, so the following preprocessor directive

```
#include <limits.h>
```

is needed to read them.

EXAMPLE 1.14 Integer Type Ranges

This program prints the limits to the ranges of the various integer types:

```
#include <iostream.h>
#include <limits.h>

//  Prints the constants stored in limits.h:
main()
{
    cout << "minimum char = " << CHAR_MIN << endl;
    cout << "maximum char = " << CHAR_MAX << endl;
    cout << "minimum short = " << SHRT_MIN << endl;
    cout << "maximum short = " << SHRT_MAX << endl;
    cout << "minimum int = " << INT_MIN << endl;
    cout << "maximum int = " << INT_MAX << endl;
    cout << "minimum long = " << LONG_MIN << endl;
    cout << "maximum long = " << LONG_MAX << endl;
    cout << "minimum signed char = " << SCHAR_MIN << endl;
    cout << "maximum signed char = " << SCHAR_MAX << endl;
    cout << "maximum unsigned char = " << UCHAR_MAX << endl;
    cout << "maximum unsigned short = " << USHRT_MAX << endl;
    cout << "maximum unsigned = " << UINT_MAX << endl;
    cout << "maximum unsigned long = " << ULONG_MAX << endl;
    return 0;
}
```

```
minimum char = -128
maximum char = 127
minimum short = -32768
maximum short = 32767
minimum int = -2147483648
maximum int = 2147483647
minimum long = -2147483648
maximum long = 2147483647
minimum signed char = -128
maximum signed char = 127
maximum unsigned char = 255
maximum unsigned short = 65535
maximum unsigned = 4294967295
maximum unsigned long = 4294967295
```

This output is from a UNIX workstation. It shows that, on this system, there are really only six distinct integer types:

`char`	range −128 to 127 (1 byte)
`short`	range −32,768 to 32,767 (2 bytes)
`int`	range −2,147,483,648 to 2,147,483,647 (4 bytes)
`unsigned char`	range 0 to 255 (1 byte)
`unsigned short`	range 0 to 65,535 (2 bytes)
`unsigned`	range 0 to 4,294,967,295 (4 bytes)

You can tell, for example, that `short` integers occupy 2 bytes (16 bits) on this machine, because the range 32,768 to 32,767 covers $65,536 = 2^{16}$ possible values. (Recall that a *byte* is 8 bits, the standard storage unit for characters.)

On a PC running Borland C++, this program produces the same ranges except for `int` and `unsigned` which have

`int`	range −32,768 to 32,767 (2 bytes)
`unsigned`	range 0 to 65,535 (2 bytes)

1.13 SIMPLE ARITHMETIC OPERATORS

An *operator* is a symbol that "operates" on one or more expressions, producing a value that can be assigned to a variable. We have already encountered the output operator `<<` and the assignment operator `=`.

Some of the simplest operators are the operators that do arithmetic: `+`, `-`, `*`, `/`, and `%`. These operate on integer types to produce another integer type: `m + n` produces the sum `m` plus `n`, `m - n` produces the difference `m` minus `n`, `-n` produces the negation of `n`, `m*n` produces the product `m` times `n`, `m/n` produces the integer quotient when `m` is divided by `n`, and `m%n` produces the integer remainder when `m` is divided by `n`. These six operators are summarized in the following table and illustrated in the example below.

Table 1.1 Integer Arithmetic Operators

Operator	Description	Example
+	Add	m + n
-	Subtract	m - n
-	Negate	-n
*	Multiply	m*n
/	Divide	m/n
%	Remainder	m%n

EXAMPLE 1.15 Integer Operators

This program illustrates the use of the six arithmetic operators:

```cpp
#include <iostream.h>
// Tests arithmetic operators:
main()
{
    int m = 38, n = 5;
    cout << m << " + " << n << " = " << (m + n) << endl;
    cout << m << " - " << n << " = " << (m - n) << endl;
    cout <<        " -" << n << " = " << (-n)    << endl;
    cout << m << " * " << n << " = " << (m * n) << endl;
    cout << m << " / " << n << " = " << (m / n) << endl;
    cout << m << " % " << n << " = " << (m % n) << endl;
    return 0;
}
```

```
38 + 5 = 43
38 - 5 = 33
   - 5 = -5
38 * 5 = 190
38 / 5 = 7
38 % 5 = 3
```

Note that $38/5 = 7$ and $38\%5 = 3$. These two operations together provide complete information about the ordinary division of 38 by 5: $38 \div 5 = 7.6$. The resulting integer part is $35 \div 5 = 7$, and the fractional part is $3 \div 5 = 0.6$. The integer quotient 7 and the integer remainder 3 can be recombined with the dividend 38 and the divisor 5 in the following relation: $7 \times 5 + 3 = 38$.

The integer quotient and remainder operators are more complicated if the integers are not positive. Of course, the divisor should never be zero. But if either m or n is negative, then m/n and m%n may give different results on different machines. The only requirement is that

    q*n + r == m

where $q = m/n$ and $r = m\%n$.

For example, –14 divided by 5 is –2.8. For the integer quotient, this could be rounded to –3 or to –2. If your computer rounds the quotient q to –3, then the integer remainder r will be 1. But if your computer rounds q to –2, then r will be –4.

EXAMPLE 1.16 Division with Negative Integers

This program is used to determine how the computer handles the division of negative integers:

```
#include <iostream.h>
// Tests quotient and remainder operators:
main()
{
    int m = -14, n = 5, q = m/n, r = m%n;
    cout << "m = " << m << endl;
    cout << "n = " << n << endl;
    cout << "q = " << q << endl;
    cout << "r = " << r << endl;
    cout << "q*n + r = " << "(" << q << ")*(" << n << ") + "
         << r << " = " << q*n + r << " = " << m << endl;
    return 0;
}
```

```
m = -14
n = 5
q = -2
r = -4
q*n + r = (-2)*(5) + -4 = -14 = -14
```

This shows the same results both from a UNIX workstation using a Motorola 68040 processor and from a DOS PC using an Intel Pentium processor.

1.14 OPERATOR PRECEDENCE AND ASSOCIATIVITY

C++ has a rich repertoire of operators. (Appendix C lists all 55 of them.) Since an expression may include several operators, it is important to know in what order the evaluations of the operators occurs. We are already familiar with the precedence of ordinary arithmetic operators: the `*`, `/`, and `%` operators have higher precedence than the `+` and `-` operators; *i.e.*, they are evaluated first. For example,

```
42 - 3*5
```

is evaluated as

```
42 - (3*5) = 42 - 15 = 27
```

Moreover, all the arithmetic operators have higher precedence than the assignment and output operators. For example, the statement

```
n = 42 - 3*5;
```

will assign the value 27 to `n`. First the operator `*` is invoked to evaluate `3*5`, then the operator `-` is invoked to evaluate `42 - 15`, and then the operator `=` is invoked to assign `27` to `n`.

Here is part of Table C.1 in Appendix C.

Table 1.2 Some C++ Operators

Operator	Description	Precedence	Associativity	Arity	Example
-	Negate	15	Right	Unary	`-n`
*	Multiply	13	Left	Binary	`m*n`
/	Divide	13	Left	Binary	`m/n`
%	Remainder, modulo	13	Left	Binary	`m%n`
+	Add	12	Left	Binary	`m + n`
-	Subtract	12	Left	Binary	`m - n`
<<	Bit shift left, output	11	Left	Binary	`cout << n`
=	Simple assignment	2	Right	Binary	`m = n`

It lists 8 operators that apply to integer variables. They fall into five distinct precedence levels. For example, the unary negate operator `-` has precedence level 15, and the binary multiply operator `*` has precedence level 13, so negative is evaluated before multiply. Thus the expression `m*-n` is evaluated as `m*(-n)`. Assignment operators have lower precedence than nearly all other operators, so they are usually performed last.

The column labeled "Associativity" tells what happens when several <u>different</u> operators with the same precedence level appear in the same expression. For example `+` and `-` both have precedence level 12 and are left associative, so the operators are evaluated from left to right. For example, in the expression

    8 - 5 + 4

first 5 is subtracted from 8, and then 4 is added to that sum:

    (8 - 5) + 4 = 3 + 4 = 7

The column labeled "Arity" lists whether the operator is unary or binary. *Unary* means that the operator takes only one operand. For example, the post-increment operator `++` is unary: `n++` operates on the single variable `n`. *Binary* means that the operator takes two operands. For example, the add operator `+` is binary: `m + n` operates on the two variables `m` and `n`.

1.15 THE INCREMENT AND DECREMENT OPERATORS

Of the many features C++ inherited from C, some of the most useful are the increment operator `++` and decrement operator `--`. These operators transform a variable into a statement expression that abbreviates a special form of assignment.

EXAMPLE 1.17 Increment and Decrement Operators

This shows how the increment and decrement operators work:

```
#include <iostream.h>
// Tests the increment and decrement operators:
main()
{
    int m = 44, n = 66;
    cout << "m = " << m << ", n = " << n << endl;
    ++m;
    --n;
    cout << "m = " << m << ", n = " << n << endl;
    m++;
    n--;
    cout << "m = " << m << ", n = " << n << endl;
    return 0;
}
```

```
m = 44, n = 66
m = 45, n = 65
m = 46, n = 64
```

Both the pre-increment operator `++m` and the post-increment operator `m++` have the same effect here: they add 1 to the value of `m`. Similarly, both the pre-decrement operator `--n` and the post-decrement operator `n--` have the same effect here: they subtract 1 from the value of `n`.

When used as a stand-alone expression statement, `++m` and `m++` are both equivalent to the assignment

```
m = m + 1;
```

they simply increase the value of `m` by 1. Similarly, the expression statements `--n` and `n--` are both equivalent to the assignment

```
n = n - 1;
```

they simply decrease the value of `n` by 1. (The increment operator `++` was used in the name "C++" because it "increments" the original C programming language; it has everything that C has, and more.)

However, when used as subexpressions (*i.e.,* expressions within expressions), the pre-increment operation `++m` is different from the post-increment operation `m++`. The pre-increment increases the variable <u>first</u> before using it in the larger expression, whereas the post-increment increases the value of the variable only <u>after</u> using the prior value of the variable within the larger expression.

Since the incrementing process is equivalent to a separate assignment, there are really two statements to be executed when the increment operation is used as a subexpression: the incrementing assignment and the larger enclosing statement. The difference between the pre-increment and the post-increment is simply the difference between executing the assignment before or after the enclosing statement.

EXAMPLE 1.18 Pre-Increment and Post-Increment Operators

This shows the difference between the pre-increment and the post-increment:

```
#include <iostream.h>
// Tests the increment and decrement operators:
main()
{
    int m = 66, n;
    n = ++m;
    cout << "m = " << m << ", n = " << n << endl;
    n = m++;
    cout << "m = " <<  m  << ", n = "  << n  << endl;
    cout << "m = " << m++ << endl;
    cout << "m = " <<  m  << endl;
    cout << "m = " << ++m << endl;
    return 0;
}
```

```
m = 67, n = 67
m = 68, n = 67
m = 68
m = 69
m = 70
```

In the first assignment, m is pre-incremented, increasing its value to 67, which is then assigned to n. In the second assignment, m is post-incremented, so 67 is assigned to n and then m is increased to 68.

In the third output statement, m is post-incremented, so the current value of m (68) is dropped into the output stream and then m is increased to 69. In the last output statement, m is pre-incremented, so m is increased to 70 first and then that value is dropped into the output stream.

Use of the increment and decrement operators as subexpressions can be tricky and should be used with caution. For example, the order of evaluations of expressions that involve them is not defined by the language and consequently can be unpredictable:

EXAMPLE 1.19   The Unpredictablilty of the Order of Evaluation of Subexpressions

```
#include <iostream.h>

main()
{
    int n = 5, x;
    x = ++n * --n;
    cout << "n = " << n << ", x = " << x << endl;
    cout << ++n << " " << ++n << " " << ++n << endl;
}
```

```
n = 5, x = 25
8 7 6
```

In the assignment to x, n is first increment to 6 and then decremented back to 5 before the multiply operator is evaluated, computing 5 * 5. In the last line, the three subexpressions are evaluated from right to left. The left associativity of the output operator << is irrelevant because there are no <u>other</u> operators involved that have the same precedence level.

1.16 COMPOUND ASSIGNMENT EXPRESSIONS

Increment and decrement operators abbreviate certain kinds of assignments. C++ also allows the assignment to be combined with other operators. The general syntax for these combined assignments is

```
variable op= expression
```

where op is a binary operator. The effect of the combined assignment is the same as

```
variable = variable op expression
```

For example, the combined assignment

```
n += 8;
```

has the same effect as the simple assignment

```
n = n + 8;
```

It simply adds 8 to n.

EXAMPLE 1.20 Assignment Operators

This shows how to use some of the combined operators:

```
#include <iostream.h>
// Tests combined operators:
main()
{
    int n = 44;
    n +=9;
    cout << n << endl;
    n -= 5;
    cout << n << endl;
    n *= 2;
    cout << n << endl;
    return 0;
}
```

```
53
48
96
```

The statement n += 9 adds 9 to n, the statement n -= 5 subtracts 5 from n, and the statement n *= 2 multiplies n by 2.

1.17 INTEGER OVERFLOW AND UNDERFLOW

Unlike the integers of pure mathematics, the integer objects in a computer are bounded. As we saw above, each integer type has a maximum value and a minimum value. If the value of a variable exceeds either of its bounds, we have what is called *overflow*.

EXAMPLE 1.21 Testing for Overflow

This program shows what happens when an object of type `short` overflows:

```
#include <iostream.h>
#include <limits.h>
//  Tests for overflow for type short:
main()
{
    short n = SHRT_MAX - 1;
    cout << n++ << endl;
    cout << n++ << endl;
    cout << n++ << endl;
    cout << n++ << endl;
    return 0;
}
```

```
32766
32767
-32768
-32767
```

The values "wrap around" the endpoints of 32,767 and –32,768. In other words, the value that results when 1 is added to 32,767 is –32,768. This is obviously wrong!

Most computers handle overflow this way. The values wrap around, so that the number that comes after the maximum value is the minimum value. This is the worst kind of error that can occur on a computer because normally there is no outside evidence that anything has gone wrong. As we shall see later, C++ fortunately provides mechanisms to help the programmer handle this problem.

Overflow is one kind of a *run-time error*. Another common example is division by zero. But this is not as great a problem because you will know when it happens: the program crashes! Numeric overflow is like an internal hemorrhage: you may not be aware that you are in grave danger.

1.18 THE `char` TYPE

In C++, the character type `char` is one of the integer types. This means that any variable of type `char` may be used in integer expressions just like any other integer. For example, the integer arithmetic operators apply to `char` variables:

```
char c = 54;
char d = 2*c - 7;
c += d%3;
```

The name "char" is short for "character." The name `char` is used because when variables of this type are input or output, they are interpreted as characters. Whenever a character is input, the system automatically stores its ASCII code (see Appendix A) as the value of the integer type `char`. And whenever a variable of type `char` is output, the system automatically sends the corresponding character to the output stream. This illustrated in the example below.

C++ defines three 8-bit integer types: char, signed char, and unsigned char. But only two of these are distinct. The type char will be either signed char or unsigned char, depending upon the computer. Use type char for ordinary characters. Use the type unsigned char for very short bit-string. The type signed char is not explicitly used very often; it would be a good choice if you needed to store a large quantity of very short integers that would not have to be output by means of the standard output operator <<.

EXAMPLE 1.22 Character Output

This shows how char variables are output:

```
#include <iostream.h>
// Tests output of type char:
main()
{
    char c = 64;
    cout << c++ << " ";        // prints '@' and increments c to 65
    cout << c++ << " ";        // prints 'A' and increments c to 66
    cout << c++ << " ";        // prints 'B' and increments c to 67
    cout << c++ << endl;       // prints 'C' and increments c to 68
    c = 96;
    cout << c++ << " ";        // prints ''' and increments c to 97
    cout << c++ << " ";        // prints 'a' and increments c to 98
    cout << c++ << " ";        // prints 'b' and increments c to 99
    cout << c++ << endl;       // prints 'c' and increments c to 100
    return 0;
}
```

```
@ A B C
` a b c
```

The first output statement inserts the character variable c into the output stream. Since it has the integer value 64, it is output as the character "@". (The ASCII code for the "at" symbol is 64.) Then c is immediately incremented to 65 which causes the character "A" to be output next. (The ASCII code for the letter A is 65.) The rest of the program continues in a similar way. (Note that on computers that use the EBCDIC code, the output here will be different.)

The complete ASCII code is shown in Appendix A.

EXAMPLE 1.23 Obtaining the ASCII Code

```
#include <iostream.h>
// Tests output of type char:
main()
{
    char c = 'A';
    cout << c++ << " " << int(c) << endl;      // prints 'A' and 65
    cout << c++ << " " << int(c) << endl;      // prints 'B' and 66
    cout << c++ << " " << int(c) << endl;      // prints 'C' and 67
    return 0;
}
```

```
A 65
B 66
C 67
```

As this program executes, `c` takes the values 65, 66, 67, and 68. But since character variables are printed as characters, the first thing printed on each line is the character whose ASCII code is stored in `c`. Thus, `A`, `B`, and `C` are printed. We use `int(c)` to print the numeric value of the character `c`.

The expression `int(c)` is called a *cast*. It converts `c` from `char` type to `int` type. This allows us to print the ASCII code of a character.

Review Questions

1.1 Describe the two ways to include comments in a C++ program.

1.2 What is wrong with the following "comment":

```
cout << "Hello, /* change? */ World.\n";
```

1.3 What does a declaration do?

1.4 What is the purpose of the preprocessing directive:

```
#include <iostream>
```

1.5 Is this a valid C++ program? Explain:

```
main() { 22; }
```

1.6 Where does the name of the language "C++" come from?

1.7 What's wrong with these declarations:

```
int first = 22, last = 99, new = 44, old = 66;
```

1.8 What's wrong with these declarations:

```
int x = y = 22;
```

1.9 What's wrong with this program:

```
main()
{
    n = 22;
    cout << n << endl;
}
```

1.10 For each of the following expressions, either evaluate it or explain why it is not a valid expression:

    a. `37/(5*2)`

    b. `37/5/2`

    c. `37(5/2)`

    d. `37%(5%2)`

    e. `37%5%2`

    f. `37 - 5 - 2`

    g. `(37-5)2`

1.11 Evaluate each of the following expressions, assuming in each case that `m` has the value 24 and `n` has the value 7:

    a. `m - 8 - n`

    b. `m = n = 3`

    c. `m%n`

    d. `m%n++`

    e. `m%++n`

    f. `++m - n--`

    g. `m += n -= 2`

1.12 Determine which of the following is a valid identifier. If it is not valid, tell why:

    a. `r2d2`

    b. `H2O`

    c. `secondCousinOnceRemoved`

    d. `2ndBirthday`

    e. `the_United_States_of_America`

    f. `_TIME_`

    g. `_12345`

    h. `x(3)`

    i. `cost_in_$`

Solved Problems

1.13 What is the output from the following program:

```
#include <iostream.h>
main()
{
    // cout << "Hello, World.\n";
}
```

This program has no output. The double-slash transforms the output statement into a comment.

1.14   What is wrong with the following program:

```
#include <iostream.h>
// This program prints "Hello, World.":
main()
{
    cout << "Hello, World.\n"
    return 0;
}
```

The required semicolon is missing from the end of the output statement.

1.15   Write four different C++ statements that each subtract 1 from the integer variable `n`.

```
n = n - 1;
n -= 1;
--n;
n--;
```

1.16   Write a single C++ statement that subtracts the sum of `x` and `y` from `z` and then increments `y`.

```
z -= (x + y++);
```

1.17   Write a single C++ statement that decrements the variable `n` and then adds it to `total`.

```
total += --n;
```

1.18   In each of the following, assume that `m` has the value 5 and `n` has the value 2 before the statement executes. Tell what the values of `m` and `n` will be after the statement executes the following:

a. `m *= n++;`
b. `m += --n;`

a. `n` will be 3 and `m` will be 10.
b. `n` will be 1 and `m` will be 6.

1.19   Identify and correct the error in each of the following:

a. `cout >> count;`
b. `m = ++n += 2;`

a. The output object `cout` requires the output operator `<<`.
    The statement should be `cout << count;`
b. The expression `++n` cannot be on the left side of an assignment.

1.20   Trace the following code fragment, showing the value of each variable each time it changes:

```
int x, y, z;
x = y = z = 6;
x *= y += z -= 4;
```

First, 6 is assigned to `z`, `y`, and `x`. Then `z` is decremented by 4, obtaining the value 2. Then `y` is incremented by 2, obtaining the value 8. Then `x` is multiplied by 8, obtaining the value 48.

1.21 On most UNIX workstations, the `int` type ranges from -2,147,483,648 to 2,147,483,647. How many bytes will an object of this type occupy in memory?

The range from -2,147,483,648 to 2,147,483,647 covers 4,294,967,296 values. This number is exactly 2^{32}, so each `int` requires 32 bits which is 4 bytes of memory.

1.22 How do the following two statements differ:

```
char ch = 'A';
char ch = 65;
```

Both statements have the same effect: declare `ch` to be a `char` and initialize it with the value 65. Since this is the ASCII code for `'A'`, that character constant can also be used to initialize ch to 65.

1.23 What code could you execute to find the character whose ASCII code is 100?

```
char c = 100;
cout << c;
```

1.24 How could you determine whether `char` is the same as `signed char` or `unsigned char` on your computer?

Run a program like that in Example 1.14 and compare the constants `CHAR_MAX`, `SCHAR_MAX`, and `UCHAR_MAX`.

Solved Programming Problems

1.25 Write a program that prints the first sentence of the Gettysburg Address.

Essentially, all that we need to do here is use a sequence of output statements, sending pieces of the sentence to the `cout` object:

```cpp
#include <iostream.h>

// Prints the first sentence of the Gettysburg Address:
main()
{
    cout << "\tFourscore and seven years ago our fathers\n";
    cout << "brought forth upon this continent a new nation,\n";
    cout << "conceived in liberty, and dedicated to the\n";
    cout << "proposition that all men are created equal.\n";
    return 0;
}
```

```
    Fourscore and seven years ago our fathers
brought forth upon this continent a new nation,
conceived in liberty, and dedicated to the
proposition that all men are created equal.
```

We could also have done this by chaining the pieces with a single reference to `cout`, like this:

```cpp
    cout << "\tFourscore and seven years ago our fathers\n"
         << "brought forth upon this continent a new nation,\n"
         << "conceived in liberty, and dedicated to the\n"
         << "proposition that all men are created equal.\n";
```

Note that this is a single statement, with a single semicolon.

If you want the output lines to be longer (or shorter) than the individual pieces sent to the output stream, simply adjust your placement of the endline characters '\n':

```cpp
#include <iostream.h>

// Prints the first sentence of the Gettysburg Address:
main()
{
    cout << "\tFourscore and seven years ago our fathers ";
    cout << "brought forth upon\nthis continent a new nation, ";
    cout << "conceived in liberty, and dedicated\nto the ";
    cout << "proposition that all men are created equal.\n";
    return 0;
}
```

```
    Fourscore and seven years ago our fathers brought forth upon
this continent a new nation, conceived in liberty, and dedicated
to the proposition that all men are created equal.
```

Don't forget to put a blank after the last word on each line that doesn't end with an endline character.

1.26 Write a program that prints the sum, difference, product, quotient, and remainder of two integers. Initialize the integers with the values 60 and 7.

After declaring integers m and n and initializing them with the values 60 and 7, we use one ouput statement to print their values, and then one output statement for each of the five operations:

```cpp
#include <iostream.h>

// Prints sum, difference, product, and quotient of given integers:
main()
{
    int m = 60, n = 7;
    cout << "The integers are " << m << " and " << n << endl;
    cout << "Their sum is        " << (m + n) << endl;
    cout << "Their difference is " << (m - n) << endl;
    cout << "Their product is    " << (m * n) << endl;
    cout << "Their quotient is   " << (m / n) << endl;
    cout << "Their remainder is  " << (m % n) << endl;
    return 0;
}
```

```
The integers are 60 and 7
Their sum is        67
Their difference is 53
Their product is    420
Their quotient is   8
Their remainder is  4
```

Note that the quotient 8 and remainder 4 fit the required relationship for the quotient and remainder from integer division: 60 = (8)(7) + (4).

1.27   Write a program that prints the block letter "B" in a 7 × 6 grid of stars like this:

```
*****
*    *
*    *
*****
*    *
*    *
*****
```

We use one output statement for each row in the block letter:

```cpp
#include <iostream.h>

// Prints the block letter "B" in a 7 x 6 grid:
main()
{
    cout << "*****" << endl;
    cout << "*    *" << endl;
    cout << "*    *" << endl;
    cout << "*****" << endl;
    cout << "*    *" << endl;
    cout << "*    *" << endl;
    cout << "*****" << endl;
    return 0;
}
```

Instead of adding the `endl` object to each output, we could have ended each quoted string with the endline character '\n' like this:

```cpp
cout << "*****\n";
```

Supplementary Problems

1.28   Trace the following code fragment, showing the value of each variable each time it changes:

```cpp
int x, y, z;
x = y = z = 5;
x *= y += z -= 1;
```

1.29   On most systems, the `unsigned char` type ranges from 0 to 255. How many bytes will an object of this type occupy in memory?

Supplementary Programming Problems

1.30   Write and run a program that prints your name and address.

1.31   Write and run a program that prints the first sentence of the Gettysburg Address, with no more than 40 characters per line.

1.32   Run the program in Example 1.11 on your system. Use the output to determine what different integer types are available and how many bytes each requires.

1.33   Modify the program shown in Example 1.16 to see how your computer handles the integer division of 20 divided by –7. Try to predict what the quotient and remainder will be. Then run your program to see if you were right:

1.34   Write and run a program that prints the first letter of your last name as a block letter in a 7×7 grid of stars.

1.35   Write and run a program that prints the first four lines of Shakespeare's Sonnet 18:

```
Shall I compare thee to a summer's day?
Thou art more lovely and more temperate.
Rough winds do shake the darling buds of May,
And summer's lease hath all too short a date.
```

1.36   To find out what your system does about uninitialized variables, write and run a test program that contains the following two lines:

```
int n;
cout << n << endl;
```

1.37   Write and run a program that causes negative overflow of an variable of type `short int`.

1.38   Write and run a program that causes overflow of an variable of type `int`.

1.39   Write and run a program like the one in Example 1.22 that prints the ASCII codes for only the 10 digits and the last 5 lowercase letters. Use Appendix A to check your output.

1.40   Write and run a program like the one in Example 1.22 that prints the ASCII codes for only the 10 uppercase and lowercase vowels. Use Appendix A to check your output.

Answers to Review Questions

1.1   One way is to use the Standard C style comment:

```
/* like this */
```

The other way is to use the C++ style comment:

```
// like this
```

The first begins with a slash-star and ends with a star-slash. The second begins with a double-slash and ends at the end of the line.

1.2   Everything between the double quotes will be printed, including the intended comment.

1.3   A declaration tells the compiler the name and type of the variable being declared. It also may be initialized in the declaration.

1.4   It includes the header file `iostream.h` into the source code. This includes declarations needed for input and output; *e.g.*, the output operator `<<`.

1.5   This is a valid C++ program. It contains a single statement: `22;` This is an expression statement because any constant, like 22, is a valid expression. The program does nothing.

1.6   The name refers to the C language and it increment operator ++. The name suggests that C++ is an advance over C.

1.7   The only thing wrong with these declarations is that new is a keyword. Keywords are reserved and cannot be used for variable names.

1.8   This is an intended declaration. The only way that the equals sign can be used in a declaration is to initialize a variable. The expression x = y = 22 is not a valid initialization because the variable y appears on the right side of the first equals sign. The correct syntax would be

```
int x = 22, y = 22;
```

1.9   There are two things wrong. The variable n is not declared, and cout is being used without including the <iostream.h> header file.

1.10 *a.* 37/(5*2) evaluates to 37/10 = 3

    b. 37/5/2 evaluates to (37/5)/2 = 7/2 = 3

    c. This is not valid because there is no operator between 37 and (5/2).
The intended operation was 37*(5/2), which evaluates to 37/2 = 18

    d. 37%(5%2) evaluates to 37%1 = 0

    e. 37%5%2 evaluates to (37%5)%2 = 2%2 = 0

    f. 37 - 5 - 2 evaluates to (37 - 5) - 2 = 32 - 2 = 30

    g. This is not valid because there is no operator between (37-5) and 2.
The intended operation was (37-5)*2, which evaluates to 32*2 = 64

1.11 *a.* m - 8 - n evaluates to (24 - 8) - 7 = 16 - 7 = 9

    b. m = n = 3 evaluates to 3

    c. m%n evaluates to 24%7 = 3

    d. m%n++ evaluates to 24%(7++) = 24%7 = 3

    e. m%++n evaluates to 24%(++7) = 24%8 = 0

    f. ++m - n-- evaluates to (++24) - (7--) = 25 - 7 = 8

    g. m += n -= 2 evaluates to 24 += (7 -= 2) = 24 += 5 = 29

1.12 *a.* r2d2 is a valid identifier

    b. H2O is a valid identifier

    c. secondCousinOnceRemoved is a valid identifier

    d. 2ndBirthday is <u>not</u> a valid identifier because its first character is a digit

    e. the_United_States_of_America is a valid identifier

    f. _TIME_ is a valid identifier

    g. _12345 is a valid identifier

    h. x(3) is <u>not</u> a valid identifier because it contains the characters '(' and ')'

    i. cost_in_$ is <u>not</u> a valid identifier because it contains the character '$'

Chapter 2

Conditional Statements and Integer Types

The programs in Chapter 1 all have *sequential execution*: each statement in the program executes once, in the order that they are listed. Conditional statements allow for more flexible programs where the execution of some statements depends upon conditions that change while the program is running.

This chapter describes the `if` statement, the `if ... else` statement, and the `switch` statement also shows how to include simple input into your programs.

2.1 INPUT

In C++, input is analogous to output. But instead of data flowing out to the output stream `cout`, we have data flowing in from the input stream `cin` (pronounced "see-in"). The name stands for "console input."

EXAMPLE 2.1 Integer Input

Here is a simple program that reads integer input:

```
main()
{
    int age;
    cout << "How old are you: ";
    cin >> age;
    cout << "In 10 years, you will be " << age + 10 << ".\n";
}
```

```
How old are you: 19
In 10 years, you will be 29.
```

The type shown in **boldface** in the shaded sample run is the input that is typed by the user.

The symbol `>>` is the *extraction operator*, also called the *input operator*. It is usually used with the `cin` input stream, which is usually the user's keyboard. Thus, when the statement

```
cin >> age;
```

executes, the system pauses, waiting for input. As soon as an integer is input, it is assigned to `age` and the program continues.

Notice that the preprocessor directive:

```
#include <iostream.h>
```

is missing from Example 2.1. It <u>is</u> required in any program that uses either `cin` or `cout`. But since nearly every program in this book does use either `cin` or `cout`, we will assume that you know to include this line at the beginning of your source code file. Omitting it from these examples simply saves some print space. We will also omit the `return` statement at the end of the `main()` function in all future examples.

The input object `cin` is analogous to the output object `cout`. Each is a C++ *stream* object that acts as a conduit through which bytes flow. The bytes flow into the running program through the `cin` object, and they flow out through the `cout` object. This can be visualized like this:

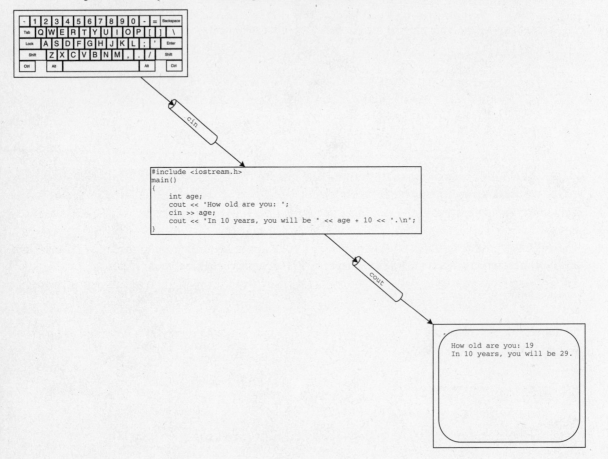

```
#include <iostream.h>
main()
{
    int age;
    cout << "How old are you: ";
    cin >> age;
    cout << "In 10 years, you will be " << age + 10 << ".\n";
}
```

```
How old are you: 19
In 10 years, you will be 29.
```

EXAMPLE 2.2 Character Input

```
main()
{
    char first, last;
    cout << "Enter your initials:\n";
    cout << "\tFirst name initial: ";
    cin >> first;
    cout << "\tLast name initial: ";
    cin >> last;
    cout << "Hello, " << first << ". " << last << ".!\n";
}
```

```
Enter your initials:
        First name initial: J
        Last name initial: H
Hello, J. H.!
```

This example illustrates a standard way to format input. The first output line alerts the user to what general input is needed. This is followed by a sequence of specific input requests, called *user prompts*. Each user prompt is indented with the tab character `\t`, and by omitting the newline character `\n` it leaves the cursor on the same line for the user to enter a response there.

EXAMPLE 2.3 Multiple Input in the Same Stream

More than one variable may be read in the same input statement:

```
main()
{
    char first, last;
    cout << "Enter your first and last initials: ";
    cin >> first >> last;
    cout << "Hello, " << first << ". " << last << ".!\n";
}
```

```
Enter your first and last initials: JH
Hello, J. H.!
```

This shows that the input stream `cin` reads the items from left to right; *i.e.*, the left-most variable is read first.

Since the `char` type is an integer type, `cin` will ignore all leading *white space* (*i.e.*, blanks, tabs, and newlines) when it reads input. So the input in this example could have been entered as

```
Enter your first and last initials: J       H
Hello, J. H.!
```

Notice that this prevents the input of blanks as characters using input operator `<<`. In later chapters, we will see more specialized methods for character input.

2.2 THE `if` STATEMENT

The `if` statement allows conditional execution. Its syntax is

```
if (condition) statement;
```

where `condition` is an integer expression and `statement` is any executable statement. The `statement` will be executed only if the `condition` has a nonzero value. (Whenever an integer expression is being evaluated as a condition, a nonzero value is interpreted to mean "true" and a zero value to mean "false.") Notice the required parentheses around the `condition`.

EXAMPLE 2.4 Testing for Divisibility

```
main()
{
    int n, d;
    cout << "Enter two integers: ";
    cin >> n >> d;
    if (n%d == 0) cout << n << " is divisible by " << d << endl;
}
```

```
Enter two integers: 24 6
24 is divisible by 6
```

This program reads two integers and then checks the value of the remainder `n % d`. In this run, the value of 24 % 6 is 0, which means that 24 is divisible by 6.

The trouble with this last example is that it doesn't do anything when `n` <u>is not</u> divisible by `d`:

```
Enter two integers: 24 5
```

To execute an alternative statement when the condition is zero, we need the `if...else` statement.

2.3 THE `if...else` STATEMENT

The `if...else` statement executes one of two alternative statements, according to the value of the specified condition. It has the syntax

```
if (condition) statement1;
else statement2;
```

where `condition` is an integer expression, and `statement1` and `statement2` are any statements. The `statement1` is executed if the `condition` has a nonzero value, and `statement2` is executed if the `condition` has a zero value.

EXAMPLE 2.5

This is the same program as in Example 2.4, except that an `else` clause has been added:

```
main()
{
    int n, d;
    cout << "Enter two integers: ";
    cin >> n >> d;
    if (n%d == 0) cout << n << " is divisible by " << d << endl;
    else cout << n << " is not divisible by " << d << endl;
}
```

```
Enter two integers: 24 5
24 is not divisible by 5
```

Since 24 % 5 == 4, the condition `(n%d == 0)` is false and the `else` clause executes.

A condition like `(n%d == 0)` is an expression whose value is interpreted as being either "false" or "true." In C++ those two values are integers: 0 means "false," and any nonzero integer means "true." Because of that correspondence, conditions can be ordinary integer expressions. In particular, the integer expression `(n%d)` itself can be used as a condition. It is nonzero (*i.e.*, "true") precisely when `n` is not divisible by `d`, we should reverse the two print statements in the previous example to make sense:

EXAMPLE 2.6

```
main()
{
    int n, d;
    cout << "Enter two integers: ";
    cin >> n >> d;
    if (n%d) cout << n << " is not divisible by " << d << endl;
    else cout << n << " is not divisible by " << d << endl;
}
```

```
Enter two integers: 24 5
24 is not divisible by 5
```

2.4 RELATIONAL OPERATORS

The next example has a condition in a more intuitive form.

EXAMPLE 2.7 Finding the Maximum of Two Integers

This program prints the larger of the two numbers input:

```
main()
{
    int m, n;
    cout << "Enter two integers: ";
    cin >> m >> n;
    if (m > n) cout << m << endl;
    else cout << n << endl;
}
```

```
Enter two integers: 22 55
55
```

In this program, the condition is (m > n). If m is greater than n, the condition is "true" and evaluates to 1; otherwise, the condition is "false" and evaluates to 0. So m is printed precisely when it is greater than n.

The symbol > is one of the *relational operators*. It is called "relational" because it evaluates how the two expressions on either side of it relate; for example, the relation 22 > 55 is false. The symbol is called an "operator" because when it is combined with expressions it produces a value. For example, when > is combined with 22 and 55 in the form 22 > 55, it produces the integer value 0, meaning "false."

There are six relational operators:

<	is less than
<=	is less than or equal to
==	is equal to
>	is greater than
>=	is greater than or equal to
!=	is not equal to

Note the double equals sign == must be used to test for equality. A common error among new C++ programmers is to use the single equals sign =. This mistake is difficult to uncover because it does not violate the syntax rules of C++.

EXAMPLE 2.8 Finding the Maximum of Three Integers

This program prints the largest of the three numbers input:

```
main()
{
    int n1, n2, n3;
    cout << "Enter three integers: ";
    cin >> n1 >> n2 >> n3;
    int max = n1;
    if (n2 > max) max = n2;
    if (n3 > max) max = n3;
    cout << "The maximum is " << max << endl;
}
```

```
Enter three integers: 22 44 66
The maximum is 66
```

```
Enter three integers: 77 33 55
The maximum is 77
```

On the first run, n1 is 22, n2 is 44, and n3 is 66. First max is assigned 22. Then, since 44 is greater than 22, max is assigned 44. Finally, since 66 is greater than 44, max is assigned 66, and that value is printed.

On the second run, n1 is 77, n2 is 33, and n3 is 55. First max is assigned 77. Then, since 33 is not greater than 77, max is unchanged. Finally, since 55 is also not greater than 77, max is again unchanged, and so the value 77 is printed.

2.5 COMPOUND STATEMENTS

A *compound statement* is a sequence of statements that is treated as a single statement. C++ identifies a compound statement by enclosing its sequence of statements in curly braces.

The next example contains the following compound statement:

```
{
    int temp = x;
    x = y;
    y = temp;
}
```

The braces that enclose the three statements form a *block*. As a compound statement, it itself qualifies as a statement and can be used wherever any other statement could be used. (Note that an entire C++ program—everything that follows main()—forms a compound statement.)

EXAMPLE 2.9 Sorting

This program reads two integers and then outputs them in increasing order:

```
main()
{
    int x, y;
    cout << "Enter two integers: ";
    cin >> x >> y;
    if (x > y) {
        int temp = x;
        x = y;
        y = temp;
    }
    cout << x << " " << y << endl;
}
```

```
Enter two integers: 66 44
44 66
```

The effect of putting the compound statement in the `if` statement this way is that all three statements inside the block will be executed if the condition is true.

These particular three statements form a *swap*; that is, they interchange the values of `x` and `y`. This construct is frequently used in programs that sort data. Such an interchange requires there three separate steps along with the temporary storage location named `temp` here.

Notice that the variable `temp` is declared inside the block. That makes it *local* to the block; *i.e.,* it only exists during the execution of the block. If the condition is false and `x` ≤ `y`, then `temp` will never exist. This is a good example of the practice of localizing objects so that they are created only when needed.

This Example 2.9 is not the most efficient way to solve the problem. If all we want to do is print the two numbers in increasing order, we could do it directly without the temp variable:

```
if (x < y) cout << x << " " << y << endl;
else cout << y << " " << x << endl;
```

The purpose of the example is to illustrate compound statements and local variable declarations.

2.6 KEYWORDS

A *keyword* in a programming language is a word that is already defined and is reserved for a single special purpose. C++ has 48 keywords. They are:

asm	continue	float	new	signed	try
auto	default	for	operator	sizeof	typedef
break	delete	friend	private	static	union
case	do	goto	protected	struct	unsigned
catch	double	if	public	switch	virtual
char	else	inline	register	template	void
class	enum	int	return	this	volatile
const	extern	long	short	throw	while

We have already seen the keywords `char`, `else`, `if`, `int`, `long`, `short`, `signed`, and `unsigned`. The remaining 40 keywords will be described subsequently.

Keywords like `if` and `else` are found in nearly every programming language. Other keywords such as `catch` and `friend` are unique to C++. The 48 keywords of C++ include all 32 of the keywords of the C language.

There are two kinds of keywords: those like `if` and `else` which serve as structure markers used to define the syntax of the language, and those like `char` and `int` which are actual names of things in the language. In some languages, the structure markers are called *reserved words* and the predefined names are called *standard identifiers*.

2.7 COMPOUND CONDITIONS

Conditions such as `n % d` and `x > y` can be combined to form compound conditions. The three *logical operators* that are used for this purpose are `&&` (and), `||` (or), and `!` (not). They are defined by

`&&`	`p && q` evaluates to 1 only when both p and q evaluate to 1
`||`	`p || q` evaluates to 1 when either p or q or both evaluate to 1
`!`	`!p` evaluates to 1 when either p evaluates to 0

For example, `(n % d || x > y)` will be true if either `n % d` is nonzero or if `x` is greater than `y` (or both), and `!(x > y)` is equivalent to `x <= y`.

The definitions of the three logical operators are usually given by the *truth tables* below.

p	q	p && q
1	1	1
1	0	0
0	1	0
0	0	0

p	q	p || q
1	1	1
1	0	1
0	1	1
0	0	0

p	!p
1	0
0	1

These show for example, that if `p` has the value 1 (for "true") and `q` has the value 0 (for "false"), then the expression `p && q` will have the value 0 and the expression `p || q` will have the value 1.

The next example solves the same problem that Example 2.8 solved, except that it uses compound conditionals:

EXAMPLE 2.10 The Maximum of Three Again

This program uses compound conditions to find the maximum of three integers:

```
main()
{
    int a, b, c;
    cout << "Enter three integers: ";
    cin >> a >> b >> c;
    if (a >= b && a >= c) cout << a << endl;
    if (b >= a && b >= c) cout << b << endl;
    if (c >= a && c >= b) cout << c << endl;
}
```

```
Enter three integers: 66 88 55
88
```

This simply checks each of the three numbers to see which is greater than or equal to the other two.

Note that Example 2.10 is no improvement over Example 2.8. Its purpose was simply to illustrate the use of compound conditionals.

Here is another example using a compound conditional:

EXAMPLE 2.11 User-Friendly Input

This program allows the user to input either a `Y` or a `y` for "yes":

```
main()
{
    char ans;
    cout << "Are you enrolled (y/n): ";
    cin >> ans;
    if (ans == 'Y' || ans == 'y') cout << "You are enrolled.\n";
    else cout << "You are not enrolled.\n";
}
```

```
Are you enrolled: N
You are not enrolled.
```

It prompts the user for an answer, suggesting a response of either `y` or `n`. But then it accepts any character and concludes that the user meant "no" unless either a `Y` or a `y` is input.

Compound conditionals that use `&&` and `||` will not even evaluate the second part of the conditional unless necessary. This is called *short-circuiting*. As the truth tables show, `(p && q)` will be false if `p` is false. So in that case there is no need to evaluate `q` if `p` is false. Similarly if `p` is true then there is no need to evaluate `q` to determine that `(p || q)` is true.

The value of short circuiting can be seen from the following example:

EXAMPLE 2.12 Short-Circuiting in a Condition

This program tests integer divisibility:

```
main()
{
    int n, d;
    cout << "Enter two positive integers: ";
    cin >> n >> d;
    if (d > 0 && n%d == 0) cout << d << " divides " << n << endl;
    else cout << d << " does not divide " << n << endl;
}
```

```
Enter two positive integers: 300 6
6 divides 300
```

```
Enter two positive integers: 300 7
7 does not divide 300
```

```
Enter two positive integers: 300 0
0 does not divide 300
```

In the first run, `d` is positive and `n%d` is zero, so the compound condition is true. In the second run, `d` is positive but `n%d` is not zero, so the compound condition is false.

In the third run, `d` is zero, so the compound condition is immediately determined to be false without evaluating the second component "`n%d == 0`". This short-circuiting prevents the program from crashing because when `d` is zero the expression `n%d` cannot be evaluated.

2.8 BOOLEAN EXPRESSIONS

A *boolean expression* is a condition that is either true or false. In the previous example the expressions `d > 0`, `n%d == 0`, and `(d > 0 && n%d == 0)` are boolean expressions. As we have seen, boolean expressions evaluate to integer values. The value 0 means "false" and every nonzero value means "true."

Since all nonzero integer values are interpreted as meaning "true," boolean expressions are often disguised. For example, the statement

```
if (n) cout << "n is not zero";
```

will print `n is not zero` precisely when `n` is not zero because that is when the boolean expression `(n)` is interpreted as "true". Here is a more realistic example:

```
if (n%d) cout << "n is not a multiple of d";
```

The output statement will execute precisely when `n%d` is not zero, and that happens precisely when `d` does not divide `n` evenly, because `n%d` is the remainder from the integer division.

The fact that boolean expressions have integer values can lead to some surprising anomalies in C++. For example, the following line might be written by a novice C++ programmer:

```
if (x >= y >= z) cout << "max = x";        // ERROR!
```

Obviously, the programmer intended to write

```
if (x >= y && y >= z) cout << "max = x";    // OK
```

The problem is that the erroneous line is syntactically correct, so the compiler will not catch the error. In fact, the program could run without any apparent error at all. This is a run-time error of the worst kind because there is no clear indication that anything is wrong.

The source of the difficulty described here is the fact that boolean expressions have numeric values. Suppose that `x` and `y` both have the value 0 and that `z` has the value 1. The expression `(x >= y >= z)` is evaluated from left to right. The first part `x >= y` evaluates to "true" which is the numeric value 1. Then that is compared to `z`, and since they are equal the complete expression evaluates to "true" even though it is really false!

The moral here is to remember that boolean expressions have numeric values, and that compound conditionals can be tricky.

Another error that novice C++ programmers are prone to make is using a single equals sign `=` when the double equals sign `==` should be. For example,

```
if (x = 0) cout << "x = 0";          // ERROR!
```

Obviously, the programmer intended to write

```
if (x == 0) cout << "x = 0";         // OK
```

The erroneous statement will first *assign* 0 to x. That assignment then has the *value* 0 which means "false" so the `cout` statement will not be executed. So even if `x` originally was zero, it will not be printed. Worse, if `x` originally was not zero, it will inadvertently be changed to zero!

Like the previous bug, this is another run time error of the worst kind. It is very difficult to detect.

2.9 NESTED CONDITIONALS

Like compound statements, conditional statements can be used wherever any other statement can be used. So a conditional statement can be used within another conditional statement. This is called *nesting* conditional statements. For example, the condition in the last example could be restated equivalently as

```
if (d > 0)
    if (n%d == 0)
        cout << d << " divides " << n << endl;
    else
        cout << d << " does not divide " << n << endl;
else
    cout << d << " does not divide " << n << endl;
```

Here extra indentation is used to help clarify the complex logic. Of course, the compiler ignores all indentation and white space. To parse the statement, it uses the following "else matching" rule:

> *Match each* else *with the last unmatched* if.

Using this rule, the compiler can easily decipher code as inscrutable as this:

```
if (a > 0) if (b > 0) ++a; else if (c > 0)
if (a < 4) ++b; else if (b < 4) ++c; else --a;
else if (c < 4) --b; else --c; else a = 0;
```

To make it readable for humans, that code should be written either like this:

```
if (a > 0)
    if (b > 0) ++a;
    else
        if (c > 0)
            if (a < 4) ++b;
            else
                if (b < 4) ++c;
                else --a;
        else
            if (c < 4) --b;
            else --c;
else
    a = 0;
```

or like this:

```
if (a > 0)
    if (b > 0) ++a;
    else if (c > 0)
        if (a < 4) ++b;
        else if (b < 4) ++c;
        else --a;
    else if (c < 4) --b;
    else --c;
else
    a = 0;
```

EXAMPLE 2.13 The Maximum of Three Again

Here is yet another way to do what was done in Example 2.8 and Example 2.10:

```
main()
{
    int a, b, c, max;
    cout << "Enter three integers: ";
    cin >> a >> b >> c;
    if (a > b)
        if (a > c) max = a;      // a > b and a > c
        else max = c;            // c >= a > b
    else
        if (b > c) max = b;      // b >= a and b > c
        else max = c;            // c >= b >= a
    cout << "The maximum is " << max << endl;
}
```

```
Enter three integers: 22 33 44
The maximum is 44
```

```
Enter three integers: 66 55 44
The maximum is 66
```

In the first run, the test `(a > b)` fails, so the second `else` executes the test `(b > c)` which also fails, thus executing the third `else` which assigns `c` to `max`. In the second run, the test `(a > b)` succeeds, and then the test `(a > c)` also succeeds, so `a` is assigned to `max`.

This program is more efficient than the one in Example 2.10 because it evaluates only two simple conditions instead of three compound conditions. Nevertheless, it should be considered inferior because its logic is more complicated. The in-line comments are really needed to clarify the logic. In the trade-off between efficiency and simplicity, the one should opt for simplicity.

Nested conditionals are by their very nature complicated. So it is usually better to avoid them whenever possible. An exception to this rule is a special form of nested conditional where all except possibly the last `else` is immediately followed by another `if`. This is a popular logical structure because it delineates in a simple way a sequence of disjoint alternatives. To clarify the logic, programmers usually line up the `else if` phrases, as shown in the next example.

EXAMPLE 2.14

This program converts a test score into its equivalent letter grade:

```
main()
{
    int score;
    cout << "Enter the test score: ";
    cin >> score;
    if (score > 100) cout << "Error: score is out of range.";
    else if (score >= 90) cout << 'A';
    else if (score >= 80) cout << 'B';
    else if (score >= 70) cout << 'C';
    else if (score >= 60) cout << 'D';
    else if (score >=  0) cout << 'F';
    else cout << "Error: score is out of range.";
}
```

```
Enter the test score: 83
B
```

```
Enter the test score: 47
F
```

```
Enter the test score: -9
Error: score is out of range.
```

The variable `score` is tested through a cascade of conditionals, continuing until one of the conditions is found to be true, or until the last `else` is reached as in the third run.

2.10 THE `switch` STATEMENT

The sequence of mutually exclusive alternatives delineated by the multiple `else if` construct can also be coded using a `switch` statement. Its syntax is

```
switch (expression) {
    case constant1: statementList1;
    case constant2: statementList2;
        :
        :
    case constantN: statementListN;
    default: statementList;
}
```

The `switch` statement evaluates the *expression* and then looks for its value among the `case` constants. If the value is found among the *constant*s listed, then the statements in that *statementList* are executed. Otherwise if there is a `default` (which is optional), then the program branches to that *statementList*. Note that the `expression` must evaluate to an integer type and that the `constants` must be integer constants (which include `chars`).

EXAMPLE 2.15

The program has the same effect as the program in Example 2.14:

```
main()
{
    int score;
    cout << "Enter the test score: ";  cin >> score;
    switch (score/10) {
        case 10:
        case  9: cout << 'A' << endl;  break;
        case  8: cout << 'B' << endl;  break;
        case  7: cout << 'C' << endl;  break;
        case  6: cout << 'D' << endl;  break;
        case  5:
        case  4:
        case  3:
        case  2:
        case  1:
        case  0: cout << 'F' << endl;  break;
        default: cout << "Error: score is out of range.\n";
    }
}
```

First the program divides the `score` by 10. In the second run where the input is 47, the expression `score/10` evaluates to 4. Then that value is located in the `case` list, and every statement from there to the next `break` is executed. That spans all the cases down to case 0 to reach the next `break` statement. This phenomenon is called a *fall through*.

2.11 THE CONDITIONAL EXPRESSION OPERATOR

C++ provides an abbreviated form of a special case of the `if...else` statement. It is called the *conditional expression operator* and uses the `?` and the `:` symbols in a special ternary format:

```
condition ? expression1 : expression2
```

Like any operator, this combines the given expressions to produce a value. The value produced is either the value of `expression1` or that of `expression2`, according to whether the `condition` is true or false. For example, the assignment statement

```
min = x < y ? x : y;
```

will assign the value of `x` to `min` if `x < y`, otherwise it assigns the value of `y` to `min`.

The conditional expression operator is generally used only when the condition and both expressions are very simple.

2.12 SCOPE

The *scope* of an identifier is that part of the program where it can be used. For example variables cannot be used before they are declared, so their scopes begin where they are declared. This is illustrated by the next example.

EXAMPLE 2.16 Scope of Variables

```
main()
{
    x = 11;   // ERROR: this is not in the scope of x
    int x;
    {
        x = 22;   // OK: this is in the scope of x
        y = 33;   // ERROR: this is not in the scope of y
        int y;
        x = 44;   // OK: this is in the scope of x
        y = 55;   // OK: this is in the scope of y
    }
    x = 66;   // OK: this is in the scope of x
    y = 77;   // ERROR: this is not in the scope of y
}
```

The scope of `x` extends from the point where it is declared to the end of `main()`. The scope of `y` extends from the point where it is declared to the end of the internal block within which it is declared.

A program may have several objects with the same name as long as their scopes are nested or disjoint. This is illustrated by the next example:

EXAMPLE 2.17 Nested and Parallel Scopes

```
int x = 11;                                          // this x is global

main()
{                                                    // begin scope of main()
    int x = 22;
    {                                      // begin scope of internal block
        int x = 33;
        cout << "In block inside main(): x = " << x << endl;
    }                                        // end scope of internal block
    cout << "In main(): x = " << x << endl;
    cout << "In main(): ::x = " << ::x << endl;
}                                                    // end scope of main()
```

```
In block inside main(): x = 33
In main(): x = 22
In main(): ::x = 11
```

There are three different objects named x in this program. The x that is initialized with the value 11 is a global variable, so its scope extends throughout the file. The x that is initialized with the value 22 has scope limited to main(). Since this is nested within the scope of the first x, it hides the first x within main(). The x that is initialized with the value 33 has scope limited to the internal block within main(), so it hides both the first and the second x within that block.

The last line in the program uses the *scope resolution operator* :: to access the global x that is otherwise hidden in main().

2.13 ENUMERATION TYPES

In addition to the predefined types such as int and char, C++ allows you to define your own special data types. This can be done in several ways, the most powerful of which use classes as described in Chapters 8-14. We consider here a much simpler kind of user-defined type.

An *enumeration type* is an integral type that is defined by the user with the syntax

```
enum typename { enumeratorlist };
```

Here enum is a C++ keyword, *typename* stands for an identifier that names the type being defined, and *enumeratorlist* stands for a list of identifiers that define integer constants. For example the following defines the enumeration type Semester, specifying three possible values that a variable of that type can have

```
enum Semester {fall, spring, summer};
```

We can then declare variables of this type:

```
Semester s1, s2;
```

and we can use those variables and those type values as we would with predefined types:

```
s1 = spring;
s2 = fall;
if (s1 == s2) cout << "Same semester.\n";
```

The actual values defined in the `enumeratorlist` are called *enumerators*. In fact, they are ordinary integer values. The values `fall`, `spring`, and `summer` defined for the `Semester` type above could have been defined like this:

```
const int fall = 0;
const int winter = 1;
const int summer = 2;
```

The values 0, 1, ... are assigned automatically when the type is defined. These default values can be overridden in the *enumeratorlist*:

```
enum Coin {penny = 1, nickel = 5, dime = 10, quarter = 25};
```

If integer values are assigned to only some of the enumerators, then the ones that follow are given consecutive values. For example,

```
enum Month {jan = 1, feb, mar, apr, may, jun, jul, aug, sep,
            oct, nov, dec};
```

will assign the numbers 1 through 12 to the twelve months.

Since enumerators are simply integer constants, it is legal to have several different enumerators with the same value:

```
enum Answer {no = 0, false = 0, yes = 1, true = 1, ok = 1};
```

This would allow the code

```
Answer ans;
    ⋮
if (ans == yes) cout << "You said it was o.k.\n";
```

to work as expected. If the value of the variable `ans` is `yes`, `true`, or `ok` (all of which equal 1), then the condition will be true and the output will occur. Note that since the integer value 1 always means "true" in a condition, this conditional statement could also be written

```
if (ans) cout << "You said it was o.k.\n";
```

Enumeration types are usually defined to make code more *self-documenting*; *i.e.*, easier to understand. Here are a few more typical examples:

```
enum Boolean {false, true};
enum Sex {female, male};
enum Day {sun, mon, tue, wed, thu, fri, sat};
enum Base {binary = 2, octal = 8, decimal = 10, hexadecimal = 16};
enum Color {red, orange, yellow, green, blue, violet};
enum Rank {two, three, four, five, six, seven, eight, nine, ten,
           jack, queen, king, ace};
enum Suit {clubs, diamonds, hearts, spades};
enum Roman {I = 1, V = 5, X = 10, L = 50, C = 100, D = 500,
            M = 1000};
```

Definitions like these can help make your code more readable. But enumerations should not be overused. Each enumerator in an enumerator list defines a new identifier. For example, the definition of `Roman` above defines the seven identifiers `I`, `V`, `X`, `L`, `C`, `D`, and `M` as specific integer constants, so these letters could not be used for any other purpose within the scope of their definition.

Note that enumerators must be valid identifiers. So for example, the following would not be valid:

```
enum Grade {F, D, C-, C, C+, B-, B, B+, A-, A};   // ERROR!
```

because the characters '+' and '–' cannot be used in identifiers. Also, the following would not be valid:

```
enum Month {jan = 1, feb, mar, apr, may, jun, jul, aug, sep,
            oct, nov, dec};
enum Base {bin = 2, oct = 8, dec = 10, hex = 16};   // ERROR!
```

because the constant `oct` is being redefined.

2.14 INTEGER TYPE CONVERSIONS

In many cases, C++ allows objects of one type to be used where another type is expected. This is called *type conversion*. The most common examples of type conversion are from one integer type to another, which we consider here, and conversion from an integer type to a floating point type, which we consider in Chapter 3.

The general idea is that one integer type may be used where another integer type is expected if the expected type has a higher "rank". For example, a `char` can be used where an `int` is expected because `int` has higher rank than `char`.

EXAMPLE 2.18 Integer Promotion

```
main()
{
    char c = 'A';
    short m = 22;
    int n = c + m;
    cout << "n = " << n << endl;
}
```
```
n = 87
```

The `char` variable `c` is initialized with the integer value 65 (the ASCII for the character `'A'`) and the `short` variable `m` is initialized with the integer value 22. In the assignment `n = c + m`, the operands `c` and `m` have different integral types, so their values 65 and 22 are both promoted to type `int` before the resulting value of 87 is assigned to `n`.

Integral promotion like this is quite common and usually occurs unnoticed. The general rule is that any integral type will be promoted to `int` whenever an integer conversion like this is necessary. An exception to that rule applies on compilers whose implementation of `int` does not cover all the values of the type being promoted. In this case the integral type will be promoted to `unsigned int` instead. For example, in Borland C++, the range of type `unsigned short` is 0 to 65,536 (see Example 1.14) which extends beyond the range of `int` (−32,768 to 32,767), so on that compiler `unsigned short` gets promoted to `unsigned int` instead of to `int`.

Since enumeration types are integral types, integral promotion applies to them too, as the next example illustrates.

EXAMPLE 2.19 Integer Promotion

```
enum Color {red, orange, yellow, green, blue, violet};

main()
{
    Color x = blue;
    cout << "x = " << x << endl;
}
```

```
x = 4
```

In the last line, the value of `x` is promoted from the enumeration type `Color` to the type `int` before it is inserted into the output stream.

Review Questions

2.1   Write a single C++ statement that prints `"Too many"` if the variable `count` exceeds 100.

2.2   What is the difference between a reserved word and a standard identifier?

2.3   What is "short-circuiting" and how is it helpful?

2.4   How is the following expression evaluated?

```
(x < y ? -1 : (x == y ? 0 : 1) );
```

2.5   What is a "fall through"?

2.6   State whether each of the following is true or false. If false, tell why.

a. `!(p || q)` is the same as `!p || !q`
b. `!!!p` is the same as `!p`
c. `p && q || r` is the same as `p && (q || r)`

2.7   What is wrong with the following code:

```
enum Semester {fall, spring, summer};
enum Season {spring, summer, fall, winter};
```

2.8   What is wrong with the following code:

```
enum Friends {"Tom", "Dick", "Harry", };
```

2.9   What is wrong with the following code:

```
if (x = 0) cout << x << " = 0\n";
else cout << x << " != 0\n";
```

2.10   What is wrong with the following code:

```
if (x < y < z) cout << x << " < " << y << " < " << z << endl;
```

2.11   What is wrong with the following code:

a. `cin << count;`
b. `if x < y min = x`
   `else min = y;`

2.12 - What is wrong with the following code:

```
cout << "Enter n: ";
cin >> n;
if (n < 0)
    cout << "That is negative. Try again.\n";
    cin >> n;
else
    cout << "o.k. n = " << n << endl;
```

Solved Problems

2.13 Construct a logical expression to represent each of the following conditions: *a.* score is greater than or equal to 80 but less than 90; *b.* answer is either 'N' or 'n'; *c.* n is even but not 8; *d.* ch is a capital letter.

a. (score >= 80 && score < 90);

b. (answer == 'N' || answer == 'n');

b. (n%2 == 0 && n != 8);

b. (ch >= 'A' && ch <= 'Z');

2.14 What is wrong with the following code:

```
if (x == 0)
    if (y == 0) cout << "x and y are both zero.\n";
else cout << "x is not zero.\n";
```

The programmer clearly intended for the second output "x is not zero.\n" to be printed if the first condition (x == 0) is false, regardless of the second condition (y == 0). That is, the else was intended to be matched with the first if. But the "else matching" rule causes it to be matched it with the second condition, which means that the output "x is not zero.\n" will be printed only when x is zero and y is not zero.

The "else matching" rule can be overridden with braces:

```
if (x == 0) {
    if (y == 0) cout << "x and y are both zero.\n";
}
else cout << "x is not zero.\n";
```

Now the else will be matched with the first if, the way the programmer had intended it to be.

2.15 What is the difference between the following two statements:

```
if (n > 2) { if (n < 6) cout << "OK"; } else cout << "NG";

if (n > 2) { if (n < 6) cout << "OK"; else cout << "NG"; }
```

In the first statement, the `else` is matched with the first `if`. In the second statement, the `else` is matched with the second `if`. If $n \leq 2$, the first statement will print NG while the second statement will do nothing. If $2 < n < 6$, both statements will print OK. If $n \geq 6$, the first statement will do nothing while the second statement will print NG.

Note that this code is difficult to read because it does not follow standard indentation conventions. The first statement should be written

```
if (n > 2) {
    if (n < 6) cout << "OK";
}
else cout << "NG";
```

The braces are needed here to override the "`else` matching" rule. This `else` is intended to match the first `if`.

The second statement should be written

```
if (n > 2)
    if (n < 6) cout << "OK";
    else cout << "NG";
```

Here the braces are not needed because the `else` is intended to be matched with the second `if`.

Solved Programming Problems

2.16 Write and run a program that reads the user's age and then prints "You are a child." if the age < 18, "You are an adult." if $18 \leq$ age < 65, and "You are a senior citizen." if age $\geq$ 65.

Here we used the `else if` construct because the three outcomes depend upon `age` being in one of three disjoint intervals:

```
main()
{
    int age;
    cout << "Enter your age: ";
    cin >> age;
    if (age < 18) cout << "You are a child.\n";
    else if (age < 65) cout << "You are an adult.\n";
    else cout << "you are a senior citizen.\n";
}
```

```
Enter your age: 44
You are an adult.
```

If control reaches the second condition `(age < 65)`, then the first condition must be false so in fact $18 \leq$ age < 65. Similarly, if control reaches the second `else`, then both conditions must be false so in fact age $\geq$ 65.

2.17 Write and run a program that reads two integers and then uses the conditional expression operator to print either "multiple" or "not" according to whether one of the integers is a multiple of the other.

An integer `m` is a multiple of an integer `n` if the remainder from the integer division of `m` by `n` is 0. So the compound condition `m % n == 0 || n % m == 0` tests whether either is a multiple of the other:

```
main()
{
    int m, n;
    cin >> m >> n;
    cout << (m % n == 0 || n % m == 0 ? "multiple" : "not") << endl;
}
```

```
30 4
not
```

```
30 5
multiple
```

The value of the conditional expression will be either `"multiple"` or `"not"`, according to whether the compound condition is true. So sending the complete conditional expression to the output stream produces the desired result.

2.18 Write and run a program that simulates a simple calculator. It reads two integers and a character. If the character is a `+`, the sum is printed; if it is a `-`, the difference is printed; if it is a `*`, the product is printed; if it is a `/`, the quotient is printed; and if it is a `%`, the remainder is printed. Use a `switch` statement.

The character representing the operation should be the control variable for the `switch` statement:

```
main()
{
    int x, y;
    char op;
    cout << "Enter two integers: ";
    cin >> x >> y;
    cout << "Enter an operator: ";
    cin >> op;
    switch (op) {
        case '+': cout << x + y << endl;  break;
        case '-': cout << x - y << endl;  break;
        case '*': cout << x * y << endl;  break;
        case '/': cout << x / y << endl;  break;
        case '%': cout << x % y << endl;  break;
    }
}
```

```
Enter two integers: 30 13
Enter an operator: %
4
```

In each of the five cases, we simply print the value of the corresponding arithmetic operation and then break.

2.19 Write and run a program that plays the game of "Rock, paper, scissors." In this game, two players simultaneously say (or display a hand symbol representing) either "rock," "paper," or "scissors." The winner is the one whose choice dominates the other. The rules are: paper dominates (wraps) rock, rock dominates (breaks) scissors, and scissors dominate (cut) paper. Use enumerated types for the choices and for the results.

First define the two `enum` types `Choice` and `Result`. Then declare variables `choice1`, `choice2`, and `result` of these types, and use an integer `n` to get the required input and assign it to them:

```
enum Choice {rock, paper, scissors};
enum Result {player1, player2, tie};

main()
{
    int n;
    Choice choice1, choice2;
    Result result;
    cout << "Choose rock (0), paper (1), or scissors (2):\n";
    cout << "Player #1: ";
    cin >> n;
    choice1 = Choice(n);
    cout << "Player #2: ";
    cin >> n;
    choice2 = Choice(n);
    if (choice1 == choice2) result = tie;
    else if (choice1 == rock)
        if (choice2 == paper) result = player2;
        else result = player1;
    else if (choice1 == paper)
        if (choice2 == rock) result = player1;
        else result = player2;
    else // (choice1 == scissors)
        if (choice2 == rock) result = player2;
        else result = player1;
    if (result == tie) cout << "\tYou tied.\n";
    else if (result == player1) cout << "\tPlayer #1 wins.\n";
    else cout << "\tPlayer #2 wins.\n";
}
```

```
Choose rock (0), paper (1), or scissors (2):
Player #1: 1
Player #2: 1
    You tied.
```

```
Choose rock (0), paper (1), or scissors (2):
Player #1: 2
Player #2: 1
    Player #1 wins.
```

```
Choose rock (0), paper (1), or scissors (2):
Player #1: 2
Player #2: 0
        Player #2 wins.
```

Through a series of nested if statements, we are able to cover all the possibilities.

2.20   Write and test a program that solves quadratic equations.

A *quadratic equation* is an equation of the form $ax^2 + bx + c = 0$, where a, b, and c are given coefficients and x is the unknown. The coefficients are real number inputs, so they should be declared of type `float` or `double`. Since quadratic equations typically have two solutions, we'll use `x1` and `x2` for the solutions to be output. These should be declared of type `double` to avoid inaccuracies from round-off error.

The solution(s) to the quadratic equation is given by the *quadratic formula*:

$$x = \frac{-b \pm \sqrt{b^2 - 4ac}}{2a}$$

But this will not apply if a is zero, so that condition must be checked separately. The formula also fails to work (for real numbers) if the expression under the square root is negative. That expression $b^2 - 4ac$ is called the *discriminant* of the quadratic. We define that as the separate variable `d` and check its sign:

```
#include <iostream.h>
#include <math.h>     // needed for the sqrt() function
// This solves the equation a*x*x + b*x + c == 0:
main()
{
    float a, b, c;
    cout << "Enter coefficients of quadratic equation: ";
    cin >> a >> b >> c;
    if (a == 0) {
        cout << "This is not a quadratic equation: a == 0\n";
        return 0;
    }
    cout << "The equation is: " << a << "x^2 + " << b
        << "x + " << c << " = 0\n";
    double d, x1, x2;
    d = b*b - 4*a*c;   // the discriminant
    if (d < 0) {
        cout << "This equation has no real solutions: d < 0\n";
        return 0;
    }
    x1 = (-b + sqrt(d))/(2*a);
    x2 = (-b - sqrt(d))/(2*a);
    cout << "The solutions are: " << x1 << ", " << x2 << endl;
}
```

```
Enter coefficients of quadratic equation: 2 1 -6
The equation is: 2x^2 + 1x + -6 = 0
The solutions are: 1.5, -2
```

```
Enter coefficients of quadratic equation: 1 4 5
The equation is: 1x^2 + 4x + 5 = 0
This equation has no real solutions: d < 0
```

```
Enter coefficients of quadratic equation: 0 4 5
This is not a quadratic equation: a == 0
```

Note how we use the `return` statement inside the conditionals to terminate the program if either `a` is zero or `d` is negative. The alternative would have be to use `else` clauses after each `if`.

Supplementary Problems

2.21 Write a single assignment statement that uses the conditional expression operator to assign the absolute value of `x` to `absx`.

2.22 Construct a logical expression to represent each of the following conditions:

a. `weight` is greater than or equal to 115 but less than 125.

b. `ch` is either `'Q'` or `'q'`.

c. `x` is even but not 26.

d. `donation` is in the range 1000–2000 or `guest` is 1.

e. `ch` is a lowercase or an uppercase letter.

2.23 Construct a truth table for each of the following boolean expressions, showing its truth value (0 or 1) for all 4 combinations of truth values of its operands `p` and `q`.

a. `!p || q`

b. `p && q || !p && !q`

c. `(p || q) && !(p && q)`

2.24 Use truth tables to determine whether the two boolean expressions in each of the following are equivalent.

a. `!(p && q)`, and `!p && !q`

b. `!!p`, and `p`

c. `!p || q`, and `p || !q`

d. `p && (q && r)`, and `(p && q) && r`

e. `p || (q && r)`, and `(p || q) && r`

2.25 Write a single C++ statement that prints "too many" if the variable `count` exceeds 100, using

a. an `if` statement;

b. the conditional expression operator.

Supplementary Programming Problems

2.26 Rewrite the "Hello World" program so that it reads the user's three initials as input and prints them instead of "World!" For example, if the user enters `R`, `W`, and `D`, the output would be `Hello, R. W. D.`

2.27 Write and run a program that reads four integers and prints them in the opposite order.

2.28 Write and run a program that reads four integers and prints the minimum and maximum. Use the conditional statements as in Example 2.8.

2.29 Write and run a program that reads a grade, A, B, C, D, or F and then prints "excellent," "good," "fair," "poor," or "failure." Use the `else if` structure.

2.30 Write and run a program that prints the truth tables for each of the boolean expressions in Problem 2.23.

2.31 Write and run a program that prints the truth tables to verify your answers to Problem 2.24.

2.32 The 1993 U.S. Tax Rate Schedule for taxpayers with single status reads:

Table 2.1 Schedule X

If the amount on Form 1040, line 37, is: Over—	But not over—	Enter on Form 1040, line 38	of the amount over—
$0	$22,100	15%	$0
22,100	53,500	$3,315.00 + 28%	22,100
53,500	115,000	12,107.00 + 31%	53,500
115,000	250,000	31,172.00 + 36%	115,000
250,000	-------	79,772.00 + 39.6%	250,000

Write and run a program that reads a dollar amount and prints the correct tax.

2.33 Write and run a program that reads a grade, A, B, C, D, or F and then prints "excellent," "good," "fair," "poor," or "failure." Use a `switch` statement.

2.34 Write and run a program that reads a character and then uses a `switch` statement to print "do" if the character is a C, "re" if it is a D, "me" if it is an E, "fa" if it is an F, "sol" if it is a G, "la" if it is an A, "ti" if it is a B, and "error" if it is any other character.

2.35 Write and run a program that reads a character and then prints: "It is a vowel" if it is a vowel, "It is an operator" if it is one of the five arithmetic operators, and "It is something else" if it is anything else. Use a `switch` statement.

2.36 Write and run a program that reads a single `char` digit and then prints the number as a literal string. For example, if the input is 7, then the output should be the word "seven". Use a `switch` statement.

2.37 Write and run a program that reads two characters and two integers. If the first character or the two characters together form one of the six relational operators, then the two integers are compared using that operator and a message describing the result is printed. For example, a run could look like this:

```
!= 33 77
33 is not equal to 77
```

2.38 Modify the program in Example 2.10 by replacing the second `if` with an `else if` and the third `if` with an `else`. How does this improve the efficiency of the program? On the average, how many conditions will be tested per run?

2.39 Write and run a program that reads three integers and prints the minimum and maximum. Use the conditional expression operator.

2.40 Modify Problem 2.18 so that it is more user-friendly. Use a `char` instead of an `int` for input, allowing the user to type in either "r", "p", or "s" for "rock," "paper," or "scissors."

Answers to Review Questions

2.1   `if (count > 100) cout << "Too many";`

2.2   A *reserved word* is a keyword in a programming language that serves to mark the structure of a statement. For example, the keywords `if` and `else` are reserved words. A *standard identifier* is a keyword that defines a type. Among the 48 keywords in C++, `if`, `else`, and `while` are reserved words, and `char`, `int`, and `float` are standard identifiers.

2.3   The term "short-circuiting" is used to describe the way C++ evaluates compound logical expressions like `(x > 2 || y > 5)` and `(x > 2 && y > 5)`. If `x` is greater than 2 in the first expression, then `y` will not even be evaluated. If `x` is less than or equal to 2 in the second expression, then `y` will not even be evaluated. In these cases only the first part of the compound expression is evaluated because that value alone determines the truth value of the compound expression.

2.4   This expression evaluates to –1 if `x < y`, it evaluates to 0 if `x == y`, and it evaluates to 1 if `x > y`.

2.5   A "fall through" in a `switch` statement is a case that does not include a `break` statement, thereby causing control to continue right on to the next case statement.

2.6   *a.* `!(p || q)` is not the same as `!p || !q`; for example, if `p` is true and `q` is false, the first expression will be false but the second expression will be true. The correct equivalent to the expression `!(p || q)` is the expression `!p && !q`.
   b. `!!!p` is the same as `!p`.
   c. `p && q || r` is <u>not</u> the same as `p && (q || r)`; for example, if `p` is false and `r` is true, the first expression will be true, but the second expression will be false: `p && q || r` <u>is</u> the same as `(p && q) || r`.

2.7   The second `enum` definition attempts to redefine the constants `spring`, `summer`, and `fall`.

2.8   Enumerators must be valid identifiers. String literals like `"Tom"` and `"Dick"` are not identifiers.

2.9   The programmer probably intended to test the condition `(x == 0)`. But by using assignment operator "`=`" instead of the equality operator "`==`" the result will be radically different from what was intended. For example, if `x` has the value 22 prior to the `if` statement, then the `if` statement will change the value of `x` to 0. Moreover, the assignment expression `(x = 0)` will be evaluated to 0 which means "false," so the `else` part of the conditional will execute, reporting that `x` is not zero!

2.10   The programmer probably intended to test the condition `(x < y && y < z)`. The code as written will compile and run, but not as intended. For example, if the prior values of `x`, `y`, and `z` are 44, 66, and 22, respectively, then the algebraic condition "$x < y < z$" is false. But as written, the code will be evaluated from left to right, as `(x < y) < z`. First the condition `x < y` will be evaluated as "true." But this has the numeric value 1, so the expression $(x < y)$ is evaluated to 1. Then the combined expression $(x < y) < z$ is evaluated as $(1) < 66$ which is also true. So the output statement will execute, erroneously reporting that $44 < 66 < 22$.

2.11   *a.* Either `cout` should be used in place of `cin`, or the extraction operator `>>` should be used in place of the insertion operator `<<`.
   b. Parentheses are required around the condition `x < y`, and a semicolon is required at the end of the `if` clause before the `else`.

2.12   There is more than one statement between the `if` clause and the `else` clause. They need to be made into a compound statement by enclosing them in braces `{ }`.

Chapter 3

Iteration and Floating Types

Iteration is the repetition of a statement or block of statements in a program. C++ has three iteration statements: the `while` statement, the `do...while` statement, and the `for` statement. Iteration statements are also called *loops* because of their cyclic nature.

3.1 THE `while` STATEMENT

The `while` statement has the syntax

```
while (condition) statement;
```

First the `condition` is evaluated. If it is nonzero (*i.e.*, true), the `statement` is executed and the `condition` is evaluated again. These two steps are repeated until the `condition` evaluates to zero (*i.e.*, is false). Note that parentheses are required around the `condition`.

EXAMPLE 3.1 Printing Cubes

This program uses a `while` loop to print cubes:

```
main()
{
    int n;
    cout << "Enter positive integers.  Terminate with 0.\n\t: ";
    cin >> n;
    while (n > 0) {
        cout << n << " cubed is " << n*n*n << "\n\t: ";
        cin >> n;
    }
}
```

```
Enter positive integers.  Terminate with 0.
        : 2
2 cubed is 8
        : 5
5 cubed is 125
        : 7
7 cubed is 343
        : 0
```

The first value input for `n` is 2. The `while` statement tests the condition `(n > 0)`. Since the condition is true, the two statements inside the loop are executed. The second statement reads 5 into `n`. At the end of the loop, control returns to the condition `(n > 0)`. Since it is still true, the two statements inside the loop are executed again. Each time control reaches the end of the loop, the condition is tested again. After the third iteration, `n` is 0, and the condition is false. That terminates the loop.

Most C++ programmers indent all the statements that lie inside a loop. This makes it easier to see the logic of the program.

EXAMPLE 3.2 Sum of Squares

This program uses a `while` loop to find the sum of the squares of the integers from 1 to n:

$$\sum_{i=1}^{n} i^2 = 1^2 + 2^2 + 3^2 + \cdots + n^2$$

```
main()
{
    int i = 1, n, sum = 0;
    cout << "Enter a positive integer: ";  cin >> n;
    while (i <= n) {
        sum += i*i;
        i++;
    }
    cout << "The sum of the first " << n << " squares is "
        << sum << endl;
}
```

```
Enter a positive integer: 4
The sum of the first 4 squares is 30
```

```
Enter a positive integer: 6
The sum of the first 6 squares is 91
```

The first run computes the sum of the first 4 squares: $1 + 4 + 9 + 16 = 30$. The second run computes the sum of the first 6 squares: $1 + 4 + 9 + 16 + 25 + 36 = 91$.

When you want several statements to execute within a loop, you need to use braces `{ }` to combine them into a compound statement. Example 3.2 illustrates the standard way to format a compound statement in a loop. The left brace ends the loop's header line. The right brace stands on a line by itself directly below the "w" of the `while` keyword. And the statements within the compound statement are all indented.

Of course, the compiler doesn't care how the code is formatted. It would accept this format:

```
    while (i <= n) { sum += i*i; i++; }
```

But most C++ programmers find the displayed format easier to read. Some C programmers also like to put the left brace on a line by itself, directly below the "w" of the `while` keyword.

3.2 THE do...while STATEMENT

The `do...while` statement is almost the same as the `while` statement. Its syntax is

```
    do statement while (condition);
```

The only difference is that the `do...while` statement executes the `statement` <u>first</u> and then evaluates the `condition`. These two steps are repeated until the `condition` evaluates to zero (*i.e*, is false). A `do...while` loop will always iterate at least once, regardless of the value of the `condition`, because the statement executes before the `condition` is evaluated the first time.

EXAMPLE 3.3 The Factorial Function

This program computes the factorial function: $n! = (n)(n-1)\ldots(3)(2)(1)$.

```
main()
{
    int n, f = 1;
    cout << "Enter a positive integer: ";  cin >> n;
    cout << n << " factorial is ";
    do {
        f *= n;
        n--;
    } while (n > 1);
    cout << f << endl;
}
```

```
Enter a positive integer: 5
5 factorial is 120
```

```
Enter a positive integer: 8
8 factorial is 40320
```

The program initializes f to 1 and then multiplies it by the input number n and all the positive integers that are less than n. So 5! = (5)(4)(3)(2)(1) = 120, and 8! = (8)(7)(6)(5)(4)(3)(2)(1) = 40,320.

3.3 THE for STATEMENT

A loop is controlled by three separate parts: an *initialization*, a *continuation condition*, and an *update*. For example, in the program in Example 3.3, the loop control variable is n; its initialization is cin >> n, its continuation condition is n > 1, and its update is n--. When these three parts are simple, the loop can be set up as a for loop, which is usually simpler than its equivalent while loop and do...while loop.

The syntax for the for statement is

```
for (initialization; continuation condition; update) statement;
```

The initialization, the continuation condition, or the update may be empty.

EXAMPLE 3.4 Sum of Squares Again

This program has the same effect as the one in Example 3.2:

```
main()
{
    int n, sum = 0;
    cout << "Enter a positive integer: ";
    cin >> n;
    for (int i = 1; i <= n; i++)
        sum += i*i;
    cout << "The sum of the first " << n << " squares is "
        << sum << endl;
}
```

Here the initialization is int i = 1, the continuation condition is i <= n, and the update is i++.

It is customary to localize the declaration of the control variable in the initialization part of a for loop. For example, the control variable i in the program above is declared to be an int within the initialization part int i = 1. This is a nice feature of C++. However, once the control variable is declared this way, it should not be redeclared in a later for loop. For example,

```
for (int i = 0; i < 100; i++)
    sum += i*i;
for (int i = 0; i < 100; i++) // ERROR: i has already been declared
    cout << i*i*i;
```

The same control variable can be used again; it just cannot be redeclared:

```
for (i = 0; i < 100; i++)      // OK
    cout << i*i*i;
```

If you have the choice between a for loop and a while or do..while loop, you should probably use the for loop. As the next example illustrates, a for loop is usually easier to understand.

EXAMPLE 3.5 The Factorial Function Again

Compare this program with the one in Example 3.3:

```
main()
{
    int n, f = 1;
    cout << "Enter a positive integer: ";  cin >> n;
    for (int i = 2; i <= n; i++)
        f *= i;
    cout << n << " factorial is " << f << endl;
}
```

This computes the factorial by multiplying 1 by the factors 2, 3, …, $n-1$, n. It won't run any faster than the version done with the while loop, but the code is more succinct.

EXAMPLE 3.6 The Extreme Values in a Sequence

This program reads a sequence of positive integers, terminated by the integer 0. It then prints the smallest and largest numbers in the sequence.

```
main()
{
    int n, min, max;
    cout << "Enter positive integers.  Terminate input with 0:\n";
    cin >> n;
    for (min = max = n; n > 0; ) {
        if (n < min) min = n;           // min and max are the smallest
        else if (n > max) max = n;      // and largest of the n that
        cin >> n;                       // have been read so far
    }
    cout << "min = " << min << " and max = " << max << endl;
}
```

```
Enter positive integers.  Terminate input with 0:
55
22
88
66
0
min = 22 and max = 88
```

Notice that the initialization part of the `for` loop `min = max = n` is the equivalent of two assignments, and the update part is empty. Also notice the use of the in-line comment that spans three lines. It describes a *loop invariant*, a condition on the variables that should be true on every iteration of the loop.

A *sentinel* is a special value of an input variable that is used to terminate the input loop. In the example above, the value 0 is used as a sentinel.

EXAMPLE 3.7 More than One Control Variable

This program shows how a `for` loop may use more than one control variable:

```
main()
{
    for (int m = 1, n = 8; m < n; m++, n--)
        cout << "m = " << m << ", n = " << n << endl;
}
```

```
m = 1, n = 8
m = 2, n = 7
m = 3, n = 6
m = 4, n = 5
```

The initialization part of the `for` loop declares the two control variables `m` and `n`, initializing `m` to 1 and `n` to 8. The update part uses the comma operator to include two update expressions: `m++` and `n--`. The loop continues as long as `m < n`. (Note that the comma in the initialization part of the `for` loop is not the comma operator; it is used there as part of an initialization list.)

3.4 THE `break` STATEMENT

We have already seen the `break` statement used in the `switch` statement. It is also used in loops. When it executes, it terminates the loop, "breaking out" of the iteration at that point.

EXAMPLE 3.8 Breaking Out of an Infinite Loop

This `while` loop is equivalent to the one in Example 3.2:

```
while (1) {
    if (i > n) break;      // loop stops here when i > n
    sum += i*i;
    i++;
}
```

As long as `(i <= n)`, the loop will continue, just as in Example 3.2. But as soon as `(i > n)`, the `break` statement executes, immediately terminating the loop.

EXAMPLE 3.9 Controlling Input with a Sentinel

This program reads a sequence of positive integers, terminated by 0, and prints their average:

```
main()
{
    int n, count = 0, sum = 0;
    cout << "Enter positive integers.  Terminate input with 0:\n";
    for ( ; ; ) {
        cout << "\t" << count + 1 << ": ";
        cin >> n;
        if (n == 0) break;
        ++count;
        sum += n;
    }
    cout << "The average of the " << count << " numbers is "
        << float(sum)/count << endl;
}
```

```
Enter positive integers.  Terminate input with 0:
        1: 7
        2: 4
        3: 5
        4: 2
        5: 0
The average of the 4 numbers is 4.5
```

When 0 is input, the `break` executes, which immediately terminating the `for` loop and causes the final output statement to execute. Without the use of the break here, the `++count` statement would have to be put in a conditional or `count` would have to be decremented outside the loop or initialized to –1.

Notice that all three control parts of this `for` loop are empty: `for ( ; ; )`. This construct is pronounced "forever." Without the presence of the `break`, this would be an *infinite loop*.

3.5 THE `continue` STATEMENT

The `break` statement jumps over all the rest of the statements in the loop's block and goes to the next statement after the loop. The `continue` statement does the same thing except that, instead of terminating the loop, it goes back to the beginning of the loop's block to begin the next iteration.

EXAMPLE 3.10 Using `continue` and `break` Statements

This little program illustrates the `continue` and `break` statements:

```
main()
{
    int n;
    for (;;){
        cout << "Enter int: ";  cin >> n;
        if (n%2 == 0) continue;
        if (n%3 == 0) break;
        cout << "\tBottom of loop.\n";
    }
    cout << "\tOutside of loop.\n";
}
```

```
Enter int: 7
        Bottom of loop.
Enter int: 4
Enter int: 9
        Outside of loop.
```

When n has the value 7, both of the `if` conditions fail and control reaches the bottom of the loop. When n has the value 4, the first `if` condition is true (4 is a multiple of 2), so control skips over the rest of the statements in the loop and jumps immediately to the top of the loop again to continue with the next iteration. When n has the value 9, the first `if` condition is false (9 is not a multiple of 2) but the second `if` condition is true (9 is a multiple of 3), so control `break`s out of the loop and jumps immediately to the first statement that follows the loop.

3.6 THE `goto` STATEMENT

The `break` statement, the `continue` statement, and the `switch` statement cause the control of the program to branch to a location other than where it normally would go. The destination of the branch is determined by the context: `break` goes to the next statement outside the loop, `continue` goes to the loop's continue condition, and `switch` goes to the correct case constant. All three of these statements are called *jump statements* because they cause the control of the program to "jump over" other statements.

The `goto` statement is another kind of jump statement. Its destination is specified by a label within the statement.

A *label* is simply an identifier followed by a colon, either at the beginning of a statement. Labels work like the `case` statements inside a `switch` statement: they specify the destination of the jump.

EXAMPLE 3.11 Breaking Out of Nested Loops

This program illustrates the correct way to break out of nested loops.

```
main()
{
    int a, b, c;
    cin >> a >> b >> c;
    for (int i = 0; i < a; i++) {
        for (int j = 0; j < b; j++)
            for (int k = 0; k < c; k++)
                if (i*j*k > 100) goto esc;
                else cout << i*j*k << " ";
esc: cout << endl;
    }
}
```

When the `goto` is reached inside the innermost loop, program control jumps out to the output statement at the bottom of the outermost loop.

There are other ways to achieve this nested loop exit. One way would be to reset the loop control variables by replacing the `if` statement inside the `k`-loop with

```
if (i*j*k > 100) j = k = b + c;
else cout << i*j*k << " ";
```

This will cause both the `j`-loop and the `k`-loop to terminate because their continue conditions, `j < b` and `k < c`, will be false. This is a "hacker's method" because it artificially sets the values of the control variables `j` and `k` to achieve the desired outcome as a *side effect*.

Another approach is to use a "done flag" within the continue conditions of the `for` loops like this:

```
int done = 0;
for (int i = 0; i < a && !done; i++) {
    for (int j = 0; j < b && !done; j++)
        for (int k = 0; k < c && !done; k++)
            if (i*j*k > 100) done = 1;
            else cout << i*j*k << " ";
}
```

But this too is somewhat artificial and cumbersome. The `goto` is really the best way to terminate nested loops.

It is easy to overuse the `goto` statement, as the next example illustrates.

EXAMPLE 3.12 Overusing `goto` **Statements**

This nonsense program shows how the use of `goto` statements can lead to "spaghetti code":

```
main()
{
    int n;
    cout << "Enter n: ";
    cin >> n;
s1: cout << "Now at step 1 with n = " << n << endl;
    --n;
    if (n < 2) return 0;
s2: cout << "Now at step 2 with n = " << n << endl;
    if (n < 7) goto s4;
s3: cout << "Now at step 3 with n = " << n << endl;
    if (n % 2 == 0) goto s1;
s4: cout << "Now at step 4 with n = " << n << endl;
    n -= 2;
    if (n > 4) goto s1;
    else goto s3;
}
```

```
Enter n: 9
Now at step 1 with n = 9
Now at step 2 with n = 8
Now at step 3 with n = 8
Now at step 1 with n = 8
Now at step 2 with n = 7
Now at step 3 with n = 7
Now at step 4 with n = 7
Now at step 1 with n = 5
Now at step 2 with n = 4
Now at step 4 with n = 4
Now at step 3 with n = 2
Now at step 1 with n = 2
```

As `n` decreases from 9 to 2, the `goto` statements send program control back and forth among the four output statements labelled `s1`, `s2`, `s3`, and `s4`:

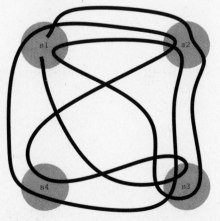

The imprudent use of `goto`s leads to unstructured *spaghetti code* which is difficult to debug.

3.7 REAL NUMBER TYPES

C++ supports three real number types: `float`, `double`, and `long double`. On most systems, `double` uses twice as many bytes as `float`. Typically, `float` uses 4 bytes, `double` uses 8 bytes, and `long double` uses 8, 10, 12, or 16 bytes.

Types that are used for real numbers are called "floating-point" types because of the way they are stored internally in the computer. On most systems, a number like 123.45 is first converted to binary form:

$$123.45 = 1111011.01110011_2$$

Then the point is "floated" so that all the bits are on its right. In this example, the floating-point form is obtained by floating the point 7 bits to the left, producing a mantissa 2^7 times smaller. So the original number is

$$123.45 = 0.111101101110011_2 \times 2^7$$

This number would be represented internally by storing the mantissa `0.111101101110011` and the exponent 7 separately. For a 32-bit `float` type, the mantissa is stored in a 23-bit segment and the exponent in an 8-bit segment, leaving 1 bit for the sign of the number. For a 64-bit `double` type, the mantissa is stored in a 52-bit segment and the exponent in an 11-bit segment.

The next example can be used on any computer to determine how many bytes it uses for each type. The program uses the `sizeof` operator which returns the size in bytes of the type specified.

EXAMPLE 3.13 Using the `sizeof` Operator

This program tells you how much space each of the 12 fundamental types uses:

```
main () {
    cout << "Number of bytes used:\n";
    cout << "\t          char: " <<          sizeof(char) << endl;
    cout << "\t         short: " <<          sizeof(short) << endl;
    cout << "\t           int: " <<           sizeof(int) << endl;
    cout << "\t          long: " <<          sizeof(long) << endl;
    cout << "\t unsigned char: " <<  sizeof(unsigned char) << endl;
    cout << "\tunsigned short: " << sizeof(unsigned short) << endl;
    cout << "\t  unsigned int: " <<   sizeof(unsigned int) << endl;
    cout << "\t unsigned long: " <<  sizeof(unsigned long) << endl;
    cout << "\t   signed char: " <<   sizeof(signed char) << endl;
    cout << "\t         float: " <<          sizeof(float) << endl;
    cout << "\t        double: " <<         sizeof(double) << endl;
    cout << "\t   long double: " <<    sizeof(long double) << endl;
}
```

The output below shows the sizes for a typical UNIX workstation. On this machine, `int` and `long` are equivalent, `unsigned int` and `unsigned long` are equivalent, and `double` and `long double` are equivalent. In other words, 'long' is no different from 'regular' on this computer.

```
Number of bytes used:
                  char: 1
                 short: 2
                   int: 4
                  long: 4
         unsigned char: 1
        unsigned short: 2
          unsigned int: 4
         unsigned long: 4
           signed char: 1
                 float: 4
                double: 8
           long double: 8
```

The next program can be used to investigate floating-point types on any computer system. It reads the values of various constants from the `float.h` header file. To access it, the program must include the preprocessor directive:

```
#include <float.h>
```

This is like the `#include <iostream.h>` directive that we always include in order to use the `cin` and `cout` objects.

EXAMPLE 3.14 Reading from the `float.h` File

This program tells you the precision and magnitude range that the `float` type has on your system:

```
main () {
    int fbits = 8*sizeof(float);          // each byte contains 8 bits
    cout << "float uses:\t" << fbits << " bits:\n\t\t"
        <<       FLT_MANT_DIG - 1 << " bits for its mantissa\n\t\t "
        << fbits - FLT_MANT_DIG << " bits for its exponent\n\t\t "
        <<                    1 << " bit for its sign\n"
        << "         to obtain: " << FLT_DIG << " sig. digits\n"
        << " with minimum value: " << FLT_MIN << endl
        << "  and maximum value: " << FLT_MAX << endl;
}
```

```
float uses:      32 bits:
                 23 bits for its mantissa
                 8 bits for its exponent
                 1 bit for its sign
         to obtain: 6 sig. digits
 with minimum value: 1.17549e-38
  and maximum value: 3.40282e+38
```

The constants `FLT_MANT_DIG`, `FLT_DIG`, `FLT_MIN`, and `FLT_MAX` are defined in the `float.h` header file.

This output is from a UNIX workstation. It shows that the 32 bits it uses to store a `float` are partitioned into 3 parts: 23 bits for the mantissa, 8 bits for the exponent, and 1 bit for the sign. The 23-bit mantissa produces a floating-point value with 6 significant digits, and the 8-bit exponent yields a range in magnitude from about 10^{-37} to about 3×10^{38}.

All floating-point arithmetic is done in `double` precision. So the only time you should use `float` instead of `double` is when you are storing large quantities of real numbers and are concerned about storage space or access time.

3.8 TYPE CONVERSIONS

We saw in Chapter 2 how one integer type can be converted automatically to another. C++ also converts integral types into floating point types when they are expected. For example,

```
int n = 22;

float x = 3.14159;

x += n;              // the value 22 is automatically converted to 22.0

cout << x - 2 << endl; // value 2 is automatically converted to 2.0
```

Converting from integer to float like this is what one would expect and is usually taken for granted. But converting from a floating point type to an integral type is not automatic.

In general, if `T` is one type and `v` is a value of another type, then the expression

```
T(v)
```

converts `v` to type `T`. This is called *type casting*. For example, if `expr` is a floating-point expression and `n` is a variable of type `int`, then

```
n = int(expr);
```

converts the value of `expr` to type `int` and assigns it to `n`. The effect is to remove the real number's fractional part, leaving only its whole number part to be assigned to `n`. For example, 2.71828 would be converted to 2. Note that this is *truncating*, not *rounding*.

EXAMPLE 3.15 Simple Type Casting

This program converts a `double` to an `int`:

```
main()
{
    double v = 1234.56789;
    int n = int(v);
    cout << "v = " << v << ", n = " << n << endl;
}
```

```
v = 1234.57, n = 1234
```

The `double` value 1234.56789 is converted to the `int` value 1234.

When one type is to be converted to a "higher" type, the type case operator is not needed. We saw this kind of *type promotion* among integral types in Chapter 2. Here's a simple example of *promotion* from `char` all the way up to `double`:

EXAMPLE 3.16 Promotion of Types

This program promotes a `char` to a `short` to an `int` to a `float` to a `double`:

```
main()
{
    char c = 'A';      cout << "  char c = " << c << endl;
    short k = c;       cout << " short k = " << k << endl;
    int m = k;         cout << "   int m = " << m << endl;
    long n = m;        cout << "  long n = " << n << endl;
    float x = n;       cout << " float x = " << x << endl;
    double y = x;      cout << "double y = " << y << endl;
}
```

```
   char c = A
 short k = 65
   int m = 65
  long n = 65
 float x = 65
double y = 65
```

The integer value of the character `'A'` is its ASCII code 65. This integer is stored as a `char` in `c`, as a `short` in `k`, as an `int` in `m`, and as an `long` in `n`. This value is then converted to the floating point value 65.0 and stored as a `float` in `x` and as a `double` in `y`. Notice that `cout` prints the integer `c` as a character, and that it prints the real numbers `x` and `y` as integers because their fractional parts are 0.

Because it is so easy to convert between integer types and real types in C++, it is easy to forget the distinction between them. In general, integers are used for counting discrete things, while reals are used for measuring on a continuous scale. This means that integer values are exact, while real values are approximate.

In the C programming language, the syntax for casting `v` as type `T` is `(T) v`. C++ inherits this form also, so we could have done `n = int(v)` as `n = (int) v`.

3.9 ROUNDOFF ERROR

In a computer, even the simplest floating-point values tend to be imprecise. This imprecision is called *roundoff error*.

EXAMPLE 3.17 Roundoff Error

This program does some simple arithmetic to illustrate roundoff error:

```
main()
{
    double x = 1000/3.0;    cout << "x = " << x << endl;
    double y = x - 333.0;   cout << "y = " << y << endl;
    double z = 3*y - 1.0;   cout << "z = " << z << endl;
    if (z == 0) cout << "z == 0.\n";
    else cout << "z does not equal 0.\n";
}
```

```
x = 333.333
y = 0.333333
z = -5.68434e-14
z does not equal 0.
```

In exact arithmetic, the variables would have the values $x = 333\ 1/3$, $y = 1/3$, and $z = 0$. But 1/3 cannot be represented exactly as a floating-point value. The inaccuracy is reflected in the residue value for z.

This example also illustrates an inherent problem with using floating-point types within conditional tests of equality. The test (z == 0) will <u>fail</u> even is z is very nearly zero, which is likely to happen when z should algebraically be zero. So it is better to avaoid tests for equality with floating-point types.

3.10 THE E-FORMAT FOR FLOATING-POINT VALUES

When input or output, floating-point values may be specified in either of two formats: *fixed-point* and *scientific*. The output in Example 3.16 illustrates both: 333.333 has fixed-point format, and -5.68434e-14 has scientific format.

In scientific format, the letter e stands for "exponent on 10." So -5.68434e-14 means -5.68434×10^{-14}, which equals -0.0000000000000568434. Obviously, the scientific format is more efficient for very small or very large numbers.

Floating-point values with magnitude in the range 0.1 to 999,999 will normally be printed in fixed-point format; all others will be printed in scientific format.

EXAMPLE 3.18 Scientific Format

This program shows how floating-point values may be input in scientific format:

```
#include <iostream.h>
main()
{
    double x;
    cout << "Enter float: ";  cin >> x;
    cout << "Its reciprocal is: " << 1/x << endl;
}
```

```
Enter float: 234.567e89
Its reciprocal is: 4.26317e-92
```

You can use either e or E in the scientific format.

3.11 CONSTANTS, VARIABLES, AND OBJECTS

An *object* is a contiguous region of memory that has an address, a size, a type, and a value. The *address* of an object is the memory address of its first byte. The *size* of an object is simply the number of bytes that it occupies in memory. The *value* of an object is the constant determined by the actual bits stored in its memory location and by the object's type which prescribes how those bits are to be interpreted.

For example, with GNU C++ on a UNIX workstation, the object n defined by

```
int n = 22;
```

has the memory address 0x3fffcd6, the size 4, the type int, and the value 22. (The memory address is a hexadecimal number. See Appendix G.)

The type of an object is determined by the programmer. The value of an object may also be determined by the programmer at compile time, or it may be determined at run-time. The size of an object is determined by the compiler. For example, in GNU C++ an int has size 4, while in Borland C++ its size is 2. The address of an object is determined by the computer's operating system at run-time.

Some objects do not have names. We will see examples of such anonymous objects in Chapters 4 and 5. A *variable* is an object that has a name. The object defined above is a variable with name 'n'.

The word "variable" is used to suggest that the object's value can be changed. An object whose value cannot be changed is called a *constant*. Constants are declared by preceding its type specifier with the keyword const, like this:

```
const int n = 22;
```

Constants must be initialized when they are declared.

EXAMPLE 3.19 The const Specifier

This program illustrates constant definitions:

```
main()
{
    const char BEEP = '\b';
    const int MAXINT = 2147483647;
    int n = MAXINT/2;
    const float KM_PER_MI = 1.60934;
    const double PI = 3.14159265358979323846;
}
```

Constants are usually defined for values like π that will be used more than once in a program but not changed.

It is customary to use all capital letters in constant identifiers to distinguish them from other kinds of identifiers. A good compiler will replace each constant symbol with its numeric value.

3.12 GENERATING PSEUDO-RANDOM NUMBERS

One of the most important applications of computers is the *simulation* of real-world systems. Most high-tech research and development is heavily dependent upon this technique for studying how systems work without actually having to interact with them directly.

Simulation requires the computer generation of random numbers to model the uncertainty of the real world. Of course, computers cannot actually generate truly random numbers because computers are *deterministic*: given the same input, the same computer will always produce the same output. But it is possible to generate numbers that appear to be randomly generated; *i.e.*, numbers that are uniformly distributed within a given interval and for which there is no discernible pattern. Such numbers are called *pseudo-random numbers*.

The Standard C header file `<stdlib.h>` defines the function `rand()` which generates pseudo-random integers in the range 0 to `RAND_MAX`, which is a constant that is also defined in `<stdlib.h>`. Each time the `rand()` function is called, it generates another `unsigned` integer in this range.

EXAMPLE 3.20 Generating Pseudo-Random Numbers

```
#include <iostream.h>
#include <stdlib.h>

main()
{
    for (int i = 0; i < 8; i++)
        cout << rand() << endl;
    cout << "RAND_MAX = " << RAND_MAX << endl;
}
```

```
1103527590
377401575
662824084
1147902781
2035015474
368800899
1508029952
486256185
RAND_MAX = 2147483647
```

```
1103527590
377401575
662824084
1147902781
2035015474
368800899
1508029952
486256185
RAND_MAX = 2147483647
```

On each run, the computer generates 8 `unsigned` integers that are uniformly distributed in the interval 0 to `RAND_MAX`, which is 2,147,483,647 on this computer. Unfortunately each run produces the same sequence of numbers. This is because they are generated from the same "seed."

Each pseudo-random number is generated from the previously generated pseudo-random number by applying a special "number crunching" function that is defined internally. The first pseudo-random number is generated from an internally defined variable, called the *seed* for the sequence. By default, this seed is initialized by the computer to be the same value every time the program is run. To overcome this violation of pseudo-randomness, we can use the `srand()` function to select our own seed.

EXAMPLE 3.21 Generating Pseudo-Random Numbers

```
#include <iostream.h>
#include <stdlib.h>

main()
{
    unsigned seed;
    cout << "Enter seed: ";
    cin >> seed;
    srand(seed);                           // initializes the seed
    for (int i = 0; i < 8; i++)
        cout << rand() << endl;
}
```

```
Enter seed: 0
12345
1406932606
654583775
1449466924
229283573
1109335178
1051550459
1293799192
```

```
Enter seed: 1
1103527590
377401575
662824084
1147902781
2035015474
368800899
1508029952
486256185
```

```
Enter seed: 12345
1406932606
654583775
1449466924
229283573
1109335178
1051550459
1293799192
794471793
```

The line `srand(seed)` assigns the value of the variable `seed` to the internal "seed" used by the `rand()` function to initialize the sequence of pseudo-random numbers that it generates. Difference seeds produce difference results.

Note that the `seed` value 12345 used in the third run of the program is the first number generated by `rand()` in the first run. Consequently the first through seventh numbers generated in the third run are the same as the second through eighth numbers generated in the first run. Also note that the sequence generated in the second run is the same as the one produced in Example 3.20. This suggests that, on this computer, the default seed value is 1.

The problem of having to enter a `seed` value interactively can be overcome by using the computer's system clock. The *system clock* keeps track of the current time in seconds. The `time()` function defined in the header file `<time.h>` returns the current time as an `unsigned` integer. This then can be used as the seed for the `rand()` function.

EXAMPLE 3.22 Generating Pseudo-Random Numbers

```
#include <iostream.h>
#include <stdlib.h>
#include <time.h>

main()
{
    unsigned seed = time(NULL);          // uses the system clock
    cout << "seed = " << seed << endl;
    srand(seed);                          // initializes the seed
    for (int i = 0; i < 8; i++)
        cout << rand() << endl;
}
```

```
seed = 808148157
1877361330
352899587
1443923328
1857423289
200398846
1379699551
1622702508
715548277
```

```
seed = 808148160
892939769
1559273790
1468644255
952730860
1322627253
1305580362
844657339
440402904
```

On the first run, the `time()` function returns the integer 808,148,157 which is used to "seed" the random number generator. The second run is done 3 seconds later, so the `time()` function returns the integer 808,148,160 which generates a completely different sequence.

In many simulation programs, one needs to generate random integers that are uniformly distributed in a given range. The next example illustrates how to do that.

EXAMPLE 3.23 Generating Pseudo-Random Numbers

```
#include <iostream.h>
#include <stdlib.h>
#include <time.h>

main()
{
    unsigned seed = time(NULL);
    cout << "seed = " << seed << endl;
    srand(seed);
    int min, max;
    cout << "Enter minimum and maximum: ";
    cin >> min >> max;                    // lowest and highest numbers
    int range = max - min + 1;            // number of numbers in range
    for (int i = 0; i < 20; i++) {
        int r = rand()/100%range + min;
        cout << r << " ";
    }
    cout << endl;
}
```

```
seed = 808237677
Enter minimum and maximum: 1 100
85 57 1 10 5 73 81 43 46 42 17 44 48 9 3 74 41 4 30 68
```

```
seed = 808238101
Enter minimum and maximum: 22 66
63 29 56 22 53 57 39 56 43 36 62 30 41 57 26 61 59 26 28
```

The first run generates 20 integers uniformly distributed between 1 and 100. The second run generates 20 integers uniformly distributed between 22 and 66.

In the `for` loop, we divide `rand()` by 100 first to strip way the two right-most digits of the random number. This is to compensate for the problem that this particular random number generator has of producing numbers that alternate odd and even. Then `rand()/100%range` produces random numbers in the range 0 to `range-1`, and `rand()/100%range + min` produces random numbers in the range `min` to `max`.

A much better approach to generating pseudo-random numbers is described in Problem 8.20.

Review Questions

3.1 What is the minimum number of iterations that

a. a `while` loop could make?

b. a `do...while` loop could make?

3.2 What is wrong with the following loop:

```
while (n <= 100)
    sum += n*n;
```

3.3   If `s` is a compound statement, and `e1`, `e2`, and `e3` are expressions, then what is the difference between the program fragment:

```
for (e1; e2; e3)
    s;
```

and the fragment:

```
        e1;
        while (e2) {
            s;
            e3;
        }
```

3.4   What is wrong with the following program:

```
main()
{
    const double pi;
    int n;
    pi = 3.14159265358979;
    n = 22;
}
```

3.5   What is an "infinite loop," and how can it be useful?

3.6   How can a loop be structured so that it terminates with a statement in the middle of its block?

3.7   What why should tests for equality with floating-point variables be avoided?

Solved Problems

3.8   Trace the following code fragment, showing the value of each variable each time it changes:

```
int x, y, z;
x = y = z = 6;
x *= y += z -= 4;
```

First, 6 is assigned to `z`, `y`, and `x`. Then `z` is decremented by 4, obtaining the value 2. Then `y` is incremented by 2, obtaining the value 8. Then `x` is multiplied by 8, obtaining the value 48.

3.9   Assuming that `e` is an expression and `s` is a statement, convert each of the following `for` loops into an equivalent `while` loop:

a. `for ( ; e; ) s`

b. `for ( ; ; e) s`

a. `while (e) s;`

b. `while (1) { s; e;},`
     assuming that `s` contains no `continue` statement. (See Exercise 3.3.)

3.10   Convert the following `for` loop into a `while` loop:

```
for (int i = 1; i <= n; i++)
    cout << i*i;

int i = 1;
while (i <= n) {
    cout << i*i;
    i++;
}
```

3.11   Describe the output from the following program:

```
main()
{
    for (int i = 0; i < 8; i++)
        if (i%2 == 0) cout << i + 1 << endl;
        else if (i%3 == 0) cout << i*i << endl;
        else if (i%5 == 0) cout << 2*i - 1 << endl;
        else cout << i << endl;
}
```

```
1       1       3       9       5       9       7       7
```

3.12   Describe the output from the following program:

```
main()
{
    for (int i = 0; i < 8; i++) {
        if (i%2 == 0) cout << i + 1 << endl;
        else if (i%3 == 0) continue;
        else if (i%5 == 0) break;
        cout << "End of program.\n";
    }
    cout << "End of program.\n";
}
```

```
1
End of program.
End of program.
3
End of program.
5
End of program.
End of program.
```

3.13   In a 32-bit `float` type, 23 bits are used to store the mantissa and 8 bits are used to store the exponent.

a. How many significant digits of precision does the 32-bit `float` type yield?

b. What is the range of magnitude for the 32-bit `float` type?

a. The 23 bits hold the 2nd through 24th bit of the mantissa. The first bit must be a 1, so it is not stored. Thus 24 bits are represented. These 24 bits can hold 2^{24} numbers. And $2^{24} = 16,777,216$, which has 7 digits with full range, so 7 complete digits can be represented. But the last digit is in doubt because of rounding. Thus, the 32-bit `float` type yields 6 significant digits of precision.

b. The 8 bits that the 32-bit `float` type uses for its exponent can hold $2^8 = 256$ different numbers. Two of these are reserved for indicating underflow and overflow, leaving 254 numbers for exponents. So an exponent can range from –126 to +127, yielding a magnitude range of $2^{-126} = 1.175494 \times 10^{-38}$ to $2^{127} = 1.70141 \times 10^{38}$.

Solved Programming Problems

3.14 Write a program that converts inches to centimeters. For example, if the user enters 16.9 for a length in inches, the output would be `42.926` cm. (One inch equals 2.54 centimeters.)

We use two variables of type `float`:

```
main()
{
    float inches, cm;
    cout << "Enter length in inches: ";
    cin >> inches;
    cm = 2.54*inches;
    cout << inches << " inches = " << cm << " centimeters.\n";
}
```

```
Enter length in inches: 16.9
16.9 inches = 42.926 centimeters.
```

Simply read the input into `inches`, convert it to centimeters in `cm`, and output it.

3.15 Write a program to find the integer square root of a given number. That is the largest integer whose square is less than or equal to the given number.

We use an "exhaustive" algorithm here: find <u>all</u> the positive integers whose square is less than or equal to the given number; then the largest of those is the integer square root:

```
main()
{
    float x;
    cout << "Enter a positive number: ";
    cin >> x;
    for (int n = 1; n*n <= x; n++)
        ;                                        // the null statement
    cout << "The integer square root of " << x << " is "
        << n-1 << endl;
}
```

```
Enter a positive number: 1234.56
The integer square root of 1234.56 is 35
```

We start with `n = 1` and continue to increment `n` until `n*n > x`. When the `for` loop terminates, `n` is the smallest integer whose square is greater than `x`, so `n-1` is the integer square root of `x`.

Notice the use of the *null statement* in the `for` loop. Everything that needs to be done in the loop is done within the control parts of the loop. But the semicolon is still necessary at the end of the loop.

3.16 Write and run a program that directly implements the quotient operator `/` and the remainder operator `%` for the division of positive integers.

The algorithm used here, applied to the fraction `n/d`, repeatedly subtracts the `d` from the `n` until `n` is less than `d`. At that point, the value of `n` will be the remainder, and the number `q` of iterations required to reach it will be the quotient:

```
main()
{
    int n, d, q, r;
    cout << "Enter numerator: ";
    cin >> n;
    cout << "Enter denominator: ";
    cin >> d;
    for (q = 0, r = n; r > d; q++) r -= d;
    cout << n << " / " << d << " = " << q << endl;
    cout << n << " % " << d << " = " << r << endl;
    cout << "(" << q << ")(" << d << ") + (" << r << ") = "
         << n << endl;
}
```

```
Enter numerator: 30
Enter denominator: 7
30 / 7 = 4
30 % 7 = 2
(4) (7) + (2) = 30
```

This run iterated 4 times: $30 - 7 = 23$, $23 - 7 = 16$, $16 - 7 = 9$, and $9 - 7 = 2$. So the quotient is 4, and the remainder is 2. Note that the following relationship must always be true for integer division:

```
(quotient)(denominator) + (remainder) = numerator
```

3.17 Write and run a program that reverses the digits of a given positive integer.

The trick here is to strip off the digits one at a time from the given integer and "accumulate" them in reverse in another integer:

```
main()
{
    long m, d, n = 0;
    cout << "Enter a positive integer: ";
    cin >> m;
    while (m > 0) {
        d = m % 10;    // d will be the right-most digit of m
        m /= 10;       // then remove that digit from m
        n = 10*n + d;  // and append that digit to n
    }
    cout << "The reverse is " << n << endl;
}
```

```
Enter a positive integer: 123456
The reverse is 654321
```

In this run, `m` begins with the value 123,456. In the first iteration of the loop, `d` is assigned the digit 6, `m` is reduced to 12,345, and `n` is increased to 6. On the second iteration, `d` is assigned the digit 5, `m` is reduced to 1,234, and `n` is increased to 65. On the third iteration, `d` is assigned the digit 4, `m` is reduced to 123, and `n` is increased to 654. This continues until, on the sixth iteration, `d` is assigned the digit 1, `m` is reduced to 0, and `n` is increased to 654,321.

3.18 Rewrite the `for` loop in Example 3.6, using the conditional expression operator in place of the if statements.

The conditional expression `(n < min ? n : min)` evaluates to `n` if `n < min`, and it evaluates to `min` otherwise. So assigning that value to `min` is equivalent to the first line of the `for` loop in the example. Similarly, the assignment `max = (n > max ? n : min)` is equivalent to the second line in the other `for` loop.

```
for (min = max = n; n > 0; ) {
    min = (n < min ? n : min);   // min and max are the smallest
    max = (n > max ? n : min);   // and largest of the n that
    cin >> n;                    // have been read so far
}
```

Note that in this version we did not use an equivalent to the `else if`.

3.19 Implement the *Euclidean Algorithm* for finding the greatest common divisor of two given positive integers.

The Euclidean Algorithm transforms a pair of positive integers (m, n) into a pair $(d, 0)$ by repeatedly dividing the larger integer by the smaller integer and replacing the larger with the remainder. When the remainder is 0, the other integer in the pair will be the greatest common divisor of the original pair (and of all the intermediate pairs).

For example, if m is 532 and n is 112, then the Euclidean Algorithm reduces the pair (532,112) to (28,0) by

$$(532,112) \rightarrow (112,84) \rightarrow (84,28) \rightarrow (28,0)$$

So 28 is the greatest common divisor of 532 and 112. This result can be verified from the facts that $532 = 28 \cdot 19$ and $112 = 28 \cdot 8$.

The reason that the Euclidean Algorithm works is that each pair in the sequence has the same set of divisors, which are precisely the factors of the greatest common divisor. In the example above, that common set of divisors is $\{1, 2, 4, 7, 14, 28\}$. The reason that this set of divisors is invariant under the reduction process is that when $m = n \cdot q + r$, a number is a common divisor of m and n if and only if it is a common divisor of n and r.

```
main()
{                                   // begin scope of main()
    int m, n, r;
    cout << "Enter two positive integers: ";
    cin >> m >> n;
    if (m < n) { int temp = m; m = n; n = temp; }   // make m >= n
    cout << "The g.c.d. of " << m << " and " << n << " is ";
    while (n > 0) {
        r = m % n;
        m = n;
        n = r;
    }
    cout << m << endl;
}
```

```
Enter two positive integers: 532 112
The g.c.d. of 532 and 112 is 28
```

3.20   Write and test a program that reads a given number of pairs (x, y) of real numbers and then computes the *least-squares regression line* for the data set. Use the equation $y = mx + b$ where

$$m = \frac{(\sum xy) - \bar{y}(\sum x)}{(\sum xx) - \bar{x}(\sum x)}$$

$$b = \bar{y} - m\bar{x}$$

and $\bar{x}$ is the mean (average) of the x's and $\bar{y}$ is the mean of the y's.

   We use `double` precision floats to minimize roundoff error:

```
main()
{
    int n;                                    //  number of data points
    double x, y, sumX = 0.0, sumY = 0.0, sumXX = 0.0, sumXY = 0.0;
    cout << "How many points: ";
    cin >> n;
    cout << "Enter " << n << " pairs, one pair per line:\n";
    for (int i = 1; i <= n; i++) {
        cout << '\t' << i << ": ";
        cin >> x >> y;
        sumX += x;          // accumulate the sum of the x's in sumX
        sumY += y;          // accumulate the sum of the y's in sumY
        sumXX += x*x;       // accumulate the sum of x*x in sumXX
        sumXY += x*y;       // accumulate the sum of x*y in sumXY
    }
    double meanX = sumX/n;
    double meanY = sumY/n;
    double m = (sumXY - meanY*sumX)/(sumXX - meanX*sumX);
    double b = meanY - meanX*m;
    cout << "The equation of the regression line is:\n"
            "\ty = " << m << "x + " << b << endl;
}
```

```
How many points: 4
Enter 4 pairs, one pair per line:
        1: 1.0 5555.04
        2: 2.0 6666.07
        3: 3.0 7777.05
        4: 4.0 8888.09
The equation of the regression line is:
        y = 1111.01x + 4444.03
```

Each of the four sums `sumX`, `sumY`, `sumXX`, and `sumXY` is accumulated within the input loop. Then the averages `meanX` and `meanY` are computed. Then they are used in the formula to compute the slope `m` and the y-intercept `b` of the regression line.

   The output from this program is very useful. The regression line is the straight line that best fits the given data. That is, among all possible straight lines, the one given by the equation

$$y = 1111.01x + 4444.03$$

is the best fitting line, in the sense that the sum of the squares of the y-distances from the data points to the line is minimal. The value of this result is that it can be used for *interpolation* (and extrapolation). For example, to guess at the probable y-value corresponding to the x-value 3.2, simply substitute that into the following equation: $y = 1111.01(3.2) + 4444.03 = 3555.03 + 4444.03 = 7999.26$.

3.21   Use the Monte Carlo simulation method to compute π.

The *Monte Carlo simulation* method is named after the casino in Monaco. It consists of picking points at random and counting those that satisfy certain criteria. It can be used to compute π by simulating the tossing of darts at a circular dart board mounted on a square:

If the darts are equally likely to hit any point in the square, then the proportion that hit inside the circle will approximate the ratio of the area of the circle to that of the square. If the square has sides of length 2.0, then that ratio is $(\pi\,r^2)/(s^2) = (\pi\,1.0^2)/(2.0^2) = \pi/4$, so 4 times that ratio will approximate π.

It is easier to use the quarter circle of radius 1.0 that lies in the first quadrant.   This way, the ran-

domly selected coordinates will all be in the range 0.0 to 1.0. The area of the square is $1.0^2 = 1.0$ and the area of the quarter circle is $(\pi\,1.0^2)/4 = \pi/4$, so the ratio is still $\pi/4$.

```cpp
#include <iostream.h>
#include <stdlib.h>
#include <time.h>

main()
{
    const long int tosses = 1000;      // toss 1000 darts
    long int hits = 0;
    float x, y;
    unsigned seed = time(NULL);
    srand(seed);
    for(long int i = 0; i < tosses; i++) {
        x = float(rand())/RAND_MAX;
        y = float(rand())/RAND_MAX;
        if (x*x + y*y < 1) ++hits;
    }
    cout << 4.0*hits/tosses << endl;
}
```

```
3.142
```

```
3.13504
```

Both runs produce an estimate of π that is correct to 3 significant digits. This accuracy can be improved by tossing more darts, but at the expense of more running time.

3.22   Simulate the Monty Hall game.

The *Monte Hall game* is named after the host of a television game show in which a contestant could win a new car by guessing the right door that the car was behind. It became a popular puzzle in the 1990s because the best playing strategy is counterintuitive. The contestant chooses one door. Then Monty opens one of the other doors that does not have the car behind it. At that point in the game, the contestant has the option of changing his choice to the third door. Most people are surprised to learn that the contestant is twice as likely to win the car if he does change his choice. This fact can be demonstrated using conditional probabilities. But for most people, a computer simulation is more convincing.

```cpp
#include <iostream.h>
#include <stdlib.h>
#include <time.h>

main()
{
    cout << "This is the Monty Hall Game.\nYou see three doors "
         << " before you. One of them has a new car behind it.\n"
         << "You will choose one of the doors. Then, before you "
         << "get to see which\ndoor has the  car behind it, Monty "
         << "will give you the chance to change\nyour choice after "
         << "showing you that one of the other doors has\nnothing "
         << "behind it.\n";
    unsigned seed = time(NULL);
    srand(seed);
    int car, choice, open, option;
    car = rand()%3 + 1;                    // random integer from 1 to 3
    cout << "Which door do you choose (1|2|3): ";
    cin >> choice;
    if (car == 1 && choice == 1) { open = 3; option = 2; }
    if (car == 1 && choice == 2) { open = 3; option = 1; }
    if (car == 1 && choice == 3) { open = 2; option = 1; }
    if (car == 2 && choice == 1) { open = 3; option = 2; }
    if (car == 2 && choice == 2) { open = 1; option = 3; }
    if (car == 2 && choice == 3) { open = 1; option = 2; }
    if (car == 3 && choice == 1) { open = 2; option = 3; }
    if (car == 3 && choice == 2) { open = 1; option = 3; }
    if (car == 3 && choice == 3) { open = 2; option = 1; }
    cout << "Monty shows that there is no car behind door number "
         << open << ".\nDo you want to change your choice to door "
         << "number " << option << "? (y|n): ";
    char answer;
    cin >> answer;
    if (answer == 'y' || answer == 'Y') choice = option;
    cout << "Door number " << car << " has the car behind it.\n"
         << "Since your final choice was door number " << choice;
    if (choice == car) cout << ", you won the car!\n";
    else cout << ", you did not win.\n";
}
```

```
This is the Monty Hall Game.
You see three doors before you. One of them has a new car behind it.
You will choose one of the doors. Then, before you get to see which
door has the car behind it, Monty will give you the chance to change
your choice after showing you that one of the other doors has
nothing behind it.
Which door do you choose (1|2|3): 3
Monty shows that there is no car behind door number 1.
Do you want to change your choice to door number 2? (y|n): n
Door number 2 has the car behind it.
Since your final choice was door number 3, you did not win.
```

3.23 Apply the Babylonian Algorithm to compute the square root of 2.

The *Babylonian Algorithm* (so called because it was used by the ancient Babylonians) computes $\sqrt{2}$ by repeated replacing one estimate x with the closer estimate $(x + 2/x)/2$. Note that this is simply the average of x and $2/x$.

```
#include <iostream.h>
#include <math.h>  // needed for the fabs() function

main()
{
    const double tolerance = 5e-8;
    double x = 2.0;
    while (fabs(x*x - 2.0) > tolerance) {
        cout << x << endl;
        x = (x + 2.0/x)/2.0;  // average of x and 2/x
    }
    cout << "x = " << x << ", x*x = " << x*x << endl;
}
```

```
2
1.5
1.41667
1.41422
x = 1.41421, x*x = 2
```

We use a "tolerance" of `5e-8` (= 0.00000005) to ensure accuracy to 7 decimal places. The `fabs()` function (for "floating-point absolute value"), defined in the `<math.h>` header file, returns the absolute value of the expression passed to it. So the loop continues until `x*x` is within the given tolerance of 2.

Supplementary Problems

3.24 Convert the following `for` loop into a `while` loop:
```
for (int i = 20; i > 10; i--)
    cout << i*i;
```

3.25 Run the program in Example 3.13 to find the sizes of the 12 fundamental C++ types on your system.

3.26 Run the program in Example 3.14 to find the precision and magnitude range for `floats` on your system.

3.27 Describe the output from the following fragment:
```
int f0 = f1 = f2 = 1;
for (int i = 0; i < 10; i++) {
    f0 = f1;
    f1 = f2;
    f2 = f0 + f1;
    cout << f2 << endl;
}
```

3.28 Describe the output from the following fragment:

```
for (int i = 0; i < 8; i++)
    if (i%2 == 0) cout << i + 3 << endl;
    else if (i%3 == 0) cout << 2*i - 1 << endl;
    else if (i%5 == 0) cout << i*i << endl;
    else cout << i << endl;
```

3.29 Describe the output from the following fragment:

```
int i = 0;
while (++i <= 9) {
    if (i == 5) continue;
    cout << i << endl;
}
```

3.30 Describe the output from the following fragment:

```
int i = 0;
while (i < 5) {
    if (i < 2) {
        i += 2;
        continue;
    }
    else cout << ++i << endl;
    cout << "Bottom of loop.\n";
}
```

3.31 In a 64-bit `double` type, 52 bits are used to store the mantissa and 11 bits are used to store the exponent.

a. How many significant digits of precision does the 64-bit `double` type yield?

b. What is the range of magnitude for the 64-bit `double` type?

Supplementary Programming Problems

3.32 Write a program that reads a temperature in Celsius degrees and prints the equivalent in Fahrenheit degrees. For example, if the user enters 75.4 for a temperature in Celsius, the output would be `135.72 degrees Fahrenheit`.

3.33 Write a program that converts centimeters to inches. For example, if the user enters 52.7 for a length in centimeters, the output would be `20.748 in`.

3.34 Write a program that converts pounds to kilograms. For example, if the user enters 160 for a weight in pounds, the output would be `72.5748 kg`. (One pound equals 0.453592 kilograms.)

3.35 Write a program that reads the radius of a sphere and prints its surface area and volume.

3.36   Modify and run the program in Example 3.1 so that it also prints the square of `n-1` and the square of `n`.

3.37   Modify the program in Example 3.1 so that it uses a `do...while` loop.

3.38   Modify the program in Example 3.1 so that it uses a `for` loop.

3.39   Write and run a program like the one in Example 3.2 that prints the sum of the first *n* cubes.

3.40   Modify the program in Example 3.3 so that it uses a `while` loop to compute factorials.

3.41   Modify the program in Example 3.3 so that it uses a `for` loop to compute factorials

3.42   Modify the program in Example 3.3 so that it uses a `while` loop to compute factorials with a control variable inside the loop that increments instead of decrementing `n`.

3.43   Modify the program in Example 3.3 so that it uses a `do...while` loop to compute factorials with a control variable inside the loop that increments instead of decrementing `n`.

3.44   Modify the program in Example 3.3 so that it uses a `for` loop with a control variable inside the loop that increments instead of `n` decrementing.

3.45   Write and run a program that reads a positive integer `n` and then reads `n` more integers and prints their sum. Use a `do...while` loop.

3.46   Write and run a program that reads a positive integer `n` and then reads `n` more integers and prints their sum. Use a `for` loop.

3.47   Write and run a program that reads a sequence of integers until a negative integer is input, and then prints the sum of the positive integers.

3.48   Modify the program in Example 3.14 so that it prints the precision and magnitude range of the `long double` type. Simply replace `float` with `long double`, and `FLT` with `LDBL`.

3.49   Write and run a program that reads a positive integer `n` and then prints a triangle of asterisks in that number of rows. Use a `for` loop. For example, if `n` is 4, then the output would be

```
*
**
***
****
```

3.50   Write and run a program that reads a positive integer `n` and then prints a diamond of asterisks in 2*n*–1 rows. Use a `for` loop. For example, if `n` is 4, then the output would be

```
   *
  ***
 *****
*******
 *****
  ***
   *
```

3.51 Write and run a program that directly implements the quotient operator / and the remainder operator % for the division of a negative integer by a positive integer. See Problem 3.16 and Example 1.16.

3.52 Redo Problem 3.19 using a `do...while` loop instead of the `while` loop.

3.53 Write and run a program that directly implements the quotient operator / and the remainder operator % for the division of any integer (positive, negative, or zero) by any nonzero integer. See Problem 3.16 and Problem 3.51.

3.54 Modify the Integer Square Root program in Problem 3.15 so that it runs more efficiently. Use the *Binary Search Algorithm* in place of the *Linear Search Algorithm*. First see if the given positive integer `x` is less than 9; if it isn't, output either 0 (if `x` < 1) or 1 (if `x` < 4) or 2, and return. If `x` $\geq$ 9, then its integer square root is between 2 and `x`/2. Split that interval, and then compare `x` with `n*n` where `n` is the midpoint of that interval. Use the comparison to determine in which half of the interval the solution lies. Repeat the process on that subinterval. Use only integers for the endpoints and midpoints of the intervals. When the midpoint is 1 more than its left endpoint, it will be the solution.

3.55 Modify the program in Example 3.14 so that it prints the precision and magnitude range of the `double` type.

3.56 Modify the Quadratic Equation program in Problem 2.20 so that it prints the equation in a form more like that used in mathematics. For example, if `a` is 1, `b` is 0, and `c` is –3, then it would print `x^2 - 3 = 0` instead of `1x^2 + 0x + -3 = 0`.

3.57 Modify the Quadratic Equation program in Problem 2.20 so that it correctly handles the special cases where $a = 0$, $b = 0$, and/or $c = 0$. For example, it would report that the 1.25 is the solution to $4x - 5 = 0$, that 0 is the solution to $4x = 0$, that there is no solutions to $5 = 0$, and that all reals are solutions to $0 = 0$.

3.58 Write and test a program that inputs 3 positive integers `day`, `month`, and `year`, and then prints the date that they represent, the number of days in that month, and a statement about whether that year is a leap year. For example, if the 3 inputs are 6, 4, and 1997, then the program would print `April 6, 1997` (for 4/6/97), `April has 30 days`, and `1997 is not a leap year`.

3.59 Write and test a program that inputs 4 positive integers `day`, `month`, `year`, and `days`, and then prints two dates, the date represented by the given `day`, `month`, and `year`, and the date that occurs `days` later. For example, if the 4 inputs are 6, 4, 1997, and 100, then the two dates printed would be `April 6, 1997` (for 4/6/97), and `July 15, 1997` (for 4/6/97 + 100 days).

3.60 Modify the Linear Regression program (Problem 3.20) so that, after computing the equation of the regression line, it allows the user to interpolate by inputting *x*-values and outputting the corresponding *y*-values computed from the equation.

3.61 Modify the Monte Hall game (Problem 3.22) so that the user can play the game repeatedly in a single run of the program. Count the number of times the player wins, and print the percentage of wins at the end of the program.

3.62 Modify the Babylonian Algorithm program (Problem 3.23) so that it computes the square root of a positive number `t` that is input interactively. Average the iterate `x` with `(x + t/x)/2`.

Answers to Review Questions

3.1 The minimum number of iterations that
a. a `while` loop could make is 0;
b. a `do...while` loop could make is 1.

3.2 It is an infinite loop: the control variable `n` does not change.

3.3 There is no difference between these two fragments, unless `s` contains a `continue` statement. For example, the following `for` statement will iterate 4 times and then terminate normally, but the `while` statement will be an infinite loop:

```
for (i = 0; i < 4; i++)
    if (i == 2) continue;


i = 0;
while (i < 4) {
    if (i == 2) continue;
    i++;
}
```

3.4 The constant `pi` is not initialized. All constants must be given values when they are declared.

3.5 An "infinite loop" is one that never terminates. Such a loop is generally considered bad programming because the program containing it will terminate normally. However, an apparent infinite loop like the following can be useful:

```
while (1) {
    cin >> n;
    if (n == 0) break;
    process(n);
}
```

The `break` statement will terminate the loop as soon as 0 is input. This is useful because it allows the code to be a little more brief than if the condition `(n == 0)` were used directly with the `while` clause.

3.6 The `break` statement can be used to terminate a loop from within the middle of its block. The example above illustrates this technique.

3.7 Due to roundoff error, the exact value of a `float` or `double` is not likely to be what you would expect. So a conditional like
    `if (z == c) ...`
should be avoided.

Chapter 4

Functions

Most useful programs are much larger than the programs that we have considered so far. To make large programs manageable, programmers modularize them into subprograms. These subprograms are called functions. They can be compiled and tested separately and reused in different programs. This modularization is characteristic of successful object-oriented software.

4.1 STANDARD C LIBRARY FUNCTIONS

The *Standard C Library* is a collection of pre-defined functions and other program elements which are accessed through *header files*. We have used some of these already: the INT_MAX constant defined in <limits.h> (Example 1.14), the rand() function defined in <stdlib.h> (Example 3.21), and the time() function defined in <time.h> (Example 3.22). The common mathematical functions are defined in the <math.h> header file. Our first example illustrates the use of one of these mathematical functions.

EXAMPLE 4.1 The Square Root Function sqrt()

The square root of a given positive number is the number whose square is the given number. The square root of 9 is 3 because the square of 3 is 9. We can think of the square root function as a "black box." When you put in a 9, out comes a 3. When the number 2 is input, the number 1.41421 is output. This function has the same input-process-output nature that complete programs have. However, the processing step is hidden: we do not need to know what the function does to 2 to produce 1.41421. All we need to know is that the output 1.41421 does have the square root property: its square is the input 2.

Here is a simple program that uses the predefined square root function:

```
#include <iostream.h>
#include <math.h>
// Test-driver for the sqrt function:
main()
{
    for (int i = 0; i < 6; i++)
        cout << "\t" << i << "\t" << sqrt(i) << endl;
}
```

```
    0       0
    1       1
    2       1.41421
    3       1.73205
    4       2
    5       2.23607
```

This program prints the square roots of the numbers 0 through 5. Each time the expression `sqrt(i)` is evaluated in the `for` loop, the `sqrt` function is executed. Its actual code is hidden away within the Standard C Library. In using it, we may confidently assume that the expression `sqrt(i)` will be replaced by the actual square root of whatever value `i` has at that moment.

Notice the directive `#include <math.h>` on the second line. This is necessary for the compiler to find the definition of the `sqrt` function. It tells the compiler that the function is declared in the `<math.h>` header file.

A function like `sqrt()` is executed by using its name as a variable in a statement, like this:

```
y = sqrt(x);
```

This is called *invoking* or *calling* the function. Thus in Example 4.1, the code `sqrt(i)` *calls* the `sqrt` function. The expression `i` in the parentheses is called the *argument* or *actual parameter* of the function call, and we say that it is *passed by value* to the function. So when `i` is 3, the value 3 is passed to the `sqrt` function by the call `sqrt(i)`.

This process is illustrated by the following diagram:

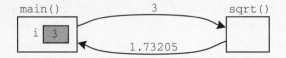

The variable `i` is declared in `main()`. During the fourth iteration of the `for` loop, its value is 3. That value is passed to the `sqrt()` function which then returns the value 1.73205.

EXAMPLE 4.2 Testing an Identity from Trigonometry

Here is another program that uses the `<math.h>` header file. Its purpose is to allow an empirical verification of the standard trigonometric identity $\sin 2x = 2\sin x\cos x$:

```
#include <iostream.h>
#include <math.h>
// Program to test trigonometric identity sin 2x = 2 sin x cos x:
main()
{
    for (float x = 0; x < 2; x += 0.2)
        cout << "\t" << x << "\t\t" << sin(2*x) << "\t"
            << 2*sin(x)*cos(x) << endl;
}
```

```
0          0        0
0.2        0.389418     0.389418
0.4        0.717356     0.717356
0.6        0.932039     0.932039
0.8        0.999574     0.999574
1          0.909297     0.909297
1.2        0.675463     0.675463
1.4        0.334988     0.334988
1.6        -0.0583744   -0.0583744
1.8        -0.442521    -0.442521
```

The program prints x in the first column, $\sin 2x$ in the second column, and $2\sin x \cos x$ in the third column. For each value of x tested, $\sin 2x = 2\sin x\cos x$. Of course, this does not prove the identity. It merely provides convincing empirical evidence of its truth.

Function values may be used like ordinary variables in an expression. Thus we can write

```
y = sqrt(2);
cout << 2*sin(x)*cos(x);
```

We can even "nest" function calls, like this:

```
y = sqrt(1 + 2*sqrt(3 + 4*sqrt(5)))
```

Most of the mathematical functions that you find on a pocket calculator are declared in the `<math.h>` header file, including all those shown in Table 4.1.

Table 4.1 Some `<math.h>` Functions

Function	Description	Example
acos(x)	inverse cosine of x (in radians)	acos(0.2) returns 1.36944
asin(x)	inverse sine of x (in radians)	asin(0.2) returns 0.201358
atan(x)	inverse tangent of x (in radians)	atan(0.2) returns 0.197396
ceil(x)	ceiling of x (rounds up)	ceil(3.141593) returns 4.0
cos(x)	cosine of x (in radians)	cos(2) returns -0.416147
exp(x)	exponential of x (base e)	exp(2) returns 7.38906
fabs(x)	absolute value of x	fabs(-2) returns 2.0
floor(x)	floor of x (rounds down)	floor(3.141593) returns 3.0
log(x)	natural logarithm of x (base e)	log(2) returns 0.693147
log10(x)	common logarithm of x (base 10)	log10(2) returns 0.30103
pow(x,p)	x to the power p	pow(2,3) returns 8.0
sin(x)	sine of x (in radians)	sin(2) returns 0.909297
sqrt(x)	square root of x	sqrt(2) returns 1.41421
tan(x)	tangent of x (in radians)	tan(2) returns -2.18504

Notice that every mathematical function returns a `double` type. If it is passed an integer, the `int` is promoted to a `double` before it is processed by the function.

Table 4.2 lists some of the more useful header files in the Standard C Library.

Table 4.2 Some of the Header Files in the Standard C Library

Header File	Description
<assert.h>	Declares the assert() function
<ctype.h>	Declares functions to test characters
<float.h>	Declares constants relevant to floats
<limits.h>	Defines the integer limits on your local system
<math.h>	Declares mathematical functions
<stdio.h>	Declares functions for standard input and output
<stdlib.h>	Declares utility functions
<string.h>	Declares functions for processing strings
<time.h>	Declares time and date functions

These are Standard C header files. They are used the same way that Standard C++ header files such as `<iostream.h>` are used. For example, if you want to use the random number function rand() from the <stdlib.h> header file, include the following preprocessor directive at the beginning of your main program file:

```
#include <stdlib.h>
```

The Standard C Library is described in greater detail in Chapter 14.

4.2 USER-DEFINED FUNCTIONS

The great variety of functions provided by the C and C++ libraries is still not sufficient for most programming tasks. Programmers also need to be able to define their own functions.

EXAMPLE 4.3 A `cube()` Function

Here is a simple example of a user-defined function:

```
//  Returns the cube of the given integer:
int cube(int x)
{
    return x*x*x;
}
```

The function returns the cube of the integer passed to it. Thus cube(2) would return 8.

A user-defined function has two parts: its header and its body. The *header* of a function specifies its return type, name, and parameter list. In Example 4.3, the return type is int, the name is cube, and the parameter list is int x. Thus the header for the cube function is

```
int cube(int x)
```

The *body* of a function is the block of code that follows its header. It contains the code that performs the function's action, including the return statement that specifies the value that the function sends back to the place where it was called. The body of the cube function is

```
{
    return x*x*x;
}
```

This is about as simple a body as a function could have. Usually the body is much larger. But the function's header typically fits on a single line.

A function's *return statement* serves two purposes: it terminates the function, and it returns a value to the calling program. Its syntax is

```
return expression;
```

where *expression* is any expression whose value could be assigned to a variable whose type is the same as the function's return type.

4.3 TEST DRIVERS

Whenever you create your own function, you should immediately test it with a simple program. Such a program is called a *test driver* for the function. Its only purpose is to test the function. It is a temporary, *ad hoc* program that should be "quick and dirty." That means that you need not include all the usual niceties such as user prompts, output labels, and documentation. Once you have used it to test your function thoroughly you can discard it.

EXAMPLE 4.4 A Test Driver for the `cube()` Function

Here is a complete program, consisting of our `cube` function followed by a test driver:

```
// Returns the cube of the given integer:
int cube(int x)
{
    return x*x*x;
}

// Test driver for the cube function:
main()
{
    int n = 1;
    while (n != 0) {
        cin >> n;
        cout << cube(n) << endl;
    }
}
```

```
5
125
-6
-216
0
0
```

This reads integers and prints their cubes until the user inputs the sentinel value 0. Each integer read is passed to the `cube` function by the call `cube(n)`. The value returned by the function replaces the expression `cube(n)` and then is passed to the output object `cout`.

Note that we omitted the `#include <iostream.h>` directive. This directive of course is required for every program that uses cin or cout. It is omitted from further examples only to save space.

We can visualize the relationship between the `main()` function and the `cube()` function like this:

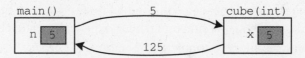

The `main()` function passes the value 5 to the `cube()` function, and the `cube()` function returns the value 125 to the `main()` function. The actual parameter `n` is passed by value to the formal parameter `x`. This simply means that `x` is assigned the value of n when the function is called.

Note that the `cube()` function is defined above the `main()` function in the example. This is because the C++ compiler must know about the `cube()` function before it is used in `main()`.

The next example shows a user-defined function named `max()` which returns the larger of the two `ints` passed to it. This function has two arguments.

EXAMPLE 4.5 A Test Driver for the `max()` Function

Here is a function with two parameters. It returns the larger of the two values passed to it:

```
//  Returns the larger of the two given integers:
int max(int x, int y)
{
    if (x < y) return y;
    else return x;
}

main()
{
    int m, n;
    do {
        cin >> m >> n;
        cout << max(m,n) << endl;
    } while (m != 0);
}
```

Notice that the function has more than one `return` statement. The first one that is reached terminates the function and returns the indicated value to the calling program.

A `return` statement is like a `break` statement. It is a jump statement that jumps out of the function that contains it. Although usually found at the end of the function, a `return` statement may be put anywhere that any other statement could appear within a function.

4.4 FUNCTION DECLARATIONS AND DEFINITIONS

The last two examples illustrate one method of defining a function in a program: the complete definition of the function is listed above the main program. This is the simplest arrangement and is good for test drivers.

Another, more common arrangement is to list only the function's header above the main program, and then list the function's complete definition (header and body) below the main program. This is illustrated in the next example.

In this arrangement, the function's declaration is separated from its definition. A function *declaration* is simply the function's header, followed by a semicolon. A function *definition* is the complete function: header and body. A function declaration is also called a function *prototype*.

A function declaration is like a variable declaration; its purpose is simply to provide the compiler with all the information it needs to compile the rest of the file. The compiler does not need to know how the function works (its body). It only needs to know the function's name, the number and types of its parameters, and its return type. This is precisely the information contained in the function's header.

Also like a variable declaration, a function declaration must appear above any use of the function's name. But the function definition, when listed separately from the declaration, may appear anywhere outside the `main()` function and is usually listed after it or in a separate file.

The variables that are listed in the function's parameter list are called *formal parameters* or *formal arguments*. They are local variables that exist only during the execution of the function.

Their listing in the parameter list constitutes their declaration. In the example above, the formal parameters are x and y.

The variables that are listed in the function's calls are called the *actual parameters* or *actual arguments*. Like any other variable in the main program, they must be declared before they are used in the call. In the example above, the actual parameters are m and n.

In these examples, the actual parameters are *passed by value*. This means that their values are assigned to the function's corresponding formal parameters. So in the previous example, the value of m is assigned to x and the value of n is assigned to y. When passed by value, actual parameters may be constants or general expressions. For example, the max() function could be called by max(44,5*m-n). This would assign the value 44 to x and the value of the expression 5*m-n to y.

EXAMPLE 4.6 The `max()` Function with Declaration Separate from Definition

This program is the same test driver for the same max() function as above. But here the function's declaration appears above the main program and the function's definition follows it:

```
int max(int, int);

//  Test driver for the max function:
main()
{
    int m, n;
    do {
        cin >> m >> n;
        cout << max(m,n) << endl;
    } while (m != 0);
}

//  Returns the larger of the two given integers:
int max(int x, int y)
{
    if (x < y) return y;
    else return x;
}
```

Notice that the formal parameters, x and y, are listed in the header in the definition (as usual) but not in the declaration.

Note that there is really not much difference between a function declaration and a variable declaration, especially if the function has no parameters. For example, in a program that processes strings, you might need a variable named length to store the length of a string. But a reasonable alternative would be to have a function that computes the length of the string wherever it is needed, instead of storing and updating the value. The function would be declared as

```
int length();
```

whereas the variable would be declared as

```
int length;
```

The only difference is that the function declaration includes the parentheses (). In reality, the two alternatives are quite different, but syntactically they are nearly the same when they are used.

In cases like this, one can regard a function as a kind of an "active variable;" *i.e.,* a variable that can do things.

4.5 SEPARATE COMPILATION

Function definitions are often compiled independently in separate files. For example, all the functions declared in the Standard C Library are compiled separately. One reason for separate compilation is "information hiding"—that is, information that is necessary for the complete compilation of the program but not essential to the programmer's understanding of the program is hidden. Experience shows that information hiding facilitates the understanding and thus success of large software projects.

EXAMPLE 4.7 The `max()` Function Compiled Separately

This shows one way that the `max` function and its test driver could be compiled separately. The test driver is in a file named `test_max.c` and the function is in a separate file named `max.c`.

`test_max.c`

```
int max(int, int);

//  Test driver for the max function:
main()
{
    int m, n;
    do {
        cin >> m >> n;
        cout << max(m,n) << endl;
    } while (m != 0);
}
```

`max.c`

```
//  Returns the larger of the two given integers:
int max(int x, int y)
{
    if (x < y) return y;
    else return x;
}
```

The actual commands that you would use to compile these files together depend upon your local system. In UNIX you could use these commands:

```
$ c++ -c max_c
$ c++ -c test_max.c
$ c++ -o test_max test_max.o max.o
$ test_max
```

(Here the dollar sign is the system prompt.) The first command compiles the `max` function, the second command compiles the test driver separately, the third command links them together to produce the executable module `test_max`, which is then run by the command on the fourth line.

One advantage of compiling functions separately is that they can be tested separately before the program(s) that call them are written. Once you know that the `max` function works properly, you can forget about <u>how</u> it works and save it as a "black box" ready to be used whenever it is needed. This is how the functions in the math library are used. It is the "off-the-shelf software" point of view.

Another advantage of separate compilation is the ease with which one module can be replaced by another equivalent module. For example, if you happen to discover a better way to compute the maximum of two integers, you can compile and test that function, and then link that module with whatever programs were using the previous version of the `max()` function.

4.6 LOCAL VARIABLES AND FUNCTIONS

A *local variable* is simply a variable that is declared inside a block. It is accessible only from within that block. Since the body of a function itself is a block, variables declared within a function are local to that function; they exist only while the function is executing. A function's formal parameters (arguments) are also regarded as being local to the function.

The next two examples show functions with local variables.

EXAMPLE 4.8 The `factorial()` Function

The factorial of a positive integer n is the number $n!$ obtained by multiplying n by all the positive integers less than n:

$$n! = (n)(n-1) \cdots (3)(2)(1)$$

For example, $5! = (5)(4)(3)(2)(1) = 120$.

Here is an implementation of the factorial function:

```
int factorial(int n)
{
    if (n < 0) return 0;
    int f = 1;
    while (n > 1)
        f *= n--;
    return f;
}
```

This function has two local variables: `n` and `f`. The parameter `n` is local because it is declared in the function's parameter list. The variable `f` is local because it is declared within the body of the function.

Here is a test driver for the factorial function:

```
int factorial(int);

main()
{
    for (int i = -1; i < 6; i++)
        cout << " " << factorial(i);
    cout << endl;
}
```

```
 0 1 1 2 6 24 120
```

This program could be compiled separately, or it could be placed in the same file with the function and compiled together.

EXAMPLE 4.9 The Permutation Function

A *permutation* is an arrangement of elements taken from a finite set. The permutation function $P(n,k)$ gives the number of different permutations of any k items taken from a set of n items. One way to compute this function is by the formula

$$P(n, k) = \frac{n!}{(n-k)!}$$

For example,

$$P(5, 2) = \frac{5!}{(5-2)!} = \frac{5!}{3!} = \frac{120}{6} = 20$$

So there are 20 different permutations of 2 items taken from a set of 5.

The code below implements this formula for the permutation function:

```
//  Returns P(n,k), the number of permutations of k from n:
int perm(int n, int k)
{
    if (n < 0 || k < 0 || k > n) return 0;
    return factorial(n)/factorial(n-k);
}
```

Notice that the condition `(n < 0 || k < 0 || k > n)` is used to handle the cases where either parameter is out of range. In these cases the function returns an "impossible" value, 0, to indicate that its input was erroneous. That value would then be recognized by the calling program as an "error flag."

Here is a test driver for the `perm()` function:

```
int perm(int,int);

main()
{
    for (int i = -1; i < 8; i++) {
        for (int j = -1; j <= i+1; j++)
            cout << " " << perm(i,j);
        cout << endl;
    }
}
```

```
0 0
0 1 0
0 1 1 0
0 1 2 2 0
0 1 3 6 6 0
0 1 4 12 24 24 0
0 1 5 20 60 120 120 0
0 1 6 30 120 360 720 720 0
0 1 7 42 210 840 2520 5040 5040 0
```

4.7 void FUNCTIONS

A function need not return a value. In other programming languages, such a function is called a *procedure* or a *subroutine*. In C++, such a function is identified simply by placing the keyword void where the function's return type would be.

A type specifies a set of values. For example, the type short specifies the set of integers from –32,768 to 32,767. The void type specifies the empty set. Consequently, no variable can be declared with void type. A void function is simply one that returns no value.

EXAMPLE 4.10 A printDate() Function

This function prints the date in literal form, given its month, day, and year in numeric form:

```cpp
void printDate(int, int, int);

main()
{
    int month, day, year;
    do {
        cin >> month >> day >> year;
        printDate(month,day,year);
    } while (month > 0);
}

void printDate(int m, int d, int y)
{
    if (m < 1 || m > 12 || d < 1 || d > 31 || y < 0) {
        cout << "Error: parameter out of range.\n";
        return;
    }
    switch (m) {
        case  1:   cout << "January ";     break;
        case  2:   cout << "February ";    break;
        case  3:   cout << "March ";       break;
        case  4:   cout << "April ";       break;
        case  5:   cout << "May ";         break;
        case  6:   cout << "June ";        break;
        case  7:   cout << "July ";        break;
        case  8:   cout << "August ";      break;
        case  9:   cout << "September ";   break;
        case 10:   cout << "October ";     break;
        case 11:   cout << "November ";    break;
        case 12:   cout << "December ";    break;
    }
    cout << d << ", " << y << endl;
}
```

The printDate() function returns no value. Its only purpose is to print the date. So its return type is void. The function uses a switch statement to print the month as a literal, and it prints the day and year as integers.

```
12 7 1941
December 7, 1941
5 16 1994
May 16, 1994
0 0 0
Error: parameter out of range.
```

Note that the function returns without printing anything if the parameters are obviously out of range (*e.g.*, m > 12 or y < 0). But impossible values such as February 19, 1996 would be printed. Corrections for these anomalies are left as exercises.

Since a void function does not return a value, it need not include a return statement. If it does have a return statement, then it should appear simply as

```
    return;
```

with no expression following the keyword return. In this case, the purpose of the return statement is simply to terminate the function.

A function with no return value is an action. Accordingly, it is usually best to use a verb phrase for its name. For example, the above function is named printDate instead of some noun phrase like date.

4.8 BOOLEAN FUNCTIONS

In some situations it is helpful to use a function to evaluate a condition, typically within an if statement or a while statement. Such functions are called *boolean functions*, after the British logician George Boole (1815-1864).

EXAMPLE 4.11 Classifying Characters

The following program classifies the 128 ASCII characters:

```
#include <iostream.h>
#include <ctype.h>

//  Prints the category to which the given character belongs:
void printCharCategory(char c)
{
    cout << "The character [" << c << "] is a ";
    if      (isdigit(c)) cout << "digit.\n";
    else if (islower(c)) cout << "lower-case letter.\n";
    else if (isupper(c)) cout << "capital letter.\n";
    else if (isspace(c)) cout << "white space character.\n";
    else if (iscntrl(c)) cout << "control character.\n";
    else if (ispunct(c)) cout << "punctuation mark.\n";
    else                 cout << "Error.\n";
}

main()
{
    for (int c = 0; c < 128; c++)
        printCharCategory(c);
}
```

The void function printCharCategory() calls the six boolean functions isdigit(), islower(), isupper(), isspace(), iscntrl(), and ispunct(). Each of these functions is predefined in the <ctype.h> header file. These functions are used to test objects' character type (*i.e.,* "c type").

Here is part of the output:

```
The character [] is a control character.
The character [ ] is a white space character.
The character [!] is a punctuation mark.
The character ["] is a punctuation mark.
The character [#] is a punctuation mark.
```

The complete output contains 128 lines.

This example illustrates several new ideas. The main idea is the use of the boolean functions isdigit(), islower(), isupper(), isspace(), iscntrl(), and ispunct(). For example, the call isspace(c) tests the character c to determine whether it is a white space character. (There are six *white space characters*: the *horizontal tab character* \t, the *newline character* \n, the *vertical tab character* \v, the *form feed character* \f, the *carriage return character* \r, and the *space character.*) If c is any of these characters, then the function returns 1 for "true"; otherwise it returns 0 for "false." Placing the call as the condition in the if statement causes the corresponding output statement to execute if and only if c is one of these characters.

Each character is tested within the printCharCategory() function. Although the program could have been written without this separate function, its use modularizes the program making it more structured. We are conforming here to the general programming principle that recommends that every task be relegated to a separate function.

EXAMPLE 4.12 A Function to Test Primality

Here is a boolean function to test whether a given integer is a prime number.

```
//  Returns 1 if n is prime, 0 otherwise:
int isPrime(int n)
{
    float sqrtp = sqrt(p);
    if (p < 2) return 0;    // 2 is the first prime
    if (p == 2) return 1;
    if (p % 2 == 0) return 0;  // 2 is the only even prime
    for (int d = 3; d <= sqrtp; d += 2)
        if (p % d == 0) return 0;
    return 1;
}
```

It works by looking for a divisor d of the given number n. It tests divisibility by the value of the condition (n % d == 0). This will be true precisely when d is a divisor of n. In that case, n cannot be a prime number, so the function immediately returns 0 for "false." If the for loop finishes without finding any divisor of n, then the function returns 1 for "true."

We can stop searching for divisors once we get past the square root of n because if n is a product d*a, then one of these factors must be less than or equal to the square root of n. We define that to be a constant so that it only has to be evaluated once; if we had used the condition d <= sqrt(n) to control the for loop, it would re-evaluate that square root at the end of each iteration.

It is also more efficient to check for even numbers `(n == 2)` first. This way, once we get to the for loop, we need only check for odd divisors. This is done by incrementing the divider `d` by 2 on each iteration.

Here is a test driver and a test run for the `isPrime()` function:

```
int isPrime(int);

main()
{
    for (int n = 1; n < 50; n++)
    if (isPrime(n)) cout << n << " ";
    cout << endl;
}
```
```
2  3  5  7  11  13  17  19  23  29  31  37  41  43  47
```

Notice that, like the "c-type" functions in the previous example, a verb phrase is used for the name of this function. The name "`isPrime`" makes the function's use more readable for humans. For example, the code

```
if (isPrime(n)) . . .
```

is almost the same as the ordinary English phrase "if `n` is prime."

It should be clear that this function is not optimal. In searching for divisors, we need only check prime numbers, because every composite (non-prime) number is a unique product of primes. But how can we use only prime values for `d`? The answer is to store the primes as we find them. But that requires using an array, so we'll have to wait until Chapter 5 to do that.

EXAMPLE 4.13 A Leap Year Function

A leap year is a year in which one extra day (February 29) is added to the regular calendar. Most of us know that the leap years are the years that are divisible by 4. For example, 1992 and 1996 are leap years. Most people, however, do not know that there is an exception to this rule: centennial years are not leap years. For example, 1800 and 1900 were not leap years. Furthermore, there is an exception to the exception: centennial years which are divisible by 400 are leap years. Thus, the year 2000 will be a leap year.

Here is a boolean function that implements this definition:

```
// Returns 1 if y is a leap year, 0 otherwise:
int isLeapYear(int y)
{
    return y % 4 == 0 && y % 100 != 0 || y % 400 == 0;
}
```

The compound condition `y % 4 == 0 && y % 100 != 0 || y % 400 == 0` will be true precisely when `y` is divisible by 4 but not by 100 unless it is also divisible by 400. In these cases the function returns 1; in all other cases it returns 0.

Here is a test driver and test run for the function:

```
int isLeapYear(int);

// Test driver for the isLeapYear function:
main()
{
    int n;
    do {
        cin >> n;
        if (isLeapYear(n)) cout << n << " is a leap year.\n";
        else cout << n << " is not a leap year.\n";
    } while (n > 1);
}
```

```
1995
1995 is not a leap year.
1996
1996 is a leap year.
1990
1990 is not a leap year.
2000
2000 is a leap year.
0
0 is a leap year.
```

4.9 I/O FUNCTIONS

Functions are particularly useful for encapsulating tasks that require messy details that are not very germane to the primary task of the program. For example, in processing personnel records, you might have a program that requires interactive input of a user's age. By relegating this task to a separate function, you can encapsulate the details needed to ensure correct data entry without distracting the main program.

We have already seen examples of output functions. The only purpose the `printDate` function in Example 4.10 was to print the date represented by its input parameters. Instead of sending information back to the calling function, it sends its information to the standard output (*i.e.,* the computer screen). An input function like the one described above is analogous. Instead of receiving its information through its parameters, it reads it from standard input (*i.e.,* the keyboard).

Example 4.14 illustrates an input function. The `while (1)` control of the loop in this example makes it look like an infinite loop: the condition `(1)` is always "true." But the loop is actually controlled by the `return` statement which not only terminates the loop but also terminates the function.

EXAMPLE 4.14 A Function for Reading the User's Age

Here is a simple function that prompts the user for his/her age and then returns it. It is "robust" in the sense that it rejects any unreasonable integer input. It repeatedly requests input until it receives an integer in the range 1 to 120:

```
int age()
{
    int n;
    while (1) {
        cout << "How old are you: ";
        cin >> n;
        if (n < 0) cout << "\a\tYour age could not be negative.";
        else if (n > 120) cout << "\a\tYou could not be over 120.";
        else return n;
        cout << "\n\tTry again.\n";
    }
}
```

As soon as the input received from `cin` is acceptable, the function terminates with a `return` statement, sending the input back to the calling function. If the input is not acceptable (`n < 0` or `n > 120`), then the *system beep* is sounded by printing the character `'\a'` and a comment printed. Then the user is asked to "Try again."

Note that this is an example of a function whose `return` statement is not at the end of the function.

Here is a test driver and output from a sample run:

```
// Prompts the user to input her/her age, and returns that value:
int age();

//  Test driver for the age() function:
main()
{
    int a = age();
    cout << "\nYou are " << a << " years old.\n";
}
```

```
How old are you: -10
        Your age could not be negative.
        Try again.
How old are you: 200
        You could not be over 120.
        Try again.
How old are you: 19

You are 19 years old.
```

Notice that the function's parameter list is empty. But even though it has no input parameters, the parentheses `()` must be included both in the function's header and in every call to the function.

4.10 PASSING BY REFERENCE

Until now, all the parameters that we have seen in functions have been *passed by value*. That means that the expression used in the function call is evaluated first and then the resulting value is assigned to the corresponding parameter in the function's parameter list before the function begins executing. For example, in the call cube(x), if x has the value 4, then the value 4 is passed to the local variable n before the function begins to execute its statements. Since the value 4 is used only locally inside the function, the variable x is unaffected by the function. Thus the variable x is a *read-only* parameter.

The pass-by-value mechanism allows for more general expressions to be used in place of an actual parameter in the function call. For example the cube function could also be called as cube(3), or as cube(2*x-3), or even as cube(2*sqrt(x)-cube(3)). In each case, the expression within the parentheses is evaluated to a single value and then that value is passed to the function.

The read-only, pass-by-value method of communication is usually what we want for functions. It makes the function more self-contained, protecting against accidental side effects. However, there are some situations where a function needs to change the value of the parameter passed to it. That can be done by passing it *by reference*.

To pass a parameter by reference instead of by value, simply append an ampersand & to the type specifier in the functions parameter list. This makes the local variable a reference to the actual parameter passed to it. So the actual parameter is *read-write* instead of read-only. Then any change to the local variable inside the function will cause the same change to the actual parameter that was passed to it.

EXAMPLE 4.15 The swap() Function

This little function is widely used in sorting data:

```
//  Swaps x and y so that each ends up with the other's value:
void swap(float& x, float& y)
{
    float temp = x;
    x = y;
    y = temp;
}
```

Its sole purpose is to interchange the two objects that are passed to it. This is accomplished by declaring the formal parameters x and y as reference variables: float& x, float& y. The reference operator & makes x and y synonyms for the actual parameters passed to the function.

Here is a test driver and output from a sample run:

```cpp
void swap(float&, float&);

// Test driver for the swap function:
main()
{
    float a = 27, b = -5.041;
    cout << a << " " << b << endl;
    swap(a,b);
    cout << a << " " << b << endl;
}
```

```
27 -5.041
-5.041 27
```

When the call `swap(a,b)` executes, the function creates its local references `x` and `y`, so that `x` is the function's local name for `a`, and `y` is the function's local name for `b`. Then the local variable `temp` is declared and initialized with the value of `a`, `a` is assigned the value of `b`, and `b` is assigned the value of `temp`. Consequently, `a` ends up with the value –5.041, and `b` ends up with the value 27.0.

Note that the function declaration:

```cpp
void swap(float&, float&);
```

includes the reference operator & for each reference parameter, even though the parameters themselves are omitted.

Some C++ programmers write the reference operator `&` as a prefix to the parameter, like this:

```cpp
void swap(float &x, float &y)
```

instead of as a suffix to its type as we do. The compiler will accept float& x, float &x, float & x, or even float&x. It's mostly a matter of taste.

EXAMPLE 4.16 Passing By Value and Passing By Reference

This example shows the difference between passing by value and passing by reference.

```cpp
void f(int x, int& y) { x = 88; y = 99; }

main()
{
    int a = 22, b = 33;
    cout << "a = " << a << ", b = " << b << endl;
    f(a,b);
    cout << "a = " << a << ", b = " << b << endl;
}
```

```
a = 22, b = 33
a = 22, b = 99
```

The call `f(a,b)` passes `a` by value to `x` and `b` by reference to `y`. So `x` is a local variable which is assigned `a`'s value of 22, while `y` is an alias for the variable `b` whose value is 33. The function assigns 88 to `x`, but that has no effect on `a`. But when it assigns 99 to `y`, it is really assigning 99 to `b`. Thus, when the function terminates, `a` still has its original value 22, while `b` has the new value 99. The actual parameter `a` is read-only, while the actual parameter `b` is read-write.

This table summarizes the differences between passing by value and passing by reference:

Table 4.3 Passing By Value Versus Passing By Reference

Passing By Value	Passing By Reference
`int x;`	`int &x;`
Formal parameter `x` is a local variable.	Formal parameter `x` is a local reference.
It is a duplicate of the actual parameter.	It is a <u>synonym</u> for the actual parameter.
It cannot change the actual parameter.	It can change the actual parameter.
Actual parameter may be a constant, a variable, or an expression.	Actual parameter must be a variable.
Actual parameter is read-only.	`Actual parameter is read-`write.

A common situation where reference parameters are needed is where the function has to return more than one value. It can only return one value directly with a `return` statement. So if more than one value must be returned, reference parameters can do the job.

EXAMPLE 4.17 Computing the Area and Circumference of a Circle

This function returns through its two reference parameters the `area` and the `circumference` of a circle whose radius has the given length `r`:

```
void computeCircle(double& area, double& circumference, double r)
{
    const double pi = 3.141592653589793;
    area = pi*r*r;
    circumference = 2*pi*r;
}
```

Here is a test driver and output from a sample run:

```
void computeCircle(double&, double&, double);

main()
{
    double r, a, c;
    cout << "Enter radius: ";
    cin >> r;
    computeCircle(a, c, r);
    cout << "area = " << a << ", circumference = " << c << endl;
}
```

```
Enter radius: 100
area = 31415.9, circumference = 628.319
```

Note that the output parameters `area` and `circumference` are listed first in the parameter list, to the left of the input parameter `r`. This standard C style is consistent with the format of assignment statements: `q = p`, where the information (the value) flows <u>from</u> the read-only variable `p` on the right <u>to</u> the read-write variable `q` on the left.

4.11 PASSING BY CONSTANT REFERENCE

There are two good reasons for passing a parameter by reference. If the function has to change the value of the actual parameter, as the `swap()` function did, then it must be passed by reference. Also, if the actual parameter that is passed to a function takes up a lot of storage space (for example, a one-megabyte graphics image), then it is more efficient to pass it by reference to prevent it from being duplicated. However, this also allows the function to change the value (*i.e.*, contents) of the actual parameter. If you don't want the function to change its contents (for example, if the purpose of the function is to print the object), then passing by reference can be risky. Fortunately, C++ provides a third alternative: passing by *constant reference*. It works the same way as passing by reference, except that the function is prevented from changing the value of the parameter. The effect is that the function has access to the actual parameter by means of its formal parameter alias, but the value of that formal parameter may not be changed during the execution of the function. A parameter that is passed by value is called "read-only" because it cannot write (*i.e.*, change) the contents of that parameter.

EXAMPLE 4.18 Passing By Constant Reference

This illustrates the three ways to pass a parameter to a function:

```
void f(int x, int& y, const int& z)
{
    x += z;
    y += z;
    cout << "x = " << x << ", y = " << y << ", z = " << z << endl;
}
```

The first parameter `a` is passed by value, the second parameter `b` is passed by reference, and the third parameter `c` is passed by constant reference:

```
main()
{
    int a = 22, b = 33, c = 44;
    cout << "a = " << a << ", b = " << b << ", c = " << c << endl;
    f(a,b,c);
    cout << "a = " << a << ", b = " << b << ", c = " << c << endl;
}
```

```
a = 22, b = 33, c = 44
x = 66, y = 77, z = 44
a = 22, b = 77, c = 44
```

The function changes the formal parameters `x` and `y`, but it would not be able to change `z`. The function's change of x has no effect upon the actual parameter `a` because it was passed by value. The function's change of `y` has the same effect upon the actual parameter `b` because it was passed by reference.

Passing parameters by constant reference is used mostly in functions that process large objects, such as arrays and class instances that are described in later chapters. Objects of fundamental types (integers, floats, *etc*.) are usually passed either by value (if you don't want the function to change them) or by reference (if you do want the function to change them).

4.12 INLINE FUNCTIONS

A function involves substantial overhead. Extra time and space have to be used to invoke the function, pass parameters to it, allocate storage for its local variables, store the current variables and the location of execution in the main program, *etc*. In some cases, it is better to avoid all this by specifying the function to be `inline`. This tells the compiler to replace each call to the function with explicit code for the function. To the programmer, an inline function appears the same as an ordinary function, except for the use of the `inline` specifier.

EXAMPLE 4.19 An `inline` Cube Function

This is the same `cube()` function that we had in EXAMPLE 4.1:

```
inline int cube(int n)
{
    return n*n*n;
}
```

The only difference is the `inline` designation in the function's header. The compiler is told to replace the expression `cube(n)` in the main program with the actual code `n*n*n`. So the following program is compiled

```
main()
{
    cout << cube(4) << endl;
    int x, y;
    cin >> x;
    y = cube(2*x-3);
}
```

the result will be as though the program itself had really been

```
main()
{
    cout << (4)*(4)*(4) << endl;
    int x, y;
    cin >> x;
    y = (2*x-3)*(2*x-3)*(2*x-3);
}
```

When the compiler replaces the `inline` function call with the function's actual code, we say that it *expands* the inline function.

Note that the C++ Standard does not actually require the compiler to expand `inline` functions. It only "advises" the compiler to do so. One that doesn't follow this "advice" could still be validated as a Standard C++ compiler. On the other hand, some Standard C++ compilers may expand some simple functions even if they are not declared to be `inline`.

4.13 SCOPE

The *scope* of a name consists of that part of the program where it can be used. It begins where the name is declared. If that declaration is inside a function (including the `main()` function), then the scope extends to the end of the innermost block that contains the declaration.

A program may have several objects with the same name as long as their scopes are nested or disjoint. This is illustrated by the next example which is an elaboration of Example 2.17.

EXAMPLE 4.20 Nested and Parallel Scopes

In this example, `f()` and `g()` are global functions, and the first `x` is a global variable. So their scope includes the entire file. This is called *file scope*. The second `x` is declared inside `main()` so it has *local scope*; *i.e.*, it is accessible only from within `main()`. The third `x` is declared inside an internal

```
void f();                                            // f() is global
void g();                                            // g() is global
int x = 11;                                          // this x is global

main()
{                                                    // begin scope of main()
    int x = 22;
    {                                        // begin scope of internal block
        int x = 33;
        cout << "In block inside main(): x = " << x << endl;
    }                                         // end scope of internal block
    cout << "In main(): x = " << x << endl;
    cout << "In main(): ::x = " << ::x << endl; // accesses global x
    f();
    g();
}                                                    // end scope of main()
```

block, so its scope is restricted to that internal block. Each `x` scope overrides the scope of the previously declared `x`, so there is no ambiguity when the identifier x is referenced. The *scope resolution operator* `::` is used to access the last `x` whose scope was overridden; in this case, the global `x` whose value is 11:

```
void f()
{                                                    // begin scope of f()
    int x = 44;
    cout << "In f(): x = " << x << endl;
}                                                    // end scope of f()

void g()
{                                                    // begin scope of g()
    cout << "In g(): x = " << x << endl;
}                                                    // end scope of g()
```
```
In block inside main(): x = 33
In main(): x = 22
In main(): ::x = 11
In f(): x = 44
In g(): x = 11
```

The `x` initialized with 44 has scope limited to the function `f()` which is parallel to `main()`; but its scope is also nested within the global scope of the first `x`, so its scope overrides that of both the first x within `f()`. In this example, the only place where the scope of the first `x` is not overridden is within the function `g()`.

4.14 OVERLOADING

C++ allows you to use the same name for different functions. As long as they have different parameter type lists, the compiler will regard them as different functions. To be distinguished, the parameter lists must either contain a different number of parameters, or there must be at least one position in their parameter lists where the types are different.

EXAMPLE 4.21 Overloading the `max()` Function

An earlier example defined a `max()` function for two integers. Here we define two other `max()` functions in the same program:

```
int max(int, int);

int max(int, int, int);

double max(double, double);

main()
{
    cout << max(99,77) << " " << max(55,66,33) << " "
        << max(3.4,7.2) << endl;
}

int max(int x, int y)
{
    return (x > y ? x : y);
}

//  Returns the maximum of the three given integers:
int max(int x, int y, int z)
{
    int m = (x > y ? x : y);
    return (z > m ? z : m);
}

//  Returns the maximum of the two given real numbers:
double max(double x, double y)
{
    return (x > y ? x : y);
}
```

```
99 66 7.2
```

Three different functions, all named `max`, are defined here. The compiler checks their parameter lists to determine which one to use on each call. For example, the first call passes two `int`s, so the version that has two `ints` in its parameter list is called. (If that version had been omitted, then the system would promote the two ints 99 and 77 to the doubles 99.0 and 77.0 and then pass them to the version that has two doubles in its parameter list.)

Overloaded functions are widely used in C++. Their value will become more apparent with the use of classes in Chapter 8.

4.15 THE `main()` AND `exit()` FUNCTIONS

Every C++ program requires a function named `main()`. In fact, we can think of the complete program itself as being made up of the `main()` function together with all the other functions that are called either directly or indirectly from it. The program starts by calling `main()`.

Although not required, most C++ compilers expect the main() function to have return type `int`. Since this is the default return type for any function, it need not be specified. So we usually just write

```
main()
```

instead of

```
int main()
```

In either case, most compilers will allow the `return` statement to be omitted, although some may give a warning if it is omitted. If it is included, it must return an integer.

Some C++ programmers prefer to declare `main()` a `void` function like this:

```
void main()
```

This is acceptable to most compilers, although some will issue a warning and then automatically change `main()` to `int` type. If the compiler does accept `main()` as a `void` function, then of course any `return` statement should appear simply as

```
return;
```

since in this case `main()` has no return type.

If you want to terminate the program from within a function other than the `main()` function, you cannot simply use a `return` statement. The `return` statement will only terminate the current function and return control to the invoking function. Fortunately, there is another way to terminate the program and it can be used anywhere within any function. That is the `exit()` function that is defined in the `<stdlib.h>` header file.

EXAMPLE 4.22 Using the `exit()` Function to Terminate a Program

```
#include <iostream.h>
#include <stdlib.h>

double reciprocal(double x)
{
    if (x == 0) exit(1);
    return 1.0/x;
}

main()
{
    double x;
    cin >> x;
    cout << reciprocal(x);
}
```

If the user enters 0 for `x`, the program will terminate from within the `reciprocal()` function without attempting to divide by it.

4.16 DEFAULT ARGUMENTS

C++ allows a function to have a variable number of arguments. This is done by providing default values for the optional arguments.

EXAMPLE 4.23 Default Parameters

This function evaluates the third degree polynomial $a_0 + a_1x + a_2x^2 + a_3x^3$. The actual evaluation is done using Horner's Algorithm, grouping the calculations as $a_0 + (a_1 + (a_2 + a_3x)x)x$ for greater efficiency:

```
double p(double, double, double =0, double =0, double =0);

main()
{
    double x = 2.0003;
    cout << "p(x, 7) = " << p(x, 7) << endl;
    cout << "p(x, 7, 6) = " << p(x, 7, 6) << endl;
    cout << "p(x, 7, 6, 5) = " << p(x, 7, 6, 5) << endl;
    cout << "p(x, 7, 6, 5, 4) = " << p(x, 7, 6, 5, 4) << endl;
}

double p(double x, double a0, double a1, double a2, double a3)
{
    return a0 + (a1 + (a2 + a3*x)*x)*x;
}
```

The call `p(x, a0, a1, a2, a3)` evaluates the third-degree polynomial $a_0 + a_1x + a_2x^2 + a_3x^3$. But since `a1`, `a2`, and `a3` all have the default value 0, the function can also be called by `p(x, a0)` to evaluate the constant polynomial a_0^3, or by `p(x, a0, a1)` to evaluate the first-degree polynomial $a_0 + a_1x$, or by `p(x, a0, a1, a2)` to evaluate the second-degree polynomial $a_0 + a_1x + a_2x^2$.

Note how the default values are given in the function prototype.

Here is the output from the test run:

```
p(x, 7) = 7
p(x, 7, 6) = 19.0018
p(x, 7, 6, 5) = 39.0078
p(x, 7, 6, 5, 4) = 71.0222
```

For example the call `p(x, 7, 6, 5)`, which is equivalent to the call `p(x, 7, 6, 5, 0)`, evaluates the second degree polynomial $7 + 6\,x + 5\,x^2$.

In the example above, the function may be called with 2, 3, 4, or 5 arguments. So the effect of allowing default parameter values is really to allow a variable number of actual parameters passed to the function.

If a function has default parameter values, then the function's parameter list must show all the parameters with default values to the right of all the parameters that have no default values, like this:

```
void f(int a, int b, int c=4, int d=7, int e=3);   // OK
void g(int a, int b=2, int c=4, int d, int e=3);   // ERROR
```

The "optional" parameters must all be listed last.

Review Questions

4.1   What are the advantages of using functions to modularize a program?

4.2   What is the difference between a function's declaration and its definition?

4.3   Where can the declaration of a function be placed?

4.4   When does a function need an `include` directive?

4.5   What is the advantage of putting a function's definition in a separate file?

4.6   What is the advantage of compiling a function separately?

4.7   What are the differences between passing a parameter by value and by reference?

4.8   What are the differences between passing a parameter by reference and by constant reference?

4.9   Why is a parameter that is passed by value referred to as "read-only"? Why is a parameter that is passed by reference referred to as "read-write"?

4.10 What is wrong with the following declaration:

```
int f(int a, int b=0, int c);
```

Solved Problems

4.11 In Example 4.13, the following expression was used to test whether y is a leap year:

```
y % 4 == 0 && y % 100 != 0 || y % 400 == 0
```

This expression is not the most efficient form. If y is not divisible by 4, it will still test the condition $y \% 400 == 0$ which would have to be false. C++ implements "short circuiting," which means that subsequent parts of a compound condition are tested only when necessary. Find an equivalent compound condition that is more efficient due to short circuiting.

The compound condition

```
y%4 == 0 && (y % 100 != 0 || y % 400 == 0)
```

is equivalent and more efficient. The two can be seen to be equivalent by checking their values in the four possibilities, represented by the four y values 1995, 1996, 1900, and 2000. This condition is more efficient because if y is not divisible by 4 (the most likely case), then it will not test y further.

4.12 Describe how a `void` function with one reference parameter can be converted into an equivalent non-`void` function with one value parameter.

Convert the reference parameter into a return value. For example, the function

```
void f(int& n)
{
    n *= 2;
}
```

is equivalent to the function

```
int g(int n)
{
    return 2*n;
}
```

These two functions are invoked differently:

```
int x = 22, y = 33;
f(x);
y = g(y);
```

But in both cases, the effect is to double the value of the parameter.

Solved Programming Problems

4.13 Write a simple program like the one in Example 4.2 to check the identity: $\cos 2x = 2\cos^2 x - 1$.

This is similar to Example 4.2:

```
#include <iostream.h>
#include <math.h>

main()
{
    for (float x = 0; x < 1; x += 0.1)
        cout << cos(2*x) << '\t' << 2*cos(x)*cos(x) - 1 << endl;
}
```

```
1           1
0.980067        0.980067
0.921061        0.921061
0.825336        0.825336
0.696707        0.696707
0.540302        0.540302
0.362358        0.362358
0.169967        0.169967
-0.0291997      -0.0291997
-0.227202       -0.227202
```

Each value in the first column matches the corresponding value in the second column, showing that the identity is true for the 10 values of `x` tested.

4.14 A more efficient way to compute the permutations function $P(n,k)$ is by the formula

$$P(n, k) = (n)(n-1)(n-2)...(n-k+2)(n-k+1)$$

This means the product of the k integers from n down to $n - k + 1$. Use this formula to rewrite and test the `perm()` function from Example 4.9.

To compute a product of `k` integers, we use a `for` loop that iterates `k` times. Each time, p is multiplied by n which is then decremented. The result is that 1 is multiplied by `n`, `n-1`, `n-2`, *etc.*, down to `n-k+1`:

```
int perm(int, int);

main()
{
    for (int i = -1; i < 8; i++) {
        for (int j = -1; j <= i+1; j++)
            cout << " " << perm(i,j);
        cout << endl;
    }
}

//  Returns P(n,k), the number of permutations of k from n:
int perm(int n, int k)
{
    if (n < 0 || k < 0 || k > n) return 0;
    int p = 1;
    for (int i = 1; i <= k; i++, n--)
        p *= n;
    return p;
}
```

The resulting output is the same as in Example 4.9.

```
0 0
0 1 0
0 1 1 0
0 1 2 2 0
0 1 3 6 6 0
0 1 4 12 24 24 0
0 1 5 20 60 120 120 0
0 1 6 30 120 360 720 720 0
0 1 7 42 210 840 2520 5040 5040 0
```

4.15 The *combination function* $C(n,k)$ gives the number of different (unordered) k-element subsets that can be found in a given set of n elements. The function can be computed from the formula

$$C(n, k) = \frac{n!}{k!\,(n-k)!}$$

Implement this formula.

This is a straightforward implementation of the formula:

```cpp
int comb(int, int);

main()
{
    for (int i = -1; i < 8; i++) {
        for (int j = -1; j <= i+1; j++)
            cout << " " << comb(i,j);
        cout << endl;
    }
}


int factorial(int);

//  Returns C(n,k), the number of combinations of k from n:
int comb(int n, int k)
{
    if (n < 0 || k < 0 || k > n) return 0;
    return factorial(n)/(factorial(k)*factorial(n-k));
}
```

```
0 0
0 1 0
0 1 1 0
0 1 2 1 0
0 1 3 3 1 0
0 1 4 6 4 1 0
0 1 5 10 10 5 1 0
0 1 6 15 20 15 6 1 0
0 1 7 21 35 35 21 7 1 0
```

Note that the `factorial()` function must be declared above the `comb()` function because it is used by that function. But it does not need to be declared above the `main()` function because it is not used there.

4.16 Write and test the `digit()` function:

```
int digit(int n, int k)
```

This function returns the kth digit of the positive integer n. For example, if n is the integer 29,415, then the call `digit(n, 0)` would return the digit 5, and the call `digit(n, 2)` would return the digit 4. Note that the digits are numbered from right to left beginning with the "zeroth digit."

This removes the right-most digit of n k times. This reduces n to an integer whose right-most digit is the same as the kth digit of the original integer. That digit is then obtained as the remainder from division by 10:

```
int digit(int, int);

main()
{
    int n, k;
    cout << "Integer: ";
    cin >> n;
    do {
        cout << "Digit: ";
        cin >> k;
        cout << "The " << k << "th digit of " << n << " is "
             << digit(n, k) << endl;
    } while (k > 0);
}

// Returns the kth digit of the integer n:
int digit(int n, int k)
{
    for (int i = 0; i < k; i++)
        n /= 10;  // remove right-most digit
    return n % 10;
}
```

```
Integer: 123456789
Digit: 8
The 8th digit of 123456789 is 1
Digit: 4
The 4th digit of 123456789 is 5
Digit: 1
The 1th digit of 123456789 is 8
Digit: 0
The 0th digit of 123456789 is 9
```

This run was on a computer whose `int`s can hold 9-digit integers.

4.17 The ancient Greeks classified numbers geometrically. For example, a number was called "triangular" if that number of pebbles could be arranged in a symmetric triangle. The first eight triangular numbers are 1, 3, 6, 10, 15, 21, 28, and 36:

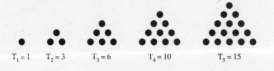

$T_1 = 1$ $T_2 = 3$ $T_3 = 6$ $T_4 = 10$ $T_5 = 15$

Write and test the boolean function:

```
int isTriangular(int n)
```

This function returns 1 if the given integer n is a triangular number, and 0 otherwise.

The argument n is triangular if and only if it is a sum of consecutive integers $1 + 2 + 3 + \cdots$. So we just have to compute these sums until we find one that is greater than or equal to n. If that sum is equal to n, then n is a triangular number; otherwise, it isn't:

```cpp
int isTriangular(int);

main()
{
    int n;
    do {
        cin >> n;
        if (isTriangular(n)) cout << n << " is triangular.\n";
        else cout << n << " is not triangular.\n";
    } while (n > 0);
}

//  Returns 1 if n is a triangular number (1, 3, 6, 10, 15, etc.):
int isTriangular(int n)
{
    int i = 0, sum = 0;
    while (sum < n)
        sum += ++i ;
    if (sum == n) return 1;
    else return 0;
}
```

```
10
10 is triangular.
8
8 is not triangular.
6
6 is triangular.
2
2 is not triangular.
1
1 is triangular.
0
0 is triangular.
```

4.18 Write a maximum function for three integers that uses the maximum for two integers.

We assume that the `max(int, int)` function is already available:

```cpp
int max(int, int);

int max(int x, int y, int z)
{
    int max(int,int);
    return max(max(x,y),z);
}
```

4.19 Write a function that converts rectangular coordinates to polar coordinates.

Every point in the coordinate plane has a unique pair (x, y) of rectangular coordinates and a unique pair (r, θ) of polar coordinates with $r \geq 0$ and $0 \leq \theta < 2\pi$. The following function converts from rectangular to polar coordinates. Since the output consists of more than one variable, the two output variables r and t are passed by reference:

```
void rectangularToPolar(double& r, double& t, double x, double y)
{
    const double pi = 3.1415926535897932385;
    r = sqrt(x*x + y*y);
    if (x > 0)
        if (y >= 0) t = atan(y/x);
        else t = atan(y/x) + 2*pi;
    else if (x == 0)
        if (y > 0)  t = pi/2;
        else if (y == 0) t = 0;
        else t = 3*pi/2;
    else t = atan(y/x) + pi;
}
```

4.20 Simulate the game of craps.

The *game of craps* is played with two dice. Each time the pair of dice is tossed, the sum of the two numbers that come up is used. That sum will be an integer in the range 2 to 12 since the faces of each die are numbers 1 to 6. The player wins immediately if he tosses a 7 or an 11, and he loses immediately if he tosses a 2, 3, or 12. If he tosses a 4, 5, 6, 8, 9, or 10, then that number becomes his "point." He then repeats tossing the dice until he wins by making his point or he loses by tossing a 7.

```
#include <iostream.h>
#include <stdlib.h>
#include <time.h>

void initializeSeed();
int toss();
void win();
void lose();

main()
{
    initializeSeed();
    int point = toss();
    if (point == 2 || point == 3 || point == 12) lose();
    if (point == 7 || point == 11) win();
    int t;
    for(;;) {
        t = toss();
        if (t == 7) lose();
        if (t == point) win();
    }
}
```

```
void initializeSeed()
{
    unsigned seed = time(NULL);
    srand(seed);
}

int toss()
{
    int die1 = rand()/10%6 + 1;
    int die2 = rand()/10%6 + 1;
    int t = die1 + die2;
    cout << "\tYou tossed a " << t << endl;
    return t;
}

void win()
{
    cout << "\tYou won.\n";
    exit(0);
}

void lose()
{
    cout << "\tYou lost.\n";
    exit(0);
}
```

```
    You tossed a 4
    You tossed a 6
    You tossed a 7
    You lost.
```

```
    You tossed a 8
    You tossed a 3
    You tossed a 6
    You tossed a 3
    You tossed a 8
    You won.
```

```
    You tossed a 7
    You won.
```

```
    You tossed a 5
    You tossed a 8
    You tossed a 2
    You tossed a 3
    You tossed a 11
    You tossed a 9
    You tossed a 8
    You tossed a 7
    You lost.
```

```
    You tossed a 12
    You lost.
```

Supplementary Programming Problems

STANDARD C LIBRARY FUNCTIONS

4.21 Write a simple program like the one in Example 4.2 to check the identity: $\cos^2 x + \sin^2 x = 1$.

4.22 Write a simple program like the one in Example 4.2 to check the identity:
$$\tan 2x = 2 \tan x /(1 - \tan^2 x).$$

4.23 Write a simple program like the one in Example 4.2 to check the identity: $\cosh^2 x - \sinh^2 x = 1$.

4.24 Write a simple program like the one in Example 4.2 to check the identity: $\operatorname{asin} x + \operatorname{acos} x = \pi/2$.

4.25 Write a simple program like the one in Example 4.2 to check the identity: $\log x^2 = 2 \log x$.

4.26 Write a simple program like the one in Example 4.2 to check the identity: $b^x = e^{(x \log b)}$.

4.27 Write a test driver to test the functions listed in Table 4.1.

USER-DEFINED FUNCTIONS

4.28 Write and test the following `area()` function that returns the area of a circle with given radius:
```
float area(float r).
```

4.29 Write and test the following `min()` function that returns the smallest of two given integers:
```
int min(int x, int y)
```

4.30 Write and test the following `min()` function that returns the smallest of three given integers:
```
int min(int x, int y, int z)
```

4.31 Write and test the following `min` function that returns the smallest of four given integers:
```
int min(int x, int y, int z, int w)
```

4.32 Write and test the following `min()` function that uses the `min(int, int)` function to find and return the smallest of three given integers:
```
int min(int x, int y, int z)
```

4.33 Write and test the following `min()` function that uses the `min(int, int)` function to find and return the smallest of four given integers:
```
int min(int x, int y, int z, int w)
```

4.34 Write and test the following `min()` function that uses the `min(int, int, int)` function to find and return the smallest of four given integers:
```
int min(int x, int y, int z, int w)
```

4.35 Write and test the following `power()` function that returns `x` raised to the power `p`, where `p` can be any nonnegative integer:
```
float power(float x, unsigned p).
```

4.36 Implement the `factorial()` function with a `for` loop. Determine which values of `n` will cause `factorial(n)` to overflow.

4.37 The combinations function $C(n,k)$ can be computed from the formula

$$C(n,k) = \frac{P(n,k)}{k!}$$

Use this formula to rewrite and test the `comb()` function implemented in Problem 4.15.

4.38 A more efficient way to compute $C(n,k)$ is shown by the formula

$$C(n,k) = (n/1)\,((n-1)/2)\,((n-2)/3)\,...\,((n-k+2)/(k-1))\,((n-k+1)/k)$$

This alternates divisions and multiplications. Use this formula to rewrite and test the `comb()` function implemented in Problem 4.15. Hint: Use a `for` loop like the one in Problem 4.14.

4.39 *Pascal's Triangle* is a triangular array of numbers that begins like this:

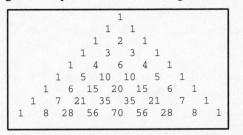

Each number in Pascal's Triangle is one of the combinations $C(n,k)$. (See Problem 4.15 and Problem 4.38.) If we count the rows and the diagonal columns starting with 0, then the number in row n and column k is $C(n,k)$. For example, the number in row number 6 and column number 2 is $C(6,2) = 15$. Write a program that uses the `comb()` function to print Pascal's Triangle down to row number 12.

4.40 Write and test a function that implements the *Euclidean Algorithm* to return the greatest common divisor of two given positive integers. See Example 3.19.

4.41 Write and test a function that uses the greatest common divisor function (Problem 4.40) to return the *least common multiple* of two given positive integers.

BOOLEAN FUNCTIONS

4.42 Write and test the following `isSquare()` function that determines whether the given integer is a square number:

```
int isSquare(int n)
```

The first ten square numbers are 1, 4, 9, 16, 25, 36, 49, 64, 81, and 100.

4.43 Write and test the following `isPentagonal()` function that determines whether the given integer is a pentagonal number:

```
int isPentagonal(int n)
```

The first ten pentagonal numbers are 1, 5, 12, 22, 35, 51, 70, 92, 117, and 145.

OVERLOADING

4.44 Write and test the following `drawSquare()` function that prints a combination of asterisks and blanks so that the asterisks form the boundary of a square of width w:

```
void drawSquare(int w).
```

4.45 Write and test the following `drawRectangle()` function that prints a combination of asterisks and blanks so that the asterisks form the boundary of a rectangle of width w and height h:

```
void drawSquare(int w, int h).
```

4.46 Write and test the following `average()` function that returns the average of four numbers:

```
float average(float x1, float x2, float x3, float x4)
```

4.47 Write and test the following `average()` function that returns the average of up to four positive numbers:

```
float average(float x1, float x2=0, float x3=0, float x4=0)
```

PASSING BY REFERENCE

4.48 Write and test the following `computeCircle()` function that returns the area a and the circumference c of a circle with given radius r:

```
void computeCircle(float& a, float& c, float r).
```

4.49 Write and test the following `computeRectangle()` function that returns the area a and the perimeter p of a rectangle with given side width w and height h:

```
void computeRectangle(float& a, float& p, float w, float h).
```

4.50 Write and test the following `computeTriangle()` function that returns the area a and the perimeter p of a triangle with given side lengths a, b, and c:

```
void computeTriangle(float& a, float& p,
                     float a, float b, float c).
```

4.51 Write and test the following `computeSphere()` function that returns the volume v and the surface area s of a sphere with given radius r:

```
void computeSphere(float& v, float& s, float r).
```

4.52 Write and test the following `computeCylinder()` function that returns the volume v and the surface area s of a cylinder with given radius r and height h:

```
void computeCylinder(float& v, float& s, float r, float h).
```

4.53 Write and test the following `frequency()` function that returns the equal temperament frequency of the given pitch p above middle C. For example, if p has the value `'F'`, then frequency would return 589 which is the nearest integer to 440(12th root of 2)^5.

```
int frequency(char p)
```

4.54 Write and test the following `computeMeans()` function that returns the arithmetic mean a, the geometric mean g, and the harmonic mean h of up to three positive numbers:

```
void computeMeans(float& a, float& g, float& h, float x1,
                  float x2=0, float x3=0)
```

FUNCTIONS WITH DEFAULT ARGUMENTS

4.55 Write and test a `polynomial()` function like the one in Example 4.23 that will evaluate polynomials up to degree 6 (*i.e.*, the highest power of *x* is x^6).

4.56 Write and test a function named `content()` that returns either the length of an interval $[x_1, x_2]$ or the area of a rectangle $[x_1, x_2] \times [y_1, y_2]$ or the volume of a parallelepiped $[x_1, x_2] \times [y_1, y_2] \times [z_1, z_2]$, according to whether the function is passed 2, 4, or 6 parameters. For example, the 4-parameter call `content(3.0, 8.0, -4.0, 6.0)` would return $(8.0 - 3.0)(6.0 - (-4.0)) = 50.0$.

4.57 Write and test a function named `dotProduct()` that returns either the product of two numbers x_1 and y_1 or the dot product of a pair of two-dimensional vectors (x_1, y_1) and (x_2, y_2) or the dot product of a pair of three-dimensional vectors (x_1, y_1, z_1) and (x_2, y_2, z_2), according to whether the function is passed 2, 4, or 6 parameters. For example, with four arguments, the call `dotProduct(3.0, 8.0, -4.0, 6.0)` would return $(3.0)(-4.0) + (8.0)(6.0) = 36.0$.

FUNCTIONS CALLING OTHER FUNCTIONS

4.58 Write and test the following `max` function that uses the `max(int, int)` function to find and return the largest of four given integers:

```
int max(int x, int y, int z, int w)
```

4.59 Write and test the following `min` function that uses the `min(int, int, int)` function to find and return the smallest of four given integers:

```
int min(int x, int y, int z, int w)
```

MODULARIZATION

4.60 Modularize the Monte Carlo program (Problem 3.23) for computing π.

4.61 Modularize the Monty Hall program (see Problem 3.22 and Problem 3.61) so that `main()` is simply a sequence of function calls:

```
main()
{
    printIntroduction();
    initializeSeed();
    int car, choice, open, option;
    car = randomInteger(1,3);
    get(choice);
    set(open, option, car, choice);
    if (change(open, option)) choice = option;
    printResults(car, choice);
}
```

4.62 Modify the Monte Hall program (Problem 4.60) so that it plays the game 6000 times. Use the "no switch" strategy on the first 3000 games and the "switch" strategy on the second 3000 games. Keep track of what fraction the player wins with each strategy, and print the results.

4.63 Modify the craps program (Problem 3.22) so that it plays the game 3600 times. Print the number and percentage of wins.

Answers to Review Questions

4.1 A separately compiled function can be regarded as independent "black box" which performs a specific task. Once the function has been thoroughly tested, the programmer need not be concerned about how it works. This frees the programmer to concentrate on the development of the main program. Moreover, if a better way of implementing the function is found later, it can replace the previous version without affecting the main program.

4.2 A function's declaration (also called it *prototype*) is essentially only the function's header. A function's definition is the complete function: header and body block. The declaration provides only the information needed to call the function: its name, its parameter types, and its return type; it is the *interface* between the function and its caller. The definition gives all the information about the function, including the details of how it works; it is the function's *implementation*.

4.3 A function may be declared anywhere as long as its declaration is above all references to the function. So the declaration must come before any calls to it, and if its definition is separate then it too must come after its declaration.

4.4 An `include` directive is used to include other files. Typically, function declarations and/or definitions are listed in a separate "header" file (with `.h` file extension). If only the declarations are in the header file, then the definitions would be compiled separately in other files.

4.5 The advantage of putting a function's definition in a separate header file is that it doesn't have to be brought into the editor when changes are made to the functions that call it.

4.6 The advantage of compiling a function separately is that it does not need to be recompiled when the functions that call it are recompiled.

4.7 A parameter passed by value is duplicated by its corresponding actual parameter.   A parameter passed by reference is simply renamed by its corresponding actual parameter.

4.8 A parameter passed by constant reference cannot be changed by the function to which it is passed.

4.9 A parameter that is passed by value cannot be changed (rewritten).

4.10 The function has a default value for a parameter (b) that precedes a parameter (c) with no default value. This violates the requirement that all default parameters be listed last in the functions parameter list.

Chapter 5

Arrays

5.1 INTRODUCTION

An *array* is a sequence of objects all of which have the same type. The objects are called the *elements* of the array and are numbered consecutively 0, 1, 2, 3, ... These numbers are called *index values* or *subscripts* of the array. The term "subscript" is used because as a mathematical sequence, an array would be written with subscripts: a_0, a_1, a_2, ... These numbers locate the element's position within the array, thereby giving *direct access* into the array.

If the name of the array is `a`, then `a[0]` is the name of the element that is in position 0, `a[1]` is the name of the element that is in position 1, *etc*. In general, the *i*th element is in position *i*–1. So if the array has *n* elements, their names are `a[0]`, `a[1]`, `a[2]`, ..., `a[n-1]`.

Here is how you should imagine an array:

a	11.11	33.33	55.55	77.77	99.99
	0	1	2	3	4

This shows an array named `a` with 5 elements: `a[0]` contains 11.11, `a[1]` contains 33.33, `a[2]` contains 55.55, `a[3]` contains 77.77, and `a[4]` contains 99.99. The diagram actually represents a region of the computer's memory because an array is always stored this way with its elements in a contiguous sequence.

The method of numbering the *i*th element with index *i*–1 is called *zero-based indexing*. Its use has the effect that the index of an array element is always the same as the number of "steps" from the initial element `a[0]` to that element. For example, element `a[3]` is 3 steps from element `a[0]`. The advantage of this method will become more apparent in Chapter 6 when we see the relationship between arrays and pointers.

5.2 PROCESSING ARRAYS

Virtually all useful programs use arrays. One reason that arrays are so useful is that they allow a single name with a variable index to be used in place of many different names. This makes it easy to do many things that would be far more difficult without arrays.

EXAMPLE 5.1 Printing a Sequence in Order

This program reads 4 numbers and then prints them in reverse order:

```
main()
{
    double a[4];
    cout << "Enter 4 real numbers:\n";
    for (int i = 1; i <= 4; i++) {
        cout << i << ": ";
        cin >> a[i-1];
    }
    cout << "Here they are in reverse order:\n";
    for (i = 3; i >= 0; i--)
        cout << "\ta[" << i << "] = " << a[i] << endl;
}
```

The declaration `double a[4]` declares `a` to be an array of 4 elements of type `double`. The first `for` loop then allows the user to enter real numbers into these 4 components. Then the second for loop prints these stored numbers in reverse order.

Here is a sample run:

```
Enter 4 real numbers:
1: 1.618
2: 2.718
3: 3.142
4: 4.444
Here they are in reverse order:
        a[3] = 4.444
        a[2] = 3.142
        a[1] = 2.718
        a[0] = 1.618
```

The array looks like this:

```
a  1.618  2.718  3.142  4.444
    0      1      2      3
```

The next example works the same way. But it uses a symbolic constant for the size of the array. This makes the code easier to modify.

EXAMPLE 5.2 Using a Symbolic Constant to Declare and Process an Array

```
main()
{
    const int size = 4;
    double a[size];
    cout << "Enter " << size << " real numbers:\n";
    for (int i = 1; i <= size; i++) {
        cout << i << ": ";
        cin >> a[i-1];
    }
    cout << "Here they are in reverse order:\n";
    for (i = size-1; i >= 0; i--)
        cout << "\ta[" << i << "] = " << a[i] << endl;
}
```

The constant integer `size` is initialized with the value 4. It is then used to declare the array `a`, to prompt the user, and to control both `for` loops. The program works the same as the previous version.

The format for an array declaration is

```
type array-name[array-size];
```

where `type` is the array's element type and `array-size` is the number of elements. The declaration in Example 5.2

```
double a[size];
```

declares `a` to be an array of 4 elements, each of type `double`. Standard C++ requires `array-size` to be a positive integer constant. As we did in Example 5.2, it is customary to define the `array-size` as a separate constant:

```
const int size = 4;
```

5.3 INITIALIZING AN ARRAY

In C++, an arrays can be initialized with a single *initializer list*, like this:

```
float a[4] = {22.2, 44.4, 66.6, 88.8};
```

The values in the list are assigned to the elements of the array in the order that they are listed.

EXAMPLE 5.3 Initializing an Array

This shows how to initialize an array explicitly:

```
main()
{
    double a[4] = {22.2, 44.4, 66.6, 88.8};
    for (int i = 0; i < 4; i++)
        cout << "a[" << i << "] = " << a[i] << endl;
}
```

```
    a[0] = 22.2
    a[1] = 44.4
    a[2] = 66.6
    a[3] = 88.8
```

The array's initializer list contains 4 values, the same number as the size of the array specified in the array's declaration.

If the array has more elements than values listed in its initializer list, then the remaining elements are initialized to zero.

EXAMPLE 5.4

Here the array has 4 elements, but its initializer list has only 2 values:

```
main()
{
    double a[4] = {22.2, 44.4};
    for (int i = 0; i < 4; i++)
        cout << "a[" << i << "] = " << a[i] << endl;
}
```

```
    a[0] = 22.2
    a[1] = 44.4
    a[2] = 0.0
    a[3] = 0.0
```

The last 2 elements, which are not given values from the initializer list, are assigned the default value 0.

If an array declaration does not include an initializer list, then its elements may contain unexpected "garbage" values.

EXAMPLE 5.5

Here the array has no initializer:

```
main()
{
    double a[4];
    for (int i = 0; i < 4; i++)
        cout << "a[" << i << "] = " << a[i] << endl;
}
```

```
    a[0] = 2.122e-314
    a[1] = 2.05154e-289
    a[2] = 3.31558e-316
    a[3] = 7.48088e-309
```

The contents of the uninitialized array are unpredictable.

When an array has an explicit initialization, its size specifier may be omitted from its declaration. For example, in the program in Example 5.6, the declaration

```
        float a[4] = {22.2, 44.4, 66.6, 88.8};
```

is equivalent to the declaration

```
        float a[] = {22.2, 44.4, 66.6, 88.8};
```

The size is determined to be the number of values in the initializer list.

5.4 PASSING AN ARRAY TO A FUNCTION

The code `float a[]` that is used to declare an array with an initializer list tells the compiler two things: the name of the array is `a`, and the array's elements will have type `float`. The symbol `a` stores the array's memory address. So the code `float a[]` provides all the information that the compiler needs to declare the array. The size of the array (*i.e.*, the number of elements in the array) does not need to be conveyed to the compiler.

The code that is used to pass an array to a function includes the array's element type and its name. This is illustrated in the next example. It includes two functions that process arrays. In both parameter lists, the array a[] is declared in the parameter list as

```
double a[]
```

The actual number of elements has to be passed by means of a separate integer variable.

When a function is passed an array this way, it is actually passed only the address of the memory cell where the array starts. This value is represented by the array's name `a`. The function can then change the contents of the array by directly accessing the memory cells where the array's elements are stored. So, although the name of the array is passed by value, its elements can be changed just as if they had been passed by reference.

EXAMPLE 5.6 Array I/O Functions

This program illustrates how arrays are passed to functions:

```
const int size = 100;

void getArray(double [], int&);

void printArray(const double [], const int);

main()
{
    double a[size];
    int n;
    getArray(a,n);
    cout << "The array has " << n << " elements.\nThey are:\n";
    printArray(a,n);
}

void getArray(double a[], int& n)
{
    n = 0;
    cout << "Enter data.  Terminate with 0:\n";
    for (n = 0; n < size; n++) {
        cout << n << ": ";
        cin >> a[n];
        if (a[n] == 0) break;
    };
}
```

```
void printArray(const double a[], const int n)
{
    for (int i = 0; i < n; i++)
        cout << '\t' << i << ": " << a[i] << endl;
}
```

```
Enter data.   Terminate with 0:
0: 22.22
1: 55.55
2: 88.88
3: 0
The array has 3 elements.
They are:
        0: 22.22
        1: 55.55
        2: 88.88
```

Note how the functions are called getArray(a,n); printArray(a,n); they are passed the array's name a and an integer variable n. Also note that the for loop in the input function prevents the user from entering more than size numbers into the array.

The input function getArray() changes the formal parameter size, so it is passed by reference. The formal parameter a is passed the <u>address</u> of the first element in the array, and this address is not changed, so a is passed by value. Since a is the name of an array (indicated by a[]), the function can still change the values of the array's elements.

The output function printArray() makes no changes to its parameters, so they are designated in the parameter list as const.

EXAMPLE 5.7 The sum **Functions**

This little function is quite useful:

```
// Returns the sum of the first n elements of the specified array:
double sum(const double a[], const int n)
{
    double s = 0.0;
    for (int i = 0; i < n; i++)
        s += a[i];
    return s;
}
```

Like the printArray() function in Example 5.10, this function does not change the values of its parameters, so each is passed as a const.

5.5 C++ DOES NOT CHECK THE RANGE OF AN ARRAY INDEX

In some programming languages, an index variable will not be allowed to go beyond the bounds set by the array's definition. For example, in Pascal, if an array a is defined to be indexed from 0 to 4, then the reference a[5] will cause the program to crash. This security mechanism is not present in C++ (or C). As the next example shows, the index variable may run far beyond its defined range without any error being detected by the computer.

EXAMPLE 5.8 Index Out of Range

This run of the previous test driver tries to sum the first 30 elements of a 5-element array:

```
Sum how many elements: 30
The sum of the array's first 30 elements is 8.60012e+257
```

The array only has 5 elements. Once the index variable i exceeds the value 4 in the function's for
loop, the reference a[i] is accessing memory cells that are not part of the array. Their contents are
unpredictable. In this run, the function adds the 5 elements to get a sum of 275.75, and then continues to
add another 25 "garbage values." The 30 numbers add up to 8.10012×10^{257}, without any indication from
the computer that anything is wrong.

It is the programmer's responsibility to ensure that index values are kept in range. In some
cases, the computer will let you know if the index is out of range. The next example shows what
could happen on a UNIX workstation if the index gets too far out of range.

EXAMPLE 5.9 Segmentation Fault

On this run, the index is so far out of range that it goes beyond that part of memory allocated to the
running program:

```
Sum how many elements: 300
Segmentation fault
```

This run-time error message means that the system has tried to access part of memory that lies outside the
"segment" allocated to the process that is currently running.

The next example shows one way that the programmer can protect against range errors.

EXAMPLE 5.10 Protecting against Range Errors

```
// Returns the sum of the first n elements of the specified array:
double sum(const double a[], const int n)
{
    if (n*sizeof(double) > sizeof(a))
        return 0;
    double s = 0.0;
    for (int i = 0; i < n; i++)
        s += a[i];
    return s;
}
```

This function first checks the size of the parameter n. Since sizeof(double) returns the size of the
array's elements, n will be out of range precisely when n*sizeof(double) > sizeof(a). In this
case, the function returns 0, signalling that it cannot compute the requested sum.

5.6 THE LINEAR SEARCH ALGORITHM

Computers are probably used more for the storage and retrieval of information than for any
other purpose. Data is often stored in a sequential structure such as an array. The simplest way

to find an object in an array is start at the beginning and inspect each element, one after the other, until the object is found. This method is called the *Linear Search Algorithm*.

EXAMPLE 5.11 The Linear Search

This program tests a function that implements the Linear Search Algorithm:

```
void search(int& found, int& location, int a[], int n, int target);

main()
{
    int a[] = {55, 22, 99, 66, 44, 88, 33, 77}, target, found, loc;
    do {
        cout << "Target: ";
        cin >> target;
        search(found,loc,a,8,target);
        if (found) cout << target << " is at a[" << loc << "].\n";
        else cout << target << " was not found.\n";
    } while (target != 0);
}

//  Linear Search:
void search(int& found, int& location, int a[], int n, int target)
{
    found = location = 0;
    while (!found && location < n)
        found = (a[location++] == target);
    --location;
}
```

```
Target: 33
33 is at a[6].
Target: 44
44 is at a[4].
Target: 50
50 was not found.
Target: 0
0 was not found.
```

In each iteration of the search loop, the current element `a[location]` is compared with `target`. The loop continues until a match is found or all the elements have been checked. Each iteration increments the index `location`, after it is accessed. So if the loop terminates because a match was found, `locator` must be decremented to the index where `target` was found.

Note that the `search()` function has three "input parameters" (`a`, `n`, and `target`) and two "output parameters" (`found` and `location`). We follow the conventional practice of listing the "output parameters" in front of the "input parameters."

5.7 THE BUBBLE SORT ALGORITHM

The Linear Search Algorithm is not very efficient. It obviously would not be a good way to find a name in the telephone book. We can do this common task more efficiently because the names are sorted in alphabetical order. To use an efficient searching algorithm on a sequential data structure such as an array, we must first sort the structure to put its element in order.

There are many algorithms for sorting an array. Although not as efficient as most others, the Bubble Sort is one of the simplest sorting algorithms. It proceeds through a sequence of iterations, each time moving the next largest item into its correct position. On each iteration, it compares each pair of consecutive elements, moving the larger element up.

EXAMPLE 5.12 The Bubble Sort

This program tests a function that implements the Bubble Sort Algorithm. It is compiled with the `swap` function shown in Example 4.15:

```
void print(float [], const int);
void sort(float [], const int);

main()
{
    float a[8] = {55.5, 22.5, 99.9, 66.6, 44.4, 88.8, 33.3, 77.7};
    print(a, 8);
    sort(a, 8);
    print(a, 8);
}

void print(float a[], const int n)
{
    for (int i = 0; i < n-1; i++) {
        cout << a[i] << ", ";
        if ((i+1)%16 == 0) cout << endl;
    }
    cout << a[n-1] << endl;
}

void swap(float& x, float& y)

// Bubble Sort:
void sort(float a[], const int n)
{
    for (int i = n-1; i > 0; i--)
        for (int j = 0; j < i; j++)
            if (a[j] > a[j+1]) swap(a[j],a[j+1]);
}
```

```
55 22 99 66 44 88 33 77
22 33 44 55 66 77 88 99
```

The `sort()` function uses two nested loops. The inside `for` loop compares pairs of adjacent elements and swaps them whenever they are in reverse order. This way, each element "bubbles up" past all the elements that are less than it.

5.8 THE BINARY SEARCH ALGORITHM

The binary search uses the "divide and conquer" strategy. It repeatedly divides the array into two pieces and refocuses on the piece that could contain the target value.

EXAMPLE 5.13 The Binary Search Algorithm

This program tests a function that implements the Binary Search Algorithm:

```
//  Binary Search:
void search(int& found, int& location, int a[], int n, int target);

main()
{
    int a[] = {22, 33, 44, 55, 66, 77, 88, 99}, target, found, loc;
    do {
        cout << "Target: ";
        cin >> target;
        search(found,loc,a,8,target);
        if (found) cout << target << " is at a[" << loc << "].\n";
        else cout << target << " was not found.\n";
    } while (target != 0);
}

void search(int& found, int& location, int a[], int n, int target)
{
    int left = 0, right = n-1;
    found = 0;
    while (!found && left <= right) {
        location = (left + right)/2;       //  the midpoint
        found = (a[location] == target);
        if (a[location] < target) left = location + 1;
        else right = location - 1;
    }
}
```

```
Target: 33
33 is at a[1].
Target: 99
99 is at a[7].
Target: 50
50 was not found.
Target: 22
22 is at a[0].
Target: 0
0 was not found.
```

On each iteration of the `while` loop, the middle element `a[location]` of the sub-array (from `a[left]` to `a[right]`) is checked for the `target`. If it is not found there, then either the left half is discarded by resetting `left = location + 1`, or the right half is discarded by resetting `right = location - 1`, according to whether `(a[location] < target)`.

The Binary Search is far more efficient than the Linear Search because each iteration reduces the search by a factor of two. For example, if the array has 1,000 elements, the Linear search could require 1,000 iterations, while the Binary search would not require more than 10.

5.9 USING ARRAYS WITH ENUMERATION TYPES

Enumeration types were described in Chapter 2. They are naturally processed with arrays.

EXAMPLE 5.14 Days of the Week

This program defines an array `high` of seven `floats`, representing the high temperatures for the seven days of a week:

```
#include <iostream.h>
main()
{
    enum Day {sun, mon, tue, wed, thu, fri, sat};
    float high[sat+1] = {88.3, 95.0, 91.2, 89.9, 91.4, 92.5, 86.7};
    for (Day day = sun; day <= sat; day++)
        cout << "The high temperature for day " << day << " was "
             << high[day] << endl;
}
```

```
The high temperature for day 0 was 88.3
The high temperature for day 1 was 95.0
The high temperature for day 2 was 91.2
The high temperature for day 3 was 89.9
The high temperature for day 4 was 91.4
The high temperature for day 5 was 92.5
The high temperature for day 6 was 86.7
```

This program defines the type `Day` so that any variable declared to have this type may be assigned any of the 7 values `sun`, `mon`, `tue`, `wed`, `thu`, `fri`, or `sat`. This type can then be used the same way that `int` or any other type is used.

The array size is `sat+1` because `sat` = 6 and the array needs 7 elements.

The variable `day`, declared as an index in the `for` loop, takes the values `sun`, `mon`, `tue`, `wed`, `thu`, `fri`, or `sat`. Remember that they are really just like the integers 0, 1, 2, 3, 4, 5, and 6.

Note that it is not possible to print the names of the symbolic constants. Thus the values of the variable `day` printed by `cout` are 0, 1, 2, *etc.*, not `sun`, `mon`, `tue`, *etc*.

The advantage of using enumeration constants this way is that they render your code "self-documenting." For example, the `for` loop control

```
for (Day day = sun; day <= sat; day++)
```

speaks for itself.

An enumeration type is really like the `short` and `char` types. But it is different in that the values for the enumeration type have been given symbolic names, and the values need not be consecutive. It is really just another way of declaring a list of integer constants.

Appendix D shows how enumeration types fit into the hierarchy of all C++ types.

EXAMPLE 5.15 Boolean Type

This shows how to implement a "boolean" type:

```
enum Boolean {false, true};

//  Prompts user for personnel information:
void getInfo(Boolean& isMarried, Boolean& spouseIsEmployed);

main()
{
    Boolean isMarried, spouseIsEmployed;
    getInfo(isMarried, spouseIsEmployed);
    if (isMarried) {
        cout << "You are married.\n";
        if (spouseIsEmployed) cout << "Your spouse is employed.\n";
        else cout << "Your spouse is not employed.\n";
    } else cout << "You are not married.\n";
}

void getInfo(Boolean& isMarried, Boolean& spouseIsEmployed)
{
    char ans;
    cout << "Are you married? ";  cin >> ans;
    isMarried = (ans == 'y' || ans == 'Y');
    if (isMarried) {
        cout << "Is your spouse employed? ";  cin >> ans;
        spouseIsEmployed = (ans == 'y' || ans == 'Y');
    } else spouseIsEmployed = false;
}
```

```
Are you married? y
Is your spouse employed? y
You are married.
Your spouse is employed.
```

```
Are you married? Y
Is your spouse employed? N
You are married.
Your spouse is not employed.
```

```
Are you married? n
You are not married.
```

Here the symbolic constant `false` has the numeric value 0, and the symbolic constant `true` has the numeric value 1. That makes these artificial boolean values consistent with standard C++ which recognizes the zero value as meaning "false" and non-zero values as meaning "true" when used in conditions such as `if (isMarried) ...` .

5.10 TYPE DEFINITIONS

Enumeration types are one way for programmers to define their own types. For example,

```
enum Color {red, orange, yellow, green, blue, violet};
```

defines the type `Color` which can then be used to declare variables like this:

```
Color shirt = blue;
Color car[] = {green, red, blue, red};
float wavelength[violet+1] = {420, 480, 530, 570, 600, 620};
```

Here, `shirt` is a variable whose value can be any one of the 6 values of the type `Color` and is initialized to have the value `blue`, `car` is an array of 4 such `Color` type variables indexed from 0 to 3, and `wavelength` is an array of 6 `float` type variables indexed from red to violet.

C++ also provides a way to rename existing types. The keyword `typedef` declares a new name (*i.e.*, an alias) for a specified type. The syntax is

```
typedef type alias;
```

where `type` is the given type and `alias` is the new name. For example, if you are used to programming in Pascal, you might want to use these type aliases:

```
typedef long Integer;
typedef double Real;
```

You could then use the names `Integer` and `Real` to declare variables of type `long int` and `double`, like this:

```
Integer n = 22;
const Real pi = 3.141592653589793;
Integer frequency[64];
```

Note the syntax for the `typedef` of an array type:

```
typedef element-type alias[];
```

It shows that the number of elements in an array is not part of its type.

A `typedef` statement does <u>not</u> define a new type; it only provides a synonym for an existing type. For example, the `celsius` function defined above could be called by

```
cout << celsius(x);
```

where `x` is declared by

```
double x = 100;
```

There is no conflict in the parameter because `Real` and `double` name the same type. This is different from an `enum` statement which does define a new integer type.

The next example shows another use for `typedef`s.

EXAMPLE 5.16 The Bubble Sort Again

This is the same program as in Example 5.12. The only change is the `typedef` of `Sequence` which is then used in the parameter lists and the declaration of `a` in `main()`:

```
typedef float Sequence[];
void sort(Sequence, const int);
void print(const Sequence, const int);

main()
{
    Sequence a = {55.5, 22.5, 99.9, 66.6, 44.4, 88.8, 33.3, 77.7};
    print(a,8);
    sort(a,8);
    print(a,8);
}

void swap(float&, float&);

//  Bubble Sort:
void sort(Sequence a, const int n)
{
    for (int i = n-1; i > 0; i--)
        for (int j = 0; j < i; j++)
            if (a[j] > a[j+1]) swap(a[j],a[j+1]);
}
void print(const Sequence a, const int n)
{
    for (int i = 0; i < n; i++)
        cout << " " << a[i];
    cout << endl;
}
```

Note the `typedef`:

```
typedef float Sequence[];
```

The brackets `[]` appear <u>after</u> the alias type name `Sequence`. Then this alias is used without brackets to declare array variables and formal parameters.

5.11 MULTIDIMENSIONAL ARRAYS

The arrays we have considered previously have all been *one-dimensional*. This means that they are *linear*; *i.e.*, sequential. But the element type of an array can be almost any type, including an array type. An array of arrays is called a *multidimensional array*. A one-dimensional array of one-dimensional arrays is called a two-dimensional array; a one-dimensional array of two-dimensional arrays is called a three-dimensional array; *etc.*

The simplest way to declare a multidimensional array is like this:

```
double a[32][10][4];
```

This is a three-dimensional array with dimensions 32, 10, and 4. The statement

```
a[25][8][3] = 99.99
```

would assign the value 99.99 to the element identified by the multi-index (25,8,3).

EXAMPLE 5.17 Reading and Printing a Two-Dimensional Array

This program shows how a two-dimensional array can be processed:

```
void read(int a[][5]);

void print(const int a[][5]);

main()
{
    int a[3][5];
    read(a);
    print(a);
}

void read(int a[][5])
{
    cout << "Enter 15 integers, 5 per row:\n";
    for (int i = 0; i < 3; i++) {
        cout << "Row " << i << ": ";
        for (int j = 0; j < 5; j++)
            cin >> a[i][j];
    }
}

void print(const int a[][5])
{
    for (int i = 0; i < 3; i++) {
        for (int j = 0; j < 5; j++)
            cout << " " << a[i][j];
        cout << endl;
    }
}
```

```
Enter 15 integers, 5 per row:
Row 0: 44 77 33 11 44
Row 1: 60 50 30 90 70
Row 2: 85 25 45 45 55
 44 77 33 11 44
 60 50 30 90 70
 85 25 45 45 55
```

Notice that in the functions' parameter lists, the first dimension is left unspecified while the second dimension (5) is specified. This is because a is stored as a one-dimensional array of 3 5-element arrays. The compiler does not need to know how many (3) of these 5-element arrays are to be stored, but it does need to know that they are 5-element arrays.

When a multi-dimensional array is passed to a function, the first dimension is not specified, while all the remaining dimensions are specified.

EXAMPLE 5.18 Reading and Printing a Two-Dimensional Array

```
    const numStudents = 3;
    const numQuizzes = 5;
    typedef int Score[numStudents][numQuizzes];
    void read(Score);
    void printQuizAverages(const Score);
    void printClassAverages(const Score);

    main()
    {
        Score score;
        cout << "Enter " << numQuizzes << " scores for each student:\n";
        read(score);
        cout << "The quiz averages are:\n";
        printQuizAverages(score);
        cout << "The class averages are:\n";
        printClassAverages(score);
    }

    void read(Score score)
    {
        for (int s = 0; s < numStudents; s++) {
            cout << "Student " << s << ": ";
            for (int q = 0; q < numQuizzes; q++)
                cin >> score[s][q];
        }
    }

    void printQuizAverages(const Score score)
    {
        for (int s = 0; s < numStudents; s++) {
            float sum = 0.0;
            for (int q = 0; q < numQuizzes; q++)
                sum += score[s][q];
            cout << "\tStudent " << s << ": " << sum/numQuizzes << endl;
        }
    }

    void printClassAverages(const Score score)
    {
        for (int q = 0; q < numQuizzes; q++) {
            float sum = 0.0;
            for (int s = 0; s < numStudents; s++)
                sum += score[s][q];
            cout << "\tQuiz " << q << ": " << sum/numStudents << endl;
        }
    }
```

This uses a `typedef` to define the alias `Score` for the two-dimensional array type. This makes the function headers more readable.

The `printQuizAverages()` function prints the average of each of the 3 rows of scores, while the `printClassAverages()` function prints the average of each of the 5 columns of scores.

Here is an interactive run of the program:

```
Enter 5 quiz scores for each student:
Student 0: 8 7 9 8 9
Student 1: 9 9 9 9 8
Student 2: 5 6 7 8 9
The quiz averages are:
        Student 0: 8.2
        Student 1: 8.8
        Student 2: 7
The class averages are:
        Quiz 0: 7.33333
        Quiz 1: 7.33333
        Quiz 2: 8.33333
        Quiz 3: 8.33333
        Quiz 4: 8.66667
```

EXAMPLE 5.19 Processing a Three-Dimensional Array

This program simply counts the number of zeros in a three-dimensional array:

```
int numZeros(int a[][4][3], int n1, int n2, int n3);

main()
{
    int a[2][4][3] = { { {5,0,2}, {0,0,9}, {4,1,0}, {7,7,7} },
                       { {3,0,0}, {8,5,0}, {0,0,0}, {2,0,9} } };
    cout << "This array has " << numZeros(a,2,4,3) << " zeros:\n";
}

int numZeros(int a[][4][3], int n1, int n2, int n3)
{
    int count = 0;
    for (int i = 0; i < n1; i++)
        for (int j = 0; j < n2; j++)
            for (int k = 0; k < n3; k++)
                if (a[i][j][k] == 0) ++count;
    return count;
}
```

```
This array has 11 zeros:
```

Notice how the array is initialized: it is a 2-element array of 4-element arrays of 3 elements each. That makes a total of 24 elements. It could have been initialized like this:

```
int a[2][4][3] = {5,0,2,0,0,9,4,1,0,7,7,7,3,0,0,8,5,0,0,0,0,2,0,9};
```
or like this:
```
int a[2][4][3] = { {5,0,2,0,0,9,4,1,0,7,7,7}, {3,0,0,8,5,0,0,0,0,2,0,9} };
```
But these are more difficult to read and understand than the three-dimensional initializer list.

Also notice the three nested `for` loops. In general, processing a *d*-dimensional array is done with *d* for loops, one for each dimension.

Review Questions

5.1 How many different types can the elements of an array have?

5.2 What type and range must an array's subscript have?

5.3 What values will the elements of an array have when it is declared if it does not include an initializer?

5.4 What values will the elements of an array have when it is declared if it has an initializer with fewer values than the number of elements in the array?

5.5 What happens if an array's initializer has more values than the size of the array?

5.6 How does an `enum` statement differ from a `typedef` statement?

5.7 When a multi-dimensional array is passed to a function, why does C++ require all but the first dimension to be specified in the parameter list?

Solved Programming Problems

5.8 Write and run a program that reads an unspecified number of numbers and then prints them together with their deviations from their mean.

We can accumulate the numbers as they are read in and then compute the mean (average) just by dividing their sum by their count:

```
const int size = 100;
main()
{
    cout << "Enter data.  Terminate with 0:\n";
    double a[size], x, sum = 0.0;
    for (int n = 0; ; n++) {
        cin >> x;
        if (x == 0) break;
        a[n] = x;
        sum += x;
    };
    double mean = sum/n;
    cout << "mean = " << mean << endl;
    for (int i = 0; i < n; i++)
        cout << '\t' << a[i] << '\t' << a[i] - mean << endl;
}
```

```
Enter data.  Terminate with 0:
1.23
7.65
0
mean = 4.44
        1.23    -3.21
        7.65    3.21
```

The input loop continues until 0 is read. The deviations are printed as `a[i] - mean`.

5.9   Write and test the function

```
void insert(int a[], int& n, int x)
```

This function inserts the item x into the sorted array a of n elements and increments n. The new item is inserted at the location that maintains the sorted order of the array. This requires shifting elements forward to make room for the new x.

Our test driver defines an array of size 100 and initializes it with 10 elements in increasing order:

```
void print(int [], int);
void insert(int [], int&, int);

main()
{
    int a[100] = { 261, 288, 289, 301, 329, 333, 345, 346, 346, 350};
    int n = 10, x;
    print(a, n);
    cout << "Item to be inserted: ";
    cin >> x;
    insert(a, n, x);
    print(a, n);
}

void print(int a[], int n)
{
    for (int i = 0; i < n-1; i++) {
        cout << a[i] << ", ";
        if ((i+1)%16 == 0) cout << endl;
    }
    cout << a[n-1] << endl;
}

void insert(int a[], int& n, int x)
{
    for (int i = n; i > 0 && a[i-1] > x; i--)
        a[i] = a[i-1];
    a[i] = x;
    ++n;
}
```

```
261, 288, 289, 301, 329, 333, 345, 346, 346, 350
Item to be inserted: 300
261, 288, 289, 300, 301, 329, 333, 345, 346, 346, 350
```

```
261, 288, 289, 301, 329, 333, 345, 346, 346, 350
Item to be inserted: 400
261, 288, 289, 301, 329, 333, 345, 346, 346, 350, 400
```

```
261, 288, 289, 301, 329, 333, 345, 346, 346, 350
Item to be inserted: 200
200, 261, 288, 289, 301, 329, 333, 345, 346, 346, 350
```

The `insert()` function works from the high end of the array, searching backward for the correct location to put x. As it searches, it shifts the elements that are larger than x one place to the right to make way for x. On the first run, 300 is inserted by shifting 7 elements to the right.

The second and third runs test "boundary values;" *i.e.*, the extreme situations. One extreme is where the new item is larger than all the elements in the array. This is tested in the second run by inserting 400. The other extreme is where the new item is smaller than all the elements in the array. This is tested in the third run by inserting 200.

5.10 Write and test the function

```
int frequency(float a[], int n, int x)
```

This function counts the number of times the item x appears among the first n elements of the array a and returns that count as the frequency of x in a.

Here we initialize the array a with 40 randomly arranged integers to test the function

```
int frequency(float [], int, int);

main()
{
    float a[] = {561, 508, 400, 301, 329, 599, 455, 400, 346, 346,
                 329, 375, 561, 390, 399, 400, 401, 561, 405, 405,
                 455, 508, 473, 329, 561, 505, 329, 455, 561, 599,
                 561, 455, 346, 301, 455, 561, 399, 599, 508, 508};
    int n = 40, x;
    cout << "Item: ";
    cin >> x;
    cout << "The frequency of item " << x << " is "
        << frequency(a, n, x) << endl;
}

int frequency(float a[], int n, int x)
{
    int count = 0;
    for (int i = 0; i < n; i++)
        if (a[i] == x) ++count;
    return count;
}
```

```
Item: 508
The frequency of item 508 is 4
```

```
Item: 500
The frequency of item 500 is 0
```

The function uses a counter count. It simply compares each element of the array with the item x and increments the counter each time a match is found.

5.11 Implement the *Insertion Sort*. In this algorithm, the main loop runs from 1 to n-1. On the `ith` iteration, the element `a[i]` is "inserted" into its correct position among the sub-array from `a[0]` to `a[i]`. This is done by shifting all the elements in the sub-array that are greater than `a[i]` one position to the right. Then `a[i]` is copied into the gap between the elements less than `a[i]` and those greater. (See Problem 5.9.)

Out test driver initializes the array `a` with 8 numbers in random order:

```cpp
void print(float [], const int);
void sort(float [], const int);

main()
{
    float a[8] = {88.8, 44.4, 77.7, 11.1, 33.3, 99.9, 66.6, 22.2};
    print(a, 8);
    sort(a, 8);
    print(a, 8);
}

void print(float a[], const int n)
{
    for (int i = 0; i < n-1; i++) {
        cout << a[i] << ", ";
        if ((i+1)%16 == 0) cout << endl;
    }
    cout << a[n-1] << endl;
}

// Insertion Sort:
void sort(float a[], const int n)
{
    float temp;
    for (int i = 1; i < n; i++) { // sort {a[0],...,a[i]}:
        temp = a[i];
        for (int j = i; j > 0 && a[j-1] > temp; j--)
            a[j] = a[j-1];
        a[j] = temp;
    }
}
```

```
88.8, 44.4, 77.7, 11.1, 33.3, 99.9, 66.6, 22.2
11.1, 22.2, 33.3, 44.4, 66.6, 77.7, 88.8, 99.9
```

On the `ith` iteration of the main loop of the Insertion Sort inserts, element `a[i]` is "inserted" so that the sub-array $\{a[0],\ldots,a[i]\}$ will be in increasing order. This is done by storing `a[i]` temporarily in `temp` and then using the inner loop to shift the larger elements to the right with `a[j] = a[j-1]`. Then temp can be copied into the element `a[j]`. Note that $a[k] \leq a[j]$ for all $k \leq j$, and $a[j] \leq a[k]$ for $j \leq k \leq i$. This ensures that the sub-array $\{a[0],\ldots,a[i]\}$ is sorted.

When the last iteration of the main loop is finished, `i == n-1`, so $\{a[0],\ldots,a[n-1]\}$ is sorted.

5.12 Rewrite and test the Bubble Sort function presented in Example 5.12, as an *indirect sort*. Instead of moving the actual elements of the array, sort an index array instead.

The test driver requires a test array `a` initialized with some random numbers and an `index` array. initialized with `index[i] == i`. This ensures that `a[index[i]]` will be the same as `a[i]` initially:

```
void print(const float a[], const int n);
void sort(float a[], int index[], int n);
void print(const float a[], int index[], const int n);

main()
{
    float a[8] = {55, 22, 99, 66, 44, 88, 33, 77};
    int index[8] = {0, 1, 2, 3, 4, 5, 6, 7};
    print(a, 8);
    sort(a, index, 8);
    print(a, index, 8);
    print(a, 8);
}

void swap(int&, int&);

//  Indirect Bubble Sort:
void sort(float a[], int index[], int n)
{
    for (int i = 1; i < n; i++)
        for (int j = 0; j < n-i; j++)
            if (a[index[j]] > a[index[j+1]])
                swap(index[j],index[j+1]);
}

void print(const float a[], const int n)
{
    for (int i = 0; i < n; i++)
        cout << " " << a[i];
    cout << endl;
}

void print(const float a[], int index[], const int n)
{
    for (int i = 0; i < n; i++)
        cout << " " << a[index[i]];
    cout << endl;
}
```

```
55 22 99 66 44 88 33 77
22 33 44 55 66 77 88 99
55 22 99 66 44 88 33 77
```

The only modification needed to the Bubble Sort is to enclose each index with `index[...]`. So `j` is replaced with `index[j]`, and `j+1` is replaced with `index[j+1]`. The effect is to leave the array `a` unchanged while moving the elements of the `index` array instead.

Note that we have two overloaded `print()` function: one to print the array directly, and the other to print it indirectly using an `index` array. This allow us to check that the original array `a` is left unchanged by the indirect sort.

5.13 Implement the *Sieve of Eratosthenes* to find prime numbers. Set up an array `prime[n]` of `ints`, set a[0] = a[1] = 0 (0 and 1 are not primes), and set `a[2]` through `a[n-1]` to 1. Then for each `i` from 3 to `n-1`, set `a[i] = 0` if `i` is divisible by 2 (*i.e.*, `i%2 == 0`). Then for each `i` from 4 to `n-1`, set `a[i] = 0` if `i` is divisible by 3. Repeat this process for each possible divisor from 2 to `n/2`. When finished, all the `i`s for which `a[i]` still equals 1 are the prime numbers. They are the numbers that have fallen through the sieve.

The test driver initializes the `prime` array with 1000 zeros. Then after invoking the `sieve()` function, it prints those index numbers `i` for which `prime[i] == 1`:

```cpp
const int size = 500;
void sieve(int prime[], const int n);

main()
{
    int prime[size] = {0};
    sieve(prime,size);
    for (int i = 0; i < size; i++) {
        if (prime[i]) cout << i << " ";
        if ((i+1) % 50 == 0) cout << endl;
    }
    cout << endl;
}

//  Sets prime[i] = 1 if and only if i is prime:
void sieve(int prime[], const int n)
{
    for (int i = 2; i < n; i++)
        prime[i] = 1;        // assume all i > 1 are prime
    for (int p = 2; p <= n/2; p++) {
        for (int m = 2*p; m < n; m += p)
            prime[m] = 0;    // no multiple of p is prime
        while (!prime[p])
            ++p;                        // advance p to next prime
    }
}
```

```
2  3  5  7  11  13  17  19  23  25  29  31  35  37  41  43  47  49
53  55  59  61  65  67  71  73  77  79  83  85  89  91  95  97
101  103  107  109  113  115  119  121  125  127  131  133  137  139  143  145  149
151  155  157  161  163  167  169  173  175  179  181  185  187  191  193  197  199
203  205  209  211  215  217  221  223  227  229  233  235  239  241  245  247
251  253  257  259  263  265  269  271  275  277  281  283  287  289  293  295  299
301  305  307  311  313  317  319  323  325  329  331  335  337  341  343  347  349
353  355  359  361  365  367  371  373  377  379  383  385  389  391  395  397
401  403  407  409  413  415  419  421  425  427  431  433  437  439  443  445  449
451  455  457  461  463  467  469  473  475  479  481  485  487  491  493  497  499
```

The `sieve()` function initially sets `prime[i]` to 1 for each `i` ≥ 2. Then it resets `prime[i]` to 0 again for every multiple `m` of a prime `p`.

5.14 Write and test the function

```
void reverse(float a[], int n)
```

This function reverses the array, so that its last element becomes its first, its second-to-last element becomes its second, *etc*. Note that this is different from Example 5.1 which does not require the movement of any elements in the array.

This solution simply swaps each of the first n/2 elements with the corresponding element in the second half of the array:

```
void print(const float [], const int);
void reverse(float [], const int);

main()
{
    float a[8] = { 88.8, 44.4, 77.7, 11.1, 33.3, 99.9, 66.6, 22.2};
    print(a, 8);
    reverse(a, 8);
    print(a, 8);
}

void reverse(float a[], const int n)
{
    float temp;
    for (int i = 0; i < n/2; i++) {
        temp = a[i];
        a[i] = a[n-i-1];
        a[n-i-1] = temp;
    }
}
```

```
88.8, 44.4, 77.7, 11.1, 33.3, 99.9, 66.6, 22.2
22.2, 66.6, 99.9, 33.3, 11.1, 77.7, 44.4, 88.8
```

5.15 Write and test a function that implements the *Perfect Shuffle* of a one-dimensional array with an even number of elements. For example, it would replace {11,22,33,44,55,66,77,88} with {11,55,22,66,33,77,44,88}:

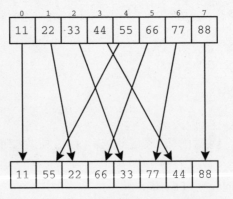

This function interleaves the first half of the array with the second half. It is easier to do this using a temporary array `temp`. Then copy `temp` back into `a`:

```
//  The Perfect Shuffle for an even number of elements:
void shuffle(float a[], int n)
{
    float temp[n];
    for (int i = 0; i < n/2; i++) {
        temp[2*i] = a[i];
        temp[2*i + 1] = n/2 + i;
    }
    for (i = 0; i < n; i++)
        a[i] = temp[i];
}
```

For the case `n == 8`, the first `for` loop copies `a[0]` into `temp[0]` and `a[4]` into `temp[1]` when `i == 0`; then it copies `a[1]` into `temp[2]` and `a[5]` into `temp[3]` when `i == 1`; then it copies `a[2]` into `temp[4]` and `a[6]` into `temp[5]` when `i == 2`; then it copies `a[3]` into `temp[6]` and `a[7]` into `temp[7]` when `i == 3`.

5.16 Write and test the function that "rotates" 90° clockwise a two-dimensional square array of `int`s. For example, it would transform the array

```
11  22  33
44  55  66
77  88  99
```

into the array

```
77  44  11
88  55  22
99  66  33
```

This solution assumes that the type `Matrix` has been defined by a `typedef`.

```
void rotate(Matrix m, const int n)
{
    Matrix temp;
    for (int i = 0; i < size; i++)
        for (int j = 0; j < size; j++)
            temp[i][j] = m[size-j-1][i];
    for (i = 0; i < size; i++)
        for (j = 0; j < size; j++)
            m[i][j] = temp[i][j];
}
```

We use a temporary array `temp` to hold the resulting rotated matrix, and then copy it back into `m`. For the case `n == 3`, the first `for` loop copies `m[2][0]` into `temp[0][0]`, `m[1][0]` into `temp[0][1]`, and `m[0][0]` into `temp[0][2]` when `i == 0`; then it copies `m[2][1]` into `temp[1][0]`, `m[1][1]` into `temp[1][1]`, and `m[0][1]` into `temp[1][2]` when `i == 1`; then it copies `m[2][2]` into `temp[2][0]`, `m[1][2]` into `temp[2][1]`, and `m[0][2]` into `temp[2][2]` when `i == 2`.

Supplementary Programming Problems

5.17 Write and run a program like the one in Example 5.2, but fills the array in reverse and then prints them in the order that they are stored. For example, the first number read is stored in the last position and is printed last.

5.18 Write and run a program like that in Problem 5.8 but computes and prints both the mean and the standard deviation of the input data. The *standard deviation* of the n numbers $a_0, \ldots, a_{n-1}$ is defined by the formula

$$\sigma = \frac{\sqrt{\displaystyle\sum_{i=0}^{n-1} (a_i - \mu)^2}}{n-1}$$

where μ is the mean of the data. This means: square each deviation `a[i]` - `mean`; sum those squares; take the square root of that sum; divide that square root by `n-1`.

5.19 Extend the program from Problem 5.18 so that it also computes and prints the Z-scores of the input data. The *Z-scores* of the n numbers $a_0, \ldots, a_{n-1}$ are defined by the formula $z_i = (a_i - \mu)/\sigma$. They normalize the given data so that it is centered about 0 and has standard deviation 1.

5.20 In the "good old days" when a grade of "C" was considered "average," teachers of large classes would often "curve" their grades according to the following distribution:

A: $1.5 \le z$
B: $0.5 \le z < 1.5$
C: $-0.5 \le z < 0.5$
D: $-1.5 \le z < -0.5$
F: $z < -1.5$

If the grades were *normally distributed* (*i.e.*, their density curve is bell-shaped), then this algorithm would produce about 7% A's, 24% B's, 38% C's, 24% D's, and 7% F's. Here the z values are the Z scores described in Problem 5.19. Extend the program from Problem 5.18 so that it prints the "curved" grade for each of the test scores read.

5.21 Write and test a function that replaces all the negative numbers in an array of integers with their absolute values.

5.22 Write and test a function that returns the minimum value stored in an array.

5.23 Write and test a function that returns the index of the minimum value stored in an array.

5.24 Write and test the following function that returns through it reference parameters both the maximum and the minimum values stored in an array.

```
void extremes(int& min, int& max, int a[], int n)
```

5.25 Write and test the following function that returns through it reference parameters both the largest and the second largest values (possibly equal) stored in an array.

```
void largest(int& max1, int& max2, int a[], int n)
```

5.26 Write and test the following function that attempts to remove an item from an array:

```
int remove(int a[], int& n, int x)
```

The function searches the first `n` elements of the array `a` for the item `x`. If `x` is found, it is removed, all the elements above that position are shifted down, `n` is decremented, and 1 is returned to indicate a successful removal. If `x` is not found, the array is left unchanged and 0 is returned to indicate "failure." (See Problem 5.9.)

5.27 Write and test the following function:

```
void rotate(int a[], int n, int k)
```

The function "rotates" the first `n` elements of the array `a`, `k` positions to the right (or `-k` positions to the left if `k` is negative). The last `k` elements are "rotated" around to the beginning of the array. For example, if `a` is the array shown below:

0	1	2	3	4	5	6	7
22	33	44	55	66	77	88	99

then the call `rotate(a, 8, 3)` would transform `a` into

0	1	2	3	4	5	6	7
77	88	99	22	33	44	55	66

Note that the call `rotate(a, 8, -5)` would have the same effect.

5.28 Write and test the following function:

```
void append(int a[], int m, int b[], int n)
```

The function appends the first `n` elements of the array `b` onto the end of the first `m` elements of the array `a`. It assumes that `a` has room for at least `m + n` elements. For example, if `a` and `b` look like this:

a

0	1	2	3	4	5	6	7	8	9	10	11	12	13
22	27	33	34	39	44	50	55	0	0	0	0	0	0

b

0	1	2	3	4	5	6	7
66	72	77	88	90	0	0	0

then the call `append(a, 8, b, 5)` would transform `a` into

a

0	1	2	3	4	5	6	7	8	9	10	11	12	13
22	27	33	34	39	44	50	55	66	72	77	88	90	0

Note that `b` is left unchanged, and only 5 elements of `a` are changed.

5.29 Write and test the following function:

```
int isPalindrome(int a[], int n)
```

The function returns 1 or 0, according to whether the first n elements of the array a form a palindrome. A *palindrome* is an array like `{22,33,44,55,44,33,22}` that remains unchanged when reversed. Warning: The function should leave the array <u>unchanged</u>.

5.30 Write and test a function that adds element-wise 2 one-dimensional `int` arrays of the same size. For example, if the two given arrays are

```
22   33   44   55   and  7   4   1   -2
```

then the third array would be assigned

```
29   37   45   53
```

5.31 Write and test a function that subtracts element-wise 2 one-dimensional `int` arrays of the same size. For example, if the two given arrays are

    22 33 44 55 and 7 4 1 -2

then the third array would be assigned:

    15 29 43 57

5.32 Write and test a function that multiplies element-wise 2 one-dimensional `int` arrays of the same size. For example, if the two given arrays are

    2   4   6   8 and 7 4 1 -2

then the third array would be assigned

    14 16   6 -16

5.33 One reason that the version of the Bubble Sort presented in Example 5.12 is inefficient is that it will perform the same number of comparisons on an array of *n* elements regardless of how ordered its elements are initially. Even if the array is already completely sorted, this version of the Bubble Sort will still make about $n^2/2$ comparisons. Modify this version so that the main `while` loop stops as soon as it has a complete iteration with no swaps. Use a flag (*i.e.*, an `int` variable that stops the loop when its value is 1) named `sorted` that is set to 0 at the beginning of each iteration of the main loop and then is set to 1 if a swap is made.

5.34 Rewrite and test the `sort()` function presented in Example 5.12, using the Selection Sort instead of the Bubble Sort. The *Selection Sort* of an array of `n` elements goes through `n-1` iterations, each time selecting out the next largest element `a[j]` and swapping it with the element that is in the position where `a[j]` should be. So on the first iteration it selects the largest of all the elements and swaps it with `a[n-1]`, and on the second iteration it selects the largest from the remaining unsorted elements `a[0],...,  a[n-2]` and swaps it with `a[n-2]`, *etc*. On its *i*th iteration it selects the largest from the remaining unsorted elements `a[0], ..., a[n-i]` and swaps it with `a[n-i]`.

5.35 Implement the *Indirect Selection Sort*. (See Problem 5.12.)

5.36 Implement the *Indirect Insertion Sort*. (See Problem 5.11.)

5.37 Write and test a function that computes the median value stored in a sorted array. The *median* is the middle number.

5.38 Write and test a function that computes the *k*th percentile of a sorted array. The *k*th *percentile* is the number that is *k*% of the way from the beginning of the sorted array. For example, the 75th percentile is the number *x* in the array for which 75% of the elements *y* have $y \le x$. The median is the 50th percentile.

5.39 Write a program to determine how many repeated perfect shuffles it takes to restore an array to its original order. (See Problem 5.15.)

5.40 Implement the perfect shuffle for an array of any size, even or odd.

5.41 Write and test the following function:

```
void prepend(int a[], int m, int b[], int n)
```

The function prepends the first `n` elements of the array `b` ahead of the first `m` elements of the array `a`. It assumes that `a` has room for at least `m + n` elements.

5.42 Write and test a function that "transposes" a two-dimensional square array of ints. For example, it would transform the array

```
11   22   33
44   55   66
77   88   99
```

into the array

```
11  44  77
22  55  88
33  66  99
```

5.43 Write and test a function that "zeros out" the diagonals of a two-dimensional square array of ints. For example, it would transform the array

```
11   12   13   14   15
21   22   23   24   25
31   32   33   34   35
41   42   43   44   45
51   52   53   54   55
```

into the array

```
 0   12   13   14    0
21    0   23    0   25
31   32    0   34   35
41    0   43    0   45
 0   52   53   54    0
```

5.44 Write and test a function that returns the *trace* (*i.e.*, the sum of the main diagonal elements) of a two-dimensional square array of ints. For example, it would return 46 for the array

```
11   22   33
40   20   60
35   25   15
```

5.45 Write and test a function that compares 2 two-dimensional int arrays of the same size and assigns –1, 0, or 1 to each element of a third array of the same size according to whether the corresponding element of the first array is less than, equal to, or greater than the corresponding element of the second array. For example, if the two given arrays are

```
22   44   66              33   44   55
50   50   50              50   50   80
```

then the third array would be assigned

```
-1    0    1
 0    0   -1
```

5.46 Write and test a function that computes the "outer product" of 2 one-dimensional int arrays. The (i, j) element of the resulting two-dimensional array will be the product of the ith element of the first array with the jth element of the second array. For example, if the two given arrays are

```
20   30   40                  3   -2
```

then the third array would be assigned

```
 60   90  120
-40  -60  -80
```

5.47 A *minimax* or *saddle point* in a two-dimensional array is an element that is the minimum of its row and the maximum of its column, or vice verse. For example, in the following array

```
11   22   33   33
99   55   66   77
77   44   99   22
```

the element 33 is a minimax because it is the maximum of row 0 and the minimum of column 2. The element 55 is another minimax because it is the minimum of row 1 and the maximum of column 1. Write and test a program that reads the integers m and n, and then reads an m-by-n matrix, and then prints the location and value of each minimax in the matrix. For example, it would print

```
a[0,2] = 33 is a minimax
a[1,1] = 55 is a minimax
```

for the matrix shown above.

5.48 Write and test a function that creates Pascal's Triangle in the square matrix passed to it. For example, if it is passed the two-dimensional array a and the integer 4, then it would load the following into a:

```
1   0   0   0   0
1   1   0   0   0
1   2   1   0   0
1   3   3   1   0
1   4   6   4   1
```

Answers to Review Questions

5.1 Only one: all of an array's elements must be the same type.

5.2 An array's subscript must be an integer type with range from 0 to $n-1$, where n is the array's size.

5.3 In the absence of an initializer, the elements of an array will have unpredictable initial values.

5.4 If the array's initializer has fewer values than the array size, then the specified values will be assigned to the lowest numbered elements and the remaining elements will automatically be initialized to zero.

5.5 It is an error to have more initial values than the size of the array.

5.6 An enum statement defines an enumeration type which is a new unsigned integer type. A typedef merely defines a synonym for an existing type.

5.7 When a multi-dimensional array is passed to a function, all dimensions except the first must be specified so that the compiler will be able to compute the location of each element of the array.

Chapter 6

Pointers and References

6.1 INTRODUCTION

When a variable is declared, three fundamental attributes are associated with it: its *name*, its *type*, and its *address* in memory. For example, the declaration

```
int n;
```

associates the name `n`, the type `int`, and the address of some location in memory where the value of `n` is to be stored. Suppose that address is `0x3fffd14`. (This is *hexadecimal notation*; it is explained in Appendix G.) Then we can visualize `n` like this:

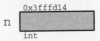

The box represents the variable's storage location in memory. The variable's name is on the left of the box, the variable's address is above the box, and the variable's type is below the box.

If the value of the variable is known, then it is shown inside the box:

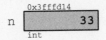

The value of a variable is accessed by means of its name. For example, we can print the value of `n` with the statement

```
cout << n;
```

The address of a variable is accessed by means of the *address operator* `&`. For example, we can print the address of `n` with the statement

```
cout << &n;
```

The address operator `&` "operates" on the variable's name to produce its address. It has precedence level 15 (see Appendix C) which is the same level as the logical NOT operator `!` and pre-increment operator `++`.

EXAMPLE 6.1 Printing Pointer Values

This shows how both the *value* and the *address* of a variable can be printed:

```
main()
{
    int n = 33;
    cout << "n = " << n << endl;    // print the value of n
    cout << "&n = " << &n << endl;  // print the address of n
}
```

The output looks like this:

```
n = 33
&n = 0x3fffd14
```

You can tell that the second output `0x3fffd14` is an address by the "0x" prefix for hexadecimal format. This address is equal to the decimal number 67,108,116. (See Appendix G.)

Displaying the address of a variable this way is not very useful. The address operator `&` has other more important uses. We saw one use in Chapter 4: designating reference parameters in a function declaration. That use is closely tied to another: declaring reference variables.

6.2 REFERENCES

A *reference* is an alias, a synonym for another variable. It is declared by using the reference operator `&` appended to the reference's type.

EXAMPLE 6.2 Using References

Here `r` is declared to be a reference for `n`:

```
main()
{
    int n = 33;
    int& r = n;  //  r is a reference for n
    cout << "n = " << n << ", r = " << r << endl;
    --n;
    cout << "n = " << n << ", r = " << r << endl;
    r *= 2;
    cout << "n = " << n << ", r = " << r << endl;
}
```

```
n = 33, r = 33
n = 32, r = 32
n = 64, r = 64
```

The two identifiers `n` and `r` are different names for the same variable: they always have the same value. Decrementing `n` changes both `n` and `r` to 32. Doubling r increases both `n` and `r` to 64.

EXAMPLE 6.3 References Are Aliases

This shows that `r` and `n` have the same memory address:

```
main()
{
    int n = 33;
    int& r = n;
    cout << "&n = " << &n << ", &r = " << &r << endl;
}
```

```
&n = 0x3fffd14, &r = 0x3fffd14
```

The following diagram illustrates how references work:

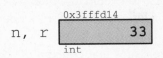

The value 33 is stored only once. The identifiers n and r are both symbolic names for the same memory location 0x3fffd14.

Like a const, a reference <u>must be initialized</u> when it is declared. That requirement should seem reasonable: a synonym must have a something for which it is an alias. In other words, every reference must have a referent.

Reference parameters were defined for functions in Chapter 4. We see now that they work the same way as reference variables: they are merely synonyms for other variables. Indeed, a reference parameter for a function is really just a reference variable whose scope is limited to the function.

We have seen that the ampersand character & has several uses in C++: when used as a prefix to a variable name, it returns the address of that variable; when used as a suffix to a type in a variable declaration, it declares the variable to be a synonym for the variable to which it is initialized; and when used as a suffix to a type in a function's parameter declaration, it declares the parameter to be a reference parameter for the variable that is passed to it. All of these uses are variations on the same theme: <u>the ampersand refers to the address</u> at which the value is stored.

6.3 POINTERS

The reference operator & returns the memory address of the variable to which it is applied. We used this in Example 6.1 to print the address. We can also store the address in another variable. The type of the variable that stores an address is called a *pointer*. If the variable has type int, then the pointer variable must have type "pointer to int," denoted by int*:

EXAMPLE 6.4 Pointer Values Are Addresses

```
main()
{
    int n = 33;
    int* p = &n;  //  p holds the address of n
    cout << "n = " << n << ", &n = " << &n << ", p = " << p << endl;
    cout << "&p = " << &p << endl;
}
```

```
n = 33, &n = 0x3fffd14, p = 0x3fffd14
&p = 0x3fffd10
```

The pointer variable p and the expression &n have the same type (pointer to int) and the same value (0x3fffd14). That value is stored at memory location 0x3fffd10:

The variable p is called a "pointer" because its value "points" to the location of another value. It is an int pointer because the value to which it points is an int.

The value of a pointer is an address. That address depends upon the state of the individual computer on which the program is running. In most cases, the actual value of that address (*e.g.*, 0x3fffd14) is not relevant to the issues that concern the programmer. So diagrams like the one above are usually drawn something like this:

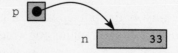

This captures the essential features of p and n: p is a pointer to n, and n has the value 33. A pointer can be thought of as a "locator": it tells where to locate another value.

Often we will need to use the pointer p alone to obtain the value to which it points. This is called "dereferencing" the pointer, and is accomplished simply by applying the star * (the asterisk) symbol as an operator to the pointer:

EXAMPLE 6.5 Dereferencing a Pointer

Here p points to the integer named n, so *p and n are the same value:

```
main()
{
    int n = 33;
    int* p = &n;  //  p points to n
    cout << "*p = " << *p << endl;
}
```
```
*p = 33
```

This shows that *p is an alias for n.

The address operator & and the dereference operator * are inverses of each other: n == *p whenever p == &n. This can also be expressed as n == *&n and p == &*p.

EXAMPLE 6.6 Referencing Is the Opposite of Dereferencing

Here p points to the integer named n and r is a reference that is initialized to the value to which p points. So p references n and r dereferences p. Therefore r is an alias for n; *i.e.*, they are different names for the same value 33:

```
main()
{
    int n = 33;
    int* p = &n;  //  p points to n
    int& r = *p;  //  r is a reference for n
    cout << "r = " << r << endl;
}
```
```
r = 33
```

This shows that r is a reference for n.

6.4 DERIVED TYPES

In Example 6.6, `p` has type pointer to `int`, and r has type reference to `int`. These types are derived from the `int` type. Like arrays, constants, and functions, these are *derived types*. Here are some declarations of derived types:

```
int& r = n;              //   r has type reference to int
int* p = &n;             //   p has type pointer to int
int a[] = {33, 66};      //   a has type array of int
const int c = 33;        //   c has type const int
int f() = { return 33; }; //  f has type function returns int
```

C++ types are classified as either fundamental or derived. (See Appendix D.) The fundamental types include enumeration types and all the number types. Each derived type is based upon some other type(s). A variable declared to have any of the derived types illustrated above (constant, array, pointer, reference, and function) is based upon a single fundamental type. A derived type that is based upon more than one fundamental type is called a *structure type*. These include structures, unions, and classes, which will be studied in later chapters.

6.5 OBJECTS AND LVALUES

The Annotated C++ Reference Manual [Ellis] states: "An *object* is a region of storage. An *lvalue* is an expression referring to an object or function." Originally, the terms "lvalue" and "rvalue" referred to things that appeared on the left and right sides of assignments. But now "lvalue" is more general.

The simplest examples of lvalues are names of objects, *i.e.,* variables:

```
int n;
n = 44;  // n is an lvalue
```

The simplest examples of things that are not lvalues are literals:

```
44 = n;  // ERROR: 44 is not an lvalue
```

But symbolic constants are lvalues:

```
const int max = 65535;  // max is an lvalue
```

even though they cannot appear on the left side of an assignment:

```
max = 21024;  // ERROR: max is constant
```

Lvalues that can appear on the left side of an assignment are called *mutable lvalues*; those that cannot are called *immutable lvalues*. A variable is a mutable lvalue; a constant is an immutable lvalue. Other examples of mutable lvalues include subscripted variables and dereferenced pointers:

```
int a[8];
a[5] = 22;   // a[5] is a mutable lvalue
int* p = &n;
*p = 77;     // *p is a mutable lvalue
```

Other examples of immutable lvalues include arrays, functions, and references.

In general, an lvalue is anything whose address is accessible. Since an address is what a reference variable needs when it is declared, the C++ syntax requirement for such a declaration specifies an lvalue:

```
type& refname = lvalue;
```

For example, this is a legal declaration of a reference:

```
int& r = n;          // OK: n is an lvalue
```

but these are illegal:

```
int& r = 44;         // ERROR: 44 is not an lvalue
int& r = n++;        // ERROR: n++ is not an lvalue
int& r = cube(n);    // ERROR: cube(n) is not an lvalue
```

6.6 RETURNING A REFERENCE

A function's return type may be a reference provided that the value returned is an lvalue which is not local to the function. This restriction means that the returned value is actually a reference to an lvalue that exists after the function terminates. Consequently that returned lvalue may be used like any other lvalue; for example, on the left side of an assignment:

EXAMPLE 6.7 Returning a Reference

```
int& max(int& m, int& n)       // return type is reference to int
{
    return (m > n ? m : n);    // m and n are non-local references
}

main()
{
    int m = 44, n = 22;
    cout << m << ", " << n << ", " << max(m,n) << endl;
    max(m,n) = 55;             // changes the value of m from 44 to 55
    cout << m << ", " << n << ", " << max(m,n) << endl;
}
```
```
44, 22, 44
55, 22, 55
```

The `max()` function returns a reference to the larger of the two variables passed to it. Since the return value is a reference, the expression `max(m,n)` acts like a reference to `m` (since `m` is larger than `n`). So assigning 55 to the expression `max(m,n)` is equivalent to assigning it to `m` itself.

EXAMPLE 6.8 Using a Function as an Array Subscript

```
float& component(float* v, int k)
{
    return v[k-1];
}

main()
{
    float v[4];
    for (int k = 1; k <= 4; k++)
        component(v,k) = 1.0/k;
    for (int i = 0; i < 4; i++)
        cout << "v[" << i << "] = " << v[i] << endl;
}
```

The output looks like this:

```
v[0] = 1
v[1] = 0.5
v[2] = 0.333333
v[3] = 0.25
```

The `component()` function allows vectors to be accessed using the scientific "1-based indexing" instead of the default "0-based indexing." So assignment `component(v,k) = 1.0/k` is really the assignment `v[k+1] = 1.0/k`. We'll see a better way to do this in Chapter 9.

6.7 ARRAYS AND POINTERS

Although pointer types are not integer types, some integer arithmetic operators can be applied to pointers. The affect of this arithmetic is to cause the pointer to point to another memory location. The actual change in address depends upon the size of the fundamental type to which the pointer points.

Pointers can be incremented and decremented like integers. However, the increase or decrease in the pointer's value is equal to the size of the object to which it points:

EXAMPLE 6.9 Traversing an Array with a Pointer

This example shows how a pointer can be used to traverse an array.

```
main()
{
    const int size = 3;
    short a[size] = {22, 33, 44};
    cout << "a = " << a << endl;
    cout << "sizeof(short) = " << sizeof(short) << endl;
    short* end = a + size;        // converts size to offset 6
    short sum = 0;
    for (short* p = a; p < end; p++) {
        sum += *p;
        cout << "\t p = " << p;
        cout << "\t *p = " << *p;
        cout << "\t sum = " << sum << endl;
    }
    cout << "end = " << end << endl;
}
```

```
a = 0x3fffd1a
sizeof(short) = 2
        p = 0x3fffd1a    *p = 22        sum = 22
        p = 0x3fffd1c    *p = 33        sum = 55
        p = 0x3fffd1e    *p = 44        sum = 99
end = 0x3fffd20
```

The second line of output shows that on this machine `short` integers occupy 2 bytes. Since `p` is a pointer to `short`, each time it is incremented it advances 2 bytes to the next `short` integer in the array. That way, `sum += *p` accumulates their sum of the integers. If `p` were a pointer to `double` and `sizeof(double)` were 8 bytes, then each time `p` is incremented it would advance 8 bytes.

Example 6.9 shows that when a pointer is incremented, its value is increased by the number size (in bytes) of the object to which it points. For example,

```
float a[8];
float* p = a;          //  p points to a[0]
++p;                   // increases the value of p by sizeof(float)
```

If floats occupy 4 bytes, then ++p; increases the value of p by 4, and p += 5; increases the value of p by 20. This is how an array can be traversed: by initializing a pointer to the first element of the array and then repeatedly incrementing the pointer. Each increment moves the pointer to the next element of the array.

We can also use a pointer for direct access into the array. For example, we can access a[5] by initializing the pointer to a[0] and then adding 5 to it:

```
float* p = a;          //  p points to a[0]
p += 5;                //  now p points to a[5]
```

So once the pointer is initialized to the starting address of the array, it works like an index.

WARNING: In C++ it is possible to access and even modify unallocated memory locations. This is risky and should generally be avoided. For example,

```
float a[8];
float* p = a[7];   // p points to last element in the array
++p;               // now p points to memory past last element!
*p = 22.2;         // TROUBLE!
```

The next example shows an even tighter connection between arrays and pointers: the name of an array itself is a const pointer to the first element of the array. It also shows that pointers can be compared.

EXAMPLE 6.10 Examining the Addresses of Array Elements

```
main()
{
    short a[] = {22, 33, 44, 55, 66};
    cout << "a = " << a << ", *a = " << *a << endl;
    for (short* p = a; p < a + 5; p++)
        cout << "p = " << p << ", *p = " << *p << endl;
}
```

```
a = 0x3fffd08, *a = 22
p = 0x3fffd08, *p = 22
p = 0x3fffd0a, *p = 33
p = 0x3fffd0c, *p = 44
p = 0x3fffd0e, *p = 55
p = 0x3fffd10, *p = 66
```

Initially, a and p are the same: they are both pointers to short and they have the same value (0x3fffd08). Since a is a constant pointer, it cannot be increment to traverse the array. Instead, we increment p and use the exit condition p < a + 5 to terminate the loop. This computes a + 5 to be the hexadecimal address 0x3fffd08 + 5*sizeof(short) = 0x3fffd08 + 5*2 = 0x3fffd08 + 0xa = 0x3fffd12, so the loop continues as long as p < 0x3fffd12.

The array subscript operator [] is equivalent to the dereference operator *. They provide direct access into the array the same way:

```
a[0] == *a
```

```
a[1] == *(a + 1)
a[2] == *(a + 2), etc.
```

So the array a could be traversed like this:

```
for (int i = 0; i < 8; i++)
    cout << *(a + i) << endl;
```

The next example illustrates how pointers can be combined with integers to move both forward and backward in memory.

EXAMPLE 6.11 Pattern Matching

In this example, the loc function searches through the first n1 elements of array a1 looking for the string of integers stored in the first n2 elements of array a2 inside it. If found, it returns a pointer to the location within a1 where a2 begins; otherwise it returns the NULL pointer.

```
short* loc(short* a1, short* a2, int n1, int n2)
{
    short* end1 = a1 + n1;
    for (short* p1 = a1; p1 < end1; p1++)
        if (*p1 == *a2) {
            for (int j = 0; j < n2; j++)
                if (p1[j] != a2[j]) break;
            if (j == n2) return p1;
        }
    return 0;
}

main()
{
    short a1[9] = {11, 11, 11, 11, 11, 22, 33, 44, 55};
    short a2[5] = {11, 11, 11, 22, 33};
    cout << "Array a1 begins at location\t" << a1 << endl;
    cout << "Array a2 begins at location\t" << a2 << endl;
    short* p = loc(a1, a2, 9, 5);
    if (p) {
        cout << "Array a2 found at location\t" << p << endl;
        for (int i = 0; i < 5; i++)
            cout << "\t" << &p[i] << ": " << p[i]
                 << "\t" << &a2[i] << ": " << a2[i] << endl;
    }
    else cout << "Not found.\n";
}
```

```
Array a1 begins at location     0x3fffd12
Array a2 begins at location     0x3fffd08
Array a2 found at location      0x3fffd16
        0x3fffd16: 11   0x3fffd08: 11
        0x3fffd18: 11   0x3fffd0a: 11
        0x3fffd1a: 11   0x3fffd0c: 11
        0x3fffd1c: 22   0x3fffd0e: 22
        0x3fffd1e: 33   0x3fffd10: 33
```

The pattern matching algorithm uses two loops. The outer loop is controlled by the pointer `p1` which points to elements in array `a1` where the inner loop will begin checking for a match with array `a2`. The inner loop is controlled by the integer `j` which is used to compare corresponding elements of the two arrays. If a mismatch is found, the inner loop aborts and the outer loop continues by incrementing `p1` to look for a match starting with the next element of `a1`. If the inner loop is allowed to finish, then the condition `(j == n2)` will be true and the current location pointed to by `p1` is returned.

In the test driver, we verify that the match has indeed been found by checking the actual addresses.

6.8 THE new OPERATOR

When a pointer is declared like this:

```
float* p;  //  p is a pointer to a float
```

it only allocates memory for the pointer itself. The value of the pointer will be some memory address, but the memory at that address is not yet allocated. This means that storage could already be in use by some other variable. In this case, `p` is uninitialized: it is not pointing to any allocated memory. Any attempt to access the memory to which it points will be an error:

```
*p = 3.14159;   // ERROR: no storage has been allocated for *P
```

A good way to avoid this problem is to initialize pointers when they are declared:

```
float x = 3.14159;  // x contains the value 3.14159
float* p = &x;      // p contains the address of x
cout << *p;         // OK: *p has been allocated
```

In this case, accessing `*p` is no problem because the memory needed to store the float 3.14159 was automatically allocated when `x` was declared; `p` points to the same allocated memory.

Another way to avoid the problem of a dangling pointer is to allocate memory explicitly for the pointer itself. This is done with the `new` operator:

```
float* q;
q = new float;      // allocates storage for 1 float
*q = 3.14159;       // OK: *q has been allocated
```

The `new` operator returns the address of a block of *s* unallocated bytes in memory, where *s* is the size of a float. (Typically, `sizeof(float)` is 4 bytes.) Assigning that address to `q` guarantees that `*q` is not currently in use by any other variables.

The first two of these lines can be combined, thereby initializing `q` as it is declared:

```
float* q = new float;
```

Note that using the `new` operator to initialize `q` only initializes the pointer itself, not the memory to which it points. It is possible to do both in the same statement that declares the pointer:

```
float* q = new float(3.14159);
cout << *q;           // ok: both q and *q have been initialized
```

In the unlikely event that there is not enough free memory to allocate a block of the required size, the `new` operator will return `0` (the NULL pointer):

```
double* p = new double;
if (p == 0) abort();  // allocator failed: insufficient memory
else *p = 3.141592658979324;
```

This prudent code calls an `abort()` function to prevent dereferencing the NULL pointer.

Consider again the two alternatives to allocating memory:

```
float x = 3.14159;                    // allocates named memory
float* p = new float(3.14159);  // allocates unnamed memory
```

In the first case, memory is allocated at compile time to the named variable x. In the second case, memory is allocated at run time to an unnamed object that is accessible through *p.

6.9 THE delete OPERATOR

The delete operator reverses the action of the new operator, returning allocated memory to the free store. It should only be applied to pointers that have been allocated explicitly by the new operator:

```
float* q = new float(3.14159);
delete q;                 // deallocates q
*q = 2.71828;             // ERROR: q has been deallocated
```

Deallocating q returns the block of sizeof(float) bytes to the free store, making it available for allocation to other objects. Once q has been deallocated, it should not be used again until after it has been reallocated. A deallocated pointer, also called a *dangling pointer*, is like an uninitialized pointer: it doesn't point to anything.

A pointer to a constant cannot be deleted:

```
const int * p = new int;
delete p;                 // ERROR: cannot delete pointer to const
```

This restriction is consistent with the general principle that constants cannot be changed.

Using the delete operator for fundamental types (char, int, float, double, *etc.*) is generally not recommended because little is gained at the risk of a potentially disastrous error:

```
float x = 3.14159;  // x contains the value 3.14159
float* p = &x;      // p contains the address of x
delete p;           // RISKY: p was not allocated by new
```

This would deallocate the variable x, a mistake that can be very difficult to debug.

6.10 DYNAMIC ARRAYS

An array name is really just a constant pointer that is allocated at compile time:

```
float a[20];        // a is a const pointer to a block of 20 floats
float* const p = new float[20];   // so is p
```

Here, both a and p are constant pointers to blocks of 20 floats. The declaration of a is called *static binding* because it is allocated at compile time; the symbol is bound to the allocated memory even if the array is never used while the program is running.

In contrast, we can use a non-constant pointer to postpone the allocation of memory until the program is runnning. This is generally called *run-time binding* or *dynamic binding*:

```
float* p = new float[20];
```

An array that is declared this way is called a *dynamic array*.

Compare the two ways of defining an array:

```
float a[20];                    // static array
float* p = new float[20];  // dynamic array
```

The static array `a` is created at compile time; its memory remains allocated thoughout the run of the program. The dynamic array `p` is created at run time; its memory allocated only when its declaration executes. Furthermore, the memory allocated to the array `p` is deallocated as soon as the `delete` operator is invoked on it:

```
delete [] p;                    // deallocates the array p
```

Note that the subscript operator `[]` must be included this way, because `p` is an array.

EXAMPLE 6.12 Using Dynamic Arrays

The `get()` function here creates a dynamic array

```
void get(double*& a, int& n)
{
    cout << "Enter number of items: ";  cin >> n;
    a = new double[n];
    cout << "Enter " << n << " items, one per line:\n";
    for (int i = 0; i < n; i++) {
        cout << "\t" << i+1 << ": ";
        cin >> a[i];
    }
}

void print(double* a, int n)
{
    for (int i = 0; i < n; i++)
        cout << a[i] << " ";
    cout << endl;
}

main()
{
    double* a;       // a is simply an unallocated pointer
    int n;
    get(a, n);       // now a is an array of n doubles
    print(a, n);
    delete [] a;     // now a is simply an unallocated pointer again
    get(a, n);       // now a is an array of n doubles
    print(a, n);
}
```

```
Enter number of items: 4
Enter 4 items, one per line:
        1: 44.4
        2: 77.7
        3: 22.2
        4: 88.8
44.4 77.7 22.2 88.8
Enter number of items: 2
Enter 2 items, one per line:
        1: 3.33
        2: 9.99
3.33 9.99
```

Inside the `get()` function, the `new` operator allocates storage for `n` doubles after the value of `n` is obtained interactively. So the array is created "on the fly" while the program is running.

Before `get()` is used to create another array for `a`, the current array has to be deallocated with the `delete` operator. Note that the subscript operator `[]` must be specified when deleting an array.

Note that the array parameter `a` is *a pointer that is passed by reference*:

```
void get(double*& a, int& n)
```

This is necessary because the `new` operator will change the value of `a` which is the address of the first element of the newly allocated array.

6.11 USING `const` WITH POINTERS

A pointer to a constant is different from a constant pointer. This distinction is illustrated in the following example.

EXAMPLE 6.13 Constant Pointers, Pointer Constants, and Constant Pointer Constants

This fragment declares four variables: a pointer `p`, a constant pointer `cp`, a pointer `pc` to a constant, and a constant pointer `cpc` to a constant:

```
int * p;                  // a pointer to an int
++(*p);                   // ok: increments int *p
++p;                      // ok: increments pointer p
int * const cp;           // a constant pointer to an int
++(*cp);                  // ok: increments int *cp
++cp;                     // illegal: pointer cp is constant
const int * pc;            // a pointer to a constant int
++(*pc);                  // illegal: int *pc is constant
++pc;                     // ok: increments pointer pc
const int * const cpc;    // a constant pointer to a constant int
++(*cpc);                 // illegal: int *cpc is constant
++cpc;                    // illegal: pointer cpc is constant
```

Note that the reference operator `*` may be used in a declaration with or without a space on either side. Thus, the following three declarations are equivalent:

```
int* p;     // indicates that p has type int* (pointer to int)
int * p;    // style sometimes used for clarity
int *p;     // old C style
```

6.12 ARRAYS OF POINTERS AND POINTERS TO ARRAYS

The elements of an array may be pointers. Here is an array of 4 pointers to type `double`:

```
double* p[4];
```

Its elements can allocated like any other pointer:

```
p[2] = new double(3.141592653589793);
```

We can visualize this array like this:

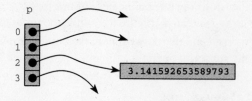

The next example illustrates a useful application of pointer arrays. It shows how to sort a list indirectly by changing the pointers to the elements instead of moving the elements themselves. This is equivalent to the Indirect Bubble Sort shown in Problem 5.12.

EXAMPLE 6.14 Indirect Bubble Sort

```
// The Indirect Bubble Sort sorts the pointer array:
void sort(float* p[], int n)
{
    float* temp;
    for (int i = 1; i < n; i++)
        for (int j = 0; j < n-i; j++)
            if (*p[j] > *p[j+1]) {
                temp = p[j];
                p[j] = p[j+1];
                p[j+1] = temp;
            }
}
```

On each iteration of the inner loop, if the `floats` of adjacent pointers are out of order, then the pointers are swapped.

6.13 POINTERS TO POINTERS

A pointer may point to another pointer. For example,

```
char c = 't';
char* pc = &c;
char** ppc = &pc;
char*** pppc = &ppc;
***pppc = 'w';            // changes the value of c to 'w'
```

We can visualize these variables like this:

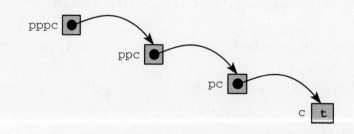

The assignment `***pppc = 'w'` refers to the contents of the address `pc` that is pointed to by the address `ppc` that is pointed to by the address `pppc`.

6.14 POINTERS TO FUNCTIONS

Like an array name, a function name is actually a constant pointer. We can think of its value as the address of the code that implements the function.

A pointer to a function is simply a pointer whose value is the address of the function name. Since that name is itself a pointer, a pointer to a function is just a pointer to a constant pointer. For example,

```
int f(int);          // declares the function f

int (*pf)(int);      // declares the function pointer pf

pf = &f;             // assigns the address of f to pf
```

We can visualize the function pointer like this:

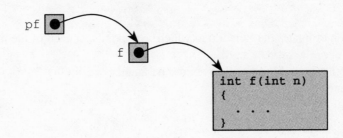

The value of function pointers is that they allow us to define functions of functions. This is done by passing a function pointer as a parameter to another function.

EXAMPLE 6.15 The Sum of a Function

The `sum()` function has two parameters: the function pointer `pf` and the integer `n`:

```
int sum(int (*)(int), int);
int square(int);
int cube(int);

main()
{
    cout << sum(square,4) << endl;    // 1 + 4 + 9 + 16
    cout << sum(cube,4) << endl;      // 1 + 8 + 27 + 64
}
```

The call `sum(square,4)` computes and returns the sum `square(1) + square(2) + square(3) + square(4)`. Since `square(k)` computes and returns `k*k`, the `sum()` function returns `1 + 4 + 9 + 16 = 30`.

Here are the function definitions and the output:

```
//   Returns the sum f(0) + f(1) + f(2) + . . . + f(n-1):
int sum(int (*pf)(int k), int n)
{
    int s = 0;
    for (int i = 1; i <= n; i++)
        s += (*pf)(i);
    return s;
}

int square(int k)
{
    return k*k;
}

int cube(int k)
{
    return k*k*k;
}
```
```
30
100
```

The sum() function evaluates the function to which pf points, at each of the integers 1 through n, and returns the sum of these n values.

Note that the declaration of the function pointer parameter pf in the sum() function's parameter list requires the dummy variable k.

6.15 NUL, NULL, AND void

The constant 0 (zero) has type int. Nevertheless, this symbol can be assigned to all the fundamental types:

```
char c = 0;       // initializes c to the char '\0'
short d = 0;      // initializes d to the short int 0
int n = 0;        // initializes n to the int 0
unsigned u = 0;   // initializes u to the unsigned int 0
float x = 0;      // initializes x to the float 0.0
double z = 0;     // initializes z to the double 0.0
```

In each case, the object is initialized to the number zero. In the case of type char, the character c becomes the *null character*; denoted by '\0' or NUL, it is the character whose ASCII code is 0.

The values of pointers are memory addresses. These addresses must remain within that part of memory allocated to the executing process, with the exception of the address 0x0. This is called the NULL pointer. The same constant applies to pointers derived from any type:

```
char* pc = 0;       // initializes pc to NULL
short* pd = 0;      // initializes pd to NULL
int* pn = 0;        // initializes pn to NULL
unsigned* pu = 0;   // initializes pu to NULL
float* px = 0;      // initializes px to NULL
double* pz = 0;     // initializes pz to NULL
```

The `NULL` pointer cannot be dereferenced. This is a common but fatal error:

```
int* p = 0;
*p = 22;            // ERROR: cannot dereference the NULL pointer
```

A reasonable precaution is to test a pointer before attempting to dereference it:

```
if (p) *p = 22;   // ok
```

This tests the condition `(p != NULL)` because that condition is true precisely when `p` is nonzero.

The name `void` denotes a special fundamental type. Unlike all the other fundamental types, `void` can only be used in a derived type:

```
void x;    // ERROR: no object can have type void
void* p;  // OK
```

The most common use of the type `void` is to specify that a function does not return a value:

```
void swap(double&, double&);
```

Another, different use of `void` is to declare a pointer to an object of unknown type:

```
void* p = q;
```

This use is most common in low-level C programs designed to manipulate hardware resources.

Review Questions

6.1   How do you access the memory address of a variable?

6.2   How do you access the contents of the memory location whose address is stored in a pointer variable?

6.3   Explain the difference between the following two uses of the reference operator `&`:

```
int& r = n;
p = &n;
```

6.4   Explain the difference between the following two uses of the indirection operator `*`:

```
int* q = p;
n = *p;
```

6.5   What is a "dangling pointer"?

6.6   What dire consequences could result from dereferencing a dangling pointer?

6.7   How can these dire consequences be avoided?

6.8   What is wrong with the following code:

```
int& r = 22;
```

6.9   What is wrong with the following code:

```
int* p = &44;
```

6.10   What is wrong with the following code:

```
char c = 'w';
char p = &c;
```

6.11 What is the difference between "static binding" and "dynamic binding"?

6.12 What is wrong with the following code:
```
char c = 'w';
char* p = c;
```

6.13 What is wrong with the following code:
```
short a[32];
for (int i = 0; i < 32; i++)
    *a++ = i*i;
```

6.14 Determine the value of each of the indicated variables after the following code executes. Assume that integers occupy 4 bytes and that m is stored in memory starting at byte 0x3fffd00.
```
int m = 44;
int* p = &m;
int& r = m;
int n = (*p)++;
int* q = p - 1;
r = *(--p) + 1;
++*q;
```
  a. m
  b. n
  c. &m
  d. *p
  e. r
  f. *q

6.15 Classify each of the following as a mutable lvalue, an immutable lvalue, or a non-lvalue:
  a. double x = 1.23;
  b. 4.56*x + 7.89
  c. const double y = 1.23;
  d. double a[8] = {0.0};
  e. a[5]
  f. double f() { return 1.23; }
  g. f(1.23)
  h. double& r = x;
  i. double* p = &x;
  j. *p
  k. const double* p = &x;
  l. double* const p = &x;

6.16 What is wrong with the following code:
```
float x = 3.14159;
float* p = &x;
short d = 44;
short* q = &d;
p = q;
```

6.17 What is wrong with the following code:

```
int* p = new int;
int* q = new int;
cout << "p = " << p << ", p + q = " << p + q << endl;
```

6.18 What is the only thing that you should ever do with the NULL pointer?

6.19 In the following declaration, explain what type p is, and describe how it might be used:

```
double**** p;
```

6.20 If x has the address 0x3fffd1c, then what will values of p and q be for each of the following:

```
double x = 1.01;
double* p = &x;
double* q = p + 5;
```

6.21 If p and q are pointers to int and n is an int, which of the following are legal:

a. p + q
b. p − q
c. p + n
d. p − n
e. n + p
f. n − q

6.22 What does it mean to say that an array is really a constant pointer?

6.23 How is it possible that a function can access every element of an array when it is passed only the address of the first element?

6.24 Explain why the following three conditions are true for an array a and an int i:

```
a[i] == *(a + i);
*(a + i) == i[a];
a[i] == i[a];
```

6.25 Explain the difference between the following two declarations:

```
double * f();
double (* f)();
```

6.26 Write a declaration for each of the following:

a. an array of 8 floats;
b. an array of 8 pointers to float;
c. a pointer to an array of 8 floats;
d. a pointer to an array of 8 pointers to float;
e. a function that returns a float;
f. a function that returns a pointer to a float;
g. a pointer to a function that returns a float;
h. a pointer to a function that returns a pointer to a float;

Solved Programming Problems

6.27 Write a function that uses pointers to copy an array of `double`.

The `copy()` function uses the `new` operator to allocate an array of `n` doubles. The pointer `p` contains the address of the first element of that new array, so it can be used for the name of the array, as in `p[i]`. Then after copying the elements of `a` into the new array, `p` is returned by the function

```
double* copy(double a[], int n)
{
    double* p = new double[n];
    for (int i = 0; i < n; i++)
        p[i] = a[i];
    return p;
}

void print(double [], int);

main()
{
    double a[8] = {22.2, 33.3, 44.4, 55.5, 66.6, 77.7, 88.8, 99.9};
    print(a, 8);
    double* b = copy(a, 8);
    a[2] = a[4] = 11.1;
    print(a, 8);
    print(b, 8);
}
```

```
22.2, 33.3, 44.4, 55.5, 66.6, 77.7, 88.8, 99.9
22.2, 33.3, 11.1, 55.5, 11.1, 77.7, 88.8, 99.9
22.2, 33.3, 44.4, 55.5, 66.6, 77.7, 88.8, 99.9
```

In this run we initialize `a` as an array of 8 doubles. We use a `print()` function to examine the contents of `a`. The the `copy()` function is called and its return value is assigned to the pointer `b` which then serves as the name of the new array. Before printing `b`, we change the values of two of `a`'s elements in order to check that `b` is not the same array as `a`, as the last two `print()` calls confirm.

6.28 Write a function that uses pointers to search for the address of a given integer in a given array. If the given integer is found, the function returns its address; otherwise it returns `NULL`.

We use a `for` loop to traverse the array. If the `target` is found at `a[i]`, then its address `&a[i]` is returned. Otherwise, `NULL` is returned:

```
int* location(int a[], int n, int target)
{
    for (int i = 0; i < n; i++)
        if (a[i] == target) return &a[i];
    return NULL;
}
```

The test driver calls the function and stores its return address in the pointer `p`. If that is nonzero (*i.e.*, not `NULL`), then it and the `int` to which it points are printed.

```
main()
{
    int a[8] = {22, 33, 44, 55, 66, 77, 88, 99}, * p, n;
    do {
        cin >> n;
        if (p = location(a, 8, n)) cout << p << ", " << *p << endl;
        else cout << n << " was not found.\n";
    } while (n > 0);
}
```

```
44
0x3fffcc4, 44
50
50 was not found.
99
0x3fffcd8, 99
90
90 was not found.
0
0 was not found.
```

6.29 Write a function that is passed an array of n pointers to floats and returns a newly created array that contains those n float values.

We use a for loop to traverse the array until p points to the target:

```
float* duplicate(float* p[], int n)
{
    float* const b = new float[n];
    for (int i = 0; i < n; i++, q++)
        b[i] = *p[i];
    return b;
}
```

```
void print(float [], int);
void print(float* [], int);
```

```
main()
{
    float a[8] = {44.4, 77.7, 22.2, 88.8, 66.6, 33.3, 99.9, 55.5};
    print(a, 8);
    float* p[8];
    for (int i = 0; i < 8; i++)
        p[i] = &a[i];   // p[i] points to a[i]
    print(p, 8);
    float* const b = duplicate(p, 8);
    print(b, 8);
}
```

```
44.4, 77.7, 22.2, 88.8, 66.6, 33.3, 99.9, 55.5
44.4, 77.7, 22.2, 88.8, 66.6, 33.3, 99.9, 55.5
44.4, 77.7, 22.2, 88.8, 66.6, 33.3, 99.9, 55.5
```

6.30   Implement a function for integrating a function by means of Riemann sums. Use the formula

$$\int_a^b f(x)\,dx = \left(\sum_{i=1}^n f(a+ih)\right)h$$

This function, named `riemann()`, is similar to the `sum()` function in Example 6.15. Its first argument is a pointer to a function that has one `double` argument and returns a `double`. In this test run, we pass it (a pointer to) the `cube()` function. The other three arguments are the boundaries `a` and `b` of the interval [a, b] over which the integration is being performed and the number `n` of subintervals to be used in the sum. The actual Riemann sum is the sum of the areas of the `n` rectangles based on these subintervals whose heights are given by the function being integrated:

```
double riemann(double (*)(double), double, double, int);
double cube(double);

main()
{
    cout << riemann(cube,0,2,10) << endl;
    cout << riemann(cube,0,2,100) << endl;
    cout << riemann(cube,0,2,1000) << endl;
    cout << riemann(cube,0,2,10000) << endl;
}

//  Returns [f(a)*h + f(a+h)*h + f(a+2h)*h + . . . + f(b-h)*h],
//  where h = (b-a)/n:
double riemann(double (*pf)(double t), double a, double b, int n)
{
    double s = 0, h = (b-a)/n, x;
    int i;
    for (x = a, i = 0; i < n; x += h, i++)
        s += (*pf)(x);
    return s*h;
}

double cube(double t)
{
    return t*t*t;
}
```

```
3.24
3.9204
3.992
3.9992
```

In this test run, we are integrating the function $y = x^3$ over the interval [0, 2]. By elementary calculus, the value of this integral is 4.0. The call `riemann(cube,0,2,10)` approximates this integral using 10 subintervals, obtaining 3.24. The call `riemann(cube,0,2,100)` approximates the integral using 100 subintervals, obtaining 3.9204. These sums get closer to their limit 4.0 as `n` increases. With 10,000 subintervals, the Riemann sum is 3.9992.

Note that the only significant difference between this `riemann()` function and the `sum()` function in Example 6.15 is that the sum is multiplied by the subinterval width `h` before being returned.

6.31 Write a function that returns the *numerical derivative* of a given function *f* at a given point *x*, using a given tolerance *h*. Use the formula

$$f'(x) = \frac{f(x+h) - f(x-h)}{2h}$$

This `derivative()` function is similar to the `sum()` function in Example 6.15, except that it implements the formula for the numerical derivative instead. It has three arguments: a pointer to the function *f*, the *x* value, and the tolerance *h*. In this test run, we pass it (pointers to) the `cube()` function and the `sqrt()` function.

```cpp
#include <iostream.h>
#include <math.h>

double derivative(double (*)(double), double, double);
double cube(double);

main()
{
        cout << derivative(cube, 1, 0.1) << endl;
        cout << derivative(cube, 1, 0.01) << endl;
        cout << derivative(cube, 1, 0.001) << endl;
        cout << derivative(sqrt, 1, 0.1) << endl;
        cout << derivative(sqrt, 1, 0.01) << endl;
        cout << derivative(sqrt, 1, 0.001) << endl;
}

//  Returns an approximation to the derivative f'(x):
double derivative(double (*pf)(double t), double x, double h)
{
    return ((*pf)(x+h) - (*pf)(x-h))/(2*h);
}

double cube(double t)
{
    return t*t*t;
}
```

```
3.01
3.0001
3
0.500628
0.500006
0.5
```

The derivative of the `cube()` function x^3 is $3x^2$, and its value at $x = 1$ is 3, so the numerical derivative should be close to 3.0 for large *h*. Similarly, the derivative of the `sqrt()` function $\sqrt{x}$ is $1/(2\sqrt{x})$, and its value at $x = 1$ is 1/2, so its numerical derivative should be close to 0.5 for large *h*.

6.32 Write a function that is passed an array of n pointers to floats and returns a pointer to the maximum of the n floats.

The pointer pmax is used to locate the maximum float. It is initialized to have the same value as p[0] which points to the first float. Then inside the for loop, the float to which p[i] points is compared to the float to which pmax points, and pmax is updated to point to the larger float when it is detected. So when the loop terminates, pmax points to the largest float:

```
float* max(float* p[], int n)
{
    float* pmax = p[0];
    for (int i = 1; i < n; i++)
        if (*p[i] > *pmax) pmax = p[i];
    return pmax;
}

void print(float [], int);
void print(float* [], int);

main()
{
    float a[8] = {44.4, 77.7, 22.2, 88.8, 66.6, 33.3, 99.9, 55.5};
    print(a, 8);
    float* p[8];
    for (int i = 0; i < 8; i++)
        p[i] = &a[i];  // p[i] points to a[i]
    print(p, 8);
    float* m = max(p, 8);
    cout << m << ", " << *m << endl;
}
```

```
44.4, 77.7, 22.2, 88.8, 66.6, 33.3, 99.9, 55.5
44.4, 77.7, 22.2, 88.8, 66.6, 33.3, 99.9, 55.5
0x3fffcd4, 99.9
```

Here we have two (overloaded) print() functions: one to print the array of pointers, and one to print the floats to which they point. After initializing and printing the array a, we define the array p and initialize its elements to point to the elements of a. The call print(p, 8) verifies that p provides *indirect access* to a. Finally the pointer m is declared and initialized with the address returned by the max() function. The last output verifies that m does indeed point to the largest float among those accessed by p.

Supplementary Problems

6.33 Write the following function that is passed an array of n pointers to floats and returns a newly created array that contains those n float values in reverse order.

```
float* mirror(float* p[], int n)
```

6.34 Write the following function that returns the number of bytes that s has to be incremented before it points to the null character '\0':

```
unsigned len(const char* s)
```

6.35 Write the following function that copies the first *n* bytes beginning with `*s2` into the bytes beginning with `*s1`, where *n* is the number of bytes that `s2` has to be incremented before it points to the null character `'\0'`:

```
void cpy(char* s1, const char* s2)
```

6.36 Write the following function that copies the first *n* bytes beginning with `*s2` into the bytes beginning at the location of the first occurrence of the null character `'\0'` after `*s1`, where *n* is the number of bytes that `s2` has to be incremented before it points to the null character `'\0'`:

```
void cat(char* s1, const char* s2)
```

6.37 Write the following function that compares at most *n* bytes beginning with `s2` with the corresponding bytes beginning with `s1`, where *n* is the number of bytes that `s2` has to be incremented before it points to the null character `'\0'`. If all *n* bytes match, the function should return 0; otherwise, it should return either -1 or 1 according to whether the byte from `s1` is less than or greater than the byte from `s2` at the first mismatch:

```
int cmp(char* s1, char* s2)
```

6.38 Write the following function that searches the *n* bytes beginning with `s` for the character `c`, where *n* is the number of bytes that `s` has to be incremented before it points to the null character `'\0'`. If the character is found, a pointer to it is returned; otherwise return NULL:

```
char* chr(char* s, char c)
```

6.39 Write the following function that returns the sum of the `floats` pointed to by the first `n` pointers in the array `p`:

```
float sum(float* p[], int n)
```

6.40 Write the following function that changes the sign of each of the negative `floats` pointed to by the first `n` pointers in the array `p`:

```
void abs(float* p[], int n)
```

6.41 Write the following function that indirectly sorts the `floats` pointed to by the first `n` pointers in the array `p` by rearranging the pointers:

```
void sort(float* p[], int n)
```

6.42 Implement the *Indirect Selection Sort* using an array of pointers. (See Problem 5.35.)

6.43 Implement the *Indirect Insertion Sort*. (See Problem 5.36.)

6.44 Implement the *Indirect Random Shuffle*. (See Problem 5.15.)

6.45 Rewrite the `sum()` function (Example 6.15) so that it applies to functions with return type `double` instead of `int`. Then test it on the `sqrt()` function (defined in `<math.h>`) and the reciprocal function.

6.46 Apply the `riemann()` function (Problem 6.30) to the following functions defined in `<math.h>`:

a. `sqrt()`, on the interval [1, 4];
b. `cos()`, on the interval [0, $\pi/2$];
c. `exp()`, on the interval [0, 1];
d. `log()`, on the interval [1, e].

6.47 Apply the `derivative()` function (Problem 6.31) to the following functions defined in `<math.h>`:

    a. `sqrt()`, at the point $x = 4$;

    b. `sin()`, at the point $x = \pi/6$;

    c. `exp()`, at the point $x = 0$;

    d. `log()`, at the point $x = 1$.

6.48 Write the following function that returns the product of the n values $f(1)$, $f(2)$, ..., and $f(n)$. (See Example 6.15.)

```
int product(int (*pf)(int k), int n)
```

6.49 Implement the *Bisection Method* for solving equations. Use the following function:

```
double root(double (*pf)(double x), double a, double b, int n)
```

Here, `pf` points to a function f that defines the equation $f(x) = 0$ that is to be solved, a and b bracket the unknown root x (*i.e.*, $a \leq x \leq b$), and n is the number of iterations to use. For example, the call `root(square,1,2,100)` would return 1.414213562373095 ($= \sqrt{2}$), thereby solving the equation $x^2 = 2$. The Bisection Method works by repeatedly bisecting the interval and replacing it with the half that contains the root. It checks the sign of the product $f(a)\,f(b)$ to determine whether the root is in the interval $[a, b]$.

6.50 Implement the *Trapezoidal Rule* for integrating a function. Use the following function:

```
double trap(double (*pf)(double x), double a, double b, int n)
```

Here, `pf` points to the function f that is to be integrated, a and b bracket the interval $[a, b]$ over which f is to be integrated, and n is the number of subintervals to use. For example, the call `trap(square,1,2,100)` would return 1.41421. The Trapezoidal Rule returns the sum of the areas of the n trapezoids that would approximate the area under the graph of f. For example, if $n = 5$, then it would return the following, where $h = (b–a)/5$, the width of each trapezoid.

$$\frac{h}{2}\,[f(a) + 2f(a+h) + 2f(a+2h) + 2f(a+3h) + 2f(a+4h) + f(b)]$$

Answers to Review Questions

6.1 Apply the address operator `&` to the variable `&x`.

6.2 Apply the dereference operator `*` to the variable `*p`.

6.3 The declaration `int& r = n;` declares r to be a reference (alias) for the `int` variable n. The assignment `p = &n;` assigns the address of n to the pointer p.

6.4 The declaration `int* q = p;` declares q to be a pointer (memory address) pointing to the same `int` to which n points. The assignment `n = *p;` assigns to n the `int` to which p points.

6.5 A "dangling pointer" is a pointer that has not been initialized. It is dangerous because it could be pointing to unallocated memory, or inaccessible memory.

6.6 If a pointer pointing to unallocated memory is dereferenced, it could change the value of some unidentified variable. If a pointer pointing to inaccessible memory is dereferenced, the program will probably crash (*i.e.*, terminate abruptly).

6.7 Initialize pointers when they are declared.

6.8   You cannot have a reference to a constant; it's address is not accessible.

6.9   The reference operator `&` cannot be applied to a constant.

6.10 The variable `p` has type `char`, while the expression `&c` has type pointer to `char`. To initialize `p` to `&c`, `p` would have to be declared as type `char*`.

6.11 Static binding is when memory is allocated at compile time, as with the array declaration:
```
double a[400];
```
Dynamic binding is when memory is allocated at run time, by means of the `new` operator:
```
double* p;
p = new double[400];
```

6.12 The variable `p` has type `char*`, while the expression `c` has type `char`. To initialize `p` to `c`, `p` would have the same type as c: either both `char` or both `char*`.

6.13 The only problem is that the array name a is a constant pointer, so it cannot be incremented. The following modified code would be okay:
```
short a[32];
short* p = a;
for (int i = 0; i < 32; i++)
    *p++ = i*i;
```

6.14
   a. m = 46
   b. n = 44
   c. &m = 0x3fffd00
   d. *p = 46
   e. *r = 46
   f. *q = 46

6.15
   a. mutable lvalue;
   b. not an lvalue;
   c. immutable lvalue;
   d. immutable lvalue;
   e. mutable lvalue;
   f. immutable lvalue;
   g. mutable lvalue if return type is a non-local reference; otherwise not an lvalue;
   h. mutable lvalue;
   i. mutable lvalue;
   j. mutable lvalue, unless `p` points to a constant, in which case `*p` is an immutable lvalue;
   k. mutable lvalue;
   l. immutable lvalue;

6.16 The pointers `p` and `q` have different types: `p` is pointer to `float` while `q` is pointer to `short`. It is an error to assign the address in one pointer type to a different pointer type.

6.17 It is an error to add two pointers.

6.18 Test it to see if it is `NULL`. In particular, you should never try to dereference it.

6.19 `p` is a pointer to a pointer to a pointer to a pointer to a `double`. It could be used to represent a four-dimensional array.

6.20 The value of `p` is the same as the address of `a`: `0x3fffd1c`. The value of `q` depends upon `sizeof(double)`. If objects of type `double` occupy 8 bytes, then an offset of 8(5) = 40 is added to `p`, to give `q` the hexadecimal value `0x3fffd44`.

6.21 The only expressions among these six that are illegal are `p + q` and `n - q`.

6.22 The name of an array is a variable that contains the address of the first element of the array. This address cannot be changed, so the array name is actually a constant pointer.

6.23 In the following code that adds all the elements of the array `a`, each increment of the pointer `p` locates the next element:

```
const size = 3;
short a[size] = {22, 33, 44};
short* end = a + size;  // adds size*sizeof(short) = 6 to a
for (short* p = a; p < end; p++)
    sum += *p;
```

6.24 The value `a[i]` returned by the subscripting operator `[]` is the value stored at the address computed from the expression `a + i`. In that expression, `a` is a pointer to its base type `T` and `i` is an `int`, so the offset `i*sizeof(T)` is added to the address `a`. The same evaluation would be made from the expression `i + a` which is what would be used for `i[a]`.

6.25 The declaration `double * f();` declares `f` to be a function that returns a pointer to double. The declaration `double (* f)();` declares `*f` to be a pointer to a function that returns a double.

6.26

a. `float a[8];`
b. `float* a[8];`
c. `float (* a)[8];`
d. `float* (* a)[8];`
e. `float f();`
f. `float* f();`
g. `float (* f)();`
h. `float* (* f)();`

Chapter 7

Strings

7.1 INTRODUCTION

A *string* (also called a *character string*) is a sequence of contiguous characters in memory terminated by the `NUL` character `'\0'`. Strings are accessed by variables of type `char*` (pointer to `char`). For example, if `s` has type `char*`, then

```
cout << s << endl;
```

will print all the characters stored in memory beginning at the address `s` and ending with the first occurrence of the `NUL` character.

The C header file `<string.h>` provides a wealth of special functions for manipulating strings. For example, the call `strlen(s)` will return the number of characters in the string `s`, not counting its terminating `NUL` character. These functions all declare their string parameters as pointers to `char`. So before we study these string operations, we need to review pointers.

7.2 REVIEW OF POINTERS

A *pointer* is a memory address. For example, the following declarations define `x` to be a `float` containing the value 44.44 and `p` to be a pointer containing the address of `x`:

```
float x = 44.44;
float* p = &x;
```

If we imagine memory to be a sequence of bytes with hexadecimal addresses, then we can picture `x` and `p` like this:

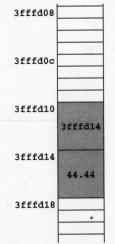

This shows `x` stored at the address `3fffd14` and `p` stored at the address `3fffd10`. The variable `x` contains the float value 44.44 and the variable `p` contains the address value

185

`3fffd14`. The value of `p` is the address of `x`: `3fffd14`. This relationship is usually represented by a diagram like this:

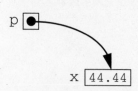

This shows two rectangles, one labeled `p` and one labeled `x`. The rectangles represent storage locations in memory. The variable `p` points to the variable `x`. We can access `x` through the pointer `p` by means of the dereference operator `*`. The statement

```
*p = 77.77;
```

changes the value of `x` to 77.77:

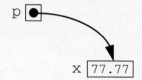

We can have more than one pointer pointing to the same object:

```
float* q = &x;
```

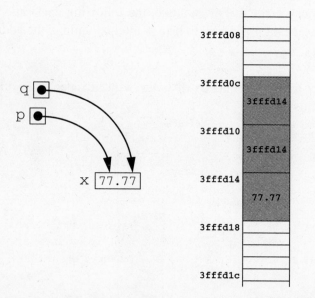

Now `*p`, `*q`, and `x` are all names for the same object whose address is shown to be `3fffd14` and whose current value is 77.77. This shows `q` at address `3fffd0c`. The value stored in `q` is the address `3fffd14` of `x`.

The example below traces these definitions on a UNIX workstation. Notice that, as these figures indicate, memory is allocated in descending order. The first object, `x`, is stored at address `3fffd14`, occupying bytes `3fffd14–3fffd17`. The second object, `p`, is stored at address `3fffd10`.

EXAMPLE 7.1 Tracing Pointers

This program defines a float x and two float pointers p and q. It prints their values and their addresses. It also prints the values of the objects that the pointer point to:

```
main()
{
    float x = 44.44;
    cout << "x = " << x << endl;
    cout << "\t&x = " << &x << endl;   //  prints address of x
    float* p = &x;                      //  p points to x
    cout << "\np = " << p << endl;
    cout << "\t&p = " << &p << endl;   //  prints address of p
    cout << "\t*p = " << *p << endl;   //  prints object p points to
    *p = 77.77;
    cout << "\np = " << p << endl;
    cout << "\t&p = " << &p << endl;
    cout << "\t*p = " << *p << endl;
    cout << "x = " << x << endl;
    cout << "\t&x = " << &x << endl;
    float* q = &x;                      //  q points to x
    cout << "\nq = " << q << endl;
    cout << "\t&q = " << &q << endl;
    cout << "\t*q = " << *q << endl;
    cout << "x = " << x << endl;
    cout << "\t&x = " << &x << endl;
}
```

```
x = 44.44         &x = 0x3fffd14

p = 0x3fffd14     &p = 0x3fffd10    *p = 44.44

p = 0x3fffd14     &p = 0x3fffd10    *p = 77.77
x = 77.77         &x = 0x3fffd14

q = 0x3fffd14     &q = 0x3fffd0c    *q = 77.77
x = 77.77         &x = 0x3fffd14
```

Notice how address values are output: 0x3fffd14 is the hexadecimal numeral 3fffd14. The prefix 0x is the standard notation used to indicate that the numeral is hexadecimal. Although there is no need to do so, one can compute the corresponding decimal value, remembering that 'a' is "hex" for 10, 'b' is 11, 'c' is 12, 'd' is 13, 'e' is 14, and 'f' is 15:

$$0x3fffd14 = 3{\times}16^6 + 15{\times}16^5 + 15{\times}16^4 + 15{\times}16^3 + 13{\times}16^2 + 1{\times}16^1 + 4{\times}16^0 = 67{,}108{,}116$$

So in this run, x is actually stored in the 4 bytes numbered 67,108,116–67,108,119. These are virtual addresses on a UNIX workstation with 20 megabytes of memory. On a DOS PC with 4 megabytes of memory, x, p, and q were stored at addresses 0x23e6, 0x23dc, and 0x23be.

If p is a pointer, then the call cout << *p will always print the value of the object to which p points, and the call cout << p will usually print the value of the address that is stored in p. The important exception to this second rule is when p is declared to have type char*.

7.3 STRINGS

In C++, a *string* is an array of characters with the following exceptional features:

- An extra component is appended to the end of the array, and its value is set to the NUL character `'\0'`. This means that <u>the total number of characters in the array is always 1 more than the string length</u>.

- The string may be initialized with a string literal, like this:

```
char str[] = "Bjarne";
```

Note that this array has 7 elements: `'B'`, `'j'`, `'a'`, `'r'`, `'n'`, `'e'`, and `'\0'`.

- The entire string may be output as a single object, like this:

```
cout << str;
```

The system will copy characters from `str` to `cout` until the NUL character `'\0'` is encountered.

- The entire string may be input as a single object, like this:

```
cin >> buffer;
```

The system will copy characters from `cin` into `buffer` until a white space character is encountered. The user must ensure that buffer is defined to be a character string long enough to hold the input.

- The functions declared in the `<string.h>` header file may be used to manipulate strings. These include the string length function `strlen()`, the string copying functions `strcpy()` and `strncpy()`, the string concatenating functions `strcat()` and `strncat()`, the string comparing functions `strcmp()` and `strncmp()`, and the token extracting function `strtok()`. These functions are described in Section 7.8.

EXAMPLE 7.2 Strings Are Terminated with the NUL Character

This little demo program shows that the NUL character `'\0'` is appended to the string:

```
main()
{
    char s[] = "ABCD";
    for (int i = 0; i < 5; i++)
        cout << "s[" << i << "] = '" << s[i] << "'\n";
}
s[0] = 'A'
s[1] = 'B'
s[2] = 'C'
s[3] = 'D'
s[4] = ''
```

When the NUL character is sent to `cout`, nothing is printed—not even a blank. This is seen by printing one apostrophe immediately before the character and another apostrophe immediately after the character.

7.4 STRING I/O

Input and output of strings is done in several ways in C++ programs. The best way is by means of string class operators as described in Chapter 10. More straightforward methods are described here.

EXAMPLE 7.3 Ordinary Input and Output of Strings

This program reads words into a 79-character buffer:

```
main()
{
    char word[80];
    do {
        cin >> word;
        if (*word) cout << "\t\"" << word << "\"\n";
    } while (*word);
}
```

```
Today's date is March 12, 1996.
        "Today's"
        "date"
        "is"
        "March"
        "12,"
        "1996."
Tomorrow is Monday.
        "Tomorrow"
        "is"
        "Monday."
^D
```

In this run, the `while` loop iterated 10 times: once for each word entered (including the **Control-D** that stopped the loop). Each word in the input stream `cin` is echoed to the output stream `cout`. Note that the output stream is not "flushed" until the input stream encounters the end of the line.

Each string is printed with a double quotation mark `"` on each side. This character must be designated by the character pair `\"` inside a string literal.

The expression `*word` controls the loop. It is the initial character in the string. It will be nonzero (*i.e.*, "true") as long as the string `word` contains a string of length greater than 0. The string of length 0, called the *empty string*, contains the NUL character `'\0'` in its first element. Pressing **Control-D** on a UNIX or Macintosh computer (**Control-Z** on a DOS PC or in VAX/VMS) sends the end-of-file character in from `cin`. This loads the empty string into `word`, setting `*word` (which is the same as `word[0]`) to `'\0'` and stopping the loop. The last line of output shows only the **Control-D** echo.

Note that punctuation marks (apostrophes, commas, periods, *etc.*) are included in the strings, but whitespace characters (blanks, tabs, newlines, *etc.*) are not.

The `do` loop in Example 7.3 could be replaced with:

```
cin >> word
while (*word) {
    cout << "\t\"" << word << "\"\n";
    cin >> word;
}
```

When **Control-D** is pressed, the call `cin >> word` assigns the empty string to `word`.

Example 7.3 and Example 7.1 illustrate an important distinction: the output operator `<<` behaves differently with pointers of type `char*` than with other pointer types. With a `char*` pointer, the operator outputs the entire character string to which the pointer points. But with any other pointer type, the operator will simply output the address of the pointer.

7.5 SOME `cin` MEMBER FUNCTIONS

The input stream object `cin` includes the input functions: `cin.getline()`, `cin.get()`, `cin.ignore()`, `cin.putback()`, and `cin.peek()`. Each of these function names includes the prefix "cin." because they are "member functions" of the `cin` object. This object-oriented principle is explained in Chapters 8 and 12.

The call `cin.getline(str,n)` reads up to `n` characters into `str` and ignores the rest.

EXAMPLE 7.4 The `cin.getline()` Function with Two Parameters

This program echoes the input, line by line:

```
main()
{
    char line[80];
    do {
        cin.getline(line, 80);
        if (*line) cout << "\t[" << line << "]\n";
    } while (*line);
}
```

```
Once upon a midnight dreary, while I pondered, weak and weary,
    [Once upon a midnight dreary, while I pondered, weak and weary,]
Over many a quaint and curious volume of forgotten lore,
    [Over many a quaint and curious volume of forgotten lore,]
^D
```

Note that the condition `(*line)` will evaluate to "true" precisely when `line` contains a non-empty string, because only then will `line[0]` be different from the NUL character (whose ASCII value is 0).

The call `cin.getline(str,n,ch)` reads all input up to the first occurrence of the delimiting character `ch` into `str`. If the specified character `ch` is the newline character `'\n'`, then this is equivalent to `cin.getline(str,n)`. This is illustrated in the next example where the delimiting character is the comma `','`.

EXAMPLE 7.5 The `cin.getline()` Function

This program echoes the input, clause by clause:

```
main()
{
    char clause[20];
    do {
        cin.getline(clause, 20, ',');
        if (*clause) cout << "\t[" << clause << "]\n";
    } while (*clause);
}
```

```
Once upon a midnight dreary, while I pondered, weak and weary,
Over many a quaint and curious volume of forgotten lore,
^D  [Once upon a midnight dreary]
    [ while I pondered]
    [ weak and weary]
    [
Over many a quaint and curious volume of forgotten lore]
    [
]
```

Notice that the invisible endline character that follows "`weary,`" is stored as the first character of the next input line. Since the comma is being used as the delimiting character, the endline character is processed just like an ordinary character.

The `cin.get()` function is used for reading input character-by-character. The call `cin.get(ch)` copies the next character from the input stream `cin` into the variable `ch` and returns 1, unless the end of file is detected in which case it returns 0.

EXAMPLE 7.6 The `cin.get()` Function

This program counts the number of occurrences of the letter 'e' in the input stream. The loop continues as long as the `cin.get(ch)` function is successful at reading characters into `ch`:

```
main()
{
    char ch;
    int count = 0;
    while (cin.get(ch))
        if (ch == 'e') ++count;
    cout << count << " e's were counted.\n";
}
```

```
Once upon a midnight dreary, while I pondered, weak and weary,
Over many a quaint and curious volume of forgotten lore,
^D
11 e's were counted.
```

The opposite of `get` is `put`. The `cout.put()` function is used for writing to the output stream `cout` character-by-character. This is illustrated in the next example.

EXAMPLE 7.7 The `cout.put()` Function

This program echoes the input stream, capitalizing each word:

```
#include <ctype.h>
main()
{
    char ch, pre = '\0';
    while (cin.get(ch)) {
        if (pre == ' ' || pre == '\n') cout.put(char(toupper(ch)));
        else cout.put(ch);
        pre = ch;
    }
}
```

The output looks like this:

```
Fourscore and seven years ago our fathers
Fourscore And Seven Years Ago Our Fathers
brought forth upon this continent a new nation,
Brought Forth Upon This Continent A New Nation,
^D
```

The variable `pre` holds the previously read character. The idea is that if `pre` is a blank or the newline character, then the next character `ch` would be the first character of the next word. In that case, `ch` is replaced by its equivalent uppercase character `ch + 'A' - 'a'`.

The header file `<ctype.h>` declares the function `toupper(ch)` which returns the uppercase equivalent of `ch` if `ch` is a lowercase letter.

The `cin.putback()` function restores the last character read by a `cin.get()` back to the input stream `cin`. The `cin.ignore()` function reads past one or more characters in the input stream `cin` without processing them. Example 7.8 illustrates these functions.

The `cin.peek()` function can be used in place of the combination `cin.get()` and `cin.putback()` functions. The call

```
ch = cin.peek()
```

copies the next character of the input stream `cin` into the `char` variable `ch` without removing that character from the input stream. Example 7.9 shows how the `peek()` function can be used in place of the `get()` and `putback()` functions.

EXAMPLE 7.8 The `cin.putback()` and `cin.ignore()` Functions

This tests a function that extracts the integers from the input stream:

```
int nextInt();

main()
{
    int m = nextInt(), n = nextInt();
    cin.ignore(80,'\n');                      //  ignore rest of input line
    cout << m << " + " << n << " = " << m+n << endl;
}

int nextInt()
{
    char ch;
    int n;
    while (cin.get(ch))
         if (ch >= '0' && ch <= '9') {  //  next character is a digit
             cin.putback(ch);           //  put it back so it can be
             cin >> n;                  //  read as a complete int
             break;
         }
    return n;
}
```
```
What is 305 plus 9416?
305 + 9416 = 9721
```

The `nextInt()` function scans past the characters in `cin` until it encounters the first digit. In this run, that digit is 3. Since this digit will be part of the first integer 305, it is put back into `cin` so that the complete integer 305 can be read into `n` and returned.

EXAMPLE 7.9 The `cin.peek()` Function

This version of the `nextInt()` function is equivalent to the one in the previous example:

```
int nextInt()
{
    char ch;
    int n;
    while (ch = cin.peek())
        if (ch >= '0' && ch <= '9') {
            cin >> n;
            break;
        }
        else cin.get(ch);
    return n;
}
```

The expression `ch = cin.peek()` copies the next character into `ch`, and returns 1 if successful. Then if `ch` is a digit, the complete integer is read into `n` and returned. Otherwise, the character is removed from `cin` and the loop continues. If the end-of-file is encountered, the expression `ch = cin.peek()` returns 0, stopping the loop.

7.6 CHARACTER FUNCTIONS DEFINED IN `<ctype.h>`

Example 7.7 illustrates the `toupper()` function. This is one of a series of character manipulation function defined in the `<ctype.h>` header file. These are summarized in Table 7.1.

Table 7.1   `<ctype.h>` Functions

`isalnum()`	`int isalnum(int c);` Returns nonzero if `c` is an alphabetic or numeric character; otherwise returns 0.
`isalpha()`	`int isalpha(int c);` Returns nonzero if `c` is an alphabetic character; otherwise returns 0.
`iscntrl()`	`int iscntrl(int c);` Returns nonzero if `c` is a control character; otherwise returns 0.
`isdigit()`	`int isdigit(int c);` Returns nonzero if `c` is a digit character; otherwise returns 0.
`isgraph()`	`int isgraph(int c);` Returns nonzero if `c` is any non-blank printing character; otherwise returns 0.
`islower()`	`int islower(int c);` Returns nonzero if `c` is a lowercase alphabetic character; otherwise returns 0.
`isprint()`	`int isprint(int c);` Returns nonzero if `c` is any printing character; otherwise returns 0.
`ispunct()`	`int ispunct(int c);` Returns nonzero if `c` is any printing character, except the alphabetic characters, the numeric characters, and the blank; otherwise returns 0.
`isspace()`	`int isspace(int c);` Returns nonzero if `c` is any white-space character, including the blank `' '`, the form feed `'\f'`, the newline `'\n'`, the carriage return `'\r'`, the horizontal tab `'\t'`, and the vertical tab `'\v'`; otherwise returns 0.
`isupper()`	`int isupper(int c);` Returns nonzero if `c` is an uppercase alphabetic character; otherwise returns 0.
`isxdigit()`	`int isxdigit(int c);` Returns nonzero if `c` is one of the 10 digit characters or one of the 12 hexadecimal digit letters: `'a'`, `'b'`, `'c'`, `'d'`, `'e'`, `'f'`, `'A'`, `'B'`, `'C'`, `'D'`, `'E'`, or `'F'`; otherwise returns 0.
`tolower()`	`int tolower(int c);` Returns the lowercase version of `c` if `c` is an uppercase alphabetic character; otherwise returns `c`.
`toupper()`	`int toupper(int c);` Returns the uppercase version of `c` if `c` is a lowercase alphabetic character; otherwise returns `c`.

Note that these functions receive an `int` parameter `c` and they return an `int`. This works because `char` is an integer type. Normally, a `char` is passed to the function and the return value is assigned to a `char`, so we regard these as character-modifying functions.

Here is a diagram that summarizes most of the `<ctype.h>` functions:

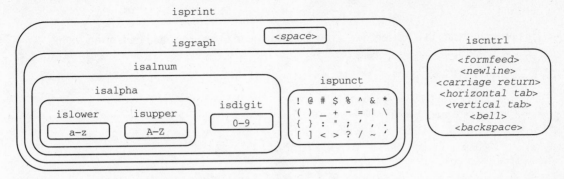

It shows, for example, that if `ch` is the character `'$'`, then `isprint(ch)`, `isgraph(ch)`, and `ispunct(ch)` will return nonzero (*i.e.*, "true"), while `isalnum(ch)`, `isalpha(ch)`, and `islower(ch)` will return zero (*i.e.*, "false")

7.7 ARRAYS OF STRINGS

Recall that a two-dimensional array is really a one-dimensional array whose components themselves are one-dimensional arrays. When those component arrays are strings, we have an array of strings.

Example 7.10 declares the two-dimensional array `name` as

```
char name[4][20];
```

This declaration allocates 80 bytes, arranged like this:

Each of the 4 rows is a one-dimensional array of 20 characters and therefore can be regarded as a character string. These strings are accessed as `name[0]`, `name[1]`, `name[2]`, and `name[3]`. In the sample run shown in Example 7.10, the data would be stored like this:

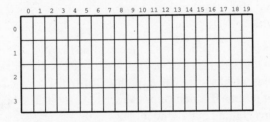

Here, the symbol ∅ represents the NUL character `'\0'`.

EXAMPLE 7.10 An Array of Strings

This program reads in a sequence of strings, storing them in an array, and then prints them:

```
main()
{
    char name[8][24];
    int count = 0;
    cout << "Enter at most 8 names with at most 23 characters:\n";
    while (cin.getline(name[count++], 24))
        ;
    --count;
    cout << "The names are:\n";
    for (int i = 0; i < count; i++)
        cout << "\t" << i << ". [" << name[i] << "]" << endl;
}
```

```
Enter at most 8 names with at most 23 characters:
George Washington
John Adams
Thomas Jefferson
^D
The names are:
        0. [George Washington]
        1. [John Adams]
        2. [Thomas Jefferson]
```

Note that all the activity in the `while` loop is done within its control condition:

```
cin.getline(name[count++],20)
```

This call to the `cin.getline()` function reads the next line into `name[count]` and then increments `count`. The function returns nonzero (*i.e.*, "true") if it was successful in reading a character string into `name[count]`. When the end-of-file is signalled (with **<Control-D>** or **<Control-Z>**), the `cin.getline()` function fails, so it returns 0 which stops the `while` loop. The body of this loop is empty, indicated by the line that contains nothing but a semicolon.

A more efficient way to store strings is to declare an array of pointers:

```
char* name[4];
```

Here, each of the 4 components has type `char*` which means that each `name[i]` is a string. This declaration does not initially allocate any storage for string data. Instead, we need to store all the data in a buffer string. Then we can set each `name[i]` equal to the address of the first character of the corresponding name in the buffer. This is done in Example 7.11. This method is more efficient because each component of `name[i]` uses only as many bytes as are needed to store the string (plus storage for one pointer). The trade-off is that the input routine needs a sentinel to signal when the input is finished.

EXAMPLE 7.11 A String Array

This program illustrates the use of the `getline()` function with the sentinel character `'$'`. It is nearly equivalent to that in Example 7.10. It reads a sequence of names, one per line, terminated by the sentinel `'$'`. Then it prints the names which are stored in the array `name`:

```
main()
{
    char buffer[80];
    cin.getline(buffer,80,'$');
    char* name[4];
    name[0] = buffer;
    int count = 0;
    for (char* p = buffer; *p != '\0'; p++)
        if (*p == '\n') {
            *p = '\0';               //  end name[count]
            name[++count] = p+1;   //  begin next name
        }
    cout << "The names are:\n";
    for (int i = 0; i < count; i++)
        cout << "\t" << i << ". [" << name[i] << "]" << endl;
}
```

```
George Washington
John Adams
Thomas Jefferson
$
The names are:
        0. [George Washington]
        1. [John Adams]
        2. [Thomas Jefferson]
```

The entire input is stored in `buffer` as the single string containing "George Washington\nJohn Adams\nThomas Jefferson\n". The `for` loop then scans through buffer using the pointer `p`. Each time `p` finds the `'\n'` character, it terminates the string in `name[count]` by appending the NUL character `'\0'` to it. Then it increments the counter `count` and stores the address `p+1` of the next character in `name[count]`.

The resulting array `name` looks like this:

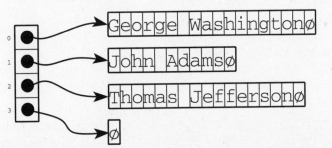

Note that the extra bytes that padded the ends of the names in Example 7.10 are not required here.

If the strings being stored are known at compile time, then the string array described above is quite a bit simpler to handle. Example 7.12 illustrates how to initialize a string array.

EXAMPLE 7.12 Initializing a String Array

This program is nearly equivalent to those in the previous two examples. It initializes the string array
`name` and then prints its contents:

```
main()
{
    char* name[] = { "George Washington",
                     "John Adams",
                     "Thomas Jefferson"
                   };
    cout << "The names are:\n";
    for (int i = 0; i < 3; i++)
        cout << "\t" << i << ". [" << name[i] << "]" << endl;
}
```

```
The names are:
        0. [George Washington]
        1. [John Adams]
        2. [Thomas Jefferson]
```

The storage of the data in the `name` array here is the same as in Example 7.11.

7.8 THE C-STRING HANDLING LIBRARY

The C header file `<string.h>`, also called the *C-String Library*, includes a family of
functions that are very useful for manipulating strings. Example 7.13 illustrates the simplest of
these functions, the *string length function*, which returns the length of the string passed to it.

EXAMPLE 7.13 The String Length Function `strlen()`

This program is a simple test driver for the `strlen()` function. The call `strlen(s)` simply
returns the number of characters in `s` that precede the first occurrence of the NUL character `'\0'`:.

```
#include <string.h>
main()
{
    char s[] = "ABCDEFG";
    cout << "strlen(" << s << ") = " << strlen(s) << endl;
    cout << "strlen(\"\") = " << strlen("") << endl;
    char buffer[80];
    cout << "Enter string: ";  cin >> buffer;
    cout << "strlen(" << buffer << ") = " << strlen(buffer) << endl;
}
```

```
strlen(ABCDEFG) = 7
strlen("") = 0
Enter string: computer
strlen(computer) = 8
```

In some ways, strings behave like fundamental objects (*i.e.*, integers and reals). For example,
they can be output to `cout` in the same way. But strings are structured objects, composed of

smaller pieces (characters). So many of the operations that are provided for fundamental objects, such as the assignment operator (=), the comparison operators (<, >, ==, <=, >=, and !=), and the arithmetic operators (+, *etc.*) are not available for strings. Some of the functions in the C String Library simulate these operations. In Chapter 8 we will learn how to write our own versions of these operations.

The next example illustrates three other string functions. These are used to locate characters and substrings within a given string.

EXAMPLE 7.14 The `strchr()`, `strrchr()`, and `strstr()` Functions

```
#include <string.h>
main()
{
    char s[] = "The Mississippi is a long river.";
    cout << "s = \"" << s << "\"\n";
    char* p = strchr(s, ' ');
    cout << "strchr(s, ' ') points to s[" << p - s << "].\n";
    p = strchr(s, 's');
    cout << "strchr(s, 's') points to s[" << p - s << "].\n";
    p = strrchr(s, 's');
    cout << "strrchr(s, 's') points to s[" << p - s << "].\n";
    p = strstr(s, "is");
    cout << "strstr(s, \"is\") points to s[" << p - s << "].\n";
    p = strstr(s, "isi");
    if (p == NULL) cout << "strstr(s, \"isi\") returns NULL\n";
}
```

Here is the output:

```
s = "The Mississippi is a long river."
strchr(s, ' ') points to s[3].
strchr(s, 's') points to s[6].
strrchr(s, 's') points to s[17].
strstr(s, "is") points to s[5].
strstr(s, "isi") returns NULL
```

The call `strchr(s, ' ')` returns a pointer to the first occurrence of the blank character `' '` within the string `s`. The expression `p - s` computes the index (offset) 3 of this character within the string. (Remember that arrays used zero-based indexing, so the initial character `'T'` has index 0.) Similarly, the character `'s'` first appears at index 6 in `s`.

The call `strrchr(s, ' ')` returns a pointer to the last occurrence of the character `'s'` within the string s; this is s[17].

The call `strstr(s, "is")` returns a pointer to the first occurrence of the substring `"is"` within the string s; this is at s[5]. The call `strstr(s, "isi")` returns the NULL pointer because `"isi"` does not occur anywhere within the string s.

There are two functions that simulate the assignment operator for strings: `strcpy()` and `strncpy()`. The call `strcpy(s1,s2)` copies string s2 into string s1. The call `strncpy(s1,s2,n)` copies the first n characters of string s2 into string s1. Both functions return s1. These are illustrated in the next two examples.

EXAMPLE 7.15 The String Copy Function `strcpy()`

This program traces call `strcpy(s1,s2)`:

```
#include <iostream.h>
#include <string.h>
main()
{
    char s1[] = "ABCDEFG";
    char s2[] = "XYZ";
    cout << "Before strcpy(s1,s2):\n";
    cout << "\ts1 = [" << s1 << "], length = " << strlen(s1) << endl;
    cout << "\ts2 = [" << s2 << "], length = " << strlen(s2) << endl;
    strcpy(s1,s2);
    cout << "After strcpy(s1,s2):\n";
    cout << "\ts1 = [" << s1 << "], length = " << strlen(s1) << endl;
    cout << "\ts2 = [" << s2 << "], length = " << strlen(s2) << endl;
}
```

```
Before strcpy(s1,s2):
        s1 = [ABCDEFG], length = 7
        s2 = [XYZ], length = 3
After strcpy(s1,s2):
        s1 = [XYZ], length = 3
        s2 = [XYZ], length = 3
```

After `s2` is copied into `s1`, they are indistinguishable: both consist of the 3 characters `XYZ`. The effect of `strcpy(s1,s2)` can be visualized like this:

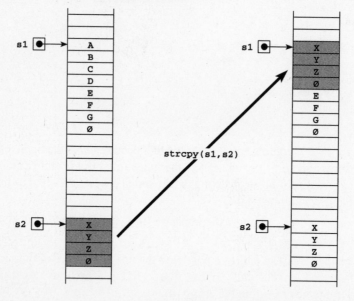

Since `s2` has length 3, `strcpy(s1,s2)` copies 4 bytes (including the NUL character, shown as ⌀), overwriting the first 4 characters of `s1`. This changes the length of `s1` to 3.

Note that `strcpy(s1,s2)` creates a duplicate of string `s2`. The resulting two copies are distinct strings. Changing one of these strings later would have no effect upon the other string.

EXAMPLE 7.16 The Second String Copy Function `strncpy()`

This program traces calls `strncpy(s1,s2,n)`:

```
#include <iostream.h>
#include <string.h>
//  Test-driver for the strncpy() function:
main()
{
    char s1[] = "ABCDEFG";
    char s2[] = "XYZ";
    cout << "Before strncpy(s1,s2,2):\n";
    cout << "\ts1 = [" << s1 << "], length = " << strlen(s1) << endl;
    cout << "\ts2 = [" << s2 << "], length = " << strlen(s2) << endl;
    strncpy(s1,s2,2);
    cout << "After strncpy(s1,s2,2):\n";
    cout << "\ts1 = [" << s1 << "], length = " << strlen(s1) << endl;
    cout << "\ts2 = [" << s2 << "], length = " << strlen(s2) << endl;
}
```

```
Before strncpy(s1,s2,2):
        s1 = [ABCDEFG], length = 7
        s2 = [XYZ], length = 3
After strncpy(s1,s2,2):
        s1 = [XYCDEFG], length = 7
        s2 = [XYZ], length = 3
```

The call `strncpy(s1,s2,2)` replaces the first 2 characters of `s1` with `XY`, leaving the rest of `s1` unchanged. The effect of `strncpy(s1,s2,2)` can be visualized like this:

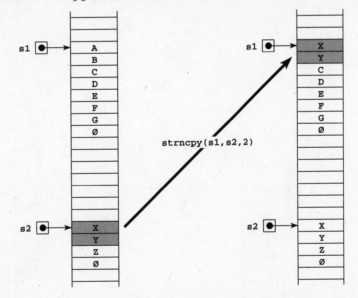

Since `s2` has length 3, `strncpy(s1,s2,2)` copies 2 bytes (excluding the NUL character ∅), over-writing the first 2 characters of `s1`. This has no effect upon the length of `s1` which is 7.

If `n < strlen(s2)`, as it is in the above example, then `strncpy(s1,s2,n)` simply copies the first `n` characters of `s2` into the beginning of `s1`. However, if `n ≥ strlen(s2)`, then strncpy(s1,s2,n) has the same effect as strcpy(s1,s2): it makes s1 a duplicate of s2 with the same length.

The strcat() and strncat() functions work the same as the strcpy() and strncpy() functions except that the characters from the second string are copied onto the end of the first string. The term "cat" comes from the word "catenate" meaning "string together."

EXAMPLE 7.17 The String Concatenation Function strcat()

This program traces call strcat(s1,s2) which appends the string s2 onto the end of string s1:

```
#include <iostream.h>
#include <string.h>
//  Test-driver for the strcat() function:
main()
{
    char s1[] = "ABCDEFG";
    char s2[] = "XYZ";
    cout << "Before strcat(s1,s2):\n";
    cout << "\ts1 = [" << s1 << "], length = " << strlen(s1) << endl;
    cout << "\ts2 = [" << s2 << "], length = " << strlen(s2) << endl;
    strcat(s1,s2);
    cout << "After strcat(s1,s2):\n";
    cout << "\ts1 = [" << s1 << "], length = " << strlen(s1) << endl;
    cout << "\ts2 = [" << s2 << "], length = " << strlen(s2) << endl;
}
```

Here is the output:

```
Before strcat(s1,s2):
        s1 = [ABCDEFG], length = 7
        s2 = [XYZ], length = 3
After strcat(s1,s2):
        s1 = [ABCDEFGXYZ], length = 10
        s2 = [XYZ], length = 3
```

The call strcat(s1,s2) appends XYZ onto the end of s1. It can be visualized like this:

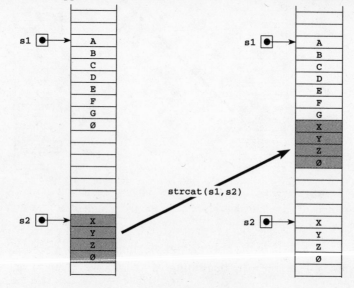

Since `s2` has length 3, `strcat(s1,s2)` copies 4 bytes (including the NUL character, shown as ∅), overwriting the NUL characters of `s1` and its following 3 bytes. The length of `s1` is increased to 10.

If any of the extra bytes following `s1` that are needed to copy `s2` are in use by any other object, then all of `s1` and its appended `s2` will be copied to some other free section of memory.

EXAMPLE 7.18 The Second String Concatenation Function `strncat()`

This program traces calls `strncat(s1,s2,n)`:

```
#include <iostream.h>
#include <string.h>
//  Test-driver for the strncat() function:
main()
{
    char s1[] = "ABCDEFG";
    char s2[] = "XYZ";
    cout << "Before strncat(s1,s2,2):\n";
    cout << "\ts1 = [" << s1 << "], length = " << strlen(s1) << endl;
    cout << "\ts2 = [" << s2 << "], length = " << strlen(s2) << endl;
    strncat(s1,s2,2);
    cout << "After strncat(s1,s2,2):\n";
    cout << "\ts1 = [" << s1 << "], length = " << strlen(s1) << endl;
    cout << "\ts2 = [" << s2 << "], length = " << strlen(s2) << endl;
}
```

The output looks like this:
```
Before strncat(s1,s2,2):
        s1 = [ABCDEFG], length = 7
        s2 = [XYZ], length = 3
After strncat(s1,s2,2):
        s1 = [ABCDEFGXY], length = 9
        s2 = [XYZ], length = 3
```
The call `strncat(s1,s2,2)` appends XY onto the end of `s1`. The effect can be visualized like this:

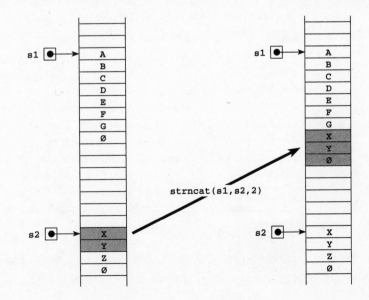

Since `s2` has length 3, `strncat(s1,s2,2)` copies 2 bytes overwriting the NUL character of `s1` and the byte that follows it. Then it puts the NUL character in the next byte to complete the string `s1`. This increases its length to 9. (If either of the extra 2 bytes had been in use by some other object, then the entire 10 characters `ABCDEFGXYØ` would have been written in some other free part of memory.)

The next example illustrates the string *tokenize function*. Its purpose is to identify "tokens" within a given string: *e.g.*, words in a sentence.

EXAMPLE 7.19 The String Tokenize Function `strtok()`

This program shows how `strtok()` is used to extract the individual words from a sentence.

```
#include <iostream.h>
#include <string.h>
// Test-driver for the strtok() function:
main()
{
    char s[] = "Today's date is March 12, 1995.";
    char* p;
    cout << "The string is: [" << s << "]\nIts tokens are:\n";
    p = strtok(s, " ");
    while (p) {
        cout << "\t[" << p << "]\n";
        p = strtok(NULL, " ");
    }
    cout << "Now the string is: [" << s << "]\n";
}
```

```
The string is: [Today's date is March 12, 1995.]
Its tokens are:
        [Today's]
        [date]
        [is]
        [March]
        [12,]
        [1995.]
Now the string is: [Today's]
```

The call `p = strtok(s, " ")` sets the pointer `p` to point to the first token in the string `s` and changes the blank that follows `"Today's"` to the NUL character `'\0'` (denoted by Ø in the following diagram). This has the effect of making both `s` and `p` the string `"Today's"`. Then each successive call `p = strtok(NULL, " ")` advances the pointer `p` to the next non-blank character that follows the new NUL character, changing each blank that it passes into a NUL character, and changing the first blank that follows `*p` into a NUL character. This has the effect of making `p` the next substring that was delimited by blanks and is now delimited by NUL characters. This continues until p reaches the NUL character that terminated the original string `s`. That makes `p` NUL (*i.e.*, 0), which stops the while loop. The combined effect upon the original string `s` of all the calls to `strtok()` is to change every blank into a NUL. This "tokenizes" the string `s`, changing it into a sequence of distinct token strings, only the first of which is identified by `s`.

Note that the `strtok()` function changes the string that it tokenizes. Therefore, if you want to use the original string after you tokenize it, you should duplicate it with `strcpy()`.

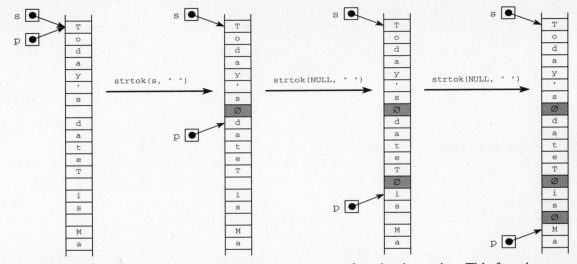

Also note that the second parameter of the `strtok()` function is a string. This function uses all the characters in this string as delimiters in the first string. For example, to identify words in s, you might use `strtok(s, " ,:;.")`.

The `strpbrk()` function also uses a string of characters as a collection of characters. It generalizes the `strchr()` function, looking for the first occurrence in the first string of <u>any</u> of the characters in the second string.

EXAMPLE 7.20 The `strpbrk()` Function

```
#include <iostream.h>
#include <string.h>
main()
{
    char s[] = "The Mississippi is a long river.";
    cout << "s = \"" << s << "\"\n";
    char* p = strpbrk(s, "nopqr");
    cout << "strpbrk(s, \"nopqr\") points to s[" << p - s << "].\n";
    p = strpbrk(s, "NOPQR");
    if (p == NULL) cout << "strpbrk(s, \"NOPQR\") returns NULL.\n";
}
```

```
s = "The Mississippi is a long river."
strpbrk(s, "nopqr") points to s[12].
strpbrk(s, "NOPQR") returns NULL.
```

The call `strpbrk(s, "nopqr")` returns the first occurrence in s of any of the five characters `'n'`, `'o'`, `'p'`, `'q'`, or `'r'`. The first of these found is the `'p'` at s[12].

The call `strpbrk(s, "NOPQR")` returns the NULL pointer because none of these five characters occurs in s.

Table 7.2 summarizes some of the most useful functions declared in `<string.h>`. Note that `size_t` is a special integer type that is defined in the `<string.h>` file.

Table 7.2   `<string.h>` Functions

`memcpy()`	`void* memcpy(void* s1, const void* s2, size_t n);` Replaces the first `n` bytes of `*s1` with the first `n` bytes of `*s2`. Returns `s`.
`strcat()`	`char* strcat(char* s1, const char* s2);` Appends `s2` to `s1`. Returns `s1`.
`strchr()`	`char* strchr(const char* s, int c);` Returns a pointer to the first occurrence of `c` in `s`. Returns `NULL` if `c` is not in `s`.
`strcmp()`	`int strcmp(const char* s1, const char* s2);` Compares `s1` with substring `s2`. Returns a negative integer, zero, or a positive integer, according to whether `s1` is lexicographically less than, equal to, or greater than `s2`.
`strcpy()`	`char* strcpy(char* s1, const char* s2);` Replaces `s1` with `s2`. Returns `s1`.
`strcspn()`	`size_t strcspn(char* s1, const char* s2);` Returns the length of the longest substring of `s1` that begins with `s1[0]` and contains <u>none</u> of the characters found in `s2`.
`strlen()`	`size_t strlen(const char* s);` Returns the length of `s`, which is the number of characters beginning with `s[0]` that precede the first occurrence of the `NUL` character.
`strncat()`	`char* strncat(char* s1, const char* s2, size_t n);` Appends the first `n` characters of `s2` to `s1`. Returns `s1`. If `n ≥ strlen(s2)`, then `strncat(s1,s2,n)` has the same effect as `strcat(s1,s2)`.
`strncmp()`	`int strncmp(const char* s1, const char* s2, size_t n);` Compares `s1` with the substring `s` of the first `n` characters of `s2`. Returns a negative integer, zero, or a positive integer, according to whether `s1` is lexicographically less than, equal to, or greater than `s`. If `n ≥ strlen(s2)`, then `strncmp(s1,s2,n)` and `strcmp(s1,s2)` have the same effect.
`strncpy()`	`char* strncpy(char* s1, const char* s2, size_t n);` Replaces the first `n` characters of `s1` with the first `n` characters of `s2`. Returns `s1`. If `n ≤ strlen(s1)`, then the length of `s1` is not affected. If `n ≥ strlen(s2)`, then `strncpy(s1,s2,n)` and `strcpy(s1,s2)` have the same effect.
`strpbrk()`	`char* strpbrk(const char* s1, const char* s2);` Returns the address of the first occurrence in `s1` of <u>any</u> of the characters in `s2`. Returns `NULL` if none of the characters in `s2` appears in `s1`.
`strrchr()`	`char* strrchr(const char* s, int c);` Returns a pointer to the <u>last</u> occurrence of `c` in `s`. Returns `NULL` if `c` is not in `s`.
`strspn()`	`size_t strspn(char* s1, const char* s2);` Returns the length of the longest substring of `s1` that begins with `s2[0]` and contains <u>only</u> characters found in `s2`.
`strstr()`	`char* strstr(const char* s1, const char* s2);` Returns the address of the first occurrence of `s2` as a substring of `s1`. Returns `NULL` if `ch` is not in `s1`.
`strtok()`	`char* strtok(char* s1, const char* s2);` Tokenizes the string `s1` into tokens delimited by the characters found in string `s2`. After the initial call `strtok(s1, s2)`, each successive call `strtok(NULL, s2)` returns a pointer to next token found in `s1`. These calls change the string `s1`, replacing each delimiter with the `NUL` character `'\0'`.

Review Questions

7.1   Consider the following declarations for `s`:

```
char s[6];
char s[6] = {'H', 'e', 'l', 'l', 'o'};
char s[6] = "Hello";
char s[];
char s[] = new char[6];
char s[] = {'H', 'e', 'l', 'l', 'o'};
char s[] = "Hello";
char s[] = new("Hello");
char* s;
char* s = new char[6];
char* s = {'H', 'e', 'l', 'l', 'o'};
char* s = "Hello";
char* s = new("Hello");
```

a. Which of these is a valid declaration of a C++ character string?

b. Which of these is a valid declaration of a C++ character string of length 5, initialized to the string `"Hello"` and allocated at compile time?

c. Which of these is a valid declaration of a C++ character string of length 5, initialized to the string `"Hello"` and allocated at run time?

d. Which of these is a valid declaration of a C++ character string as a formal parameter for a function?

7.2   What is wrong with using the statement

```
cin >> s;
```

to read the input `"Hello, World!"` into a string `s`?

7.3   What does the following code print:

```
char s[] = "123 W. 42nd St., NY, NY 10020-1095";
int count = 0;
for (char* p = s; *p; p++)
    if (isupper(*p)) ++count;
cout << count << endl;
```

7.4   What does the following code print:

```
char s[] = "123 W. 42nd St., NY, NY 10020-1095";
for (char* p = s; *p; p++)
    if (isupper(*p)) *p = tolower(*p);
cout << s << endl;
```

7.5   What does the following code print:

```
char s[] = "123 W. 42nd St., NY, NY 10020-1095";
for (char* p = s; *p; p++)
    if (isupper(*p)) (*p)++;
cout << s << endl;
```

7.6   What does the following code print:

```
char s[] = "123 W. 42nd St., NY, NY 10020-1095";
int count = 0;
for (char* p = s; *p; p++)
    if (ispunct(*p)) ++count;
cout << count << endl;
```

7.7   What does the following code print:

```
char s[] = "123 W. 42nd St., NY, NY 10020-1095";
for (char* p = s; *p; p++)
    if (ispunct(*p)) *(p-1) = tolower(*p);
cout << s << endl;
```

7.8   What is the difference between the following two statements, if `s1` and `s2` have type `char*`:

```
s1 = s2;
strcpy(s1,s2);
```

7.9   If `first` contains the string `"Rutherford"` and `last` contains the string `"Hayes"`, then what will be the effect of each of the following calls:

a. `int n = strlen(first);`
b. `char* s1 = strchr(first, 'r');`
c. `char* s1 = strrchr(first, 'r');`
d. `char* s1 = strpbrk(first, "rstuv");`
e. `strcpy(first, last);`
f. `strncpy(first, last, 3);`
g. `strcat(first, last);`
h. `strncat(first, last, 3);`

7.10   What do each of the following assign to `n`:

a. `int n = strspn("abecedarian","abcde");`
b. `int n = strspn("beefeater","abcdef");`
c. `int n = strspn("baccalaureate","abc");`
d. `int n = strcspn("baccalaureate","rstuv");`

7.11   What does the following code print:

```
char* s1 = "ABCDE";
char* s2 = "ABC";
if (strcmp(s1,s2) < 0) cout << s1 << " < " << s2 << endl;
else cout << s1 << " >= " << s2 << endl;
```

7.12   What does the following code print:

```
char* s1 = "ABCDE";
char* s2 = "ABCE";
if (strcmp(s1,s2) < 0) cout << s1 << " < " << s2 << endl;
else cout << s1 << " >= " << s2 << endl;
```

7.13 What does the following code print:

```
char* s1 = "ABCDE";
char* s2 = "";
if (strcmp(s1,s2) < 0) cout << s1 << " < " << s2 << endl;
else cout << s1 << " >= " << s2 << endl;
```

7.14 What does the following code print:

```
char* s1 = " ";
char* s2 = "";
if (strcmp(s1,s2) == 0) cout << s1 << " == " << s2 << endl;
else cout << s1 << " != " << s2 << endl;
```

Solved Problems

7.15 Explain why the following alternative to Example 7.12 does not work:

```
main()
{
    char name[10][20], buffer[20];
    int count = 0;
    while (cin.getline(buffer,20))
        name[count] = buffer;
    --count;
    cout << "The names are:\n";
    for (int i = 0; i < count; i++)
        cout << "\t" << i << ". [" << name[i] << "]" << endl;
}
```

This does not work because the assignment

```
        name[count] = buffer;
```

assigns the same pointer to each of the strings `name[0]`, `name[1]`, *etc*. Arrays cannot be assigned this way. To copy one array into another, use `strcpy()`, or `strncpy()`.

Solved Programming Problems

7.16 Write the `strcpy()` function.

This copies the string `s2` into the string `s1`:

```
char* strcpy(char* s1, const char* s2)
{
    for (char* p = s1; *s2; )
        *p++ = *s2++;
    *p = '\0';
    return s1;
}
```

The pointer p is initialized at the beginning of s1. On each iteration of the for loop, the character
*s2 is copied into the character *p, and then both s2 and p are incremented. The loop continues
until *s2 is 0 (*i.e.*, the null character '\0'). Then the null character is appended to the string s1 by
assigning it to *p. (The pointer p was left pointing to the byte after the last byte copied when the loop
terminated.)

Note that this function does not allocate any new storage. So its first argument s1 should already
have been defined to be a character string with the same length as s2.

7.17 Write the strncat() function.

This function appends up to n characters from s2 onto the end of s1. It is the same as the
strcat() function except that its third argument n limits the number of characters copied:

```
char* strncat(char* s1, const char* s2, size_t n)
{
    for (char* end = s1; *end; end++) ;        // find end of s1
    for (char* p = s2; *p && p - s2 < n; )
        *end++ = *p++;
    *end = '\0';
    return s1;
}
```

The first for loop finds the end of string s1. That is where the characters from string s2 are to be
appended. The second for loop copies characters from s2 to the locations that follow s1. Notice how
the extra condition q - s2 < n limits the number of characters copied to n: the expression q -
s2 equals the number of characters copied because it is the difference between q (which points to the
next character to be copied) and s2 (which points to the beginning of the string).

Note that this function does not allocate any new storage. It requires that string s1 have at least *k*
more bytes allocated, where *k* is the smaller of n and the length of string s2.

7.18 Write and test a function that returns the *plural* form of the singular English word passed to it.

This requires testing the last letter and the second from last letter of the word to be pluralized. We use
pointers p and q to access these letters.

```
void pluralize(char* s)
{
    int len = strlen(s);
    char* p = s + len - 1;    // last letter
    char* q = s + len - 2;    // last 2 letters
    if (*p == 'h' && (*q == 'c' || *q == 's')) strcat(p, "es");
    else if (*p == 's') strcat(p, "es");
    else if (*p == 'y')
        if (isvowel(*q)) strcat(p, "s");
        else strcpy(p, "ies");
    else if (*p == 'z')
        if (isvowel(*q)) strcat(p, "zes");
        else strcat(p, "es");
    else strcat(p, "s");
}
```

Two of the tests depend upon whether the second from last letter is a vowel, so we define a little boolean function `isvowel()` for testing that condition:

```
int isvowel(char c)
{
    return (c == 'a' || c == 'e' || c == 'i' || c == 'o'
                || c == 'u');
}
```

The test driver repeatedly reads a word, prints it, pluralizes it, and prints it again. The loop terminates when the user enters a single blank for a word:

```
#include <iostream.h>
#include <string.h>

void pluralize(char*);

main()
{
    char word[80];
    for (;;) {
        cin.getline(word, 80);
        if (*word == ' ') break;
        cout << "\tThe singular is [" << word << "].\n";
        pluralize(word);
        cout << "\t  The plural is [" << word << "].\n";
    }
}
```

```
wish
    The singular is [wish].
      The plural is [wishes].
hookah
    The singular is [hookah].
      The plural is [hookahs].
bus
    The singular is [bus].
      The plural is [buses].
toy
    The singular is [toy].
      The plural is [toys].
navy
    The singular is [navy].
      The plural is [navies].
quiz
    The singular is [quiz].
      The plural is [quizzes].
quartz
    The singular is [quartz].
      The plural is [quartzes].
computer
    The singular is [computer].
      The plural is [computers].
```

7.19   Write a program that reads a sequence of names, one per line, and then sorts and prints them.

We assume that names have no more than 25 characters and that there will be no more than 25 names. We'll read all the input in at once and store it all in a single `buffer`. Since each name will be terminated with a NUL character, the `buffer` needs to be large enough to hold 25*(20 + 1) + 1 characters (25 21-character strings plus one last NUL character).

The program is modularized into five function calls. The call `input(buffer)` reads everything into the `buffer`. The call `tokenize(name, numNames, buffer)` "tokenizes" the `buffer`, storing pointers to its names in the `name` array and returning the number of names in `numNames`. The call `print(name, numNames)` prints all the names that are stored in `buffer`. The call `sort(name, numNames)` does an *indirect sort* on the names stored in `buffer` by rearranging the pointers stored in the `name` array.

```
#include <iostream.h>
#include <string.h>

const int nameLength = 20;
const int maxNumNames = 25;
const int bufferLength = maxNumNames*(nameLength + 1);
void input(char* buffer);
void tokenize(char** name, int& numNames, char* buffer);
void print(char** name, int numNames);
void sort(char** name, int numNames);

main()
{
    char* name[maxNumNames];
    char buffer[bufferLength+1];
    int numNames;
    input(buffer);
    tokenize(name, numNames, buffer);
    print(name, numNames);
    sort(name, numNames);
    print(name, numNames);
}
```

The entire input is done by the single call `cin.getline(buffer, bufferLength, '$')`. This reads characters until the "$" character is read, storing all the characters in `buffer`.

```
// Reads up to 25 strings into buffer:
void input(char* buffer)
{
    cout << "Enter up to " << maxNumNames << " names, one per line."
         << " Terminate with \'$\'.\nNames are limited to "
         << nameLength << " characters.\n";
    cin.getline(buffer, bufferLength, '$');
}
```

The `tokenize()` function uses the `strtok()` function to scan through the `buffer`, "tokenizing" each substring that ends with the newline character `'\n'` and storing its address in the `name` array. The `for` loop continues until `p` points to the sentinel `'$'`. Notice that the function's `name` parameter is declared as a `char**` because it is an array of pointers to `char`s. Also note that the counter `n` is declared as an `int&` (passed by reference) so that its new value is returned to `main()`.

```
// Copies address of each string in buffer into name array:
void tokenize(char** name, int& n, char* buffer)
{
    char* p = strtok(buffer, "\n");            // p points to each token
    for (n = 0; p && *p != '$'; n++) {
        name[n] = p;
        p = strtok(NULL, "\n");
    }
}
```

The `print()` and `sort()` functions are similar to those seen before, except that both operate here indirectly. Both functions operate on the `name` array, using to access the names that are stored in `buffer`. Notice that the `sort()` function changes only the `name` array; the `buffer` is left unchanged.

```
// Prints the n names stored in buffer:
void print(char** name, int n)
{
    cout << "The names are:\n";
    for (int i = 0; i < n; i++)
        cout << "\t" << i+1 << ". " << name[i] << endl;
}
```

```
// Sorts the n names stored in buffer:
void sort(char** name, int n)
{
    char* temp;
    for (int i = 1; i < n; i++)                              // Bubble Sort
        for (int j = 0; j < n-i; j++)
            if (strcmp(name[j], name[j+1]) > 0) {
                temp = name[j];
                name[j] = name[j+1];
                name[j+1] = temp;
            }
}
```

```
Enter up to 25 names, one per line.  Terminate with '$'.
Names are limited to 20 characters.
Washington, George
Adams, John
Jefferson, Thomas
Madison, James
Monroe, James
Adams, John Quincy
Jackson, Andrew
$The names are:
        1. Washington, George
        2. Adams, John
        3. Jefferson, Thomas
        4. Madison, James
        5. Monroe, James
        6. Adams, John Quincy
        7. Jackson, Andrew
```

```
The names are:
        1. Adams, John
        2. Adams, John Quincy
        3. Jackson, Andrew
        4. Jefferson, Thomas
        5. Madison, James
        6. Monroe, James
        7. Washington, George
```

On this sample run the user entered 7 names and then the sentinel "$". The names were then printed, sorted, and printed again.

7.20   Write and test a function to reverse a string in place, without any duplication of characters.

The function first locates the end of the string. Then it swaps the first character with the last character, the second character with the second from last character, *etc.*:

```
void reverse(char* s)
{
    for (char* end = s; *end; end++);     // find end of s
    char temp;
    while (s < end - 1) {
        temp = *--end;
        *end = *s;
        *s++ = temp;
    }
}
```

The test driver uses the `getline()` function to read the string. Then it prints it, reverses it, and prints it again:

```
void reverse(char*);

main()
{
    char string[80];
    cin.getline(string, 80);
    cout << "The string is [" << string << "].\n";
    reverse(string);
    cout << "The string is [" << string << "].\n";
}
```

```
Today is Wednesday.
The string is [Today is Wednesday.].
The string is [.yadsendeW si yadoT].
```

Supplementary Programming Problems

7.21   Write and run the variation of the program in Example 7.3 that uses `while (cin >> word)` instead of `do..while (*word)`.

7.22   Write the `strchr()` function.

7.23 Write a function that returns the <u>number</u> of occurrences of a given character within a given string.

7.24 Write and test the `strrlen()` function.

7.25 Write and test the `strrchr()` function.

7.26 Write and test the `strstr()` function.

7.27 Write and test the `strncpy()` function.

7.28 Write and test the `strcat()` function.

7.29 Write and test the `strcmp()` function.

7.30 Write and test the `strncmp()` function.

7.31 Write and test the `strchr()` function.

7.32 Write and test the `strrchr()` function.

7.33 Write and test the `strstr()` function.

7.34 Write and test the `strspn()` function.

7.35 Write and test the `strcspn()` function.

7.36 Write and test the `strpbrk()` function.

7.37 Write a function that returns the <u>number</u> of words that contain a given character within a given string. (See Example 7.19.)

7.38 Write a (nonrecursive) function that determines whether a given string is a palindrome. (See Problem 5.29.)

7.39 First, try to predict what the following program will do to the string s. (See Example 7.19.) Then run the program to check your prediction.

```
#include <iostream.h>
#include <string.h>
//  Test-driver for the strtok() function:
main()
{
    char s[] = "###ABCD#EFG##HIJK#L#MN#####O#P#####";
    char* p;
    cout << "The string is: [" << s << "]\nIts tokens are:\n";
    p = strtok(s, "#");
    while (p) {
        cout << "\t[" << p << "]\n";
        p = strtok(NULL, "#");
    }
    cout << "Now the string is: [" << s << "]\n";
}
```

7.40 Write a program that reads one line of text and then prints it with all its letters capitalized.

7.41   Write a program that reads one line of text and then prints it with all its blanks removed.

7.42   Write a program that reads one line of text and then prints the number of vowels that were read.

7.43   Write a program that reads one line of text and then prints the number of words that were read.

7.44   Write a program that reads one line of text and then prints the number of four-letter words that were read.

7.45   Write a program that reads one line of text and then prints the same words in reverse order. For example, the input

```
today is Tuesday
```

would produce the output

```
Tuesday is today
```

7.46   Write a program that reads one line of text and then prints it with each word reversed. For example, the input

```
Today is Tuesday
```

would produce the output

```
yadoT si yadseuT
```

7.47   Write a program that reads one line of text and then prints it with the following changes: to every occurrence of "he" is added "or she"; to every occurrence of "him" is added "or her"; to every occurrence of "his" is added "or hers".

7.48   Write a program that reads up to 50 lines of text, each line containing up to 80 characters, and then prints all the lines in reverse order. For example, the input

```
All in the golden afternoon
Full leisurely we glide;
For both our oars, with little skill,
By little arms are plied.
```

would produce the output

```
By little arms are plied.
For both our oars, with little skill,
Full leisurely we glide;
All in the golden afternoon
```

7.49   Write a program that reads up to 50 lines of text, each line containing up to 80 characters, and then prints all the words on each line in reverse order. For example, the input

```
All in the golden afternoon
Full leisurely we glide;
For both our oars, with little skill,
By little arms are plied.
```

would produce the output

```
afternoon golden the in All
skill, little with oars, our both For
glide; we leisurely Full
plied. are arms little By
```

7.50 Write a program that reads up to 50 lines of text, each line containing up to 80 characters, and then prints all the words on each line in alphabetical order. For example, the input

```
All in the golden afternoon
Full leisurely we glide;
For both our oars, with little skill,
By little arms are plied.
```

would produce the output

```
afternoon All golden in the
Full glide; leisurely we
both For little oars, our skill, with
are arms By little plied.
```

7.51 Write a program that reads up to 50 lines of text, each line containing up to 80 characters, and then reformats text so that no line has more than 40 characters. For example, the input

```
"The first thing I've got to do," said Alice to herself, as she wan-
dered about in the wood, "is to grow to my right size again; and the
second thing is to find my way into that lovely garden.
```

would produce the output

```
"The first thing I've got to do," said
Alice to herself, as she wandered about
in the wood, "is to grow to my right size
again; and the second thing is to find my
way into that lovely garden.
```

7.52 Write a program that encodes and then decodes a line of text. The program should first input the *shift key* k to the encoding; this will be an integer in the range 1 to 25. Then the program will read a line of text, print it, encode it, print the resulting *cyphertext*, decode it, and then print the resulting *plaintext* to show that it is the same as the original text. The encoding and decoding should be done by separate functions. A letter is encoded simply by adding k to it, and it is decoded by subtracting k from it. Both operations must "wrap around" the end of the alphabet, so for example `'W'` would be encoded to `'B'` and `'d'` would be decoded to `'y'` if k were 6.

7.53 Write a program that plays the game of Hangman.

7.54 Write a function that prints a random sentence. Use the following arrays:

```
char* article[5] = {"a", "some", "that", "this", "the"}
char* noun[5] = {"boy", "dog", "girl", "man", "woman"};
char* verb[5] = {"barked at", "bit", "kissed", "spoke to"};
```

7.55 Write and test the following function that tallies the frequencies of each of the 26 letters (regardless of case) in the given string:

```
void tally(int frequency[], const char* s)
```

So after returning, `frequency[0]` will be the number of occurrences of either `'A'` or `'a'` in s, `frequency[1]` will be the number of occurrences of either `'B'` or `'b'` in s, *etc.*

7.56   Write and test the following function that deletes all duplicate characters in the given string:
```
void delDups(char* s)
```
For example, if `s` is the string `"ABRACADABRA"`, then after the call `delDups(s)` the string would be reduced to `"ABRCD"`.

7.57   Write and test the following function that deletes all occurrences in `s1` of characters in `s2`:
```
void del(char* s1, const char* s2)
```
For example, if `s1` is the string `"ABRACADABRA"`, and `s1` is the string `"AB"`, and then after the call `del(s1, s2)` the string `s1` would be reduced to `"RCDR"`.

Answers to Review Questions

7.1   Among the 13 declarations:
 a.   The following are valid declarations for a C++ character string:
```
char s[6];
char s[6] = {'H', 'e', 'l', 'l', 'o'};
char s[6] = "Hello";
char s[] = {'H', 'e', 'l', 'l', 'o'};
char s[] = "Hello";
char* s;
char* s = new char[6];
char* s = "Hello";
```
 b.   The following are valid declarations for a C++ character string of length 5, initialized to the string `"Hello"` and allocated at compile time:
```
char s[6] = {'H', 'e', 'l', 'l', 'o'};
char s[6] = "Hello";
char s[] = {'H', 'e', 'l', 'l', 'o'};
char s[] = "Hello";
char* s = "Hello";
```
 c.   It is not possible to initialize a string like this at run time.
 d.   The following are valid declarations for a C++ character string as a formal parameter for a function:
```
char s[];
char* s;
```

7.2   This will read only as far as the first whitespace. For the given input, it would assign `"Hello,"` to s.

7.3   This counts the number of uppercase letters in the string `s`, so the output is `6`.

7.4   This changes all uppercase letters to lowercase in the string `s`:
```
123 w. 42nd st., ny, ny 10020-1095
```
Note that to change the case of a character `*p`, it must be assigned the return value of the function:
```
*p = tolower(*p);
```

7.5   This increments all uppercase letters, changing the `W` to an `X`, the `S` to a `T`, *etc.*:
```
123 X. 42nd Tt., OZ, OZ 10020-1095
```

7.6   This counts the number of punctuation characters in the string `s`, so the output is `5`.

7.7 This changes each character that is followed by a punctuation character to that following character:

```
123 .. 42nd S.,, N,, NY 1002--1095
```

7.8 The assignment `s1 = s2` simply makes `s1` a synonym for `s2`; *i.e.*, they both point to the same character. The call `strcpy(s1,s2)` actually copies the characters of `s2` into the string `s1`, thereby duplicating the string.

7.9 *a.* This assigns the integer 10 to `n`.
    b. This assigns the substring `"rford"` to s1.
    c. This assigns the substring `"rd"` to s1.
    d. This assigns the substring `"utherford"` to s1.
    e. This copies `last` to `first`, so that `first` will also be the string `"Hayes"`.
    f. This copies the substring `"Hay"` into the first part of `first`, making it `"Hayherford"`.
    g. This appends `last` onto the end of `first`, making it `"RutherfordHayes"`.
    h. This appends the substring `"Hay"` onto the end of `first`, making it `"RutherfordHay"`.

7.10 *a.* 7.
     b. 6.
     c. 5.
     d. 7.

7.11 It prints: `ABCDE >= ABC`

7.12 It prints: `ABCDE < ABCE`

7.13 It prints: `ABCDE >=`

7.14 It prints: `! =`

Chapter 8

Classes

8.1 INTRODUCTION

A *class* is like an array: it is a derived type whose elements have other types. But unlike an array, the elements of a class may have different types. Furthermore, some elements of a class may be functions, including operators.

Although any region of storage may generally be regarded as an "object", the word is usually used to describe variables whose type is a class. Thus "object-oriented programming" involves programs that use classes. We think of an object as a self-contained entity that stores its own data and owns its own functions. The functionality of an object gives it life in the sense that it "knows" how to do things on its own.

There is much more to object-oriented programming than simply including classes in your programs. However, that is the first step. An adequate treatment of the discipline lies far beyond an introductory outline such as this.

8.2 CLASS DECLARATIONS

Here is a is declaration for a class whose objects represent rational numbers (*i.e.*, fractions):

```
class Rational {
public:
    void assign(int, int);
    double convert();
    void invert();
    void print();
private:
    int num, den;
};
```

The declaration begins with the keyword `class` followed by the name of the class and ends with the required semicolon. The name of this class is `Rational`.

The functions `assign()`, `convert()`, `invert()`, and `print()` are called *member functions* because they are members of the class. Similarly, the variables `num` and `den` are called *member data*. Member functions are also called *methods* and *services*.

In this class, all the member functions are designated as `public`, and all the member data are designated as `private`. The difference is that `public` members are accessible from outside the class, while `private` members are accessible only from within the class. Preventing access from outside the class is called "information hiding." It allows the programmer to compartmentalize the software which makes it easier to understand, to debug, and to maintain.

The following example shows how this class could be implemented and used.

EXAMPLE 8.1 Implementing the Rational Class

```
class Rational {
public:
    void assign(int, int);
    double convert();
    void invert();
    void print();
private:
    int num, den;
};

main()
{
    Rational x;
    x.assign(22,7);
    cout << "x = ";  x.print();
    cout << " = " << x.convert() << endl;
    x.invert();
    cout << "1/x = ";  x.print();  cout << endl;
}

void Rational::assign(int numerator, int denominator)
{
    num = numerator;
    den = denominator;
}

double Rational::convert()
{
    return double(num)/den;
}
void Rational::invert()
{
    int temp = num;
    num = den;
    den = temp;
}

void Rational::print()
{
    cout << num << '/' << den;
}
```
```
x = 22/7 = 3.14286
1/x = 7/22
```

Here x is declared to be an object of the Rational class. Consequently, it has its own internal data members num and den, and it has the ability to call the four class member functions assign(), convert(), invert(), and print(). Note that a member function like invert() is called by prefixing its name with the name of its owner: x.invert(). Indeed, a member function can only be called this way. We say that the object x "owns" the call.

An object like x is declared just like an ordinary variable. Its type is Rational. We can think of this type as a "user-defined type." C++ allows us to extend the definition of the programming language by adding the new Rational type to the collection of predefined numeric types int, float, *etc*. We can envision the object x like this:

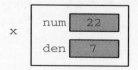

Notice the use of the specifier Rational: as a prefix to each function name. This is necessary for each member function definition that is given outside of its class definition. The *scope resolution operator* :: is used to tie the function definition to the Rational class. Without this specifier, the compiler would not know that the function being defined is a member function of the Rational class. This can be avoided by including the function definitions within declaration, as shown below in Example 8.2.

When an object like the Rational object x in Example 8.1 is declared, we say that the class has been *instantiated*, and we call the object an *instance* of the class. And just as we may have many variables of the same type, we may also have may instances of the same class:

```
Rational x, y, z;
```

EXAMPLE 8.2   A Self-Contained Implementation of the Rational Class

Here's the same Rational class with the definitions of its member functions included within the class declaration:

```
class Rational {
public:
    void assign(int n, int d) { num = n; den = d; }
    double convert() { return double(num)/den; }
    void invert() { int temp = num; num = den; den = temp; }
    void print() { cout << num << '/' << den; }
private:
    int num, den;
};
```

In most cases, the preferred style is to define the member functions outside of the class declaration, using the scope resolution operator as shown in Example 8.1. That format physically separates the function declarations from their definitions, consistent with the general principle of information hiding. In fact, the definitions are often put in a separate file and compiled separately. The point is that application programs that use the class need only know <u>what</u> the objects can do; they do not need to know <u>how</u> the objects do it. The function declarations tell what they do; the function definitions tell how they do it. This of course is how the predefined types (int, double, *etc*.) work: we know what the result should be when we divide one float by another, but we don't really know how the division is done (*i.e.*, what algorithm is implemented). More importantly, we don't want to know. Having to think about those details would distract us from the task at hand. This point of view is often called *information hiding* and is an important principle in object-oriented programming.

When the member function definitions are separated from the declarations, as in Example 8.1, the declaration section is called the *class interface*, and the section containing the member function definitions is called the *implementation*. The interface is the part of the class that the programmer needs to see in order to use the class. The implementation would normally be concealed in a separate file, thereby "hiding" that information that the user (*i.e.*, the programmer) does not need to know about. These class implementations are typically done by implementors who work independently of the programmers who will use the classes that they have implemented.

8.3 CONSTRUCTORS

The `Rational` class defined in Example 8.1 uses the `assign()` function to initialize its objects. It would be more natural to have this initialization occur when the objects are declared. That's how ordinary (predefined) types work:

```
int n = 22;
char* s = "Hello";
```

C++ allows this simpler style of initialization to be done for class objects using constructor functions.

A *constructor* is a member function that is called automatically when an object is declared. A constructor function must have the same name as the class itself, and it is declared without return type. The following example illustrates how we can replace the `assign()` function with a constructor.

EXAMPLE 8.3   A Constructor Function for the `Rational` Class

```
class Rational {
public:
    Rational(int n, int d) { num = n; den = d; }
    void print() { cout << num << '/' << den; }
private:
    int num, den;
};

main()
{
    Rational x(-1,3), y(22,7);
    cout << "x = ";
    x.print();
    cout << " and y = ";
    y.print();
}
```

```
x = -1/3 and y = 22/7
```

The constructor function has the same effect as the `assign()` function had in Example 8.1: it initializes the object by assigning the specified values to its member data. When the declaration of x executes, the constructor is called automatically and the integers -1 and 3 are passed to its parameters n and d. The function then assigns these values to x's num and den data members. So the declarations

```
    Rational x(-1,3), y(22,7);
```

are equivalent to the three lines

```
    Rational x, y;
    x.assign(-1,3);
    y.assign(22,7);
```

A class's constructor "constructs" the class objects by allocating and initializing storage for the objects and by performing any other tasks that are programmed into the function. It literally creates a live object from a pile of unused bits.

We can visualize the relationships between the Rational class itself and its instantiated objects like this:

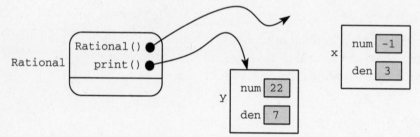

The class itself is represented by a rounded box containing its member functions. Each function maintains a pointer, named "this", which points to the object that is calling it. The snapshot here represents the status during the execution of the last line of the program, when the object y is calling the print() function: y.print(). At that moment, the "this" pointer for the constructor points to no object because it is not being called.

A class may have several constructors. Like any other overloaded function, these are distinguished by their distinct parameter lists.

EXAMPLE 8.4   Adding More Constructors to the Rational Class

```
    class Rational {
    public:
        Rational() { num = 0; den = 1; }
        Rational(int n) { num = n; den = 1; }
        Rational(int n, int d) { num = n; den = d; }
        void print() { cout << num << '/' << den; }
    private:
        int num, den;
    };

    main()
    {
        Rational x, y(4), z(22,7);
        cout << "x = ";
        x.print();
        cout << "\ny = ";
        y.print();
        cout << "\nz = ";
        z.print();
    }
```

The output looks like this:

```
x = 0/1
y = 4/1
z = 22/7
```

This version of the `Rational` class has three constructors. The first has no parameters and initializes the declared object with the default values 0 and 1. The second constructor has one integer parameter and initializes the object to be the fractional equivalent to that integer. The third constructor is the same as in Example 8.2.

Among the various constructors that a class may have, the simplest is the one with no parameters. It is called the *default constructor*. If this constructor is not explicitly declared in the class definition, then the system will automatically create it for the class. That is what happens in Example 8.1.

8.4 CONSTRUCTOR INITIALIZATION LISTS

Most constructors do nothing more than initialize the object's member data. Consequently, C++ provides a special syntactical device for constructors that simplifies this code. The device is an *initialization list*.

Here is the third constructor in Example 8.2, rewritten using an initialization list:

```
Rational(int n, int d) : num(n), den(d) { }
```

The assignment statements in the function's body that assigned `n` to `num` and `d` to `den` are removed. Their action is handled by the initialization list shown in boldface. Note that the list begins with a colon and precedes the function body which is now empty.

Here is the `Rational` class with its three constructors rewritten using initializer lists.

EXAMPLE 8.5   Using Initializer Lists in the `Rational` Class

```
class Rational {
public:
    Rational() : num(0), den(1) { }
    Rational(int n) : num(n), den(1) { }
    Rational(int n, int d) : num(n), den(d) { }
private:
    int num, den;
};
```

Of course, these three separate constructors are not necessary. They can be combined into a single constructor, using default parameter values:

EXAMPLE 8.6   **Using Default Parameter Values in the `Rational` Class Constructor**

```
class Rational {
public:
    Rational(int n=0, int d=1) : num(n), den(d) { }
private:
    int num, den;
};


main()
{
    Rational x, y(4), z(22,7);
}
```

Here, `x` will represent 0/1, `y` will represent 4/1, and `z` will represent 22/7.

Recall that the default values are used when actual parameters are not passed. So in the declaration of the `Rational` object `x` where no values are passed, the formal parameter `n` is given the default value 0 which is then assigned to `x.num`, and the formal parameter `d` is given the default value 1 which is then assigned to `x.den`. In the declaration of the object `y` where only the value 4 is passed, the formal parameter `n` is given that value 4 which is then assigned to `y.num`, and the formal parameter `d` is given the default value 1 which is then assigned to `y.den`. No default values are used in the declaration of `z`.

8.5 ACCESS FUNCTIONS

Although a class's member data are usually declared to be `private` to limit access to them, it is also common to include `public` member functions that provide read-only access to the data. Such functions are called *access functions*.

EXAMPLE 8.7   **Access Functions in the `Rational` Class**

```
class Rational {
public:
    Rational(int n=0, int d=1) : num(n), den(d) { }
    int numerator() const { return num; }
    int denominator() const { return den; }
private:
    int num, den;
};


main()
{
    Rational x(22,7);
    cout << x.numerator() << '/' << x.denominator() << endl;
}
```

```
22/7
```

The functions `numerator()` and `denominator()` return the values of the `private` member data.

Note the use of the `const` keyword in the declarations of the two access functions. This allows the functions to be applied to constant objects. (See Section 8.9.)

8.6 PRIVATE MEMBER FUNCTIONS

Class member data are usually declared to be `private` and member functions are usually declared to be `public`. But this dichotomy is not required. In some cases, it is useful to declare one or more member functions to be `private`. As such, these functions can only be used within the class itself; *i.e.*, they are local *utility functions*.

EXAMPLE 8.8   Using `private` Member Functions `gcd()` and `reduce()`

```
class Rational {
public:
    Rational(int n=0, int d=1) : num(n), den(d) { reduce(); }
    void print() { cout << num << '/' << den << endl; }
private:
    int num, den;
    int gcd(int j, int k) { if (k==0) return j; return gcd(k,j%k); }
    void reduce() { int g = gcd(num, den); num /= g; den /= g; }
};

main()
{
    Rational x(100,360);
    x.print();
}
```

5/18

This version includes two `private` functions. The `gcd()` function returns the greatest common divisor of the two integers passed to it. The `reduce()` function uses the `gcd()` to reduce the fraction num/den to lowest terms. Thus the fraction 100/360 is stored as the object 5/18.

Instead of having a separate `reduce()` function, we could have done the actual reduction within the constructor. But there are two good reasons for doing it this way. Combining the construction with the reduction would violate the software principle that separate tasks should be handled by separate functions. Moreover, the `reduce()` function will be needed later to reduce the results of arithmetic operations performed on `Rational` objects.

Note that the keywords `public` and `private` are called *access specifiers*; they specify whether the members are accessible outside the class definition. The keyword `protected` is the third access specifier. It will be described in Chapter 11.

8.7 THE COPY CONSTRUCTOR

Every class has at least two constructors. These are identified by their unique declarations:

```
X();            // default constructor
X(const X&);    // copy constructor
```

where X is the class identifier. For example, these two special constructors for a `Widget` class would be declared:

```
Widget();                    // default constructor
Widget(const Widget&);  // copy constructor
```

The first of these two special constructors is called the *default constructor*; it is called automatically whenever an object is declared in the simplest form, like this:

```
Widget x;
```

The second of these two special constructors is called the *copy constructor*; it is called automatically whenever an object is copied (*i.e.*, duplicated), like this:

```
Widget y(x);
```

If either of these two constructors is not defined explicitly, then it is automatically defined implicitly by the system.

Note that the copy constructor takes one parameter: the object that it is going to copy. That object is passed by constant reference because it should not be changed.

When the copy constructor is called, it copies the complete state of an existing object into a new object of the same class. If the class definition does not explicitly include a copy constructor (as all the previous examples have not), then the system automatically creates one by default. The ability to write your own copy constructor gives you more control over your software.

EXAMPLE 8.9   Adding a Copy Constructor to the `Rational` Class

```
class Rational {
public:
    Rational(int n=0, int d=1) : num(n), den(d) { reduce(); }
    Rational(const Rational& r) : num(r.num), den(r.den) { }
    void print() { cout << num << '/' << den; }
private:
    int num, den;
    int gcd(int m, int n) { if (n==0) return m; return gcd(n,m%n); }
    void reduce() { int g = gcd(num, den); num /= g; den /= g; }
};

main()
{
    Rational x(100,360);
    Rational y(x);
    cout << "x = ";  x.print();  cout << ", y = ";  y.print();
}
```

```
x = 5/18, y = 5/18
```

The copy constructor copies the `num` and `den` fields of the parameter `r` into the object being constructed. When `y` is declared, it calls the copy constructor which copies `x` into `y`.

Note the required syntax for the copy constructor: it must have one parameter, which has the same class as that being declared, and it must be passed by constant reference: `const X&`.

The copy constructor is called automatically whenever

- an object is copied by means of a declaration initialization;

- an object is passed by value to a function;

- an object is returned by value from a function.

EXAMPLE 8.10 Tracing Calls to the Copy Constructor

```
class Rational {
public:
    Rational(int n, int d) : num(n), den(d) { }
    Rational(const Rational& r) : num(r.num), den(r.den)
        { cout << "COPY CONSTRUCTOR CALLED\n"; }
private:
    int num, den;
};

Rational f(Rational r) // calls the copy constructor, copying ? to r
{
    Rational s = r;     // calls the copy constructor, copying r to s
    return s;           // calls the copy constructor, copying s to ?
}

main()
{
    Rational x(22,7);
    Rational y(x);      // calls the copy constructor, copying x to y
    f(y);
}
```

```
COPY CONSTRUCTOR CALLED
COPY CONSTRUCTOR CALLED
COPY CONSTRUCTOR CALLED
COPY CONSTRUCTOR CALLED
```

In this example, the copy constructor is called four times. It is called when y is declared, copying x to y; it is called when y is passed by value to the function f, copying y to r; it is called when s is declared, copying r to s; and it is called when the function f returns by value, even though nothing is copied there. Note that the initialization of s looks like an assignment. But as part of a declaration it calls the copy constructor just as the declaration of y does.

If you do not include a copy constructor in your class definition, then the compiler generates one automatically. This "default" copy constructor will simply copy objects bit-by-bit. In many cases, this is exactly what you would want. So in these cases, there is no need for an explicitly defined copy constructor.

However, in some important cases, a bit-by-bit copy will not be adequate. The String class, defined in Chapter 10, is a prime example. In objects of that class, the relevant data member holds only a pointer to the actual string, so a bit-by-bit copy would only duplicate the pointer, not the string itself. In cases like this, it is essential that you define your own copy constructor.

8.8 THE CLASS DESTRUCTOR

When an object is created, a constructor is called automatically to manage its birth. Similarly, when an object comes to the end of its life, another special member function is called automatically to manage its death. This function is called a *destructor*.

Each class has exactly one destructor. If it is not defined explicitly in the class definition, then like the default constructor, the copy constructor, and the assignment operator, the destructor is created automatically.

EXAMPLE 8.11 Including a Destructor in the `Rational` Class

```
class Rational {
public:
    Rational() { cout << "OBJECT IS BORN.\n"; }
    ~Rational()  { cout << "OBJECT DIES.\n"; }
private:
    int num, den;
};

main()
{
    {
        Rational x;                       // beginning of scope for x
        cout << "Now x is alive.\n";
    }                                      // end of scope for x
    cout << "Now between blocks.\n";
    {
        Rational y;
        cout << "Now y is alive.\n";
    }
}
```

```
OBJECT IS BORN.
Now x is alive.
OBJECT DIES.
Now between blocks.
OBJECT IS BORN.
Now y is alive.
OBJECT DIES.
```

The output here shows when the constructor and the destructor are called.

The class destructor is called for an object when it reaches the end of its scope. For a local object, this will be at the end of the block within which it is declared. For a `static` object, it will be at then end of the `main()` function.

Although the system will provide them automatically, it is considered good programming practice always to define the copy constructor, the assignment operator, and the destructor within each class definition.

8.9 CONSTANT OBJECTS

It is good programming practice to make an object constant if it should not be changed. This is done with the `const` keyword:

```
const char blank = ' ';
const int maxint = 2147483647;
const double pi = 3.141592653589793;
void init(float a[], const int size);
```

Like variables and function parameters, objects may also be declared to be constant:

```
const Rational pi(22,7);
```

However, when this is done, the C++ compiler restricts access to the object's member functions. For example, with the `Rational` class defined previously, the `print()` function could not be called for this object:

```
pi.print();    // error: call not allowed
```

In fact, unless we modify our class definition, the only member functions that could be called for `const` objects would be the constructors and the destructor. To overcome this restriction, we must declare as constant those member functions that we want to be able to use with `const` objects.

A function is declared constant by inserting the `const` keyword between its parameter list and its body:

```
void print() const { cout << num << '/' << den << endl; }
```

This modification of the function definition will allow it to be called for constant objects:

```
const Rational pi(22,7);
pi.print();    // o.k. now
```

8.10 STRUCTURES

The C++ `class` is a generalization of the C `struct` (for "structure") which is a class with only `public` members and no functions. One normally thinks of a class as a structure that is given life by means of its member functions and which enjoys information hiding by means of `private` data members.

To remain compatible with the older C language, C++ retains the `struct` keyword which allows `struct`s to be defined. However, a C++ `struct` is essentially the same as a C++ `class`. The only significant difference between a C++ `struct` and a C++ `class` is with the default access specifier assigned to members. Although not recommended, C++ classes can be defined without explicitly specifying its member access specifier. For example,

```
class Rational {
    int num, den;
};
```

is a valid definition of a `Rational` class. Since the access specifier for its data members `num` and `den` is not specified, it is set by default to be `private`. If we make it a `struct` instead of a `class`

```
struct Rational {
    int num, den;
};
```

then the data members are set by default to be `public`. But this could be corrected simply by specifying the access specifier explicitly:

```
struct Rational {

private:

    int num, den;

};
```

So the difference between a `class` and a C++ `struct` is really just cosmetic.

8.11 POINTERS TO OBJECTS

In many applications, it is advantageous to use pointers to objects (and `structs`). Here is a simple example:

EXAMPLE 8.12   Using Pointers to Objects

```
class X {
public:
    int data;
};

main()
{
    X* p = new X;
    (*p).data = 22;              // equivalent to: p->data = 22;
    cout << "(*p).data = " << (*p).data << " = " << p->data << endl;
    p->data = 44;
    cout << "  p->data = " << (*p).data << " = " << p->data << endl;
}
```

```
(*p).data = 22 = 22
  p->data = 44 = 44
```

Since `p` is a pointer to an `X` object, `*p` is an `X` object, and `(*p).data` accesses its (`public`) data member `data`. Note that parentheses are required in the expression `(*p).data` because the direct member selection operator ".". has higher precedence than the dereferencing operator "*". (See Appendix C.)

The two notations

```
(*p).data

p->data
```

have the same meaning. When working with pointers objects, the "arrow" symbol "->" is preferred because it is simpler and it suggests "the thing to which `p` points."

Here is a more important example:

EXAMPLE 8.13 A Node Class for Linked Lists

This defines a Node class each of whose objects contain an int data member and a next pointer. The program allows the user to create a linked list in reverse. Then it traverses the list, printing each data value.

```
class Node {
public:
    Node(int d, Node* p=0) : data(d), next(p) { }
    int data;
    Node* next;
};

main()
{
    int n;
    Node* p;
    Node* q=0;
    while (cin >> n) {
        p = new Node(n, q);
        q = p;
    }
    for ( ; p->next; p = p->next )
        cout << p->data << " -> ";
    cout << "*\n";
}
```

```
88 77 66 55 44 33 22^D
22 -> 33 -> 44 -> 55 -> 66 -> 77 -> *
```

First note that the definition of the Node class includes two references to the class itself. This is allowed because each reference is actually a pointer to the class. Also note that the constructor initializes both data members.

The while loop continues reading ints into n until the user enters the end-of-file character (**Control-D** on Mac and UNIX systems, and **Control-Z** on DOS and VAX systems). Within the loop, it gets a new node, inserts the int into its data member, and connects the new node to the previous node (pointed to by q). Finally, the for loop traverses the list, beginning with the node pointed to by p (which is the last node constructed) and continuing until p->next is NUL (in which case, p will be pointing to the last node in the list).

The list constructed in this example can be visualized like this:

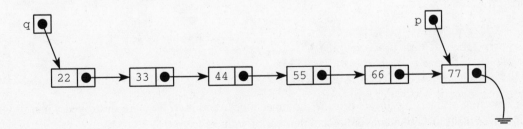

8.12 STATIC DATA MEMBERS

Sometimes a single value for a data member applies to all members of the class. In this case, it would be inefficient to store the same value in every object of the class. That can be avoided by declaring the data member to be `static`. This is done by including the `static` keyword at the beginning of the variable's declaration. It also requires that the variable be defined globally. So the syntax looks like this:

```
class X {
public:
    static int n;   // declaration of n as a static data member
};
```

```
int X::n = 0;       // definition of n
```
Static variables are automatically initialized to 0, so the explicit initialization in the definition is unnecessary unless you want it to have a non-zero initial value.

EXAMPLE 8.14 A `static` Data Member

The `Widget` class maintains a `static` data member `count` which keeps track of the number of `Widget` objects in existence globally. Each time a widget is created (by the constructor) the counter is incremented, and each time a widget is destroyed (by the destructor) the counter is decremented.

```
class Widget {
public:
    Widget() { ++count; }
    ~Widget() { --count; }
    static int count;
};
```

```
int Widget::count = 0;
```

```
main()
{
    Widget w, x;
    cout << "Now there are " << w.count << " widgets.\n";
    {
        Widget w, x, y, z;
        cout << "Now there are " << w.count << " widgets.\n";
    }
    cout << "Now there are " << w.count << " widgets.\n";
    Widget y;
    cout << "Now there are " << w.count << " widgets.\n";
}
```

```
Now there are 2 widgets.
Now there are 6 widgets.
Now there are 2 widgets.
Now there are 3 widgets.
```

Notice how four widgets are created inside the inner block, and then they are destroyed when program control leaves that block, reducing the global number of widgets from 6 to 2.

A static data member is like an ordinary global variable: only one copy of the variable exists no matter how many instances of the class exist. The main difference is that it is a data member of the class, and so may be private.

EXAMPLE 8.15 A static Data Member that is private

```
class Widget {
public:
    Widget() { ++count; }
    ~Widget() { --count; }
    int numWidgets() { return count; }
private:
    static int count;
};

int Widget::count = 0;

main()
{
    Widget w, x;
    cout << "Now there are " << w.numWidgets() << " widgets.\n";
    {
        Widget w, x, y, z;
        cout << "Now there are " << w.numWidgets() << " widgets.\n";
    }
    cout << "Now there are " << w.numWidgets() << " widgets.\n";
    Widget y;
    cout << "Now there are " << w.numWidgets() << " widgets.\n";
}
```

This works the same way as Example 8.14. But now that the static variable count is private, we need the access function numWidgets() to read count in main().

The relationships among the class, its members, and its objects can be visualized like this:

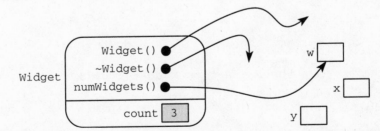

The rounded box represents the class itself which contains the three member functions and the data member count. The public members are above the line and the private member(s) are below it. Each member function maintains a pointer (named "this") which points to the object that owns the current function call. This snapshot shows the status during the execution of the last line in the program: three widgets (w, x, and y) exist, and w is calling the numWidgets() function which returns the value of the private data member count. Note that this data member resides within the class itself; the class objects have no data.

8.13 static FUNCTION MEMBERS

Like any ordinary member function, the numWidgets() function in Example 8.15 requires that it be owned by some instance of the class. But since it returns the value of the static data member count which is independent of the individual objects themselves, it doesn't matter which object calls it. We had w call it each time, but we could just as well have had x or y or z call it when they exist. Moreover, we couldn't call it at all until after some object had been created. This is rather arbitrary. Since the action of the function is independent of the actual function objects, it would be better to make the calls independent of them too. This can be done simply by declaring the function to be static.

EXAMPLE 8.16 A static Function Member

The Widget class maintains a static data member count which keeps track of the number of Widget objects in existence globally. Each time a widget is created (by the constructor) the counter is incremented, and each time a widget is destroyed (by the destructor) the counter is decremented.

```
class Widget {
public:
    Widget() { ++count; }
    ~Widget() { --count; }
    static int num() { return count; }
private:
    static int count;
};

int Widget::count = 0;

main()
{
    cout << "Now there are " << Widget::num() << " widgets.\n";
    Widget w, x;
    cout << "Now there are " << Widget::num() << " widgets.\n";
    {
        Widget w, x, y, z;
        cout << "Now there are " << Widget::num() << " widgets.\n";
    }
    cout << "Now there are " << Widget::num() << " widgets.\n";
    Widget y;
    cout << "Now there are " << Widget::num() << " widgets.\n";
}
```

```
Now there are 0 widgets.
Now there are 2 widgets.
Now there are 6 widgets.
Now there are 2 widgets.
Now there are 3 widgets.
```

Declaring the num() function to be static renders it independent of the class instances. So now it is invoked simply as a member of the Widget class using the scope resolution operator ":: ". This allows the function to be called before any objects have been instantiated.

The previous figure showing relationships among the class, its members, and should now looks like this:

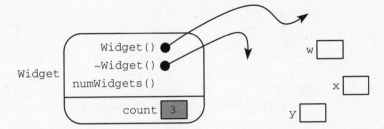

The difference is that now the member function `num()` has no "this" pointer. As a `static` member function, it is associated with the class itself, not with its instances.

Static member functions can access only `static` data from their own class.

Review Questions

8.1 Explain the difference between a `public` member and a `private` member of a class.

8.2 Explain the difference between the interface and the implementation of a class.

8.3 Explain the difference between a class member function and an application function.

8.4 Explain the difference between a constructor and a destructor.

8.5 Explain the difference between the default constructor and other constructors.

8.6 Explain the difference between the copy constructor and the assignment operator.

8.7 Explain the difference between an access function and a utility function.

8.8 Explain the difference between a `class` and a `struct` in C++.

8.9 What name must a constructor have?

8.10 What name must a destructor have?

8.11 How many constructors can a class have?

8.12 How many destructors can a class have?

8.13 How and why is the scope resolution operator `::` used in class definitions?

8.14 Which member functions are created automatically by the compiler if they are not included (by the programmer) in the class definition?

8.15 How many times is the copy constructor called in the following code:

```
Widget f(Widget u)
{
    Widget v(u);
    Widget w = v;
    return w;
}
```

```
main()
{
    Widget x;
    Widget y = f(f(x));
}
```

8.16 Why are the parentheses needed in the expression `(*p).data`?

Solved Programming Problems

8.17 Implement a `Point` class for three-dimensional points (*x*,*y*,*z*). Include a default constructor, a copy constructor, a `negate()` function to transform the point into its negative, a `norm()` function to return the point's distance from the origin (0,0,0), and a `print()` function.

```
#include <iostream.h>
#include <math.h>

class Point {
public:
    Point(float x=0, float y=0, float z=0) : x_(x), y_(y), z_(z) { }
    Point(const Point& p) : x_(p.x_), y_(p.y_), z_(p.z_)  { }
    void negate() { x_ *= -1; y_ *= -1; z_ *= -1; }
    double norm() { return sqrt(x_*x_ + y_*y_ + z_*z_); }
    void print()
        { cout << '(' << x_ << "," << y_ << "," << z_ << ")"; }
private:
    float x_, y_, z_;
};
```

In this implementation, we have used the common device of ending the name of each data member with an underscore (_). This has the advantage of making it easy to match up the names of constructor parameters (x, y, and z) with their corresponding data members (x_, y_, and z_) without conflict.

8.18 Implement a `Stack` class for stacks of `int`s. Include a default constructor, a destructor, and the usual stack operations: `push()`, `pop()`, `isEmpty()`, and `isFull()`. Use an array implementation.

```
class Stack {
public:
    Stack(int s=10) : size(s), top(-1) { a = new int[size]; }
    ~Stack() { delete [] a; }
    void push(const int& item) { a[++top] = item; }
    int pop() { return a[top--]; }
    int isEmpty() const { return top == -1; }
    int isFull() const { return top == (size-1); }
private:
    int size;  // size of array
    int top;   // top of stack
    int* a;    // array to hold stack items
};
```

In this implementation, `top` is always the index of the top element on the stack. The data member `size` is the size of the array that holds the stack items. So the stack is full when it contains that number of items. The constructor sets `size` to 10 as the default.

8.19 Implement a `Time` class. Each object of this class will represent a specific time of day, storing the hours, minutes, and seconds as integers. Include a constructor, access functions, a function `advance(int h, int m, int s)` to advance the current time of an existing object, a function `reset(int h, int m, int s)` to reset the current time of an existing object, and a `print()` function.

```
class Time {
public:
    Time(int h=0, int m=0, int s=0)
      : hr(h), min(m), sec(s) { normalize(); }
    int hours() { return hr; }
    int minutes() { return min; }
    int seconds() { return sec; }
    void advance(int, int, int);
    void reset(int, int, int);
    void print() { cout << hr << ":" << min << ":" << sec; }
private:
    int hr, min, sec;
    void normalize();
};

void Time::normalize()
{
    min += sec/60;
    hr += min/60;
    hr = hr % 24;
    min = min % 60;
    sec = sec % 60;
}



void Time::advance(int h=0, int m=0, int s=1)
{
    hr += h;
    min += m;
    sec += s;
    normalize();
}

void Time::reset(int h=0, int m=0, int s=0)
{
    hr = h;
    min = m;
    sec = s;
    normalize();
}
```

Here we have used a utility function `normalize()` which normalizes the `Time` object so that its three data members are in the correct range: $0 \le sec < 60$, $0 \le min < 60$, and $0 \le hr < 24$.

8.20 Implement a `Random` class for generating pseudo-random numbers.

This class uses the utility function `randomize()` which implements the *Linear Congruential Algorithm* introduced by D. H. Lehmer in 1949. It updates the `seed_` using the multiplier constant `mult_` and the modulus constant `mod_`. Their values are consistent with those recommended by Donald E. Knuth in his seminal work *The Art of Computer Programming*.

```cpp
#include <iostream.h>
#include <limits.h>
#include <time.h>
const unsigned long mult_ = 234567821;
const unsigned long mod_ = ULONG_MAX;           // = 4,294,967,295
const int max_ = INT_MAX;                // = 2,147,483,647 or 32,767

class Random {
public:
    Random() { seed_ = time(NULL); }
    Random(unsigned long seed) : seed_(seed) { randomize(); }
    int integer(int max=max_) { randomize();  return seed_ % max_; }
    int integer(int min, int max)
        { randomize();  return min + seed_ % (max - min + 1); }
    double real() { randomize();  return double(seed_)/double(mod_);
}
private:
    unsigned long seed_;
    void randomize() { seed_ = (mult_*seed_ + 1) % mod_; }
};

main()
{
    Random random;
    for (int i = 1; i <= 10; i++) {
        int m = random.integer();
        int n = random.integer(1, 99);
        double x = random.real();
        cout << "\t" << m << "\t" << n << "\t" << x << endl;
    }
}
```

1078943744	71	0.0791259
1253709367	94	0.252766
705325754	31	0.698051
67134329	37	0.805397
1908776228	10	0.81263
1076073003	11	0.949527
1849257406	82	0.158744
902847182	22	0.872112
771227400	11	0.603844
460755423	1	0.879149

Our test driver makes 10 calls to each of the three random number functions, generating 10 pseudo-random integers in the range 0 to 2,147,483,647, 10 pseudo-random integers in the range 1 to 99, and 10 pseudo-random real numbers in the range 0.0 to 1.0.

8.21 Implement a `Person` class. Each object of this class will represent a human being. Data members should include the person's name, year of birth, and year of death. Include a default constructor, a destructor, access functions, and a print function.

```cpp
#include <iostream.h>
#include <string.h>

class Person {
public:
    Person(const char*, int, int);
    ~Person() { delete [] name_; }
    char* name() { return name_; }
    int born() { return yob_; }
    int died() { return yod_; }
    void print();
private:
    int len_;
    char* name_;
    int yob_, yod_;
};

Person::Person(const char* name=0, int yob=0, int yod=0)
    : len_(strlen(name)),
      name_(new char[len_+1]),
      yob_(yob),
      yod_(yod)
{
    memcpy(name_, name, len_+1);
}

void Person::print()
{
    cout << "\tName: " << name_ << endl;
    if (yob_) cout << "\tBorn: " << yob_ << endl;
    if (yod_) cout << "\tDied: " << yod_ << endl;
}
```

To keep the object self-contained, `name_` is stored as a separate string. To facilitate this separate storage, we save its length in the data member `len_` and use the `memcpy()` function (defined in `string.h`) to copy the string `name` into the string `name_`. Then the destructor uses the delete operator to de-allocate this storage.

8.22 Implement a `String` class. Each object of this class will represent a character string. Data members are the length of the string and the actual character string. In addition to constructors, destructor, access functions, and a print function, include a "subscript" function.

```cpp
class String {
public:
    String(short =0);                    // default constructor
    String(const char*);                 // constructor
    String(const String&);               // copy constructor
    ~String() { delete [] data; }        // destructor
    int length() const { return len; }   // access function
```

```
        char* convert() { return data; }     // access function
        char character(short i) { char c = data[i]; return c; }
        void print() { cout << data; }
    private:
        short len;      // number of (non-null) characters in string
        char* data;     // the string
    };

    String::String(short size) : len(size)
    {
        data = new char[len+1];
        for (int i=0; i < len; i++) data[i] = ' ';
        data[len] = '\0';
    }


    String::String(const char* str) : len(strlen(str))
    {
        data = new char[len+1];
        memcpy(data, str, len+1);
    }


    String::String(const String& str) : len(str.len)
    {
        data = new char[len+1];
        memcpy(data, str.data, len+1);
    }
```

This implementation includes three constructors: the default constructor with optional parameter size, a constructor that allows an object to be initialized with an ordinary C string, and the copy constructor. The second access function is named convert() because it actually converts from type String to char* type. The "subscript" function is named character() because it returns one character in the string—the one indexed by the parameter i.

8.23 Implement a Matrix class for 2-by-2 matrices:

$$\begin{bmatrix} a & b \\ c & d \end{bmatrix}$$

Include a default constructor, a copy constructor, an inverse() function that returns the inverse of the matrix, a det() function that returns the determinant of the matrix, a Boolean function isSingular() that returns 1 or 0 according to whether the determinant is zero, and a print() function.

```
    class Matrix {
    public:
        Matrix(double a=0, double b=0, double c=0, double d=0 )
          : a_(a), b_(b), c_(c), d_(d) { }
        Matrix(const Matrix& m)
          : a_(m.a_), b_(m.b_), c_(m.c_), d_(m.d_)  { }
        double det() { return a_*d_ - b_*c_; }
        int isSingular() { return det() == 0; }
        Matrix inverse();
        void print();
```

```
class Matrix {
public:
    Matrix(double a=0, double b=0, double c=0, double d=0 )
      : a_(a), b_(b), c_(c), d_(d) { }
    Matrix(const Matrix& m)
      : a_(m.a_), b_(m.b_), c_(m.c_), d_(m.d_)  { }
    double det() { return a_*d_ - b_*c_; }
    int isSingular() { return det() == 0; }
    Matrix inverse();
    void print();
private:
    double a_, b_, c_, d_;
};

Matrix Matrix::inverse()
{
    double k = 1/det();
    Matrix temp(k*d_,-k*b_,-k*c_,k*a_);
    return temp;
}

void Matrix::print()
{
    cout << a_ << "   " << b_ << '\n' << c_ << "   " << d_ << "\n";
}
```

Supplementary Programming Problems

8.24 Implement a `Point` class for two-dimensional points (*x*, *y*). Include a default constructor, a copy constructor, a `negate()` function to transform the point into its negative, a `norm()` function to return the point's distance from the origin (0,0), and a `print()` function.

8.25 Implement a `Circle` class. Each object of this class will represent a circle, storing its radius and the *x* and *y* coordinates of its center as `floats`. Include a default constructor, access functions, an `area()` function, and a `circumference()` function.

8.26 Modify the `Circle` class (Problem 8.25) so that its data members are the `float radius` and the two-dimensional `Point center`.

8.27 Implement a `Sphere` class. Each object of this class will represent a sphere with data members `float radius` and the three-dimensional `Point center`. Include a default constructor, access functions, an `surfaceArea()` function, and a `volume()` function.

8.28 Modify the `Stack` class (Problem 8.17) adding the member function `count()` which returns the number of items on the stack.

8.29 Modify the `Stack` class (Problem 8.17) adding the member function `print()` which prints the contents of the stack.

8.30 Modify the `Stack` class (Problem 8.17) so that it holds items of type `float` instead of `int`.

8.31 Modify the `Stack` class (Problem 8.17) so that it holds items of type `Rational`.

8.32 Write a program that tests the application function

```
void reverse(Stack);
```

which reverses the items on the stack passed to it. This function should use two local stacks to do its job.

8.33 Implement a `Queue` class for holding `int`s. A queue is like a stack (see Problem 8.17) except that items are inserted at one end (called the `rear`) and removed from the other end (called the `front`). Include a default constructor, a destructor, and the usual queue operations: `insert()`, `remove()`, `isEmpty()`, and `isFull()`. Use an array implementation.

8.34 Modify the `Queue` class (Problem 8.33) adding the member functions `count()` which returns the number of items on the queue, and `print()` which prints its contents.

8.35 Modify the `Queue` class (Problem 8.33) so that it holds items of type `Rational`.

8.36 Write a program that tests the application function

```
void reverse(Queue);
```

which reverses the items on the queue passed to it. This function should use a local stacks to do its job.

8.37 Modify the `Time` class (Problem 8.19) using the number of seconds elapsed since midnight as the only data member. Include a function `advance(int s)` to advance the existing time by `s` seconds, and a function `secondsElapsedSince(int h, int m, int s)` that returns the number of seconds that have elapsed from the given time to the time stored.

8.38 Implement a `Date` class with member data for the month, day, and year. Each object of this class will represent a specific A.D. date, storing the month, day, and year as integers. Include a default constructor, a copy constructor, access functions, a function `reset(int y, int m, int d)` to reset the date for an existing object, a function `advance(int y, int m, int d)` to advance an existing date by `y` years, `m` months, and `d` days, and a `print()` function. Use a `normalize()` utility function to ensure that the data members are in the correct range: $1 \leq$ year, $1 \leq$ month ≤ 12, $1 \leq$ day $\leq$ `daysIn(month)`, where `daysIn(int month)` is another utility function that returns the number of days in `month`. Ignore leap years.

8.39 Modify the `Date` class (Problem 8.38) to accommodate leap years. A year is a leap year if it is divisible by 400, or if it is divisible by 4 but not by 100. For example, the years 1996 and 2000 are leap years, but the years 1995 and 1900 are not.

8.40 Modify the `Date` class (Problem 8.39) using the number of days elapsed since the date January 1, 1 A.D. as the only data member. Include a function `advance(int d)` to advance the existing date by `d` days, and a function `daysElapsedSince(int y, int m, int d)` that returns the number of days that have elapsed from the given date passed to the date stored.

8.41 Modify the `Date` class (Problem 8.40) adding the function `weekDay()` that returns an integer in the range 0 to 6 for Sunday through Saturday. Use Zeller's Algorithm:

```
if (month < 3) { mp = 0; yp = year - 1; }
else { mp = int(0.4*month + 2.3); yp = year; }
t = int(yp/4) - int(yp/100) + int(yp/400);
return (365*year + 31*(month - 1) + day + t - mp) % 7;
```

Modify the `print()` function so that it also prints the name of the day of the week.

8.42 Modify the `Person` class (Problem 8.21) to include the following member functions:

```
int isLiving();

int age(int year);
```

The `isLiving()` function returns 0 or 1 according to whether `yod_` is zero. The `age()` function returns the persons current age based upon the current `year` passed to it, or it returns the person's age at death if `yod_` is not zero.

8.43 Implement an `Employee` class by modifying the `Person` class (Problem 8.21). Include data members for Social Security Number number, monthly salary, and tax rate. Include a member function `tax()` that returns the amount of tax paid.

8.44 Implement a `Student` class by modifying the `Person` class (Problem 8.21). Include data members for student identification number, major program, grade point average, and credits earned. Include a member function `update(int credit, char grade)` that processes the given information (`credit` and `grade`) for one course, using it to update the student's grade point average, and credits earned.

8.45 Implement an `Address` class for storing a residential address.

8.46 Modify the `Person` class (Problem 8.21) by adding an `address` data member with type `Address` class (Problem 8.45).

8.47 Modify the `Person` class (Problem 8.21) replacing the declarations `int yob_, yod_` with:

```
Date dob_, dod_;
```

for "date of birth" and "date of death" (see Problem 8.38).

8.48 Implement a `Computer` class with data members for the computer type (*e.g.*, `"PC"`), the CPU (*e.g.*, `"Intel Pentium"`), the operating system (*e.g.*, `"DOS"`), the number of megabytes of memory (*e.g.*, `8`), the number of gigabytes of disk space (*e.g.*, `1.2`), the type of printer that it has, whether it has a CD-ROM, whether it has Internet access, its purchase price, and year of purchase. Include a default constructor, a destructor, access functions, and a `print()` function.

8.49 Implement the `Rational` class with its `den` member declared to be `unsigned` instead of `int`. This allows for more than twice as many objects because `unsigned` allows more than twice as many possible positive integer values as does `int`.

8.50 Implement the following additional member functions for the `Rational` class:

```
Rational plus(Rational);

Rational minus(Rational);

Rational times(Rational);

Rational dividedBy(Rational);
```

So, for example, the call `x.minus(y)` would subtract the `Rational` object `y` from the `Rational` object `x`. Note that this simulates the operator `-=` for the `Rational` class.

8.51 Implement the following additional member functions for the `Rational` class:

```
int isEqualTo(Rational);
int isGreaterThan(Rational);
int isLessThan(Rational);
```

So, for example, the call `x.isGreaterThan(y)` would return 1 or 0 according to whether the `Rational` object `x` is greater than the `Rational` object `y`. Note that this simulates the operator `>` for the `Rational` class.

8.52 Implement the following additional constructor for the `Rational` class:

```
Rational(Float);
```

So, for example, the declaration `Rational x(3.14)` would construct the `Rational` object `x` that represents the fraction 157/50.

8.53 Implement a `Complex` class for complex numbers. Each object of this class will represent a complex number $x + y$ **i**, storing the real part x and the imaginary part y as real numbers of type `double`. Include a default constructor, a copy constructor, access functions, a `norm()` function that returns the norm (magnitude) of the complex number, an `isEqualTo(Complex)` function, and arithmetic functions `plus(Complex)`, `minus(Complex)`, `times(Complex)`, and `dividedBy(Complex)`.

8.54 Implement the following additional constructor for the `Complex` class (Problem 8.25):

```
Complex(Rational);
```

So, for example, the declarations

```
Rational x(22,7);
Complex z(x);
```

would construct the `Rational` object `x` that represents the fraction 22/7 and the `Complex` object `z` that represents the real number 3.14159.

8.55 Implement the following additional functions for the `Point` class (Problem 8.17):

```
float dot(Point);
Point cross(Point);
```

The `dot()` function returns the dot product (scalar product), and the `cross()` function returns the cross product (vector product).

8.56 Modify the `String` class (Problem 8.21) by adding a constructor that allows an object to be initialized with a single character, constructing a string of length 1 containing that character.

8.57 Modify the `String` class (Problem 8.21) by adding the function

```
String substr(short start, short length);
```

This function returns the `String` object that contains the substring of the owner indexed from start to `start + length - 1`. For example, if `s` represents the string `"ABCDEFGHIJK"`, then `s.substr(2,5)` would return the object that represents the string `"CDEFG"`, and `s.substr(8,7)` would return the object that represents the string `"IJK"`. Note that the value of start is the length of the omitted prefix.

8.58 Modify the `Matrix` class (Problem 8.23) so that it represents 3-by-3 matrices.

8.59 Implement a `Quaternion` class for hypercomplex numbers (also called "hamiltonians"). Each object of this class will represent a hypercomplex number $t + x\,\mathbf{i} + y\,\mathbf{j} + z\,\mathbf{k}$, where each of the components t, x, y, and z has type `double`. Include a default constructor, a copy constructor, access functions, a `norm()` function that returns the norm (magnitude) of the hypercomplex number, an `isEqualTo(Quaternion)` function, and arithmetic functions `plus(Quaternion)`, `minus(Quaternion)`, and `times(Quaternion)`, where multiplication is defined by the following rules: $\mathbf{i}^2 = \mathbf{j}^2 = \mathbf{k}^2 = -1$, $\mathbf{i}\,\mathbf{j} = \mathbf{k} = -\mathbf{j}\,\mathbf{i}$, $\mathbf{j}\,\mathbf{k} = \mathbf{i} = -\mathbf{k}\,\mathbf{j}$, and $\mathbf{k}\,\mathbf{i} = \mathbf{j} = -\mathbf{i}\,\mathbf{k}$.

8.60 Write a program like the one in Example 8.2, except insert the new nodes at the end of the list so that the data values can be input in the same order as they are output.

Answers to Review Questions

8.1 A `public` member is accessible from outside the class; a `private` member is not.

8.2 The class interface consists of the member data and the member function prototypes (*i.e.* just the function declarations). The class implementation contains the definitions of the member functions.

8.3 A class member function is part of the class, so it has access to the class's `private` parts. An application function is declared outside the class, and so it does <u>not</u> have access to the class's `private` parts.

8.4 A constructor is a class member function that executes automatically whenever an object of that class is instantiated (*i.e.*, constructed). A destructor is a class member function that executes automatically whenever the scope of that object terminates (*i.e.*, is destructed).

8.5 The default constructor is the unique constructor that has no parameters (or the one whose parameters all have default values).

8.6 A class's copy constructor executes whenever an object of that class is copied by any mechanism except direct assignment. This includes initialization, passing a parameter by value, and returning by value.

8.7 An access function is a `public` class member function that returns the value of one of the class's data members. A utility function is a `private` class member function that is used only within the class to perform "technical" tasks.

8.8 A `class` and a `struct` in C++ are essentially the same. The only significant difference is that the default access level for a class of `private`, while that for a struct is `public`.

8.9 Every class constructor must have the same name as the class itself.

8.10 Every class destructor must have the same name as the class itself, prefixed with a tilde (~).

8.11 There is no limit to the number of constructors that a class may have. But since multiple constructors are function overloads, they all must be distinguishable by their parameter lists.

8.12 A class can only one destructor.

8.13 The scope resolution operator `::` used in general "to resolve external references." It is used in a class definition whenever the definition of a member function is given outside the scope of the class definition.

8.14 There are four class member functions that are created automatically by the compiler if they are not included (by the programmer) in the class definition: the default constructor, the copy constructor, the destructor, and the overloaded assignment operator.

8.15 The copy constructor is called 7 times in this code. Each call to the function `f` requires 3 calls to the copy constructor: when the parameter is passed by value to `u`, when `v` is initialized, and when `w` is returned by value. The seventh call is for the initialization `y`.

8.16 The parentheses are needed in the expression `(*p).data` because the direct member selection operator "`.`" has higher precedence than the dereferencing operator "`*`". (See Appendix C.)

Chapter 9

Overloading Operators

9.1 INTRODUCTION

C++ includes a rich store of 45 operators. They are summarized in Appendix C. These operators are defined automatically for the fundamental types (`int`, `float`, *etc.*). When you define a class, you are actually creating a new type. Most of the C++ operators can be overloaded to apply to your new class type. This chapter describes how to do that.

9.2 OVERLOADING THE ASSIGNMENT OPERATOR

Of all the operators, the assignment operator `=` is probably used the most. Its purpose is to copy one object to another. Like the default constructor, the copy constructor, and the destructor, the assignment operator is created automatically for every class that is defined. But also like those other three member functions, it can be defined explicitly in the class definition.

EXAMPLE 9.1   Adding an Assignment Operator to the `Rational` Class

Here is a class interface for the `Rational` class, showing the default constructor, the copy constructor, and the assignment operator:

```
class Rational {
public:
    Rational(int =0, int =1);        // default constructor
    Rational(const Rational&);       // copy constructor
    void operator=(const Rational&); // assignment operator
    // other declarations go here
private:
    int num;
    int den;
};
```

Note the required syntax for the assignment operator. The name of this member function is `operator=`. Its argument list is the same as that of the copy constructor: it contains a single argument of the same class, passed by constant reference.

Here is the implementation of the overloaded assignment operator:

```
void Rational::operator=(const Rational& r)
{
    num = r.num;
    den = r.den;
}
```

It simply copies the member data from the object `r` to the object that owns the call.

249

9.3 THE this POINTER

C++ allows assignments to be chained together, like this:

```
x = y = z = 3.14;
```

This is executed first by assigning 3.14 to z, then to y, and finally to x. But, as Example 9.1 shows, the assignment operator is really a function named operator=. In this chain, the function is called three times. On its first call, it assigns 3.14 to z, so the input to the function is 3.14. On its second call, it assigns 3.14 to y, so its input again must be 3.14. So that value should be the output (*i.e.*, return value) of the first call. Similarly, the output of the second call should again be 3.14 to serve as the input to the third call. The three calls to this function are nested, like this:

```
f(x, f(y, f(z, 3.14)))
```

The point is that the assignment operator is a function that should return the value it assigns. Therefore, instead of the return type void, the assignment operator should return a reference to the same type as the object being assigned

```
Rational& operator=(Rational& r)
```

This allows assignments to be chained together.

EXAMPLE 9.2   The Preferred Function Prototype for an Overloaded Assignment Operator

```
class Rational {
public:
    Rational(int =0, int =1);                 // default constructor
    Rational(const Rational&);                // copy constructor
    Rational& operator=(const Rational&);     // assignment operator
    // other declarations go here
private:
    int num;
    int den;
    // other declarations go here
};
```

The preferred syntax for the prototype of an overloaded assignment operator in a class T is

```
T& operator=(const T&);
```

The return type is a reference to an object of the same class T. But then this means that the function should return the object that is being assigned, in order for the assignment chain to work. So when the assignment operator is being overloaded as a class member function, it should return the object that owns the call. Since there is no other name available for this owner object, C++ defines a special pointer, named this, which points to the owner object.

We can envision the this pointer like this:

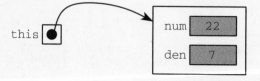

Now we can give the correct implementation of the overloaded assignment operator:

EXAMPLE 9.3 Implementation of the Assignment Operator for the `Rational` **Class**

```
Rational& Rational::operator=(const Rational& r)
{
    num = r.num;
    den = r.den;
    return *this;
}
```

Now assignments for the `Rational` class can be chained together:

```
Rational x, y, z(22,7);
x = y = z;
```

The correct implementation for an overloaded assignment operator in a class `T` is

```
T& T::operator=(const T& t)
{
    // assign each member datum of t to the
    // corresponding member datum of the owner
    return *this;
}
```

Finally, note that an assignment is different from an initialization, even though they both use the equals sign:

```
Rational x(22,7);   // this is an initialization
Rational y(x);      // this is an initialization
Rational z = x;     // this is an initialization
Rational w;
w = x;              // this is an assignment
```

An initialization calls the copy constructor. An assignment calls the assignment operator.

9.4 OVERLOADING ARITHMETIC OPERATORS

All programming languages provide the standard arithmetic operators `+`, `-`, `*`, and `/` for numeric types. So it is only natural to define these for user-defined numeric types like the `Rational` class. In older programming languages like C and Pascal, this is done by defining functions like this:

```
Rational product(Rational x, Rational y)
{
    Rational z(x.num*y.num, x.den*y.den);
    return z;
}
```

This works. But the function has to be called in the conventional way:

```
z = product(x,y);
```

C++ allows such functions to be defined using the standard arithmetic operator symbols, so that they can be called more naturally:

```
z = x*y;
```

Like most operators in C++, the multiplication operator has a function name that uses the reserved word `operator`: its name is "`operator*`". Using this in place of "`product`" in the code above, we would expect the overloaded function to look something like this:

```
Rational operator*(Rational x, Rational y)
{
    Rational z(x.num*y.num, x.den*y.den);
    return z;
}
```

But this is not a member function. If it were, we would have to set it up as in Problem 8.50, with only one argument. The `operator*` function requires two arguments.

Since the overloaded arithmetic operators cannot be member functions, they cannot access the `private` member data `num` and `den`. Fortunately, C++ allows an exception to this rule so that we can complete our definitions of the overloaded arithmetic functions. The solution is to declare the function as a *friend* of the Rational class.

A `friend` function is a nonmember function that is given access to all members of the class within which it is declared. So it has all the privileges of a member function without actually being a member of the class. This attribute is used mostly with overloaded operators.

EXAMPLE 9.4 Declaring the Multiplication Operator as a `friend` Function

Here is the `Rational` class declaration with the overloaded multiplication operator declared as a friend function:

```
class Rational {
    friend Rational operator*(const Rational&, const Rational&);
public:
    Rational(int =0, int =1);
    Rational(const Rational&);
    Rational& operator=(const Rational&);
    // other declarations go here
private:
    int num;
    int den;
    // other declarations go here
};
```

Note that the function prototype is inserted inside the class declaration, above the `public` section. Also note that the two arguments to the function are both passed by constant reference.

Now we can implement this nonmember just as we had expected:

```
Rational operator*(const Rational& x, const Rational& y)
{
    Rational z(x.num * y.num, x.den * y.den);
    return z;
}
```

Note that the keyword `friend` is not used in the function implementation. Also note that the scope resolution prefix `Rational::` is not used because this is not a member function.

Here is a little program that uses our improved `Rational` class:

EXAMPLE 9.5 The `Rational` Class with Assignment and Multiplication Operators

```
#include "Rational.h"

main()
{
    Rational x(22,7), y(-3,8), z;
    z = x;                              // assignment operator is called
    z.print();  cout << endl;
    x = y*z;                            // multiplication operator is called
    x.print();  cout << endl;
}
```

```
22/7
-33/28
```

Note that the `reduce()` function was called from within the overloaded multiplication operator to reduce -66/56 to -33/58. (See Example 8.2.)

9.5 OVERLOADING THE ARITHMETIC ASSIGNMENT OPERATORS

C++ allows your to combine arithmetic operations with the assignment operator; for example, using `x *= y` in place of `x = x * y`. These combination operators can all be overloaded for use in your own classes.

EXAMPLE 9.6 The `Rational` Class with an Overloaded `*=` Operator

```
class Rational {
public:
    Rational(int =0, int =1);
    Rational& operator=(const Rational&);
    Rational& operator*=(const Rational&);
    // other declarations go here
private:
    int num, den;
    // other declarations go here
};

Rational& Rational::operator*=(const Rational& r)
{
    num = num*r.num;
    den = den*r.den;
    return *this;
}
```

The operator `operator*=` has the same syntax and nearly the same implementation as the basic assignment operator `operator=`. By returning `*this`, the operator can be chained, like this:

```
x *= y *= z;
```

It is also important to ensure that overloaded operators perform consistently with each other. For example, the following two lines should have the same effect, even though they call different operators:

```
x = x*y;
x *= y
```

9.6 OVERLOADING THE RELATIONAL OPERATORS

The six relational operators `<`, `>`, `<=`, `>=`, `==`, and `!=` can be overloaded the same way that the arithmetic operators are overloaded: as `friend` functions.

EXAMPLE 9.7 Overloading the Equality Operator `==` in the `Rational` Class

Like other `friend` functions, the equality operator is declared above the `public` section of the class:

```
class Rational {
    friend int operator==(const Rational&, const Rational&);
    friend Rational operator*(const Rational&, const Rational&);
    // other declarations go here
public:
    Rational(int =0, int =1);
    Rational(const Rational&);
    Rational& operator=(const Rational&);
    // other declarations go here
private:
    int num;
    int den;
    // other declarations go here
};

int operator==(const Rational& x, const Rational& y)
{
    return (x.num * y.den == y.num * x.den);
}
```

The test for equality of two fractions a/b and c/d is equivalent to the test $a*d == b*c$. So we end up using the equality operator for `int`s to define the equality operator for `Rational`s.

Note that the relational operators return an `int` type, representing either "true" (1) or "false" (0).

9.7 OVERLOADING THE STREAM OPERATORS

C++ allows you to overload the stream insertion operator `>>` for customizing input and the stream deletion operator `<<` for customizing output. Like the arithmetic and relational operators, these should also be declared as `friend` functions.

For a class `T` with data member `d`, the syntax for the output operator is

```
friend ostream& operator<<(ostream& ostr, const T& t)
    { return ostr << t.d; }
```

Here, `ostream` is a standard class defined (indirectly) in the `iostream.h` header file. Note that all the parameters and the return value are passed by reference.

This function can then be called using the same syntax that we used for fundamental types:

```
cout << "x = " << x << ", y = " << y << endl;
```

Here is an example of how custom output can be written:

EXAMPLE 9.8 Overloading the Output Operator `<<` **the** `Rational` **Class**

```
#include <iostream.h>

class Rational {
    friend ostream& operator<<(ostream&, const Rational&);
public:
    Rational(int n=0, int d=1) : num(n), den(d) { }
    // other declarations go here
private:
    int num, den;
    // other declarations go here
};

main()
{
    Rational x(22,7), y(-3,8);
    cout << "x = " << x << ", y = " << y << endl;
}

ostream& operator<<(ostream& ostr, const Rational& r)
{
    return ostr << r.num << '/' << r.den;
}
```

```
x = 22/7, y = -3/8
```

When the second line of `main()` executes, the expression `cout << "x = "` executes first. This calls the standard output operator `<<`, passing the standard output stream `cout` and the string `"x = "` to it. As usual, this inserts the string into the output stream and then returns a reference to `cout`. This return value is then passed with the object `x` to the overloaded `<<` operator. This call to `operator<<` executes with `cout` in place of `ostr` and with `x` in place of `r`. The result is the execution of the line

```
return ostr << r.num << '/' << r.den;
```

which inserts `22/7` into the output stream and returns a reference to `cout`. Then another call to the standard output operator `<<` and another call to the overloaded operator are made, with the output (a reference to `cout`) of each call cascading into the next call as input. Finally the last call to the standard output operator `<<` is made, passing `cout` and `endl`. This flushes the stream, causing the complete line

```
x = 22/7, y = -3/8
```

to be printed.

The syntax for overloading the input operator for a class `T` with data member `d` is

```
friend istream& operator>>(istream& istr, T& t)
    { return istr >> t.d; }
```

Here, `istream` is another standard class defined (indirectly) in the `iostream.h` header file.
Here is an example of how custom input can be written:

EXAMPLE 9.9 Overloading the Input Operator `>>` **in the** `Rational` **Class**

```
#include <iostream.h>

class Rational {
    friend istream& operator>>(istream&, Rational&);
    friend ostream& operator<<(ostream&, const Rational&);
public:
    Rational(int n=0, int d=1) : num(n), den(d) { }
    // other declarations go here
private:
    int num, den;
    int gcd(int, int);
    void reduce();
};

main()
{
    Rational x, y;
    cin >> x >> y;
    cout << "x = " << x << ", y = " << y << endl;
}

istream& operator>>(istream& istr, Rational& r)
{
    cout << "\t Numerator: ";  istr >> r.num;
    cout << "\tDenominator: ";  istr >> r.den;
    r.reduce();
    return istr;
}
```

```
        Numerator: -10
      Denominator: -24
        Numerator: 36
      Denominator: -20
x = 5/12, y = -9/5
```

This version of the input operator includes user prompts to facilitate input. It also includes a call to the utility function `reduce()`. Note that, as a `friend`, the operator can access this private function.

9.8 CONVERSION OPERATORS

In our original implementation of the `Rational` class (Example 8.1) we defined the member function `convert()` to convert from type `Rational` to type `double`:

```
double convert() { return double(num)/den; }
```

This requires the member function to be called as

```
x.convert();
```

In keeping with our goal to make objects of the `Rational` class behave like objects of fundamental types (*i.e.*, like ordinary variables), we would like to have a conversion function that could be called with a syntax that conforms to ordinary type conversions:

```
n = int(t);
y = double(x);
```

This can be done with a conversion operator.

Our `Rational` class already has the facility to convert an object from `int` to `Rational`:

```
Rational x(22);
```

This is handled by the default constructor, which assigns 22 to `x.num` and 1 to `x.den`. This constructor also handles direct type conversions from type `int` to type `Rational`:

```
x = Rational(22);
```

Constructors of a given class are used to convert from another type to that class type.

To convert from the given class type to another type requires a different kind of member function. It is called a *conversion operator*, and it has a different syntax. If `type` is the type to which the object is to be converted, then the conversion operator is declared as

```
operator type();
```

For example, a member function of the `Rational` class that returns an equivalent `float` would be declared as

```
operator float();
```

Or, if we want it to convert to type `double`, then we would declare it as

```
operator double();
```

And, if we want it to be usable for constant `Rational`s (like `pi`), then we would declare it as

```
operator double() const;
```

Recall that, in our original implementation of the `Rational` class (Example 8.1) we defined the member function `convert()` for this purpose.

EXAMPLE 9.10   Adding a Conversion Operator to the `Rational` Class

```
#include <iostream.h>

class Rational {
    friend istream& operator>>(istream&, Rational&);
    friend ostream& operator<<(ostream&, const Rational&);
public:
    Rational(int n=0, int d=1) : num(n), den(d) { }
    operator double() const;
    // other declarations go here
private:
    int num, den;
    // other declarations go here
};

main()
{
    Rational x(-5,8);
    cout << "x = " << x << ", double(x) = " << double(x) << endl;
    const Rational p(22,7);
    const double pi = double(p);
    cout << "p = " << p << ", pi = " << pi << endl;
}
```

```
Rational::operator double() const
{
    return double(num)/den;
}
```

```
x = -5/8, double(x) = -0.625
p = 22/7, pi = 3.14286
```

First we use the conversion operator `double()` to convert the `Rational` object `x` into the double -0.625. Then we use it again to convert the constant `Rational` object `p` into the constant double pi.

9.9 OVERLOADING THE INCREMENT AND DECREMENT OPERATORS

The increment operator `++` and the decrement operator `--` each have two forms: prefix and postfix. Each of these four forms can be overloaded. We'll examine the overloading of the increment operator here. Overloading the decrement operator works the same way.

When applied to integer types, the pre-increment operator simply adds 1 to the value of the object being incremented. This is a unary operator: its single argument is the object being incremented. The syntax for overloading it for a class named `T` is simply

```
T operator++();
```

So for our `Rational` class, it is declared as

```
Rational operator++();
```

EXAMPLE 9.11 Adding a Pre-Increment Operator to the `Rational` Class

This example adds an overloaded pre-increment operator `++` to our `Rational` class. Although we can make this function do whatever we want, it should be consistent with the action that the standard pre-increment operator performs on integer types. That adds 1 to the current value of the object before that value is used in the expression. This is equivalent to adding its denominator to its numerator:

$$\frac{22}{7} + 1 = \frac{22+7}{7} = \frac{29}{7}$$

So, we simply add `den` to `num` and then return `*this`, which is the object itself:

```
class Rational {
    friend ostream& operator<<(ostream&, const Rational&);
public:
    Rational(int n=0, int d=1) : num(n), den(d) { }
    Rational operator++();
    // other declarations go here
private:
    int num, den;
    // other declarations go here
};
```

```
main()
{
    Rational x(22,7), y = ++x;
    cout << "y = " << y << ", x = " << x << endl;
}


Rational Rational::operator++()
{
    num += den;
    return *this;
}
```

```
y = 29/7, x = 29/7
```

Postfix operators have the same function name as the prefix operators. For example, both the pre-increment operator and the post-increment operator are named `operator++`. To distinguish them, C++ specifies that the prefix operator has one argument and the postfix operator has two arguments. (When used, they both appear to have one argument.) So the correct syntax for the prototype for an overloaded post-increment operator is

```
T operator++(int);
```

The required argument must have type `int`. This appears a bit strange because no integer is passed to the function when it is invoked. The integer argument is thus a *dummy argument*, required only so that the postfix operator can be distinguished from the corresponding prefix operator.

EXAMPLE 9.12 Adding a Post-Increment Operator to the `Rational` Class

To be consistent with the ordinary post-increment operator for integer types, this overloaded version should not change the value of `x` until after it has been assigned to `y`. To do that, we need a temporary object to hold the contents of the object that owns the call. This is done by assigning `*this` to `temp`. Then this object can be returned after adding `den` to `num`.

```
class Rational {
    friend ostream& operator<<(ostream&, const Rational&);
public:
    Rational(int n=0, int d=1) : num(n), den(d) { }
    Rational operator++();          // pre-increment
    Rational operator++(int);       // post-increment
    // other declarations go here
private:
    int num, den;
    // other declarations go here
};


main()
{
    Rational x(22,7), y = x++;
    cout << "y = " << y << ", x = " << x << endl;
}
```

```
Rational Rational::operator++(int)
{
    Rational temp = *this;
    num += den;
    return temp;
}
```

```
y = 22/7, x = 29/7
```

Note that the dummy argument in the `operator++` function is an unnamed `int`. It need not be named because it is not used. But it must be declared to distinguish the post-increment from the pre-increment operator.

9.10 OVERLOADING THE SUBSCRIPT OPERATOR

Recall that, if `a` is an array, then the expression `a[i]` really means nothing more than `*(a+i)`. This is because `a` is actually the address of the initial element in the array, so `a+i` is the address of the ith element, since the number of bytes added to `a` is `i` times the size of each array element.

The symbol `[]` denotes the *subscript operator*. Its name derives from the original use of arrays, where `a[i]` represented the mathematical symbol a_i. When used as `a[i]`, it has two operands: `a` and `i`. The expression `a[i]` is equivalent to `operator[](a, i)`. And as an operator, `[]` can be overloaded.

EXAMPLE 9.13   Adding a Subscript Operator to the `Rational` Class

```
#include <iostream.h>
#include <stdlib.h>      // defines the exit() function

class Rational {
    friend ostream& operator<<(ostream&, const Rational&);
public:
    Rational(int n=0, int d=1) : num(n), den(d) { }
    int& operator[](int);
    // other declarations go here
private:
    int num, den;
    // other declarations go here
};

main()
{
    Rational x(22,7);
    cout << "x = " << x << endl;
    cout << "x[1] = " << x[1] << ", x[2] = " << x[2] << endl;
}
```

```
int& Rational::operator[](int i)
{
    if (i == 1) return num;
    if (i == 2) return den;
    cerr << "ERROR: index out of range\n";
    exit(0);
}
```

```
x = 22/7
x[1] = 22, x[2] = 7
```

The expression `x[1]` calls the subscript operator, passing 1 to i, which returns `x.num`. Similarly, `x[2]` returns `x.den`. If `i` has any value other than 1 or 2, then an error message is sent to `cerr`, the standard error stream, and then the `exit()` function is called.

This example is artificial. There is no advantage to accessing the fields of the `Rational` object `x` with `x[1]` and `x[2]` instead of `x.num` and `x.den`. However, there are many important classes where the subscript is very useful. (See Problem 9.14.)

Note that the subscript operator is an access function, since it provides `public` access to `private` member data.

Review Questions

9.1 How is the `operator` keyword used?

9.2 What does `*this` always refer to?

9.3 Why can't the `this` pointer be used in nonmember functions?

9.4 Why should the overloaded assignment operator return `*this`?

9.5 What is the difference between the effects of the following two declarations:
```
Rational y(x);
Rational y = x;
```

9.6 What is the difference between the effects of the following two lines:
```
Rational y = x;
Rational y;  y = x;
```

9.7 Why can't `**` be overloaded as an exponentiation operator?

9.8 Why should the stream operators `<<` and `>>` be overloaded as `friend` functions?

9.9 Why should the arithmetic operators `+`, `-`, `*`, and `/` be overloaded as `friend` functions?

9.10 How is the overloaded pre-increment operator distinguished from the overloaded post-increment operator?

9.11 Why is the `int` argument in the implementation of the post-increment operator left unnamed?

9.12 What mechanism allows the overloaded subscript operator `[]` to be used on the left side of an assignment statement, like this: `v[2] = 22`?

Solved Programming Problems

9.13 Implement the binary subtraction operator, the unary negation operator, and the less-than operator `<` for the `Rational` class (see Example 9.1).

All three of these operators are implemented as `friend` functions to give them access to the `num` and `den` data members of their owner objects:

```
class Rational {
    friend Rational operator-(const Rational&, const Rational&);
    friend Rational operator-(const Rational&);
    friend int operator<(const Rational&, const Rational&);
public:
    Rational(int =0, int =1);
    Rational(const Rational&);
    Rational& operator=(const Rational&);
    // other declarations go here
private:
    int num, den;
    int gcd(int, int)
    int reduce();
};
```

The binary subtraction operator simply constructs and returns a `Rational` object `z` that represents the difference `x - y`:

```
Rational Rational::operator-(const Rational& x, const Rational& y)
{
    Rational z(x.num*y.den - y.num*x.den, x.den*y.den);
    z.reduce();
    return z;
}
```

Algebraically, the subtraction *a/b - c/d* is performed using the common denominator *bd*:

$$\frac{a}{b} - \frac{c}{d} = \frac{ad - bc}{bd}$$

So the numerator of `x - y` should be `x.num*y.den - y.num*x.den` and the denominator should be `x.den*y.den`. The function constructs the `Rational` object `z` with that numerator and denominator.

This algebraic formula can produce a fraction that is not in reduced form, even if x and y are. For example, $1/2 - 1/6 = (1{\cdot}6 - 2{\cdot}1)/(2{\cdot}6) = 4/12$. So we call the `reduce()` utility function before returning the resulting object `z`.

The unary negation operator overloads the symbol "–". It is distinguished from the binary subtraction operator by its parameter list; it has only one parameter:

```
Rational Rational::operator-(const Rational& x)
{
    Rational y(-x.num, x.den);
    return y;
}
```

To negate a fraction *a/b* we simply negate its numerator: *(-a)/b*. So the newly constructed `Rational` object `y` has the same denominator as `x` but its numerator is `-x.num`.

The less-than operator is easier to do if we first modify our default constructor to ensure that every object's `den` value is positive. Then we can use the standard equivalence for the less-than operator:

$$\frac{a}{b} < \frac{c}{d} \Leftrightarrow ad < bc$$

```cpp
int operator<(const Rational& x, const Rational& y)
{
    return (x.num*y.den < y.num*x.den);
}

Rational::Rational(int n=0, int d=1) : num(n), den(d)
{
    if (d == 0) n = 0;
    else if (d < 0) { n *= -1; d *= -1; }
    reduce();
}
```

The modification ensuring that `den > 0` could instead be done in the `reduce()` function, since that utility should be called by every member function that allows `den` to be changed. However, none of our other member functions allows the sign of `den` to change, so by requiring it to be positive when the object is constructed we don't need to check the condition again.

9.14 Implement a `Vector` class, with a default constructor, a copy constructor, a destructor, and overloaded assignment operator, subscript operator, equality operator, stream insertion operator, and stream extraction operator.

Here is the class declaration:

```cpp
#include <iostream.h>

class Vector {
    friend int operator==(const Vector&, const Vector&);
    friend ostream& operator<<(ostream&, const Vector&);
    friend istream& operator>>(istream&, Vector&);
public:
    Vector(int =1, double =0.0);              // default constructor
    Vector(const Vector&);                    // copy constructor
    ~Vector();                                // destructor
    const Vector& operator=(const Vector&);   // assignment operator
    double& operator[](int) const;            // subscript operator
private:
    int size;
    double* data;
};
```

Here is the implementation of the overloaded equality operator:

```cpp
int operator==(const Vector& v, const Vector& w)
{
    if (v.size != w.size) return 0;
    for (int i = 0; i < v.size; i++)
        if (v.data[i] != w.data[i]) return 0;
    return 1;
}
```

It is a nonmember function which returns 1 or 0 according to whether the two vectors v and w are equal. If their sizes are not equal, then it returns 0 immediately. Otherwise it checks the corresponding elements of the two vectors, one at a time. If there is any mismatch, then again it returns 0 immediately. Only if the entire loop finishes without finding any mismatches can we conclude that the two vectors are equal and return 1.

Here is the implementation of the overloaded stream extraction operator:

```
ostream& operator<<(ostream& ostr, const Vector& v)
{
    ostr << '(';
    for (int i = 0; i < v.size-1; i++) {
        ostr << v[i] << ", ";
        if ((i+1)%8 == 0) cout << "\n ";
    }
    return ostr << v[i] << ")\n";
}
```

This prints the vector like this: (1.11111, 2.22222, 3.33333, 4.44444, 5.55556). The conditional inside the loop allows the output to "wrap" around several lines neatly if the vector has more than 8 elements.

The output is sent to ostr which is just a local name for the output stream that is passed to the function. That would be cout if the function is called like this: cout << v;.

In the last line of the function, the expression ostr << v[i] << ")\n" makes two calls to the (standard) stream extraction operator. Those two calls return ostr as the value of this expression, and so that object ostr is then returned by this function.

Here is the overloaded stream insertion operator:

```
istream& operator>>(istream& istr, Vector& v)
{
    for (int i = 0; i < v.size; i++) {
        cout << i << ": ";
        istr >> v[i];
    }
    return istr;
}
```

This implementation prompts the user for each element of the vector v. It could also be implemented without user prompts, simply reading the elements one at a time.

Notice that the elements are read from the input stream istr, which is the first parameter passed in to the function. When the function is called like this: cin >> v; the standard input stream cin will be passed to the parameter istr, so the vector elements are actually read from cin. The argument istr is simply a local name for the actual input stream which probably will be cin. Notice that this argument is also returned, allowing a cascade of calls like this: cin >> u >> v >> w;.

Here is the implementation of the default constructor:

```
Vector::Vector(int sz=1, double t=0.0) : size(sz)
{
    data = new double[size];
    for (int i = 0; i < size; i++)
        data[i] = t;
}
```

The declaration `Vector u;` would construct the vector `u` having 1 element with the value 0.0; the declaration `Vector v(4);` would construct the vector `v` with 4 elements all with the value 0.0; and the declaration `Vector w(8, 3.14159);` would construct the vector `w` with 8 elements all with the value 3.14159.

This constructor uses the initialization list `size(sz)` to assign the argument `sz` to the data member `size`. Then it uses the `new` operator to allocate that number of elements to the array `data`. Finally, it initializes each element with the value `t`.

The copy constructor is almost the same as the default constructor:

```
Vector::Vector(const Vector& v) : size(v.size)
{
    data = new double[v.size];
    for (int i = 0; i < size; i++)
        data[i] = v.data[i];
}
```

It uses the data members of the vector argument `v` to initialize the object being constructed. So it assigns `v.size` to the new object's `size` member, and it assigns `v.data[i]` to the elements of the new object's `data` member.

The destructor simply restores the storage allocated to the `data` array and then sets `data` to `NULL` and `size` to 0:

```
Vector::~Vector()
{
    delete [] data;
    data = NULL;
    size = 0;
}
```

The overloaded assignment operator creates a new object that duplicates the vector `v`:

```
const Vector& Vector::operator=(const Vector& v)
{
    if (&v != this) {
        delete [] data;
        size = v.size;
        data = new double[v.size];
        for (int i = 0; i < size; i++)
            data[i] = v.data[i];
    }
    return *this;
}
```

The condition `(&v != this)` determines whether the object that owns the call is different from the vector `v`. If the address of `v` is the same as `this` (which is the address of the current object), then they are the same object and nothing needs to be done. This check is a safety precaution to guard against the possibility that an object might, directly or indirectly, be assigned to itself, like this: `w = v = w;`.

Before creating a new object, the function restores the allocated data array. Then it copies the vector `v` the same way that the copy constructor did.

The overloaded subscript operator simply returns the `ith` component of the object's `data` array:

```
double& Vector::operator[](int i) const
{
    return data[i];
}
```

Supplementary Programming Problems

9.15 Implement the addition and division operators for the `Rational` class (see Example 9.1).

9.16 Implement the operators `+=`, `-=`, and `/=` for the `Rational` class (see Example 9.1).

9.17 Implement the other five relational operators (`<`, `>`, `<=`, `>=`, and `!=`) for the `Rational` class (see Example 9.1).

9.18 Rewrite the overloaded input operator for the `Rational` class (Example 9.9) so that, instead of prompting for the numerator and denominator, it reads a fraction type as "`22/7`".

9.19 Implement a conversion operator in the `Rational` class to convert to `float` type.

9.20 Implement a conversion operator in the `Rational` class to <u>round</u> to `int` type.

9.21 Implement pre-decrement and post-decrement operator in the `Rational` class.

9.22 Implement an exponentiation operator for the `Rational` class with prototype:

```
Rational operator&&(const Rational&, const unsigned&);
```

For example, if `x` represents the fraction 2/5, then `x&&4` would return the `Rational` that represents the fraction 16/625.

9.23 Implement an exponentiation operator for the `Rational` class with prototype:

```
Rational operator&&(const Rational&, const int&);
```

For example, if `x` represents the fraction 2/5, then `x&&-4` would return the `Rational` that represents the fraction 625/16. (See Problem 9.22.)

9.24 Implement addition for the `Vector` class (Problem 9.14) by overloading the `+` operator.

9.25 Implement subtraction for the `Vector` class (Problem 9.14) by overloading the `-` operator.

9.26 Implement scalar multiplication for the `Vector` class (Problem 9.14) by overloading the `*` operator. If `t` is a double and `v` is a vector, then `t*v` would return the `Vector` obtained by multiplying each element of `v` by `t`.

9.27 Implement an inner product (*i.e.*, the "dot product") for the `Vector` class (Problem 9.14) by overloading the `*` operator. If `v` and `w` are vectors, then `v*w` would return the `double` obtained by summing the products of the corresponding elements of `v` and `w`:

$$ v \bullet w = \sum_{i=0}^{n-1} v_i w_i = v_0 w_0 + v_1 w_1 + \cdots + v_{n-1} w_{n-1} $$

9.28 Implement a norm function for the `Vector` class (Problem 9.14). If `v` is a vector, then `v.norm()` would return the square root of `v*v` (see Problem 9.27).

9.29 Modify the `Vector` class (Problem 9.14) so that its objects are all three-dimensional (physical) vectors with subscripts ranging from 1 to 3. Include vector addition (Problem 9.24), vector subtraction (Problem 9.25), scalar multiplication (Problem 9.26), the inner product (Problem 9.27), the norm function (Problem 9.28), and a cross-product function:

$$v \times w = (v_2 w_3 - v_3 w_2, v_3 w_1 - v_1 w_3, v_1 w_2 - v_2 w_1)$$

9.30 Implement an overloaded assignment operator `=` for the `Time` class (see Problem 8.19).

9.31 Implement overloaded stream insertion operator `<<` and stream extraction operator `>>` for the `Time` class (see Problem 8.19).

9.32 Implement overloaded pre-increment operator `++` and pre-decrement operator `--` for the `Time` class (see Problem 8.19), where "increment" means to add one second.

9.33 Implement an overloaded operator `+=` for the `Time` class (see Problem 8.19) that adds one time to another.

9.34 Implement an overloaded assignment operator `=` for the `Point` class (see Problem 8.17).

9.35 Implement overloaded stream insertion operator `<<` and stream extraction operator `>>` for the `Point` class (see Problem 8.17).

9.36 Implement overloaded comparison operators `==` and `!=` for the `Point` class (see Problem 8.17).

9.37 Implement overloaded addition operator `+` and subtraction operator `-` for the `Point` class (see Problem 8.17).

9.38 Implement an overloaded multiplication operator `*` to return the dot product of two `Point` objects (see Problem 8.55).

9.39 Implement an overloaded bitwise AND operator `&` to return the cross product of two `Point` objects (see Problem 8.55).

9.40 Implement a conversion operator that converts a `Point` object (see Problem 8.17) into a `Vector` object (see Problem 9.14).

9.41 Implement a conversion operator that converts a `Vector` object (see Problem 9.14) into a `Point` object (see Problem 8.17).

9.42 Implement an overloaded assignment operator `=` for the `Person` class (see Problem 8.21).

9.43 Implement overloaded stream insertion operator `<<` and stream extraction operator `>>` for the `Person` class (see Problem 8.21).

9.44 Implement overloaded comparison operators `==` and `!=` for the `Person` class (see Problem 8.21).

9.45 Implement an overloaded assignment operator `=` for the `Matrix` class (see Problem 8.23).

9.46 Implement overloaded stream insertion operator `<<` and stream extraction operator `>>` for the `Matrix` class (see Problem 8.23).

9.47 Implement overloaded comparison operators `==` and `!=` for the `Matrix` class (see Problem 8.23).

9.48 Implement overloaded addition operator `+` and subtraction operator `-` for the `Matrix` class (see Problem 8.23).

9.49 Implement a conversion operator that converts a `Matrix` object (see Problem 8.23) into a `Vector` object (see Problem 9.14).

9.50 Implement a conversion operator that converts a `Vector` object (see Problem 9.14) into a `Matrix` object (see Problem 8.23).

9.51 Implement an overloaded assignment operator `=` for the `Date` class (see Problem 8.38).

9.52 Implement overloaded stream insertion operator `<<` and stream extraction operator `>>` for the `Date` class (see Problem 8.38).

9.53 Implement overloaded pre-increment operator `++` and pre-decrement operator `--` for the `Date` class (see Problem 8.38), where "increment" means to add one day.

9.54 Implement an overloaded operator `+=` for the `Date` class (see Problem 8.38) that adds one date to another.

9.55 Implement overloaded stream insertion operator `<<` and stream extraction operator `>>` for the `Address` class (see Problem 8.45). Include user prompts for the input.

9.56 Implement overloaded stream insertion operator `<<` and stream extraction operator `>>` for the `Computer` class (see Problem 8.48). Include user prompts for the input.

9.57 Implement an overloaded assignment operator `=` for the `Complex` class (see Problem 8.53).

9.58 Implement overloaded stream insertion operator `<<` and stream extraction operator `>>` for the `Complex` class (see Problem 8.53).

9.59 Implement overloaded comparison operators `==` and `!=` for the `Complex` class (see Problem 8.53).

9.60 Implement overloaded addition operator `+` and subtraction operator `-` for the `Complex` class (see Problem 8.54).

9.61 Implement overloaded multiplication operator `*` and division operator `/` for the `Complex` class (see Problem 8.54).

9.62 Overload the NOT operator `!` to return the norm for the `Complex` class (see Problem 8.53). The *norm* of a complex number is the square root of the sum of the squares of its real and imaginary parts. So if `z` represents the complex number 3 - 4**i**, then `!z` would return 5. Note that this is a unary operator.

9.63 Overload the bitwise NOT operator `~` to return the conjugate for the `Complex` class (see Problem 8.53). The *conjugate* of a complex number is the same complex number except with the sign of its imaginary part reversed. So if `z` represents the complex number 3 - 4**i**, then `~z` would return the `Complex` object that represents 3 + 4**i**. Note that this is a unary operator.

9.64 Implement a conversion operator that converts a `Point` object (see Problem 8.17) into a `Complex` object (see Problem 8.59).

9.65 Implement a conversion operator that converts a `Complex` object (see Problem 8.53) into a `Point` object (see Problem 8.17).

9.66 Implement the overloaded division operator `/` for the `Complex` class (see Problem 8.54) using the norm operator `!` (see Problem 9.62) and the conjugate operator `~` (see Problem 9.62). The quotient of two complex numbers is computed by the formula

$$\frac{u}{v} = \frac{u \cdot \bar{v}}{|v|}$$

where $\bar{v}$ is the conjugate of v and $|v|$ is the norm of v.

9.67 Implement an overloaded assignment operator `=` for the `Quaternion` class (see Problem 8.59).

9.68 Implement overloaded stream insertion operator `<<` and stream extraction operator `>>` for the `Quaternion` class (see Problem 8.59).

9.69 Implement overloaded comparison operators `==` and `!=` for the `Quaternion` class (see Problem 8.59).

9.70 Implement overloaded addition operator `+` and subtraction operator `-` for the `Quaternion` class (see Problem 8.59).

9.71 Overload the NOT operator `!` to return the norm for the `Quaternion` class (see Problem 8.59). The *norm* of a quaternion is the square root of the sum of the squares of its real and imaginary parts. So if `z` represents the quaternion 3 - 4**i** +12**k**, then `!z` would return 13. Note that this is a unary operator.

9.72 Overload the bitwise NOT operator `~` to return the conjugate for the `Quaternion` class (see Problem 8.59). The *conjugate* of a quaternion is the same quaternion except with the sign of its imaginary parts reversed. So if `z` represents the complex number 3 - 4**i** +12**k**, then `~z` would return the `Quaternion` object that represents 3 + 4**i** -12**k**. Note that this is a unary operator.

9.73 Implement the overloaded division operator `/` for the `Quaternion` class (see Problem 8.59) using the norm operator `!` (see Problem 9.62) and the conjugate operator `~` (see Problem 9.72). The quotient of two quaternions is computed by the formula

$$\frac{u}{v} = \frac{u \cdot \bar{v}}{|v|}$$

where $\bar{v}$ is the conjugate of v and $|v|$ is the norm of v.

9.74 Implement a conversion operator that converts a `Point` object (see Problem 8.17) into a `Quaternion` object (see Problem 8.59).

9.75 Implement a conversion operator that converts a `Quaternion` object (see Problem 8.59) into a `Point` object (see Problem 8.17).

9.76 Implement a conversion operator that converts a `Complex` object (see Problem 8.53) into a `Quaternion` object (see Problem 8.59).

9.77 Implement a constructor that converts a `Complex` object (see Problem 8.53) into a `Quaternion` object (see Problem 8.59).

Answers to Review Questions

9.1 The `operator` keyword is used to form the name of a function that overloads an operator. For example, the name of the function that overloads the assignment operator `=` is "`operator=`".

9.2 The keyword `this` is a pointer to the object that owns the call of the member function in which the expression appears.

9.3 The expression `*this` always refers to the object that owns the call of the member function in which the expression appears. Therefore, it can only be used within member function.

9.4 The overloaded assignment operator should return `*this` so that the operator can be used in a cascade of calls, like this: `w = x = y = z;`

9.5 The declaration `Rational y(x);` calls the default constructor; the declaration `Rational y = x` calls the copy constructor.

9.6 The declaration `Rational y = x;` calls the copy constructor. The code `Rational y; y = x;` calls the default constructor and then the assignment operator.

9.7 The symbol `**` cannot be overloaded as an operator because it is not a C++ operator.

9.8 The stream operators `<<` and `>>` should be overloaded as `friend` functions because their left operands should be stream objects. If an overloaded operator is a member function, then its left operand is `*this`, which is an object of the class to which the function is a member.

9.9 The arithmetic operators `+`, `-`, `*`, and `/` should be overloaded as `friend` functions so that their left operands can be declared as `const`. This allows, for example, the use of an expression like `22 + x`. If an overloaded operator is a member function, then its left operand is `*this`, which is not `const`.

9.10 The overloaded pre-increment operator has no arguments. The overloaded post-increment operator has one (dummy) argument, of type `int`.

9.11 The `int` argument in the implementation of the post-increment operator is left unnamed because it is not used. It is a dummy argument.

9.12 By returning a reference, the overloaded subscript operator `[]` can be used on the left side of an assignment statement, like this: `v[2] = 22`. This is because, as a reference, `v[2]` is an lvalue.

Chapter 10

A `String` Class

10.1 INTRODUCTION

Chapter 7 described the way that character strings are handled using C-style programming: each string is implemented as a pointer `p` to a `char` in memory. The actual string of characters that `p` represents are held in a contiguous block beginning with byte `*p` and terminated with the `NUL` character `'\0'`. To distinguish this representation from that which will be defined in this chapter, we will refer to the former as "C-strings."

Chapter 7 also described the `string.h` header file. It defines many functions that operate on C-strings. The `String` class defined in this chapter will include functions that perform equivalent operations on `String` objects. Indeed, many of these new operations will be implemented using functions from the `string.h` header file.

The character string abstract data type is an ideal candidate for implementation as a C++ class, encapsulating the data and functionality in individualized objects. This chapter shows one way to do that. Such an implementation allows us to use strings as objects of a `String` class.

10.2 THE `String` CLASS INTERFACE

There are generally two methods for delimiting an un-indexed sequence of objects. One method is to use a trailer or terminating object to signal the end of the sequence. C-strings are implemented this way, using the `NUL` character `'\0'` as the trailer. It is also the method by which the DOS and UNIX operating systems store records in a file, using the end-of-line character `'\n'` as the trailer. The other method is to store the length of the sequence with the sequence. This is how the VAX/VMS operating system stores records in a file. It is also how we will implement our `String` class:

```
unsigned len;    // the number of (non-NUL) characters stored
char* buf;       // the actual character string
```

Here, `len` will be the length of the sequence of characters and `buf` will be the "buffer" that holds them. Actually, `buf` is a C-string, so it really is just a pointer to a byte in memory.

For example, suppose that `name` and `state` are `String` objects representing the C-strings `"T. Jefferson"` and `"Virginia"`. Then we can visualize them like this:

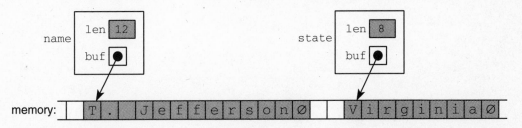

This implementation will improve the efficiency of some string operations. For example, to determine that `"ABCDEFGHIJKLMNOPQRSTUVWXY"` and `"ABCDEFGHIJKLMNOPQRSTUVWXYZ"` are not equal requires examining all 51 characters. But since we are storing the strings' lengths in our `String` class, the comparison operator need only compare the integers 25 and 26 to determine that these two strings are not equal.

Here is the class interface for a `String` class:

```
#include <iostream.h>

class String {
    friend int operator==(const String&, const String&);
    friend int operator!=(const String&, const String&);
    friend int operator<(const String&, const String&);
    friend int operator<=(const String&, const String&);
    friend int operator>(const String&, const String&);
    friend int operator>=(const String&, const String&);
    friend ostream& operator<<(ostream&, const String&);
    friend istream& operator>>(istream&, String&);
    friend String operator+(const String&, const String&);
public:
    String(unsigned =0);                        // default constructor
    String(char, unsigned);             // constructor
    String(const char*);                // constructor
    String(const String&);              // copy constructor
    ~String();                          // destructor
    String& operator=(const String&);   // assignment operator
    String& operator+=(const String&);  // append operator
    operator char*() const;             // conversion operator
    char& operator[](unsigned) const;   // subscript operator
    unsigned length() const;            // access function
private:
    unsigned len;    // the number of (non-NUL) characters stored
    char* buf;       // the actual character string
};
```

Note that this interface is very similar to that of the `Vector` class (Problem 9.14).

10.3 THE CONSTRUCTORS AND DESTRUCTOR

Here is the implementation of the default constructor:

```
String::String(unsigned n) : len(n)
{
    buf = new char[len+1];
    for (int i = 0; i < len; i++ )
        buf[i] = ' ';
    buf[len] = '\0';
}
```

It constructs a `String` object containing `n` blanks. If no parameter is passed, then `n` takes the default value 0 and the empty string is constructed.

EXAMPLE 10.1 Testing the Default Constructor

This test driver invokes the default constructor twice: once with no parameter and once passing 4:

```
#include "String.h"

main()
{
    String s1;
    cout << "s1 = [" << s1 << "], length = " << s1.length() << endl;
    String s2(4);
    cout << "s2 = [" << s2 << "], length = " << s2.length() << endl;
}
```
```
s1 = [], length = 0
s2 = [    ], length = 4
```

The first object constructed, `s1`, is the empty string. The second object, `s2`, is a string of 4 blanks.

The second constructor creates a string of identical characters:

```
String::String(char c, unsigned n) : len(n)
{
    buf = new char[len+1];
    for (int i = 0; i < len; i++ )
        buf[i] = c;
    buf[len] = '\0';
}
```

First it uses an initialization list to assign `n` to the object's length field `len`. Then it uses the `new` operator to allocate $n+1$ characters to the object's buffer array `buf`. The `for` loop assigns the same character `c` to each of the first n elements of the `buf` array. As always, the NUL character `'\0'` is assigned to the last element of the object's buffer.

EXAMPLE 10.2 Testing the Second Constructor

This test driver invokes the constructor twice: once with one parameter and once with two:

```
#include "String.h"

main()
{
    String s1('B',1);
    cout << "s1 = [" << s1 << "], length = " << s1.length() << endl;
    String s2('B',4);
    cout << "s2 = [" << s2 << "], length = " << s2.length() << endl;
}
```
```
s1 = [B], length = 1
s2 = [BBBB], length = 4
```

First it constructs the string `s1` containing a single character `'B'`. Then it constructs the string `s2` containing four `'B'`s.

The third constructor converts a C-string into a `String` object:

```
String::String(const char* s)
{
    len = strlen(s);
    buf = new char[len+1];
    for (int i = 0; i < len; i++ )
        buf[i] = s[i];
    buf[len] = '\0';
}
```

It uses the `strlen` defined in the `string.h` header file to set the object's length field `len` to the length of the C-string `s`. Then it does the same things that the second constructor did, except that it copies the individual characters of `s` into the object's buffer.

EXAMPLE 10.3 Testing the Third Constructor

This creates the string object `s1` that represents the C-string `"Hello, World!"`:

```
#include "String.h"

main()
{
    String s1("Hello, World!");
    cout << "s1 = [" << s1 << "], length = " << s1.length() << endl;
}
```

```
s1 = [Hello, World!], length = 13
```

The string has 13 characters, including the comma, the blank, and the exclamation point (but not counting the NUL character `'\0'`).

Here is how we might visualize the object `s1`:

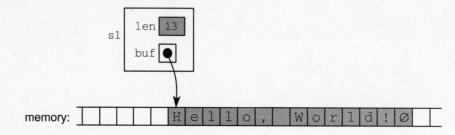

As usual, we use the symbol ∅ to represent the NUL character.

The destructor for our `String` class is typical:

```
String::~String()
{
    delete [] buf;
}
```

It simply uses the `delete` operator to restore the memory that was allocated to the object. Note that the subscript operator `[]` must be specified because `buf` is an array.

10.4 THE COPY CONSTRUCTOR

In many class definitions, instead of defining a copy constructor explicitly, the one that is automatically provided by the compiler can be used. It simply does a direct copy of each corresponding data member. This, however, will not work properly for our String class. The problem is that a direct memory copy would duplicate the buf pointer but not the string to which it points. This would result in having two different objects with the same member data. Consequently, we need to define our own copy constructor:

```
String::String(const String& s) : len(s.len)
{
    buf = new char[len+1];
    for (int i = 0; i < s.len; i++ )
        buf[i] = s.buf[i];
    buf[len] = '\0';
}
```

This works the same way as the third constructor, except that the string s that it duplicates is an existing String object instead of a C-string. Also, we can use an initialization list to assign s.len to the new object's len field. That was not possible in the third constructor because we had to invoke a function (strlen()) to obtain the length of s.

EXAMPLE 10.4 Testing the Copy Constructor

This test driver invokes the copy constructor twice: once when it initializes the object creator, and once when it initializes the object inventor:

```
#include "String.h"

main()
{
    String name("Bjarne Stroustrup");
    cout << "name = [" << name << "]\n";
    String creator = name;                  // calls the copy constructor
    cout << "creator = [" << creator << "]\n";
    String inventor = "Charles Babbage";    // calls two constructors
    cout << "inventor = [" << inventor << "]\n";
}
```

```
name = [Bjarne Stroustrup]
creator = [Bjarne Stroustrup]
inventor = [Charles Babbage]
```

First it uses the third constructor to construct the String object name which duplicates the constant C-string "Bjarne Stroustrup". Then it uses the copy constructor to create the String object creator which duplicates the String object name by being initialized by it.

The last declaration uses both constructors to construct the String object inventor. First it uses the third constructor to create a temporary String object that duplicates the constant C-string "Charles Babbage". Then it uses the copy constructor to create the String object inventor to duplicate the temporary object.

10.5 THE ASSIGNMENT OPERATOR

The assignment operator is used whenever one object is assigned to another object that has already been declared of the same class. Like the copy constructor, the assignment operator is automatically provided by the compiler if we don't write our own version. But it is unwise to rely upon the automatically generated assignment operator for classes whose objects contain pointers, because duplicating pointers does not duplicate the data to which they point.

EXAMPLE 10.5 Using the Assignment Operator Generated by the Compiler

This example shows what can go wrong when you rely upon the automatically generated assignment operator for the String class:

```
#include "String.h"

main()
{
    String myCar = "Infiniti G20";
    String yourCar = "Lexus ES300";
    cout << "\t  myCar = [" << myCar << "]\n";
    cout << "\tyourCar = [" << yourCar << "]\n";
    myCar = yourCar;                          // memberwise assignment
    cout << "After: myCar = yourCar\n";
    cout << "\t  myCar = [" << myCar << "]\n";
    cout << "\tyourCar = [" << yourCar << "]\n";
    yourCar[6] = 'L';
    cout << "After: yourCar[6] = 'L'\n";
    cout << "\t  myCar = [" << myCar << "]\n";
    cout << "\tyourCar = [" << yourCar << "]\n";
}
```

```
          myCar = [Infiniti G20]
        yourCar = [Lexus ES300]
After: myCar = yourCar
          myCar = [Lexus ES300]
        yourCar = [Lexus ES300]
After: yourCar[6] = 'L'
          myCar = [Lexus LS300]
        yourCar = [Lexus LS300]
```

The assignment operator that is generated automatically by the compiler simply uses "member-wise assignment." For our String class, that means that in the fifth statement in main(), yourCar.len is assigned to myCar.len and yourCar.buf is assigned to myCar.buf. But the buf members are pointers, so the result is that both yourCar.buf and myCar.buf point to the same C-string in memory: the one that contains "Lexus ES300". So when you buy a new Lexus LS300, it becomes my car too! In other words, the assignment myCar = yourCar in this program means that I become a co-owner of your new Lexus LS300 (and that I lost my Lexus ES300).

The following diagram illustrates the problem:

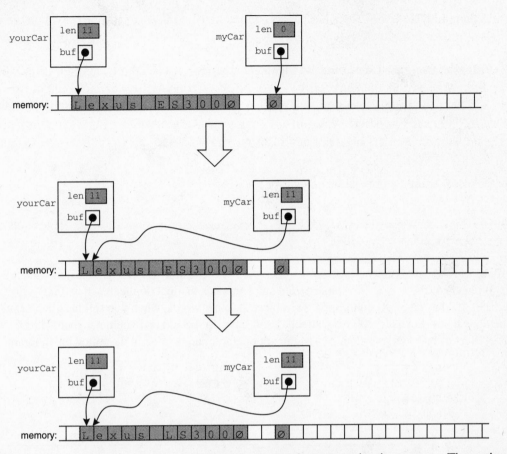

Both objects, yourCar and myCar, point to the same character string in memory. The assignment myCar = yourCar simply duplicated the integer len and the pointer buf, without duplicating the character string. So when the "E" is changed to an "L", it gets changed in both objects.

To overcome problems indicated by Example 10.5, we need to define our own assignment operator so that an assignment y = x replaces the object y with a duplicate of the object x.

Here is our own assignment operator, defined explicitly:

```
String& String::operator=(const String& s)
{
    if (&s == this) return *this;
    len = s.len;
    delete [] buf;
    buf = new char[s.len + 1];
    strcpy(buf, s.buf);
    return *this;
}
```

First it checks whether the object s is different from the object to which it is to be assigned. If they are already the same object, then nothing more needs to be done. The conditional tests whether the address of s is the same as the address (this) of the current object.

If the two objects are not the same, then we recreate the current object so that it becomes a duplicate of s. After setting len to s.len, we deallocate the memory currently assigned to buf and then allocate a new string of bytes of the correct length (s.len + 1). Then we use the strcpy() function (defined in string.h) to copy s.buf into buf and return *this.

EXAMPLE 10.6 Using the User-Defined Assignment Operator

Here is the output from the same program that we ran in Example 10.5, but which now uses our explicitly defined assignment operator:

```
          myCar = [Infiniti G20]
        yourCar = [Lexus ES300]
After: myCar = yourCar
          myCar = [Lexus ES300]
        yourCar = [Lexus ES300]
After: yourCar[6] = 'L'
          myCar = [Lexus ES300]
        yourCar = [Lexus LS300]
```

This time, when the assignment myCar = yourCar executes, it actually replaces the myCar object with a duplicate of the yourCar object. And since this is a distinct duplicate, changing yourCar[6] to the letter "L" has no effect on the myCar object. In other words, when you sell me your Lexus ES300 and then buy a new Lexus LS300 for yourself, I still have my ES300 and you have your LS300.

The effect of our own user-defined assignment operator can be seen in the following diagram:

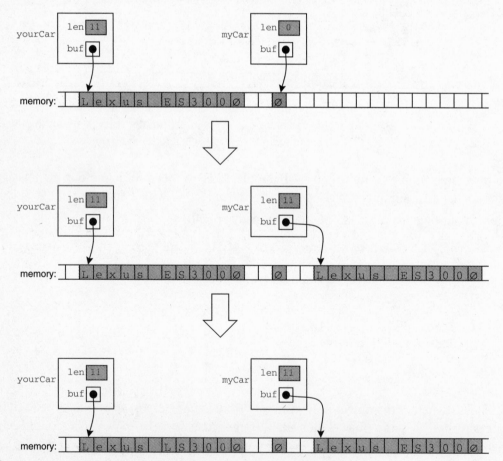

Here the new operator allocates storage for a new string in memory for the myCar object. So when the "E" is changed to an "L" in the yourCar object, it has no effect upon the myCar object.

EXAMPLE 10.7 Another Test of the Assignment Operator

```
#include "String.h"

main()
{
    String name("Babbage"), creator("Stroustrup");
    cout << "name = [" << name << "]\n";
    cout << "creator = [" << creator << "]\n";
    name = creator;                 // calls the assignment operator
    cout << "name = [" << name << "]\n";
}
```

The output looks like this:

```
name = [Babbage]
creator = [Stroustrup]
name = [Stroustrup]
```

First it uses the third constructor to construct the two String objects name and creator, representing the C-strings "Babbage" and "Stroustrup". Then it uses the assignment operator to assign the String object creator to the String object name. Notice how the length of name is adjusted.

The diagram on the next page illustrates the action of the assignment name = creator. When the function operator= is invoked, it creates the local variables this and s. The this pointer points to the object name which owns the call, and s is a reference to the object creator. The function changes this->len to 10 and resets this->buf to a newly allocated string of 11 bytes into which s.buf is copied using the strcpy() function.

10.6 THE ADDITION OPERATOR

The addition operator + is a natural choice for the concatenation function in a String class. After all, concatenation means adding two strings together to form a new string.

Here is the concatenation function for our String class:

```
String operator+(const String& s1, const String& s2)
{
    String s(s1.len + s2.len);
    strcpy(s.buf, s1.buf);
    strcat(s.buf, s2.buf);
    return s;
}
```

First it constructs a new String object s of length s1.len + s2.len. Then it uses the strcpy() and strcat() functions defined in the string.h header file to copy s1.buf to s.buf and append s2.buf to it.

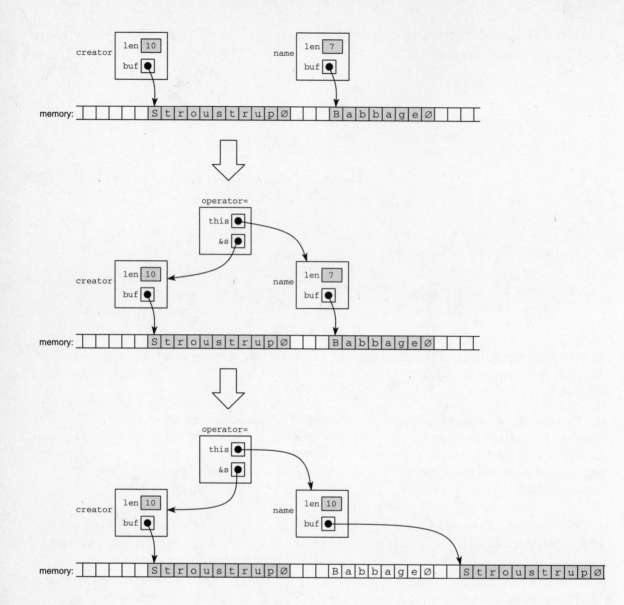

EXAMPLE 10.8 Testing the Addition Operator

```
#include "String.h"

main()
{
    String first("Bjarne"), last("Stroustrup"), blank(" ");
    cout << "first = [" << first << "], last = [" << last << "]\n";
    String name = first + " " + last;
    cout << "name = [" << name << "]\n";
}
```

```
first = [Bjarne], last = [Stroustrup]
name = [Bjarne Stroustrup]
```

In this example, we first construct the `String` objects `first` and `last`. Then we concatenate `first`, `blank`, and `last`, and assign the result to the `String` object `name`.

We can visualize the execution of this test driver like this:

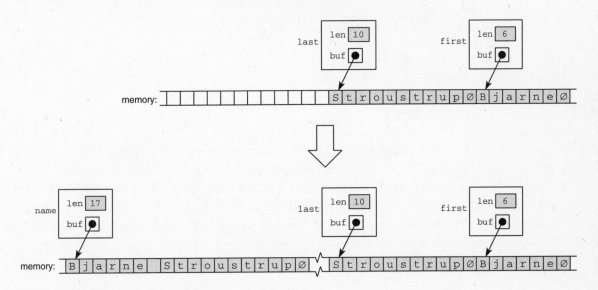

The length of the new `String` object `name` is `first.len` + `temp.len` + `last.len` = $10 + 1 + 6 = 17$, where `temp` is the temporary `String` object that represents the C-string `" "`.

10.7 AN APPEND OPERATOR

The `+=` operator is one of a series of arithmetic assignment operators that combine the arithmetic operators (`+`, `-`, `*`, *etc.*) with the assignment operator. Like most operators, the arithmetic assignment operators can be overloaded to perform whatever operations you want. However, it is unwise to define an overloaded operator to do anything that is not similar to the action of the original operator.

The `+=` operator is defined for integer types to be equivalent to the addition operator followed by the assignment operator. For example, the following two blocks have the same effect:

```
{ int n += m; }

{ int temp = m + n; int n = temp; }
```

The only difference is that the second block uses an extra `int`. In our `String` class, we overloaded the `+=` operator to preserve this meaning, so that the following two blocks will have the same effect:

```
{ String s2 += s1; }

{ String temp = s1 + s2; int s2 = temp; }
```

Here is the overloaded `+=` operator for our `String` class:

```
String& String::operator+=(const String& s)
{
    len += s.len;
    char* tempbuf = new char[len+1];
    strcpy(tempbuf, buf);
    strcat(tempbuf, s.buf);
    delete [] buf;
    buf = tempbuf;
    return *this;
}
```

First it increments its `len` field by the length of the `String` object passed to it. Then it allocates the total number of bytes needed for the new string and holds this space in the temporary C-string `tempbuf`. Then, just as it does with the addition operator (page 280), it uses the `strcpy()` and `strcat()` functions defined in the `string.h` header file to copy its `buf` to `tempbuf` and then append `s.buf` to it. Now it can release the memory allocated to its original buffer and then assign the `tempbuf` pointer to it.

EXAMPLE 10.9 Testing the `+=` Operator

This test driver invokes the `+=` operator to append the string `" (1792-1871)"` onto the `String` object `name`:

```
#include "String.h"

main()
{
    String name("Charles Babbage");
    cout << "name = [" << name << "]\n";
    name += " (1792-1871)";
    cout << "name = [" << name << "]\n";
}
```

```
name = [Charles Babbage]
name = [Charles Babbage (1792-1871)]
```

Note that the third constructor will be invoked to convert the C-string `" (1792-1871)"` into a `String` object before it is passed to the `+=` operator.

10.8 ACCESS FUNCTIONS

The operator

```
operator char*() const;
```

is a conversion operator that converts a `String` object into a C-string. It has the reverse effect of the constructor

```
String (const char*);
```

which converts a C-string into a `String` object.

This conversion operator has a very simple implementation:

```
String::operator char*() const
{
    return buf;
}
```

Its `buf` data member <u>is</u> the C-string that we want.

Note that this conversion operator is an access function: it simply provides public access to the private data member `buf`. It is not really an "inverse" of the `String (const char*)` constructor because it does not create a new C-string. As an access function, it merely provides public access to the `buf` C-string that already exists within the `String` object.

EXAMPLE 10.10 Testing the Conversion to C-String Operator

```
#include "String.h"

main()
{
    String name("John von Neumann");       // name is a String object
    cout << "name = [" << name << "]\n";
    char* s = name;                        // s is a C-string
    cout << "s = [" << s << "]\n";
}
```

```
name = [John von Neumann]
s = [John von Neumann]
```

Here is the overloaded subscript operator for our `String` class:

```
char& String::operator[](unsigned i) const
{
    return buf[i];
}
```

It simply returns the `i`th element of the object's `buf` buffer.

EXAMPLE 10.11 Testing the Subscript Operator

```
#include "String.h"

main()
{
    String name("Charles Babbage");
    cout << "name = [" << name << "]\n";
    cout << "name[8] = [" << name[8] << "]\n";
    name[8] = 'C';
    cout << "name[8] = [" << name[8] << "]\n";
    cout << "name = [" << name << "]\n";
}
```

The output looks like this:

```
name = [Charles Babbage]
name[8] = [B]
name[8] = [C]
name = [Charles Cabbage]
```

The only surprising result here is that the expression `name[8]`, which invokes the function, can be used on the left side of an assignment! This works because the expression is an *lvalue*. (See Section 6.5.)

The other access functions in our `String` class is the `length()` function:

```
unsigned String::length() const
{
    return len;
}
```

We have already tested the `length()` function. (See Example 10.1.)

10.9 THE COMPARISON OPERATORS

We have overloads for all six of the comparison operators: `==`, `!=`, `<`, `<=`, `>`, and `>=`. Fortunately, all of these are already defined for C-strings in the `string.h` header file. So their implementation for our `String` class is trivial:

```
#include <string.h>

int operator==(const String& s1, const String& s2)
{
    return (strcmp(s1.buf, s2.buf) == 0);
}

int operator!=(const String& s1, const String& s2)
{
    return (strcmp(s1.buf, s2.buf) != 0);
}

int operator<(const String& s1, const String& s2)
{
    return (strcmp(s1.buf, s2.buf) < 0);
}

int operator<=(const String& s1, const String& s2)
{
    return (strcmp(s1.buf, s2.buf) <= 0);
}
```

All six of these simply call the `strcmp()` function defined in the `string.h` header file. (See Table 7.2 on page 206.) It returns an integer whose sign indicates how the two C-strings compare: negative means that the first C-string lexicographically precedes the second; zero means that the two are equal; and positive means that the first lexicographically follows the second.

EXAMPLE 10.12 Testing the Comparison Operators

```
main()
{
    String x, y;
    cout << "Enter two strings: ";  cin >> x >> y;
    if (x == y) cout << "\t[" << x << "] == [" << y << "]\n";
    if (x != y) cout << "\t[" << x << "] != [" << y << "]\n";
    if (x <  y) cout << "\t[" << x << "] <  [" << y << "]\n";
    if (x <= y) cout << "\t[" << x << "] <= [" << y << "]\n";
    if (x >  y) cout << "\t[" << x << "] >  [" << y << "]\n";
    if (x >= y) cout << "\t[" << x << "] >= [" << y << "]\n";
}
```

```
Enter two strings: ABC AB
        [ABC]  != [AB]
        [ABC]  >  [AB]
        [ABC]  >= [AB]
```


10.10 STREAM OPERATORS

The stream operators overloaded for our `String` class are the stream insertion operator `<<` and the stream extraction operator `>>`. We have already used these in several test drivers. Here are their implementations:

```
ostream& operator<<(ostream& ostr, const String& s)
{
    return ostr << s.buf;
}

istream& operator>>(istream& istr, String& s)
{
    char buffer[256];
    istr >> buffer;
    s = buffer;
    return istr;
}
```

The overloaded stream insertion operator `<<` simply inserts the object's `buf` into the output stream `ostr` and then returns that reference. The overloaded stream extraction operator `>>` uses a temporary `buffer` string to read the input, assigns it to the reference `s`, and then returns the `istream` reference `istr`.

Note that both of these overloaded stream operators return the stream object that is passed to them. This makes these functions consistent with the corresponding predefined stream operators, allowing them to be invoked in cascades like this:

EXAMPLE 10.13 Testing the Stream Operators

```
#include "String.h"

main()
{
    String s1, s2;
    cin >> s1 >> s2;
    cout << s1 << "****" << s2 << endl;
}
```

```
Hello, World!
Hello,****World!
```

This little program makes two calls to the overloaded insertion operator, two calls to the overloaded extraction operator, and two calls to the standard (predefined) extraction operator. The first call is `operator>>(cin,s1)` which passes a reference to the `istream` object `cin` to the parameter `istr` and a reference to the `String` object `s1` to the parameter `s`. Then `"Hello,"` is read into the C-string `temp`. This is assigned to the String object s1, and then a reference to `cin` is returned. That return value is then used in the second call `operator>>(cin,s2)` which works the same way, leaving the object s2 representing `"World!"`.

The output line intermingles the two calls to the overloaded `<<` operator with the two calls to the standard `<<` operator in the cascade:

```
f( f( f( f( cout, s1 ), "****" ), s2 ), endl );
```

where `f` is `operator<<`.

Review Questions

10.1 Why couldn't the second constructor for our `String` class have a default value for its first argument, like this:

```
String(char c=' ', unsigned n=0)
```

10.2 What is wrong with using the copy constructor that is automatically provided by the compiler instead of writing our own copy constructor explicitly?

10.3 What is wrong with using the assignment operator that is automatically provided by the compiler instead of writing our own assignment operator explicitly?

10.4 In what ways is our String class more efficient than simply using C-strings? In what ways is it less efficient.

Solved Programming Problems

10.5 Implement the `String` comparison operator `==` directly, without using functions from the standard `string.h` header file.

We have the same function header. But now we have to check the object's data members directly:

```
int operator==(const String& s1, const String& s2)
{
    if (s1.len != s2.len) return 0;
    for (int i = 0; i < s1.len; i++)
        if (s1.buf[i] != s2.buf[i]) return 0;
    return 1;
}
```

Since we are storing the string lengths, we can determine immediately that the two strings are not equal if their len fields are not the same. Otherwise, we scan through the two strings in parallel, comparing corresponding characters. If a single mismatch is found, we can return 0 immediately. Only if all the corresponding characters match can we conclude that the two strings are equal and return 1.

10.6 Implement and test the following member function for the String class:

```
istream& getline(istream& istr, char c='\n');
```

This function reads a line of characters from the input stream object istr until it encounters the character c. These characters are stored in the object's buffer, and the input stream object is returned.

We have the same function header. But now we have to check the object's data members directly:

```
istream& String::getline(istream& istr, char c='\n')
{
    char temp[256];
    istr.getline(temp, 256, c);
    len = strlen(temp);
    delete [] buf;
    buf = new char[len + 1];
    strcpy(buf, temp);
    return istr;
}
```

As with the overloaded extraction operator >>, this function uses a temporary C-string buffer of 256 characters. It invokes the getline() functions defined in <iostream.h> to read the line. Then it performs the same steps that are used in the third constructor to transform the C-string buffer temp into the string object.

Here is a test driver for this function:

```
#include "String.h"

main()
{
    String s;
    s.getline(cin);
    cout << "\t[" << s << "]\n";
    s.getline(cin, '|');
    cout << "\t[" << s << "]\n";
    s.getline(cin, '|');
    cout << "\t[" << s << "]\n";
}
```

Here is the output:

```
George|Washington|
        [George|Washington|]
Thomas|Jefferson|
        [Thomas]
        [Jefferson]
```

The first call uses the default value `'\n'` for the delimiter argument `c`, so it reads the entire line. The following two calls use the character `'|'` for the delimiter, each reads only up to the next occurrence of that character. The effect is to be able to use the delimiter as a separator between input fields.

10.7 Implement and test the following member function for the `String` class:

```
int firstLocation(const String& s, unsigned k=0);
```

This searches the object's buffer, beginning with character `buf[k]` for the string `s`. If `s` is found to be a substring, then the index of its <u>first</u> occurrence is returned; otherwise –1 is returned.

In this solution, we implement a "brute force" searching method. Improvements could be made by using more efficient pattern-matching algorithms, such as the Knuth-Morris-Pratt Algorithm, the Boyer-Moore Algorithm, or the Rabin-Karp Algorithm. (See Chapter 19 in [Savitch].)

```
int String::firstLocation(const String& s, unsigned k=0)
{
    for (int i = k, j = 0; i < len && j < s.len; i++, j++)
        if (buf[i] != s.buf[j]) {
            i -= j;
            j = -1;
        }
    if (j == s.len) return i - s.len;              // substring found
    else return -1;
}
```

In this implementation, the `for` loop compares `buf[i]` with `s.buf[j]`, incrementing `i` and `j` simultaneously, and resetting `i` and `j` whenever a mismatch is found. For example, consider the call: `x.firstLocation(z)`. When `i = 5` and `j = 0`, `buf[i]` matches `s.buf[j]`; they are both `'F'`. So `i` and `j` both increment to `i = 6` and `j = 1`, and again `buf[i]` matches `s.buf[j]`; this time they are both `'G'`. So i and j both increment to `i = 7` and `j = 2`. But this time they do not match: `buf[i] = 'H'` and `s.buf[i] = 'Z'`. So `i` is reset to 5, and `j` is reset to –1. But then they both increment again before the next comparison is made, so next `buf[6]` is compared with `s.buf[0]`. They don't match, so next `buf[7]` is compared with `s.buf[0]`.

The loop terminates when either `i = len` or `j = s.len`. If `(j == s.len)`, then the substring was found, because `buf[i]` matched `s.buf[j]` for each `j` from 0 to `s.len`–1. In this case, `i` is pointing to the character immediately after the last character in the match, so `i - s.len` will point to the first character in the match and that is the location in `buf` that should be returned.

Here is a test driver for this function:

```
#include "String.h"

main()
{
    String x("ABCDEFGHIJKLABCDEFGHIJKL");
    String y("FGH");
    cout << x.firstLocation(y) << endl;
    cout << x.firstLocation(y, 8) << endl;
    cout << x.firstLocation(y, 20) << endl;
    String z("FGZ");
    cout << x.firstLocation(z) << endl;
}
```

```
5
17
-1
-1
```

Supplementary Programming Problems

10.8 Implement and test the other five comparison operators `!=`, `<`, `<=`, `>`, and `>=` for the String class directly, without using functions from the standard `string.h` header file.

10.9 Implement and test the following constructor for the String class:

```
String(const char* s, unsigned n, unsigned k=0);
```

This has the same effect as our third constructor, except that it uses n characters from the C-string s, beginning with character s[k]. For example, the declarations

```
String x("ABCDEFGHIJKL", 3);
String y("ABCDEFGHIJKL", 3, 5);
```

would construct the object x representing the substring "ABC" and the object y representing the substring "FGH".

10.10 Implement and test the following modification of the copy constructor for the String class:

```
String(const String& s, unsigned n, unsigned k=0);
```

This uses n characters from the object s, beginning with character s.buf[k]. For example, if x is a String object representing "ABCDEFGHIJKL", then

```
String y(x, 3);
String z(x, 3, 5);
```

would construct the object y representing the substring "ABC" and the object z representing the substring "FGH". (See Problem 10.9.)

10.11 Implement and test the following member function for the String class:

```
int frequency(char c);
```

This returns the number of occurrences of the character c in the string For example, is x is the string "Mississippi", then the call `frequency('i')` would return 4.

10.12 Implement and test the following member function for the `String` class:

```
void remove(unsigned n, unsigned k=0);
```

This removes `n` characters from the object, beginning with character `buf[k]`. For example,

```
String x("ABCDEFGHIJKL");
x.remove(3, 5);
```

would remove the substring `"FGH"` from the object `x`, changing it to `"ABCDEIJKL"`.

10.13 Implement and test the following member function for the `String` class:

```
void insert(const String& s, unsigned k=0);
```

This inserts the string `s` into the current object, beginning with character `buf[k]`. For example,

```
String x("ABCDEFGHIJKL");
String y("XYZ");
x.insert(y, 5);
```

would insert `"XYZ"` into the object `x`, changing it to `"ABCDEXYZFGHIJKL"`. Note that the third constructor would be invoked automatically to produce the same effect from the call:

```
x.insert("XYZ", 5);
```

Also note that `x.insert(y)` prepends `y` to `x`, and that `x.insert(y, x.n())` is equivalent to `x += y`, appending `y` to `x`.

10.14 Implement and test the following member function for the `String` class:

```
void replace(const String& s, unsigned n, unsigned k=0);
```

This replaces `n` characters from the object, beginning with character `buf[k]` with string `s`:

```
String x("ABCDEFGHIJKL");
String y("XYZ");
x.replace(y, 6, 5);
```

would replace the substring `"FGHIJK"` in the object `x` with the string `s`, changing `x` to `"ABCDEXYZL"`. Note that the third constructor would be invoked automatically to produce the same effect from the call:

```
x.replace("XYZ", 6, 5);
```

Also note that `x.replace(y, m, n);` is equivalent to

```
x.remove(6, 5);
x.insert("XYZ", 5);
```

10.15 Implement and test the following member function for the `String` class:

```
int lastLocation(const String& s, unsigned k=0);
```

This searches the object's buffer, beginning with character `buf[k]` for the string `s`. If `s` is found to be a substring, then the index of its <u>last</u> occurrence is returned; otherwise –1 is returned. For example,

```
String x("ABCDEFGHIJKLABCDEFGHIJKL");
String y("FGH");
cout << x.lastLocation(y) << endl;
cout << x.lastLocation(y, 20) << endl;
String z("FGZ");
cout << x.lastLocation(z) << endl;
```

would print 17, –1, and –1. (See Problem 10.7.)

10.16 Implement and test the following member function for the String class:

```
int location(const String& s, unsigned n=0, unsigned k=0);
```

This searches the object's buffer, beginning with character buf[k] for the string s. If s is found to be a substring, then the index of its (n+1)st occurrence is returned (in other words, the first n occurrences of the string s are ignored); otherwise –1 is returned. For example,

```
String x("ABCDEFGHIJKLABCDEFGHIJKLABCDEFGHIJKLABCDEFGHIJKL");
String y("FGH");
cout << x.location(y) << endl;
cout << x.location(y, 0, 20) << endl;
cout << x.location(y, 2) << endl;
cout << x.location(y, 2, 20) << endl;
cout << x.location(y, 4) << endl;
```

would print 5, 29, 29, –1, and –1. (See Problem 10.7.)

10.17 Implement and test the following member function for the String class:

```
int location(char c, unsigned n=0);
```

This searches the object's buffer, for the character c. If c is found, then the index of its (n+1)st occurrence is returned (in other words, the first n occurrences of the character c are ignored); otherwise –1 is returned. For example, if x represents the string "ABBCCCBBA", then the call x.location('C') would return 3, the call x.location('C', 3) would return 11, the call x.location('C', 5) would return –1, and the call x.location('D') would return –1. (See Problem 10.16.)

10.18 Implement and test the following member function for the String class:

```
int firstOf(const String& s, unsigned k=0);
```

This searches the object's buffer, beginning with character buf[k], for any character c that is in the string s. If any c is found, then the index of its <u>first</u> occurrence is returned; otherwise –1 is returned. For example, if x represents the string "ABBCCCBBA", then the call x.firstOf("CDE") would return 3, the call x.firstOf("BCD", 4) would return 6, and the call x.firstOf("XYZ") would return –1.

10.19 Implement and test the following member function for the String class:

```
int lastOf(const String& s);
```

This searches the object's buffer for any character c that is in the string s. If any c is found, then the index of its <u>last</u> occurrence is returned; otherwise –1 is returned. For example, if x represents the string "ABBCCCBBA", then the call x.lastOf("BCD") would return 7, and the call x.lastOf("XYZ") would return –1.

10.20 Implement and test the following member function for the String class:

```
int firstNotOf(const String& s, unsigned k=0);
```

This searches the object's buffer, beginning with character buf[k], for any character c that is <u>not</u> in the string s. If any c is found, then the index of its first occurrence is returned; otherwise –1 is returned. For example, if x represents the string "ABBCCCBBA", then the call x.firstNotOf("ABD") would return 3, and x.firstNotOf("ABC") would return –1.

10.21 Implement and test the following member function for the String class:

```
int lastNotOf(const String& s);
```

This searches the object's buffer, beginning with character buf[k], for any character c that is <u>not</u> in the string s. If any c is found, then the index of its last occurrence is returned; otherwise −1 is returned. For example, if x represents the string "ABBCCCBBA", then the call x.lastNotOf("ABD") would return 7, and x.lastNotOf("ABC") would return −1.

10.22 Implement and test the following member function for the String class:

```
int isPrefix(const String& s);
```

This returns 1 or 0 according to whether s is a prefix substring of the object. For example, if x = "ABCDEFGHIJKL" then isPrefix("ABC") would return 1, and isPrefix("FGH") would return 0.

10.23 Implement and test the following member function for the String class:

```
int isSufix(const String& s);
```

This returns 1 or 0 according to whether s is a suffix substring of the object. For example, if x = "ABCDEFGHIJKL" then isSuffix("JKL") would return 1, and isPrefix("FGH") would return 0.

10.24 Implement and test the following member function for the String class:

```
int capitalize();
```

This capitalizes all the words in the string. For this exercise, a "word" is defined as a maximal substring that contains no white space. Use the isspace() function defined in the ctype.h header file. (See Table 7.1 on page 194.)

10.25 Implement and test the following member function for the String class:

```
int numWords();
```

This returns the number of words in the string. For this exercise, a "word" is defined as a maximal substring that contains no white space. Use the isspace() function defined in the ctype.h header file. (See Table 7.1 on page 194.)

10.26 Implement and test the following member function for the String class:

```
int numSentences();
```

This returns the number of sentences in the string. For this exercise, a "sentence" is defined as a maximal substring that ends with a period and contains no other periods.

10.27 Implement and test the following member function for the String class:

```
void toUpper();
```

This function changes every lowercase character in the string to uppercase. For example, it would transform the string "Honey, I'm home!" into "HONEY, I'M HOME!". Use the character function toupper() defined in the ctype.h header file. (See Table 7.1 on page 194.)

10.28 Implement and test the following member function for the String class:

```
void toLower();
```

This function changes every uppercase character in the string to lowercase. For example, it would transform the string "New York, NY" into "new york, ny". Use the character function tolower() defined in the ctype.h header file. (See Table 7.1 on page 194.)

10.29 Implement and test the following member function for the String class:

```
void reverse();
```

This function reverses the string. For example, it would transform the string ABCD into DCBA.

10.30 Implement and test the following member function for the String class:

```
int isPalindrome();
```

This returns 1 or 0 according to whether the string is a palindrome (*i.e.*, it remains the same string when reversed). For example, isPalindrome("WASITELIOTSTOILETISAW") would return 1 (for "true").

10.31 The String class implemented in this chapter would be inefficient for writing a text file or for any purpose that involved many instances of the same word (like "the" or "New York"). This inefficiency can be reduced significantly by allowing many objects to share the same buf space in memory. However, using several pointers to point to the same data can cause problems. (See Questions Example 10.1 and Example 10.2.) These potential problems can be overcome by making the initial byte in buf a counter that keeps track of how many objects are using that buffer. For example, the declarations

```
String s1("France"), s2("Spain"), s3("France"), s4("France");
```

would be represented as:

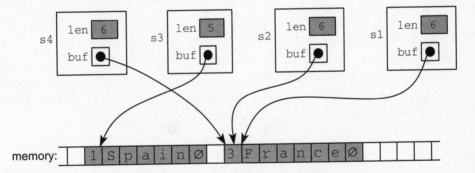

Note that each string occupies len + 2 bytes in memory. Also note that the initial byte is storing an nonnegative integer as a char, so it must remain in the range 0 to 127. Modify the String implementation in this chapter to represent strings this way. The main changes have to be made to the constructors, the destructor, and the assignment operator.

10.32 Modify the String class so that the user can set or clear a case-sensitive switch. When the switch is off, comparisons are made without regard to case, so that "NeXT" and "next" would be regarded as equal strings. One way to implement this feature is to add the static data member

```
static int sensitivity;
```

and the static function member

```
static int setSensitivity();
```

Answers to Review Questions

10.1 If the second constructor had default values for both of its arguments, then a declaration like this

```
String s;
```

would be ambiguous. Any constructor which has default values for all of its arguments is a default constructor, and a class may have only one default constructor.

10.2 The copy constructor that is automatically provided by the compiler merely duplicates the member data. This would result in different objects having their own (different) buf pointers, but they would point to the same C-string. That could be disastrous, for example, if one were changed or deleted.

10.3 See the answer to Question 10.2.

10.4 Our `String` class is more efficient when making comparisons. It is less efficient with its overloaded stream extraction operator `>>` which uses a 256-byte buffer. It would also be inefficient in a text-processing environment because of the overhead of its constructors. (See Problem 10.31.)

Chapter 11

Composition and Inheritance

11.1 INTRODUCTION

We often need to use existing classes to define new classes. The two ways to do this are called *composition* and the *inheritance*. This chapter describes both methods and shows how to decide when to use them.

11.2 COMPOSITION

Composition (also called *containment* or *aggregation*) of classes refers to the use of one or more classes within the definition of another class. When a data member of the new class is an object of another class, we say that the new class is a *composite* of the other objects.

EXAMPLE 11.1 A `Person` Class

Here is a simple definition for a class to represent people.

```
#include "String.h"

class Person {
public:
    Person(char* n="", char* nat="U.S.A.", int s=1)
      : name(n), nationality(nat), sex(s) { }
    void printName() { cout << name; }
    void printNationality() { cout << nationality; }
private:
    String name, nationality;
    int sex;
};

main()
{
    Person creator("Bjarne Stroustrup", "Denmark");
    cout << "The creator of C++ was ";
    creator.printName();
    cout << " who was born in ";
    creator.printNationality();
    cout << ".\n";
}
```

```
The creator of C++ was Bjarne Stroustrup who was born in Denmark.
```

We have used the `String` class that was defined in Chapter 10 to declare the data members `name` and `nationality` for the `Person` class. Notice that we used the `String` class's overloaded insertion operator `<<` in the `Person` class's `printName()` function.

Example 11.1 illustrates the *composition* of the `String` class within the `Person` class. The next example defines another class that we can compose with the `Person` class to improve it:

EXAMPLE 11.2 A `Date` Class

```
class Date {
    friend istream& operator>>(istream&, Date&);
    friend ostream& operator<<(ostream&, const Date&);
public:
    Date(int m=0, int d=0, int y=0) : month(m), day(d), year(y) { }
    void setDate(int m, int d, int y) { month = m; day = d; year = y;
}
private:
    int month, day, year;
};

istream& operator>>(istream& in, Date& x)
{
    in >> x.month >> x.day >> x.year;
    return in;
}

ostream& operator<<(ostream& out, const Date& x)
{
    static char* monthName[13] = {"", "January","February",
        "March", "April", "May", "June", "July", "August",
        "September", "October", "November", "December"};
    out << monthName[x.month] << ' ' << x.day << ", " << x.year;
    return out;
}

main()
{
    Date peace(11,11,1918);
    cout << "World War I ended on " << peace << ".\n";
    peace.setDate(8,14,1945);
    cout << "World War II ended on " << peace << ".\n";
    cout << "Enter month, day, and year: ";
    Date date;
    cin >> date;
    cout << "The date is " << date << ".\n";
}
```

```
World War I ended on November 11, 1918.
World War II ended on August 14, 1945.
Enter month, day, and year: 7 4 1776
The date is July 4, 1776.
```

The test driver tests the default constructor, the `setDate()` function, the overloaded insertion operator `<<`, and the overloaded extraction operator `>>`.

Now we can use the `Date` class inside the `Person` class to store a person's date of birth and date of death:

EXAMPLE 11.3 Composing the `Date` Class with the `Person` Class

```
#include "String.h"
#include "Date.h"

class Person {
public:
    Person(char* n="", int s=0, char* nat="U.S.A.")
      : name(n), sex(s), nationality(nat) { }
    void setDOB(int m, int d, int y) { dob.setDate(m, d, y); }
    void setDOD(int m, int d, int y) { dod.setDate(m, d, y); }
    void printName() { cout << name; }
    void printNationality() { cout << nationality; }
    void printDOB() { cout << dob; }
    void printDOD() { cout << dod; }
private:
    String name, nationality;
    Date dob, dod;              // date of birth, date of death
    int sex;                    // 0 = female, 1 = male
};

main()
{
    Person author("Thomas Jefferson", 1);
    author.setDOB(4,13,1743);
    author.setDOD(7,4,1826);
    cout << "The author of the Declaration of Independence was ";
    author.printName();
    cout << ".\nHe was born on ";
    author.printDOB();
    cout << " and died on ";
    author.printDOD();
    cout << ".\n";
}
```

```
The author of the Declaration of Independence was Thomas Jefferson.
He was born on April 13, 1743 and died on July 4, 1826.
```

Notice again that we have used a member function of one class to define member functions of the composed class: the `setDate()` function is used to define the `setDOB()` and `setDOD()` functions.

Composition is often referred to as a "has-a" relationship because the objects of the composite class "have" objects of the composed class as members. Each object of the `Person` class "has a" `name` and a `nationality` which are `String` objects. Composition is one way of reusing existing software to create new software.

11.3 INHERITANCE

Another way to reuse existing software to create new software is by means of inheritance (also called *specialization* or *derivation*). This is often referred to as an "is-a" relationship because every object of the class being defined "is" also an object of the inherited class.

The common syntax for deriving a class Y from a class X is

```
class Y : public X {
// ...
};
```

Here X is called the *base class* (or *superclass*) and Y is called the *derived class* (or *subclass*). The keyword public after the colon specifies *public inheritance*, which means that public members of the base class become public members of the derived class.

EXAMPLE 11.4 Deriving a Student Class from the Person Class

Students are people. So it is natural to use the People class to derive a Student class:

```
#include "Person.h"

class Student : public Person {
public:
    Student(char* n, int s=0, char* i="")
     : Person(n, s), id(i), credits(0) { }
    void setDOM(int m, int d, int y) { dom.setDate(m, d, y); }
    void printDOM() { cout << dom; }
private:
    String id;                  // student identification number
    Date dom;                   // date of matriculation
    int credits;                // course credits
    float gpa;                  // grade-point average
};
```

The Student class inherits all the public functionality of the Person class, including the Person() constructor which it uses in its constructor to initialize name in the Person class. Note that this is a private member of the Person class, so it could not be accessed directly.

Here is a test driver for the Student class:

```
#include "Student.h"

main()
{
    Student x("Ann Jones", "219360061");
    x.setDOB(5, 13, 1977);
    x.setDOM(8, 29, 1995);
    x.printName();
    cout << "\n\t        Born: ";  x.printDOB();
    cout << "\n\tMatriculated: ";  x.printDOM();  cout << endl;
}
```

```
Ann Jones
            Born: May 13, 1977
        Matriculated: August 29, 1995
```

11.4 protected CLASS MEMBERS

The `Student` class in Section 11.3 has a significant problem: it cannot directly access the `private` data members of its `Person` superclass: `name`, `nationality`, `DOB`, `DOD`, and `sex`. The lack of access on the first four of these is not serious because these can be written and read through the `Person` class's constructor and public access functions. However, there is no way to write or read a `Student`'s `sex`. One way to overcome this problem would be to make `sex` a data member of the `Student` class. But that is unnatural: `sex` is an attribute that all `Person` objects have, not just `Student`s. A better solution is to change the `private` access specifier to `protected` in the `Person` class. That will allow access to these data members from derived classes.

EXAMPLE 11.5 The Person Class with protected Data Members

These are the same class definitions that were given in Example 11.3 and Example 11.4 except that the `private` access specifier has been changed to `protected`, and we have added the access function `printSex()` to the `Student` class:

```cpp
#include "String.h"
#include "Date.h"

class Person {
public:
    Person(char* n="", int s=0, char* nat="U.S.A.")
      : name(n), sex(s), nationality(nat) { }
    void setDOB(int m, int d, int y) { dob.setDate(m, d, y); }
    void setDOD(int m, int d, int y) { dod.setDate(m, d, y); }
    void printName() { cout << name; }
    void printNationality() { cout << nationality; }
    void printDOB() { cout << dob; }
    void printDOD() { cout << dod; }
protected:
    String name, nationality;
    Date dob, dod;                 // date of birth, date of death
    int sex;                       // 0 = female, 1 = male
};

class Student : public Person {
public:
    Student(char* n, int s=0, char* i="")
      : Person(n, s), id(i), credits(0) { }
    void setDOM(int m, int d, int y) { dom.setDate(m, d, y); }
    void printDOM() { cout << dom; }
    void printSex() { cout << (sex ? "male" : "female"); }
protected:
    String id;                     // student identification number
    Date dom;                      // date of matriculation
    int credits;                   // course credits
    float gpa;                     // grade-point average
};
```

Now all five data members defined in the `Person` class are accessible from its `Student` subclass, as seen by the following test driver:

```
main()
{
    Student x("Ann Jones", 0, "219360061");
    x.setDOB(5, 13, 1977);
    x.setDOM(8, 29, 1995);
    x.setDOD(7,4,1826);
    x.printName();
    cout << "\n\t        Born: ";  x.printDOB();
    cout << "\n\t         Sex: ";  x.printSex();
    cout << "\n\tMatriculated: ";  x.printDOM();
    cout << endl;
}
```

```
Ann Jones
                Born: May 13, 1977
                 Sex: female
        Matriculated: August 29, 1995
```

The `protected` access category is a balance between `private` and `public` categories: `private` members are accessible only from within the class itself and its `friend` classes; `protected` members are accessible from within the class itself, its `friend` classes, its derived classes, and their `friend` classes; `public` members are accessible from anywhere within the file. In general, `protected` is used instead of `private` whenever it is anticipated that a subclass might be defined for the class.

A subclass inherits all the `public` and `protected` members of its base class. This means that, from the point of view of the subclass, the `public` and `protected` members of its base class appear as though they actually were declared in the subclass. For example, suppose that class `X` and subclass `Y` are defined as

```
class X {
public:
    int a;
protected:
    int b;
private:
    int c;
};

class Y : public X {
public:
    int d;
};
```

and x and y are declared as

```
    X x;

    Y y;
```

Then we can visualize objects `x` and `y` as shown below.

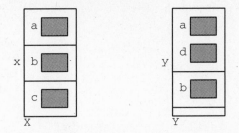

The `public` member `a` of class `X` is inherited as a `public` member of `y`, and the `protected` member `b` of class `X` is inherited as a `protected` member of `y`. But the `private` member `c` of class `X` is not inherited by `y`. (The horizontal lines in each object indicate the separate the `public`, `protected`, and `private` regions of the object.)

11.5 OVERRIDING AND DOMINATING INHERITED MEMBERS

If `Y` is a subclass of `X`, then `Y` objects inherit all the `public` and `protected` member data and member functions of `X`. For example, the `name` data and `printName()` function in the `Person` class are also members of the `Student` class.

In some cases, you might want to define a local version of an inherited member. For example, if `a` is a data member of `X` and if `Y` is a subclass of `X`, then you could also define a separate data member named `a` for `Y`. In this case, we say that the `a` defined in `Y` *dominates* the `a` defined in `X`. Then a reference `y.a` for an object `y` of class `Y` will access the `a` defined in `Y` instead of the `a` defined in `X`. To access the `a` defined in `X`, one would use `y.X::a`.

The same rule applies to member functions. If a function named `f()` is defined in `X` and another function named `f()` with the same signature is defined in `Y`, then `y.f()` invokes the latter function, and `y.X::f()` invokes the former. In this case, the local function `y.f()` *overrides* the `f()` function defined in `X` unless it is invoked as `y.X::f()`.

These distinctions are illustrated in the following example.

EXAMPLE 11.6 Dominating a Data Member and Overriding a Member Function

Here are two classes, `X` and `Y`, with `Y` inheriting from `X`.

```
class X {
public:
    void f() { cout << "X::f() executing\n"; }
    int a;
};

class Y : public X {
public:
    void f() { cout << "Y::f() executing\n"; }  // overrides X::f()
    int a;                                       // dominates X::a
};
```

But the members of `Y` have the same signatures as those in `X`. So `Y`'s member function `f()` overrides the `f()` defined in `X`, and `Y`'s data member `a` dominates the `a` defined in `X`.

Here is a test driver for the two classes:

```
main()
{
    X x;
    x.a = 22;
    x.f();
    cout << "x.a = " << x.a << endl;
    Y y;
    y.a = 44;                    // assigns 44 to the a defined in Y
    y.X::a = 66;                 // assigns 22 to the a defined in X
    y.f();                       // invokes the f() defined in Y
    y.X::f();                    // invokes the f() defined in X
    cout << "y.a = " << y.a << endl;
    cout << "y.X::a = " << y.X::a << endl;
    X z = y;
    cout << "z.a = " << z.a << endl;
}
```

```
X::f() executing
x.a = 22
Y::f() executing
X::f() executing
y.a = 44
y.X::a = 66
z.a = 66
```

Here, `y` has access to two different data members named `a` and two different functions `f()`. The defaults are the ones defined in the derived class `Y`. The scope resolution operator `::` is used in the form `X::` to override the defaults to access the corresponding members defined in the parent class `X`. When the `X` object `z` and initialized with `y`, its `X` members are used: `z.a` is assigned the value `y.X::a`.

This diagram illustrates the three objects `x`, `y`, and `z`:

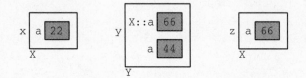

Example 11.6 and most of the remaining examples in this chapter are designed to illustrate the intricacies of inheritance. They are not intended to exemplify common programming practice. Instead, they focus on specific aspects of C++ which can then be applied to more general and practical situations. In particular, the method of dominating data members as illustrated in Example 11.6 is rather unusual. Although it is not uncommon to override function members, dominating data members of the same type is rare. More common would be the reuse of the same data name with a different type, like this:

```
class Y : public X {
public:
    double a;        // the data member a in class X had type int
}
```

In an inheritance hierarchy, default constructors and destructors behave differently from other member functions. As the following example illustrates, each constructor invokes its parent constructor before executing itself, and each destructor invokes its parent destructor after executing itself:

EXAMPLE 11.7 Parent Constructors and Destructors

```
class X {
public:
    X() { cout << "X::X() constructor executing\n"; }
    ~X() { cout << "X::X() destructor executing\n"; }
};

class Y : public X {
public:
    Y() { cout << "Y::Y() constructor executing\n"; }
    ~Y() { cout << "Y::Y() destructor executing\n"; }
};

class Z : public Y {
public:
    Z(int n) { cout << "Z::Z(int) constructor executing\n"; }
    ~Z() { cout << "Z::Z() destructor executing\n"; }
};

main()
{
    Z z(44);
}
```

```
X::X() constructor executing
Y::Y() constructor executing
Z::Z(int) constructor executing
Z::Z() destructor executing
Y::Y() destructor executing
X::X() destructor executing
```

When z is declared, the Z::Z(int) constructor is called. Before executing, it calls the Y::Y() constructor which immediately calls the X::X() constructor. After the X::X() constructor has finished executing, control returns to the Y::Y() constructor which finishes executing. Then finally the Z::Z() constructor finishes executing. The effect is that all the parent default constructors execute in top-down order.

The same thing happens with the destructors, except that each destructor executes its own code <u>before</u> calling its parent destructor. So all the parent destructors execute in bottom-up order.

Here is a more realistic example:

EXAMPLE 11.8 Parent Constructors and Destructors

Here is a demo program that uses a base class `Person` and a derived class `Student`:

```
class Person {
public:
    Person(const char* s)
        { name = new char[strlen(s)+1]; strcpy(name, s); }
    ~Person() { delete [] name; }
protected:
    char* name;
};

class Student : public Person {
public:
    Student(const char* s, const char* m) : Person(s)
        { major = new char[strlen(m)+1]; strcpy(major, m); }
    ~Student() { delete [] major; }
private:
    char* major;
};

main()
{
    Person x("Bob");
    {
        Student y("Sarah", "Biology");
    }
}
```

When `x` is instantiated, it calls the `Person` constructor which allocates 4 bytes of memory to store the string "Bob". Then `y` instantiates, first calling the `Person` constructor which allocates 6 bytes to store the string "Sarah" and then allocating 8 more bytes of memory to store the string "Biology". The scope of `y` terminates before `z` is instantiated because it is declared within an internal block. At that moment, `y`'s destructor deallocates the 8 bytes used for "Biology" and then calls the `Person` destructor which deallocates the 6 bytes used for "Sarah". Finally the `Person` destructor is called to destroy `x`, deallocating the 4 bytes used for "Bob".

11.6 private ACCESS VERSES protected ACCESS

The difference between `private` and `protected` class members is that subclasses can access `protected` members of a parent class but not `private` members. Since `protected` is more flexible, when would you want to make members `private`? The answer lies at the heart of the principle of information hiding: restrict access now to facilitate changes later. If you think you may want to modify the implementation of a data member in the future, then declaring it private will obviate the need to make any corollary changes in subclasses. Subclasses are independent of `private` data members.

EXAMPLE 11.9 The `person` Class with `protected` and `private` Data Members

Suppose that we need to know whether people (*i.e.*, `Person` objects) are high school graduates. We could just add a `protected` data member like `sex` that stores either 0 or 1. But we might decide later to replace it with data member(s) that contain more detailed information about the person's education. So, for now, we set up a `private` data member `hs` to prevent derived classes from accessing it directly:

```
class Person {
public:
    Person(char* n="", int s=0, char* nat="U.S.A.")
     : name(n), sex(s), nationality(nat) { }
    // ...
protected:
    String name, nationality;
    Date dob, dod;               // date of birth, date of death
    int sex;                     // 0 = female, 1 = male
    void setHSgraduate(int g) { hs = g; }
    int isHSgraduate() { return hs; }
private:
    int hs;                      // = 1 if high school graduate
};
```

We include `protected` access functions to allow subclasses to access the information. If we do later replace the `hs` data member with something else, we need only modify the implementations of these two access functions without affecting any subclasses.

11.7 `virtual` FUNCTIONS AND POLYMORPHISM

One of the most powerful features of C++ is that it allows objects of different types to respond differently to the same function call. This is called *polymorphism* and it is achieved by means of `virtual` functions. Polymorphism is rendered possible by the fact that a pointer to a base class instance may also point to any subclass instance:

```
class X {
    // ...
}

class Y : public X {                          // Y is a subclass if X
    // ...
}

main()
{
    X* p;              // p is a pointer to objects of base class X
    Y y;
    p = &y;            // p can also point to objects of subclass Y
}
```

So if `p` has type `X*` ("pointer to type `X`"), then `p` can also point to any object whose type is a subclass of `X`. However, even when `p` is pointing to an instance of a subclass `Y`, its type is still `X*`. So an expression like `p->f()` would invoke the function `f()` defined in the base class.

Recall that p->f() is an alternate notation for *p.f(). This invokes the member function f()
of the object to which p points. But what if p is actually pointing to an object y of a subclass of the
class to which p points, and what if that subclass Y has its own overriding version of f()? Which f()
gets executed: X::f() or Y::f()? The answer is that p->f() will execute X::f() because p
had type X*. The fact that p happens to be pointing at that moment to an instance of subclass Y is irrelevant; it's the statically defined type X* of p that normally determines its behavior.

EXAMPLE 11.10 Using `virtual` Functions

This demo program declares p to be a pointer to objects of the base class X. First it assigns p to
point to an instance x of class X. Then it assigns p to point to an instance y of the derived class Y.

```
class X {
public:
    void f() { cout << "X::f() executing\n"; }
};

class Y : public X {
public:
    void f() { cout << "Y::f() executing\n"; }
};

main()
{
    X x;
    Y y;
    X* p = &x;
    p->f();          // invokes X::f() because p has type X*
    p = &y;
    p->f();          // invokes X::f() because p has type X*
}
```

```
X::f() executing
X::f() executing
```

Two function calls p->f() are made. Both calls invoke the same version of f() that is defined in the
base class X because p is declared to be a pointer to X objects. Having p point to y has no effect on
the second call p->f().

Transform X::f() into a *virtual function* by adding the keyword "`virtual`" to its declaration:

```
class X {
public:
    virtual void f() { cout << "X::f() executing\n"; }
};
```

With the rest of the code left unchanged, the output now becomes

```
X::f() executing
Y::f() executing
```

Now the second call p->f() invokes Y::f() instead of X::f().

This example illustrates *polymorphism*: the <u>same</u> call p->f() invokes <u>different</u> functions.
The function is selected according to which class of object p points to. This is called *dynamic
binding* because the association (*i.e.*, binding) of the call to the actual code to be executed is

deferred until <u>run time</u>. The rule that the pointer's statically defined type determines which member function gets invoked is overruled by declaring the member function `virtual`.

Here is a more realistic example:

EXAMPLE 11.11 Polymorphism through `virtual` Functions

Here is a `Person` class with a `Student` subclass and a `Professor` subclass:

```
class Person {
public:
    Person(char* s) { name = new char[strlen(s+1)]; strcpy(name, s);
}
    void print() { cout << "My name is " << name << ".\n"; }
protected:
    char* name;
};

class Student : public Person {
public:
    Student(char* s, float g) : Person(s), gpa(g) { }
    void print() { cout << "My name is " << name
        << " and my G.P.A. is " << gpa << ".\n"; }
private:
    float gpa;
};

class Professor : public Person {
public:
    Professor(char* s, int n) : Person(s), publs(n) { }
    void print() { cout << "My name is " << name
        << " and I have " << publs << " publications.\n"; }
private:
    int publs;
};

main()
{
    Person* p;
    Person x("Bob");
    p = &x;
    p->print();
    Student y("Tom", 3.47);
    p = &y;
    p->print();
    Professor z("Ann", 7);
    p = &z;
    p->print();
}
```

```
My name is Bob.
My name is Tom.
My name is Ann.
```

The `print()` function defined in the base class is not `virtual`. So the call `p->print()` always invokes that same base class function `Person::print()` because `p` has type `Person*`. The pointer `p` is *statically bound* to that base class function at compile time.

Now change the base class function `Person::print()` into a `virtual` function, and run the same program:

```
class Person {
public:
    Person(char* s) { name = new char[strlen(s+1)]; strcpy(name, s);
}
    virtual void print() { cout << "My name is " << name << ".\n"; }
protected:
    char* name;
};
```

```
My name is Bob.
My name is Tom and my G.P.A. is 3.47
My name is Ann and I have 7 publications.
```

Now the pointer `p` is *dynamically bound* to the `print()` function of whatever object it points to. So the first call `p->print()` invokes the base class function `Person::print()`, the second call invokes the derived class function `Student::print()`, and the third call invokes the derived class function `Professor::print()`. We say that the call `p->print()` is *polymorphic* because its meaning changes according to circumstance.

In general, a member function should be declared as virtual whenever it is anticipated that at least some of its subclasses will define their own local version of the function.

11.8 VIRTUAL DESTRUCTORS

Virtual functions are overridden by functions that have the same signature and are defined in subclasses. Since the names of constructors and destructors involve the names of their different classes, it would seem that constructors and destructors could not be declared virtual. That is indeed true for constructors. However, an exception is made for destructors.

Every class has a unique destructor, either defined explicitly within the class definition or implicitly by the compiler. An explicit destructor may be defined to be virtual. The following example illustrates the value in defining a virtual destructor:

EXAMPLE 11.12 Memory Leak

This program is similar to Example 11.6:

```
class X {
public:
    X() { p = new int[2];  cout << "X().  "; }
    ~X() { delete [] p;  cout << "~X().\n"; }
private:
    int* p;
};
```

```
class Y : public X {
public:
    Y() { q = new int[1023];  cout << "Y(): Y::q = " << q << ".  "; }
    ~Y() { delete [] q;  cout << "~Y().  "; }
private:
    int* q;
};


main()
{
    for (int i = 0; i < 8; i++){
        X* r = new Y;
        delete r;
    }
}
```

```
X().  Y(): Y::q = 0x5821c.  ~X().
X().  Y(): Y::q = 0x5921c.  ~X().
X().  Y(): Y::q = 0x5a21c.  ~X().
X().  Y(): Y::q = 0x5b21c.  ~X().
X().  Y(): Y::q = 0x5c21c.  ~X().
X().  Y(): Y::q = 0x5d21c.  ~X().
X().  Y(): Y::q = 0x5e21c.  ~X().
X().  Y(): Y::q = 0x5f21c.  ~X().
```

Each iteration of the for loop creates a new dynamic object. As in Example 11.6, the constructors are invoked in top-down sequence: first X() and then Y(), allocating 4100 bytes of storage (using 4 bytes for each int). But since r is declared to be a pointer to X objects, only the X destructor is invoked, deallocating only 8 bytes. So on each iteration, 3992 bytes are lost! This loss is indicated by the actual values of the pointer Y::q.

To plug this leak, change the destructor ~X() into a virtual function:

```
class X {
public:
    X() { p = new int[2];  cout << "X().  "; }
    virtual ~X() { delete [] p;  cout << "~X().\n"; }
private:
    int* p;
};
```

```
X().  Y(): Y::q = 0x5a220.  ~Y().  ~X().
X().  Y(): Y::q = 0x5a220.  ~Y().  ~X().
X().  Y(): Y::q = 0x5a220.  ~Y().  ~X().
X().  Y(): Y::q = 0x5a220.  ~Y().  ~X().
X().  Y(): Y::q = 0x5a220.  ~Y().  ~X().
X().  Y(): Y::q = 0x5a220.  ~Y().  ~X().
X().  Y(): Y::q = 0x5a220.  ~Y().  ~X().
X().  Y(): Y::q = 0x5a220.  ~Y().  ~X().
```

With the base class destructor declared virtual, each iteration of the for loop calls both destructors, thereby restoring all memory that was allocated by the new operator. This allows the same memory to be reused for the pointer r.

This example illustrates what is known as a *memory leak*. In a large-scale software system, this could lead to a catastrophe. Moreover, it is a bug that is not easily located. The moral is: declare the base class destructor `virtual` whenever your class hierarchy uses dynamic binding.

As noted earlier, these examples are contrived to illustrate specific features of C++ and are not meant to exemplify typical programming practice.

11.9 ABSTRACT BASE CLASSES

A well-designed object-oriented program will include a hierarchy of classes whose interrelationships can be described by a tree diagram like the one below. The classes at the leaves of this

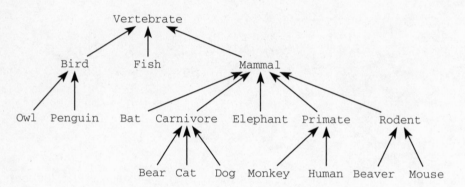

tree (*e.g.*, `Owl`, `Fish`, `Dog`) would include specific functions that implement the behavior of their respective classes (*e.g.*, `Fish.swim()`, `Owl.fly()`, `Dog.dig()`). However, some of these functions may be common to all the subclasses of a class (*e.g.*, `Vertebrate.eat()`, `Mammal.suckle()`, `Primate.peel()`). Such functions are likely to be declared `virtual` in these base classes, and then overridden in their subclasses for specific implementations.

If a `virtual` function is certain to be overridden in all of its subclasses, then there is no need to implement it at all in its base class. This is done by making the `virtual` function "pure." A *pure virtual member function* is a virtual function that has no implementation in its class. The syntax for specifying a pure virtual member function is to insert the initializer "`=0;`" in place of the functions body, like this:

```
virtual int f() =0;
```

For example, in the `Vertebrate` class above, we might decide that the `eat()` function would be overridden in every one of its subclasses, and thus declare it as a pure virtual member function within its `Vertebrate` base class:

```
class Vertebrate {
public:
    virtual void eat() =0;     // pure virtual function
};

class Fish : public Vertebrate {
public:
    void eat(); // implemented specifically for Fish class elsewhere
};
```

The individual classes in a class hierarchy are designated as either "abstract" or "concrete" according to whether they have any <u>pure</u> virtual member functions. An *abstract base class* is a class that has one or more pure virtual member functions. An *concrete derived class* is a class that does not have any pure virtual member functions. In the example above, the Vertebrate class is an abstract base class, and the Fish class is a concrete derived class. Abstract base classes cannot be instantiated.

The existence of a pure virtual member function in a class requires that every one of its concrete derived subclasses implement the function. In the example above, if the methods Vertebrate.eat(), Mammal.suckle(), and Primate.peel() were the only pure virtual functions, then the abstract base classes ("ABCs") would be Vertebrate, Mammal, and Primate, and the other 15 classes would be concrete derived classes ("CDCs"). Each of these 15 CDCs would have its own implementation of the eat() function, the 11 CDCs of the Mammal class would have their own implementation of the suckle() function, and the 2 CDCs of the Primate class would have their own implementation of the peel() function.

An ABC is typically defined during the first stages of the process of developing a class hierarchy. It lays out the framework from which the details are derived in the ABC's subclasses. Its pure virtual functions prescribe a certain uniformity within the hierarchy.

EXAMPLE 11.13 A Hierarchy of Media Classes

Here is a hierarchy of classes to represent various media objects:

The primary ABC is the Media class:

```
class Media {
public:
    virtual void print() =0;
    virtual char* id() =0;
protected:
    String title;
};
```

It has two pure virtual functions and one data member.

Here is the concrete Book subclass:

```
class Book : Media {
public:
    Book(String a="", String t="", String p="", String i="")
      : author(a), publisher(p), isbn(i) { title = t; }
    void print() { cout << title << " by " << author << endl; }
    char* id() { return isbn; };
private:
    String author, publisher, isbn;
};
```

It implements the two virtual functions using its own member data.

Here is the concrete `CD` subclass:

```
class CD : Media {
public:
    CD(String t="", String c="", String m="", String n="")
     : composer(c), make(m), number(n) { title = t; }
    void print() { cout << title << ", " << composer << endl; }
    char* id() { return make + " " + number; };
private:
    String composer, make, number;
};
```

The `CD` class will also be a CDC of the `Audio` class, which will be another ABC. So when the `Audio` class is defined, its pure virtual functions will also have to be implemented in this `CD` class.

Here is the concrete `Magazine` subclass:

```
class Magazine : Media {
public:
    Magazine(String t="", String i="", int v=0, int n=0)
     : issn(i), volume(v), number(n) { title = t; }
    void print()
        { cout << title << " Magazine, Vol. "
                << volume << ", No." << number << endl; }
    char* id() { return issn; };
private:
    String issn, publisher;
    int volume, number;
};
```

The `Magazine` class will also be a CDC of the `Periodical` class, which will be another ABC. So when the `Periodical` class is defined, its pure virtual functions will also have to be implemented in this `Magazine` class.

Here is a test driver for the four classes defined above:

```
main()
{
    Book book("Bjarne Stroustrup", "The C++ Programming Language",
        "Addison-Wesley", "0-201-53992-6");
    Magazine magazine("TIME", "0040-781X", 145, 23);
    CD cd("BACH CANTATAS", "Johann Sebastian Bach",
        "ARCHIV", "D120541");
    book.print();
    cout << "\tid: " << book.id() << endl;
    magazine.print();
    cout << "\tid: " << magazine.id() << endl;
    cd.print();
    cout << "\tid: " << cd.id() << endl;
}
```

Here is the output:

```
The C++ Programming Language by Bjarne Stroustrup
        id: 0-201-53992-6
TIME Magazine, Vol. 145, No.23
        id: 0040-781X
BACH CANTATAS, Johann Sebastian Bach
        id: ARCHIV D120541
```

Note that all the calls to the `print()` and `id()` functions are independent of their class implementations. So the implementations of these functions could be changed without making any changes to the program. For example, we could change the `Book::print()` function to

```
void print()
     { cout << title << " by " << author
             << ".\nPublished by " << publisher << ".\n"; }
```

and obtain the output

```
The C++ Programming Language by Bjarne Stroustrup.
Published by Addison-Wesley.
```

without any changes to the program.

11.10 OBJECT-ORIENTED PROGRAMMING

Object-oriented programming refers to the use of derived classes and virtual functions. A thorough treatment of object-oriented programming is beyond the scope of this book. See the books **[Bergin]**, **[Perry]**, and **[Wang]** listed in Appendix E for a more thorough treatment.

Suppose that you have three televisions, each equipped with its own video cassette recorder. Like most VCRs, yours are loaded with features and have confusing user manuals. Your three VCRs are all different, requiring different and complex operations to use them. Then one day you see on the shelf of your local electronics store a simple remote controller that can operate all kinds of VCRs. For example, it has a single "RECORD" button that causes whatever VCR it is pointed at to record the current TV program on the current tape. This marvelous device represents the essence of object-oriented programming ("OOP"): conceptual simplification of diverse *implementations* by means of a single *interface*. In this example, the interface is the remote controller, and the implementations are the (hidden) operations within the controller and the individual VCRs that carry out the requested functions ("RECORD", "STOP", "PLAY", *etc.*). The interface is the abstract base class below:

```
class VCR {
public:
    virtual void on() =0;
    virtual void off() =0;
    virtual void record() =0;
    virtual void stop() =0;
    virtual void play() =0;
};
```

and the implementations are the concrete derived classes below:

```
class Panasonic : public VCR {
public:
    void on();
    void off();
    void record();
    void stop();
    void play();
};


class Sony : public VCR {
public:
    void on();
    void off();
    void record();
    void stop();
    void play();
};


class Mitsubishi : public VCR {
public:
    void on();
    void off();
    void record();
    void stop();
    void play();
};
```

One important advantage of object-oriented systems is *extensibility*. This refers to the ease with which the system can be extended. In the example above, the VCR controller would be called "extensible" if it automatically works the same way on new VCRs that we might add in the future. The controller should not have to be modified when we extend our collection of VCRs, adding a Toshiba or replacing the Sony with an RCA.

In the object-oriented programming, we imagine two distinct points of view of the system: the view of the consumer (*i.e.*, the client or user) that shows <u>what</u> is to be done, and the view of the manufacturer (*i.e.*, the server or implementor) that shows <u>how</u> it is to be done. The consumer sees only the abstract base class, while the manufacturer sees the concrete derived classes. The customer's actions are generally called *operations*, as opposed to the manufacturer's implementations of these actions which are called generally *methods*. In C++, the actions are the pure virtual functions, and the methods are their implementations in the concrete derived classes. In this context, the abstract base class (the user's view) is called the system *interface*, and the concrete derived classes (the implementor's view) are called the system *implementation*:

This dichotomy is most effective when we use pointers to objects, as in Example 11.13. Then we can exploit dynamic binding make the system interface even more independent from the system implementation. Extensibility is facilitated by the fact that only the newly added methods need to be compiled.

The Two Views in an Object-Oriented Program

The System Interface (user's view)	The System Implementation (implementor's view)
shows <u>what</u> is done	shows <u>how</u> it is done
abstract base class	concrete derived classes
operations	methods
pure virtual functions	functions

Review Questions

11.1   What is the difference between composition and inheritance?

11.2   What is the difference between `protected` and `private` members?

11.3   How do the default constructors and destructors behave in an inheritance hierarchy?

11.4   What is a `virtual` member function?

11.5   What is a pure `virtual` member function?

11.6   What is a memory leak?

11.7   How can virtual destructors plug a memory leak?

11.8   What is an abstract base class?

11.9   What is a concrete derived class?

11.10 What is the difference between static binding and dynamic binding?

11.11 What is polymorphism?

11.12 How does polymorphism promote extensibility?

11.13 What is wrong with the following definitions:

```
class X {
protected:
    int a;
};

class Y : public X {
public:
    void set(X x, int c) { x.a = c; }
};
```

Solved Programming Problems

11.14 Implement a `Card` class, a composite `Hand` class, and a composite `Deck` class for playing poker.

First we implement a `Card` class:

```
enum Rank {two, three, four, five, six, seven, eight,
           nine, ten, jack, queen, king, ace};
enum Suit {clubs, diamonds, hearts, spades};

class Card {
    friend class Hand;
    friend class Deck;
    friend ostream& operator<<(ostream&, const Card&);
public:
    char rank() { return rank_; }
    char suit() { return suit_; }
private:
    Card() { };
    Card(Rank rank, Suit suit) : rank_(rank), suit_(suit) { };
    Card(const Card& c) : rank_(c.rank_), suit_(c.suit_) { };
    ~Card() { };
    Rank rank_;
    Suit suit_;
};
```

This class uses enumeration types for a card's 13 possible ranks and 4 possible suits. Anticipating the implementation of `Hand` and `Deck` classes, we declare them here to be `friend` classes to the `Card` class. This will allow them to access the `private` members of the `Card` class. Notice that all three constructors and the destructor are declared to be `private`. This will prevent any cards to be created or destroyed except by the `Card`'s two `friend` classes.

Here is the implementation of the overloaded insertion operator `<<` for cards:

```
ostream& operator<<(ostream& ostr, const Card& card)
{
    switch (card.rank_) {
        case two   : ostr << "two of ";    break;
        case three : ostr << "three of ";  break;
        case four  : ostr << "four of ";   break;
        case five  : ostr << "five of ";   break;
        case six   : ostr << "six of ";    break;
        case seven : ostr << "seven of ";  break;
        case eight : ostr << "eight of ";  break;
        case nine  : ostr << "nine of ";   break;
        case ten   : ostr << "ten of ";    break;
        case jack  : ostr << "jack of ";   break;
        case queen : ostr << "queen of ";  break;
        case king  : ostr << "king of ";   break;
        case ace   : ostr << "ace of ";    break;
    }
    switch (card.suit_) {
        case clubs    : ostr << "clubs";    break;
        case diamonds : ostr << "diamonds"; break;
        case hearts   : ostr << "hearts";   break;
        case spades   : ostr << "spades";   break;
    }
    return ostr;
}
```

Here is the implementation of the `Hand` class:

```
#include "Card.h"

class Hand {
    friend class Deck;
public:
    Hand(unsigned n=5) : size(n) { cards = new Card[n]; }
    ~Hand() { delete [] cards; }
    void display();
    int isPair();
    int isTwoPair();
    int isThreeOfKind();
    int isStraight();
    int isFlush();
    int isFullHouse();
    int isFourOfKind();
    int isStraightFlush();
private:
    unsigned size;
    Card* cards;
    void sort();
};
```

It uses an array to store the cards in the hand. The `sort()` function is a private utility that is called by the `Deck` class after dealing the hand. It can be implemented by any simple sort algorithm such as the Bubble Sort. The `display()` function is also straightforward, using the insertion operator `<<` that is overloaded in the `Card` class.

The eight boolean functions that identify special poker hands are not so straightforward. Here is the implementation of the `isThreeOfKind()` function:

```
int Hand::isThreeOfKind()
{
    if (cards[0].rank_ == cards[1].rank_
        && cards[1].rank_ == cards[2].rank_
        && cards[2].rank_ != cards[3].rank_
        && cards[3].rank_ != cards[4].rank_) return 1;
    if (cards[0].rank_ != cards[1].rank_
        && cards[1].rank_ == cards[2].rank_
        && cards[2].rank_ == cards[3].rank_
        && cards[3].rank_ != cards[4].rank_) return 1;
    if (cards[0].rank_ != cards[1].rank_
        && cards[1].rank_ != cards[2].rank_
        && cards[2].rank_ == cards[3].rank_
        && cards[3].rank_ == cards[4].rank_) return 1;
    return 0;
}
```

Since the hand is sorted by `rank_`, the only way there could be three cards of the same rank with the other two cards of different rank would be one of the three forms: *xxxyz*, *xyyyz*, or *xyzzz*. If any of these three forms is identified, then the function returns 1. If not it returns 0.

The `isPair()` function, the `isTwoPair()` function, the `isFullHouse()` function, and the `isFourOfKind()` function are similar to the `isThreeOfKind()` function.

The `isStraight()` function, the `isFlush()` function, and the `isStraightFlush()` function are also tricky. Here is the `isFlush()` function:

```
int Hand::isFlush()
{
    for (int i = 1; i < size; i++)
        if (cards[i].suit_ != cards[0].suit_) return 0;
    return 1;
}
```

This compares the `suit_` of each of the second through fifth cards (`card[1]` through `card[4]`). If any of these are not the same, then we know immediately that the hand is not a flush and can return 0. If the loop terminates naturally, then all four pairs match and 1 is returned.

Here is the `Deck` class:

```
#include "Random.h"
#include "Hand.h"

class Deck {
public:
    Deck();
    void shuffle();
    void deal(Hand&, unsigned =5);
private:
    unsigned top;
    Card cards[52];
    Random random;
};
```

It uses the `Random` class in its `shuffle()` function. Note that the `random` object is declared as a private member since it is used only by another member function:

```
void Deck::deal(Hand& hand, unsigned size=5)
{
    for (int i = 0; i < size; i++)
        hand.cards[i] = cards[top++];
    hand.sort();
}
```

The `top` member always locates the top of the deck; *i.e.*, the next card to be dealt. So the `deal()` function copies the top five cards off the deck into the `hand`'s `cards` array. Then it sorts the hand.

The `Deck`'s constructor initializes all 52 cards in the deck, int the order `two of clubs, three of clubs, four of clubs,..., ace of spades`:

```
Deck::Deck()
{
    for (int i = 0; i < 52; i++) {
        cards[i].rank_ = Rank(i%13);
        cards[i].suit_ = Suit(i/13);
    }
    top = 0;
}
```

So if hands are dealt without shuffling first, the first hand would be the straight flush of two through six of clubs.

Finally, here is the `shuffle()` function:

```
void Deck::shuffle()
{
    for (int i = 0; i < 52; i++) {        // do 52 random swaps
        int j = random.integer(0, 51);
        Card c = cards[i];
        cards[i] = cards[j];
        cards[j] = c;
    }
    top = 0;
}
```

It swaps the cards in each of the 52 elements with the card in a randomly selected element of the deck's `cards` array.

The implementations of the other functions are left as exercises. (See Problem 11.18.)

11.15 Implement the following class hierarchy:

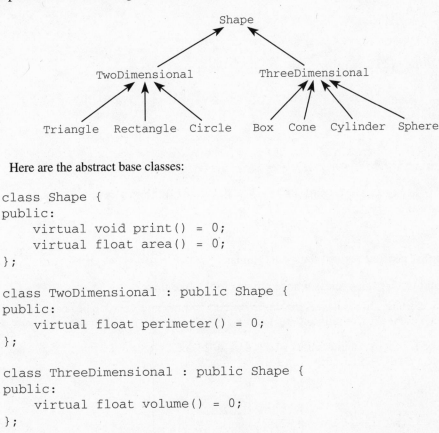

Here are the abstract base classes:

```
class Shape {
public:
    virtual void print() = 0;
    virtual float area() = 0;
};

class TwoDimensional : public Shape {
public:
    virtual float perimeter() = 0;
};

class ThreeDimensional : public Shape {
public:
    virtual float volume() = 0;
};
```

Note that the `print()` function and the `area()` function prototypes are the same for all classes in this hierarchy, so their interfaces (pure `virtual` functions) are placed in the `Shape` base class. But only two-dimensional shapes have perimeters, and only three-dimensional shapes have volumes, so their interfaces are placed in the appropriate second-level ABCs.

Here is the `Circle` class:

```
class Circle : public TwoDimensional {
public:
    Circle(float r) : radius(r) { }
    void print() { cout << "Shape is a circle.\n"; }
    float perimeter() { return 2*pi*radius; }
    float area() { return pi*radius*radius; }
private:
    float radius;
};
```

Here are two of the seven concrete derived classes:

```
class Cone : public ThreeDimensional {
public:
    Cone(float r, float h) : radius(r), height(h) { }
    void print();
    float area();
    float volume() { return pi*radius*radius*height/3; }
private:
    float radius, height;
};

void Cone::print()
{
    cout << "Cone: radius = " << radius << ", height = "
         << height << endl;
}

float Cone::area()
{
    float s = sqrt(radius*radius + height*height);
    return  pi*radius*(radius + s);
}
```

The other five concrete derived classes are similar.

11.16 Define and test a `Name` class whose objects looks like this:

Name

Then modify the `Person` class so that `name` has type `Name` instead of type `String`.

Here is the interface for the `Name` class:

```
#include "String.h"

class Name {
    friend ostream& operator<<(ostream&, const Name&);
    friend istream& operator>>(istream&, Name&);
public:
    Name(char*, char*, char*, char*, char*, char*);
    String last() { return last_; }
    String first() { return first_; }
    String middle() { return middle_; }
    String title() { return title_; }
    String suffix() { return suffix_; }
    String nick() { return nick_; }
    void last(String s) { last_ = s; }
    void first(String s) { first_ = s; }
    void middle(String s) { middle_ = s; }
    void title(String s) { title_ = s; }
    void suffix(String s) { suffix_ = s; }
    void nick(String s) { nick_ = s; }
    void dump();
private:
    String last_, first_, middle_, title_, suffix_, nick_;
};
```

Here is an implementation for the `Name` class:

```
Name::Name(char* last="", char* first="", char* middle="",
    char* title="", char* suffix="", char* nick="")
: last_(last), first_(first), middle_(middle), title_(title),
    suffix_(suffix), nick_(nick) { }

void Name::dump()
{
    cout << "\t    Last Name: " << last_   << endl;
    cout << "\t   First Name: " << first_  << endl;
    cout << "\tMiddle Names: " << middle_ << endl;
    cout << "\t        Title: " << title_  << endl;
    cout << "\t       Suffix: " << suffix_ << endl;
    cout << "\t     Nickname: " << nick_   << endl;
}

ostream& operator<<(ostream& out, const Name& x)
{
    if (x.title_ != "") out << x.title_ << " ";
    out << x.first_ << " ";
    if (x.middle_ != "") out << x.middle_ << " ";
    out << x.last_;
    if (x.suffix_ != "") out << " " << x.suffix_;
    if (x.nick_ != "") out << ", \"" << x.nick_ << "\"";
    return out;
}
```

```
istream& operator>>(istream& in, Name& x)
{
    char buffer[80];
    in.getline(buffer, 80, '|');
    x.last_ = buffer;
    in.getline(buffer, 80, '|');
    x.first_ = buffer;
    in.getline(buffer, 80, '|');
    x.middle_ = buffer;
    in.getline(buffer, 80, '|');
    x.title_ = buffer;
    in.getline(buffer, 80, '|');
    x.suffix_ = buffer;
    in.getline(buffer, 80);
    x.nick_ = buffer;
    return in;
}
```

Finally, here is the modified `Person` class:

```
#include "String.h"
#include "Date.h"
#include "Name.h"

class Person {
public:
    Person(char* n="", int s=0, char* nat="U.S.A.")
      : name(n), sex(s), nationality(nat) { }
    void setDOB(int m, int d, int y) { dob.setDate(m, d, y); }
    void setDOD(int m, int d, int y) { dod.setDate(m, d, y); }
    void printName() { cout << name; }
    void printNationality() { cout << nationality; }
    void printDOB() { cout << dob; }
    void printDOD() { cout << dod; }
protected:
    Name name;
    Date dob, dod;              // date of birth, date of death
    int sex;                    // 0 = female, 1 = male
    String nationality;
};
```

Here is a test driver for the `Name` class, with test run:

```
#include <iostream.h>
#include "Name.h"

main()
{
    Name x("Bach", "Johann", "Sebastian");
    cout << x << endl;
    x.dump();
    x.last("Clinton");
```

```
        x.first("William");
        x.middle("Jefferson");
        x.title("President");
        x.nick("Bill");
        cout << x << endl;
        x.dump();
        cin >> x;
        cout << x << endl;
        cout << "x.last   = [" << x.last()   << "]\n";
        cout << "x.first  = [" << x.first()  << "]\n";
        cout << "x.middle = [" << x.middle() << "]\n";
        cout << "x.title  = [" << x.title()  << "]\n";
        cout << "x.suffix = [" << x.suffix() << "]\n";
        cout << "x.nick   = [" << x.nick()   << "]\n";
}
```

```
Johann Sebastian Bach
            Last Name: Bach
           First Name: Johann
        Middle Names: Sebastian
                Title:
               Suffix:
             Nickname:
President William Jefferson Clinton, "Bill"
            Last Name: Clinton
           First Name: William
        Middle Names: Jefferson
                Title: President
               Suffix:
             Nickname: Bill
Tudor|Mary||Queen|I|Bloody Mary
Queen Mary Tudor I, "Bloody Mary"
x.last   = [Tudor]
x.first  = [Mary]
x.middle = []
x.title  = [Queen]
x.suffix = [I]
x.nick   = [Bloody Mary]
```

Supplementary Problems

11.17 Devise a system interface and a system implementation, similar to that for the VCR class in Section 11.10, but for a network of printers. Assume that the network includes several different kinds of printers. Your ABC should represent a generic printer.

Supplementary Programming Problems

11.18 Finish the implementation of the `Card`, `Hand`, and `Deck` classes defined in Problem 11.14, and test them.

11.19 Apply the Monte Carlo method (Problem 3.23 and Problem 4.60) to the `Deck` class (Problem 11.14) to estimate the odds of being dealt each of the eight special poker hands. Your output should look something like this:

```
How many hands: 2598960
1100606 pairs
123964 two pairs
56255 three of a kind
8726 straights
5054 flushes
3745 full houses
405 four of a kind
68 straight flushes
```

The number 2,598,960 is the actual number of different 5-card hands that could be dealt from an ordinary deck of 52 playing cards. Here are the actual number of possible different hands:

Table 11.1 Possible Poker Hands

Hand	Number of Hands
One Pair	1,098,240
Two Pairs	123,552
Three of a Kind	54,912
Straight	10,200
Flush	5,108
Full House	3,744
Four of a Kind	626
Straight Flush	40

11.20 The `shuffle()` function implemented in Problem 11.14 is not how most players shuffle cards. The common method is to interleave two halves of the deck. Done precisely, this would transform our initialized deck into the following order: two of clubs, two of hearts, three of clubs, three of hearts, ..., ace of diamonds, ace of spades. In terms of the cards initial numbers, this would be 0, 26, 1, 27, 2, 28, 3, 29, ..., 24, 50, 25, 51. This algorithm is known as the *perfect shuffle*.

a. Implement this method in place of the other, and test your resulting `Deck` class.

b. Determine empirically how many perfect shuffles it takes to restore the deck to its original ordering.

11.21 Define and test an `Address` class whose objects looks like this:

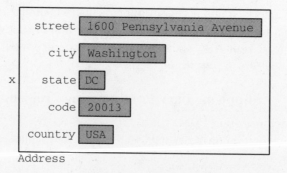

Address

Each data member should be a `String` object. Then modify the `Person` class by adding an `address` data member with type `Address`.

11.22 Define and test a `Telephone` class whose objects looks like this:

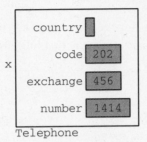

Telephone

Each data member should be a `String` object. Then modify the `Person` class by adding a `telephone` data member with type `Telephone`. Write your overloaded insertion and extraction operators so that they process the number in this format: `(202) 456-1414`.

11.23 Define and test a `Money` class whose objects represent dollar amounts. Use a `cents` data member of type `unsigned`.

11.24 Define and test a `University` class whose objects represent universities. Include the following data members:

```
String name;
Address address;
Date founded;
```

11.25 Define and test a `Degree` class whose objects represent college degrees. Include the following data members:

```
String name, discipline;
University university;
Date awarded;
```

11.26 Define and test a `Faculty` class whose objects represent universities. Include the following data members:

```
int Rank;
Money salary;
String dept, office;
Degree highestDegree;
```

11.27 Modify and test the `Student` class by adding the following data members:

```
Address campusAddress;
Telephone campusTelephone;
String school, emailAddress
Faculty advisor, degreeSought;
```

11.28 Define and test a subclass `Undergrad` that inherits from the `Student` class and includes the following data members:

```
String school, major;
Person parent;
```

11.29 Define and test a subclass `GradStudent` that inherits from the `Student` class and includes the following data members:

```
String department;
Degree lastDegree;
```

11.30 Implement the following class hierarchy, using your results of the previous problems:

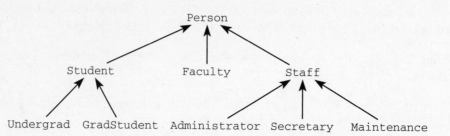

The `Person`, `Student`, and `Staff` classes should be abstract base classes; the other six classes should be concrete derived classes.

11.31 Implement the following class hierarchy:

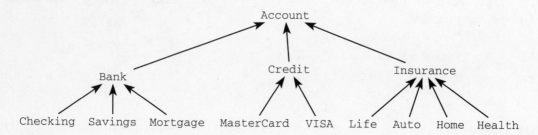

The top four (internal node) classes should be abstract base classes, and the bottom nine (leaf node) classes should be concrete derived classes.

Answers to Review Questions

11.1 Composition of classes refers to using one class to declare members of another class. Inheritance refers to deriving a subclass from a base class.

11.2 A `private` member is inaccessible from anywhere outside its class definition. A `protected` member is inaccessible from anywhere outside its class definition, with the exception that it is accessible from the definitions of derived classes.

11.3   In an inheritance hierarchy, each default constructor invokes its parent's default constructor before it executes itself, and each destructor invokes its parent's destructor after it executes itself. The effect is that all the parent default constructors execute in top-down order, and all the parent destructors execute in bottom-up order.

11.4   A `virtual` member function is a member function that can be overridden in a subclass.

11.5   A pure `virtual` function is a `virtual` member function that cannot be called directly; only its overridden functions in derived classes can be called. A pure `virtual` function is identified by the initializer `=0` at the end of its declaration.

11.6   An abstract base class is a base class which includes at least one pure `virtual` function. Abstract base classes cannot be instantiated.

11.7   A concrete derived class is a subclass of an abstract base class that can be instantiated; *i.e.*, one which contains no pure `virtual` functions.

11.8   Static binding refers to the linking of a member function call to the function itself during compile time, in contrast to dynamic binding which postpones that linking until run time. Dynamic is possible in C++ by using virtual functions and by passing to pointers to objects.

11.9   *Polymorphism* refers to the run-time binding that occurs when pointers to objects are used in classes that have `virtual` functions. The expressions `p->f()` will invoke the functions `f()` that is defined in the object to which `p` points. However, that object could belong to any one of a series of subclasses, and the selection of subclass could be made at run time. If the base-class function is `virtual`, then the selection (the "binding") of which `f()` to invoke is made at run time. So the expression `p->f()` can take "many forms."

11.10 Polymorphism promotes extensibility by allowing new subclasses and methods to be added to a class hierarchy without having to modify application programs that already use the hierarchy's interface.

11.11 The `protected` data member `a` can be accessed from the derived `Y` only if it is the member of the current object (*i.e.* only if it is `this->a`). `Y` cannot access `x.a` for any other object `x`.

Chapter 12

Stream I/O

12.1 STREAM CLASSES

The C++ programming language itself does not include any input/output (I/O) facilities. That is why we have to use the directive

```
#include <iostream.h>
```

in every program that uses I/O. The `iostream.h` header file includes the definitions for the I/O library. This chapter describes the contents of those files and how they are used.

The I/O library defines the following two class hierarchies of *stream classes*:

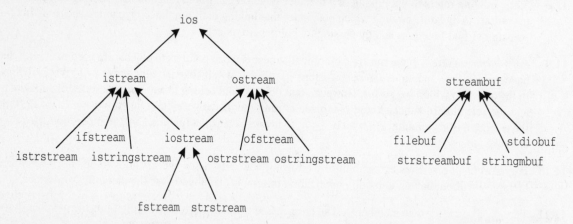

The classes that are derived from the `ios` base class are used for high-level stream processing, while the classes that are derived from the `streambuf` base class are used for low-level stream processing.

The `iostream` class is the one that we usually use for ordinary I/O. Notice that is it a subclass of both the `istream` class and the `ostream` class, both of which are subclasses of the `ios` base class. The three classes with "`fstream`" in their name are used for file processing. The four classes with "`strstr`" in their name are used for in-memory *string stream* processing. The `stdiobuf` class is used for combining C++ stream I/O with the older C I/O functions.

12.2 THE `ios` CLASS

The `ios` class serves as the base class for the other stream classes. Its primary purpose is to control the buffer for whatever stream object has been instantiated. This means that the stream controls how characters are inserted into or extracted from the buffer. To do that, the `ios` object maintains a collection of data members that control properties such as the number base (octal, decimal, hexadecimal) that is to be used, the width of the display field, the number of digits displayed for floating point numbers, *etc.* We shall examine the `protected` part of the `ios` class here in order to gain a deeper understanding of the functioning interface.

Here is part of the `ios` class:

```
class ios {
public:
    typedef unsigned long fmtflags;   // 32-bit bitstrings
    typedef unsigned char iostate;    // 8-bit bitstrings
    // other members included here
protected:
    streambuf* _strbuf;       // points to buffer
    ostream*   _tie;          // points to ostream tied to istream
    int        _width;        // width of output field
    int        _prec;         // precision for floats
    char       _fill;         // fill character for padding field
    fmtflags   _flags;        // holds all the format flags
    iostate    _state;        // holds the current io state
    ios(streambuf* _strbuf = 0, ostream* _tie = 0);
    ~ios();
};
```

The two defined types (`fmtflags` and `iostate`) are `unsigned` integer types; *i.e.*, *bits strings*. Each of the 32 bits of the data member `_flags` and each of the 8 bits of the data member `_state` can be used to represent different Boolean parameters for the stream. The default constructor and the destructor for the `ios` class are declared `protected` so that the class cannot be instantiated.

Note that the `ios` data members are all `protected`. This means that they are accessible only from within a stream's member functions; they are not accessible from user programs.

A *stream object* is an instance of a subclass of the ios class. So every stream object must have the seven data members declared in the `ios` class. Such an object `x` can be imagined like this:

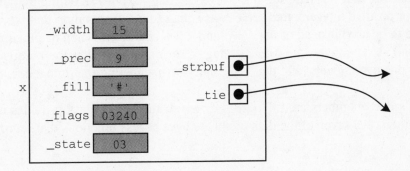

The object's seven data members include a pointer to a `streambuf`, a pointer to an `ostream`, two `int`s, a `char`, and two bit strings whose values are represented in octal. The `_width` parameter determines how wide the output field will be, the `_prec` parameter determines how many digits will be displayed for `float`s and `double`s, and the `_fill` parameter determines which character will be used for padding a justified field. If this object `x` is an output stream, then output will use a 15-character field with 9-digit precision and the character `'#'` for fill. The `_flags` and `_state` data members are bit-strings that hold many *boolean* parameters. The `_streambuf` pointer is used to connect the stream to its buffer, and the `_tie` pointer is used to "tie" an input object (like `cin`) to an output object (like `cout`).

The `_flags` member is a 32-bit string, so it can hold 32 boolean "flags". Only about half of these are used by `ios`. Those values are given symbolic names by an `enum` declaration:

```
class ios {
public:
    enum {                              // values for format flag:
        skipws    =      01,   // skip white space
        left      =      02,   // left justified in field
        right     =      04,   // right justified in field (default)
        internal  =     010,   // left and right justified
        dec       =     020,   // use number base 10 for integers
        oct       =     040,   // use number base 8 for integers
        hex       =    0100,   // use number base 16 for integers
        showbase  =    0200,   // show number base for integers
        showpoint =    0400,   // print trailing zeros for floats
        uppercase =   01000,   // use 'E', 'x' instead of 'e', 'x'
        showpos   =   02000,   // use '+' with positive integers
        scientific =  04000,   // use scientific notation for floats
        fixed     =  010000,   // use fixed point notation for floats
        unitbuf   =  020000,   // flush after each output operation
        stdio     =  040000    // flush after each character output
    };
    // other members included here
};
```

Each of these 15 constant values is a power of 2, and is represented in octal form. By adding these values for the flags that are "set," we obtain the complete flag setting for the stream object in a single octal number. For example, the `x` object shown above has the octal value `03240` for its `_format` data member. This octal number decomposes as

```
03240 = 02000 + 01000 + 0200 + 040
```

which indicates that four flags are set: the `showpos` flag (`02000`) signaling that the `+` sign is to be included for positive integers; the `uppercase` flag (`01000`) signaling that the `'E'` and `'X'` characters are to be used instead of the `'e'` and `'x'` characters when displaying numbers like `2.308E12` and `0X1204`; the `showbase` flag (`0200`) signaling that the number base is to be displayed for positive integers, and the `oct` flag (`040`) signaling that integers will be input and output in octal.

A stream's data members are all `protected`, so the `ios` class provides a set of access functions for them. All seven of the data members have access functions that return their values:

```
class ios {
public:
    // more members included here
    streambuf* rdbuf() const { return _strbuf; }
    ostream* tie() const { return _tie; }
    int width() const { return _width; }
    int precision() const { return _prec; }
    char fill() const { return _fill; }
    long flags() const { return _flags; }
    int rdstate() const { return _state; }
    // more members included here
};
```

EXAMPLE 12.1 Testing Some of the `ios` Access Functions

```
main()
{
    cout << "cout.width()    = " << cout.width() << endl;
    cout << "cout.precision() = " << cout.precision() << endl;
    cout << "cout.fill()     = [" << cout.fill() << "]" << endl;
    cout << "cin.flags()     = " << oct << cin.flags() << endl;
    cout << "cout.flags()    = " << oct << cout.flags() << endl;
}
```

```
cout.width()     = 0
cout.precision() = 6
cout.fill()      = [ ]
cin.flags()      = 20000000001
cout.flags()     = 20000000041
```

This shows that for `cout`, the default field width is 0, the default precision for floats is 6 digits, and the default fill character is the blank ' '. The octal value 20000000001 means that only the `skipws` flag (01) is set for `cin`, which means that white space (blank, tab, newline, formfeed, and return) is skipped by default. (The digit 2 in this octal value is irrelevant.) The octal value 20000000041 means that the `skipws` flag (01) and the `oct` flag (040) are set for `cout`. The `oct` flag was set by inserting the `oct` manipulator prior to the `cout.flags()` call.

Each of the four data members `_width`, `_prec`, `_fill`, and `_flags` also has an access function that can change its value:

```
class ios {
public:
    int width(int w) { int t = _width; _width = w; return t; }
    int precision(int p){ int t = _prec; _prec = p; return t; }
    char fill(char c) { char t = _fill; _fill = c; return t; }
    long flags(long f) { long t = _flags; _flags = f; return t; }
    // more members included here
};
```

These all work the same way: they return the current value after replacing it with the new value.

EXAMPLE 12.2 Changing the Fill and Width of `cout`

```
main()
{
    cout.fill('#');
    cout.width(40);
    cout << "Hello, World." << endl;
    cout << "Hello, World." << endl;
}
```

```
###########################Hello, World.
Hello, World.
```

After changing the fill character and the field width, the next item output is right-justified in a field of 40 columns with the '#' character padding on the left. Note that both the `_fill` and `_width` parameters revert back to their default values (' ' and 0) immediately after the next output.

EXAMPLE 12.3 Changing the Precision of cout

```
main()
{
    double pi = 3.14159265358979323846;
    cout << "pi = " << pi << endl;
    cout.precision(16);
    cout << "pi = " << pi << endl;
    cout << "pi = " << pi << endl;
    cout.precision(20);
    cout << "pi = " << pi << endl;
}
```

```
pi = 3.14159
pi = 3.141592653589793
pi = 3.141592653589793
pi = 3.141592653589793116
```

The default value for the _prec data member is 6. This means that floats will be displayed using 6 digits, as the first output of pi shows. Changing that to 16 causes cout to print 16 digits. That is the maximum number of digits that type double can store (on a 32-bit machine), so increasing it to 20 only results in garbage digits after the 16th. Note that, unlike the _fill and _width parameters, the precision parameter <u>does not revert back</u> to its default value after the next output.

12.3 ios FORMAT FLAGS

The width, precision, and fill parameters for a stream object are implemented with separate data members because each parameter can have more than two values. For example, any letter of the alphabet could be the fill character. But streams have many other attributes which are Boolean; *i.e.*, their value is either true or false.   These are the parameters that are listed in the first enum definition above, and are summarized in Table 12.1 below. All 15 of these flags are packed into the single data member _flags.

The next example illustrates one way to change a stream's format flags.

EXAMPLE 12.4 Using cout.flags() to Set a Stream's Format Flags

```
main()
{
    int n = 234;
    long oldf = cout.flags( ios::hex | ios::uppercase );
    cout << n << endl;
    cout.flags( ios::hex |  ios::showbase );
    cout << n << endl;
    cout.flags(oldf);
    cout << n << endl;
}
```

```
EA
0xea
234
```

The first call to `cout.flags()` sets the `hex` and `uppercase` flags, while saving all the previous settings in `oldf`. Notice that the hexadecimal form for the integer 234 is `ea`, which is printed `EA` because the uppercase flag is set. (See Appendix H for more information on hexadecimal numerals.) The second call to `cout.flags()` sets the `hex` and `showbase` flags, causing all other flags to be cleared, so that the second output prints the hexadecimal letters for `n` in lowercase and with the leading `0x` to show that the numeral is hexadecimal. The third call to `cout.flags()` restores the original (default) settings.

Table 12.1 Format Flags

Flag	Effect When Set
`ios::skipws`	Skip leading white space during formatted input. (default)
`ios::left`	Left-justify output, padding on right to make required width.
`ios::right`	Right-justify output, padding on left to make required width. (default)
`ios::internal`	Right-justify numeric output, left-justify any sign or radix, and pad the middle to make required width.
`ios::dec`	Input and output integers base 10. (default for output)
`ios::oct`	Input and output integers base 8.
`ios::hex`	Input and output integers base 16.
`ios::showbase`	Output integers with radix prefix; *e.g.*, 027 for (oct), 0x2c1 for (hex). (default)
`ios::showpoint`	Output real numbers with decimal point and trailing zeros.
`ios::uppercase`	Use uppercase letters to output hex integers and reals in scientific.
`ios::showpos`	Prefix positive integers with `'+'`.
`ios::scientific`	Output real numbers in scientific notation; *e.g.*, `1.23456e-09`
`ios::fixed`	Output real numbers with *n* digits to right of decimal point, where *n* is the precision (`_prec`)
`ios::unitbuf`	Flush the output stream after each insertion.
`ios::stdio`	Flush `stdio` and `stderr` after each insertion.

The `flags()` function sets the stream's flags to the new setting without retaining any of the previous settings. So it has the effect of clearing all the flags that are not named in the function's argument. In Example 12.4, the second call to `cout.flags()` cleared the three settings made by the first call. To set one or more flags without clearing any others, use the `setf()` function, which is one of the three other member functions defined in `ios` for accessing the format flags:

```
class ios {
public:
    // previous members included here
    long setf(long f)
        { long t = _flags; _flags |= f; return t; }
    long setf(long f, long mask)
        { long t = _flags;
          _flags = (_flags & ~mask) | (f & mask); return t; }
    long unsetf(long mask)
        { long t = _flags & mask; _flags &= ~mask; return t; }
    // more members included here
    };
```

The next example shows how to use the one-argument `setf()` function to set flags without clearing others.

EXAMPLE 12.5 Using `cout.setf()` to Set a Stream's Format Flags

This example is the same as Example 12.4 except that `setf()` is called instead of `flags()`.

```
main()
{
    int n = 234;
    long oldf = cout.setf( ios::hex | ios::uppercase );
    cout << n << endl;
    cout.setf( ios::hex |  ios::showbase );
    cout << n << endl;
    cout.flags(oldf);
    cout << n << endl;
}
```

```
EA
0XEA
234
```

The first call to `cout.setf()` sets the `hex` and `uppercase` flags, while saving all the previous settings in `oldf`, so `n` is printed in uppercase hex. The second call to `cout.setf()` sets the `hex` and `showbase` flags, leaving the `uppercase` flag set, so that the second output prints `n` is printed in uppercase hex with the leading `0x` to show that the numeral is hexadecimal. The call to `cout.flags()` restores the original (default) settings, which are lowercase decimal without showing the base.

Three subgroups of format flags are defined to facilitate avoiding a conflict between contradictory flags. Each group is identified by its *format mask*, as shown in Table 12.2.

Table 12.2 Format Flags

Mask	Flags
ios::basefield	ios::dec, ios::oct, ios::hex
ios::adjustfield	ios::left, ios::right, ios::internal
ios::floatfield	ios::scientific, ios::fixed

These definitions are part of the `ios` class:

```
class ios {
public:
    const long basefield = dec | oct | hex;
    const long adjustfield = left | right | internal;
    const long floatfield = scientific | fixed;
    // more members included here
};
```

These constants are called "masks" because they are used to "mask out" all the flags except those in its group. For example, in the implementation of the `unsetf()` function

```
long unsetf(long mask)
     { long t = _flags & mask; _flags &= ~mask; return t; }
```

the expression **_flags &= ~mask** clears all the flags in the mask, leaving all other flags unchanged. The effect of this function is to clear all the flags in the format mask and to return their previous settings:

EXAMPLE 12.6 Using `unsetf()` to Clear a Stream's Format Flags

```
main()
{
    char buffer[80];
    cin.unsetf(ios::skipws);  // clear default skipws flag
    cin >> buffer;  cout << "[" << buffer << "]\n";
    cin >> buffer;  cout << "[" << buffer << "]\n";
    cin >> buffer;  cout << "[" << buffer << "]\n";
    int n = 234;
    cout.setf( ios::hex | ios::uppercase |  ios::showbase );
    cout << n << endl;
    cout.unsetf( ios::basefield );  // clear all radix flags
    cout << n << endl;
}
```

```
  Hello, World.
[ ]
[ Hello,]
[ World.]
0XEA
234
```

The `skipws` flag is set by default, which means that ordinarily white space is skipped before reading a value into a variable. But the call to **cin.unsetf** clears this flag so that white space will not be ignored. The first three characters input are two blanks and the H, so the first read into `buffer` reads only a single blank. That is because the second blank signals an end to that input. The second read into `buffer` reads the second blank and the entire six-character string "`Hello,`". Again, input is terminated by the first blank encountered after the reading begins.

The call to **cout.unsetf** clears all the flags that are in the `basefield` group. This includes the `hex` flag that was set with the `cout.setf` call.

Warning: This use of **cout.unsetf** may not work on some older compilers (*e.g.*, version 4.5 of Microsoft Turbo C++).

The `setf()` function that takes two arguments uses a format mask in its second argument:

```
long setf(long f, long mask)
     { long t = _flags; _flags = (_flags&~mask)|(f&mask); return t; }
```

The `mask` specifies which group of flags is to be changed. The function clears all the flags in the group specified by `mask` and then sets the flag `f` if it is in that group.

EXAMPLE 12.7 Using `cout.setf()` with a Format Mask to Set a Stream's Format Flags

This example is the same as Example 12.4 except that `setf()` is called instead of `flags()`.

```
main()
{
    int n = 234;
    cout.setf( ios::hex | ios::uppercase |  ios::showbase );
    cout << n << endl;
    cout.setf( ios::oct, ios::basefield );
    cout << n << endl;
}
```

```
0XEA
0352
```

This is the correct way to change radix. To change from hexadecimal to octal, both the `oct` flag has to be set and the `hex` flag cleared. The second call to **cout.setf** does that.

12.4 `ios` STATE VARIABLES

Every stream has a `_state` data member that is defined in the `ios` class. Like the `_flags` member, the `_state` member is a bit string that holds several boolean variables. These *state variables* are specified in the `enum` definition:

```
class ios {
public:
    enum {                          // values for error state flag:
        goodbit =  0,               // all ok
        eofbit  = 01,               // end of file
        failbit = 02,               // last operation failed
        badbit  = 04                // invalid operation
    };
    // other members included here
};
```

A stream's format flags can only be changed explicitly, and only by means of the `ios` access functions described below. In contrast, a stream's state variables are changed implicitly, as a result of I/O operations. For example, when a user inputs **Control-D** (or **Control-Z** on DOS and VAX computers) to indicate end-of-file, the `cin`'s *eof flag* is set, and we say that the stream is in an *eof state*.

By adding the numeric values for the flags that are "set," we obtain the complete io state setting for the stream object in a single 8-bit number. For example, the `x` object shown above has the octal value `0` for its `_state` data member. This number decomposes as

03 = 02 + 01

which indicates that two flags are set: the `failbit` (02) signaling that the last operation failed (because input was at the end-of-file), and the `eofbit` (01).

A stream's four *state variables* (`goodbit`, `eofbit`, `failbit`, and `badbit`) can be accessed individually by their access functions (`good()`, `eof()`, `fail()`, and `bad()`). They can also be accessed collectively by the `rdstate()` function, as demonstrated by the next example.

EXAMPLE 12.8 Testing the `rdstate()` Function

```
main()
{
    cout << "cin.rdstate() = " << cin.rdstate() << endl;
    int n;
    cin >> n;
    cout << "cin.rdstate() = " << cin.rdstate() << endl;
}
```

```
cin.rdstate() = 0
22
cin.rdstate() = 0
```

```
cin.rdstate() = 0
^D
cin.rdstate() = 3
```

On the second run, the user pressed **Control-D** (or **Control-Z** on a PC or a VAX) to signal end-of-file. This sets `cin`'s `eofbit` and `failbit`, which have numeric values 1 and 2, making the (total) value of the `_state` variable 3.

The state variables can set be means of the `set()` function the same way that the single-argument `setf()` function is used to set format flags. However, state variables are generally used only to read the current state of the stream, so it is unlikely that you would want to change them directly.

The following two access functions are used to test the state of the stream within a conditional expression:

```
class ios {
public:
    operator void*() const;        // conversion operator
    int operator!() const;
    // other members included here
};
```

The first of these is a conversion operator. It returns a pointer that is NULL (*i.e.*, 0) if `_state` is nonzero and -1 otherwise. So for example, if `in` is an input stream, then the expression (`in`) will evaluate to true if none of the flags are set (*i.e.*, there is still more input), and false otherwise.

The second of these access functions overloads the negation operator. It simply calls `fail()` and returns its return value, which will be nonzero unless both the `failbit` and the `badbit` are clear. The advantage of this alternate form for determining whether the stream can be used any more is that, like the conversion operator above, this form can be used conveniently in conditional expressions. For example, if `out` is an output stream, then the expression (`!out`) will evaluate to true if either the `failbit` or the `badbit` is set (*i.e.*, the out stream will not function any more), and false otherwise.

EXAMPLE 12.9 Using the Conversion Operator `operator void*()` to Control a Loop

```
main()
{
    int n, sum=0;
    cin >> n;
    while (cin) {          // loop will continue as long as _state == 0
        sum += n;
        cin >> n;
    }
    cout << "sum = " << sum << endl;
}
```

```
44 11 22
^D
sum = 77
```

Using **Control-D** (or **Control-Z**) to terminate input is simple and convenient. Pressing this key sets the `eofbit` in the input stream. But then, if you want to use it again in the same program, it has to be cleared first. This is done with the member function `clear()`, as shown below:

EXAMPLE 12.10 Using the `clear()` Function to Clear the `eofbit`

```
main()
{
    int n, sum = 0;
    while (cin >> n)
        sum += n;
    cout << "The partial sum is " << sum << endl;
    cin.clear();
    while (cin >> n)
        sum += n;
    cout << "The total sum is " << sum << endl;
}
```

```
40 90 20 ^D
The partial sum is 150
30 50 ^D
The total sum is 230
```

When the end-of-file is detected as a result of the **Control-D**, `cin`'s `eofbit` and `failbit` are set, and the expression (`cin >> n`) returns 0. This stops the first loop and prints the partial sum. Then the call to `cin.clear()` resets the `eofbit` to 0 (*i.e.*, clears it), so that the second `while` loop can execute properly.

Warning: This use of **`cout.clear()`** may not work on some older compilers (*e.g.*, version 4.5 of Microsoft Turbo C++).

The `ios` class's `_tie` member is used to "tie" an input stream to an output stream. When an input stream is tied to an output stream, the output stream is flushed automatically whenever an operation is attempted on the input stream. This means that user prompts will work normally:

EXAMPLE 12.11 Using `cin.tie()` to Break and Reconnect the Tie of `cin` to `cout`

```
main()
{
    cout << "Press any key to continue:";
    cin.get();
    cout << "Thank you." << endl;
    cin.tie(0);                     // this breaks the tie of cin to cout
    cout << "Press any key to continue:";
    cin.get();
    cout << "Thank you." << endl;
    cin.tie(&cout);          // this reconnects the tie of cin to cout
    cout << "Press any key to continue:";
    cin.get();
    cout << "Thank you." << endl;
}
```

```
Press any key to continue:x
Thank you.
Press any key to continue:Thank you.
Press any key to continue:x
Thank you.
```

In the first I/O exchange, `cout` is flushed to prompt the user for a response, even though no `endl` or `'\n'` is passed to it. But then the call `cin.tie(0)` breaks `cin`'s tie to `cout`, so in the next I/O exchange the prompt <u>does not wait</u> for input before the next line is output. The call `cin.tie(&cout)` finally restores the tie, so that the third I/O exchange works normally again.

12.5 THE `istream` AND `ostream` CLASSES

The `istream` and `ostream` classes both inherit from the `ios` class:

```
class istream : virtual public ios { // . . . };
class ostream : virtual public ios { // . . . };
```

Making `ios` a `virtual` base class facilitates the multiple inheritance that the `iostream` class has from both the `istream` and `ostream` classes by preventing multiple copies of the `ios` class to be made for the `iostream` class.

The `istream` class defines the `cin` object and the stream extraction operator `>>` for *formatted input*. The `ostream` class defines the `cout`, `cerr`, and `clog` objects and the stream insertion operator `<<` for *formatted output*. These objects and operators are inherited by the seven subclasses shown in the diagram on page 328.

The familiar I/O operations that use the extraction and insertion operators are called *formatted I/O* because these operators recognize the types of the objects that are accessed and they format the data accordingly. For example, if `n` is an integer with value 22, then `cout << n` prints the value 22 in integer format. The `istream` and `ostream` classes also define a set of member functions for *unformatted I/O* that handles data simply as a sequence of bytes. These functions are described below and are summarized in Appendix F.

The `istream` class defines the stream extraction operator `>>` which reads data from `istream` objects, which are usually the standard input device `cin` (*i.e.*, the keyboard). If successful, this operator returns a reference to the object so that calls can be chained like this:

```
cin >> x >> y >> z;
```

If `cin` is unsuccessful, it returns 0. Under normal operation, `cin` skips white space characters (blanks, tabs, newlines, *etc.*).

EXAMPLE 12.12 Simple Use of the Extraction Operator

```
main()
{
    int m, n;
    float t;
    cin >> m >> t >> n;
    cout << "m = " << m << ", t = " << t << ", n = " << n << endl;
}
```

```
                          22

        3.14159              88
m = 22, t = 3.14159, n = 88
```

The `>>` operator will return 0 when it encounters the end-of-file character, transmitted by **Control-D** on UNIX workstations and Macintoshes and by **Control-Z** on PCs and VAX/VMS computers. This can be used to control an input loop:

EXAMPLE 12.13 Controlling an Input Loop

```
main()
{
    int n, sum = 0;
    while (cin >> n)
        sum += n;
    cout << "The sum is " << sum << endl;
}
```

```
80 70 60 50 40 30 20 10 ^Z
The sum is 360
```

12.6 UNFORMATTED INPUT FUNCTIONS

The `istream` class defines a rich collection of unformatted input functions. Many of these are summarized in Appendix F.

Several versions of the `get()` function are defined by the `istream` class. In its simplest form, it has no arguments and simply returns the next character in the input stream. Its function prototype is

```
int get();
```

This version of the function is typically used in an input loop:

EXAMPLE 12.14 Reading Characters with the `cin.get()` Function

Compare this with Example 7.6:

```
main()
{
    char c;
    while ((c = cin.get()) != EOF)
        cout << c;
    cout << endl;
}
```

```
What is in a name?
What is in a name?
Would a rose by any other name smell as sweet?
Would a rose by any other name smell as sweet?
^D
```

Each call of the `cin.get()` function reads one more character from `cin` and returns it to the variable c. Then the statement inside the loop inserts c into the output stream. These characters accumulate in a buffer until the end-of-line character is inserted. Then the buffer is flushed, and the complete line is printed just as it had been read.

The expression `(c = cin.get())` returns the value that is returned by the function call `cin.get()`. That value is compared with the integer constant `EOF`, and as long as they are unequal the loop continues.   When the end-of-file character `^D` is read, `cin.get())` returns the value of `EOF`, thereby terminating the loop.

On most computers, `EOF` has the value –1:

EXAMPLE 12.15 The Integer Constant EOF

```
main()
{
    cout << "EOF = " << EOF << endl;
}
```

```
EOF = -1
```

Another form of the `get()` function reads the next character from the input stream into its char parameter that is passed by reference:

```
istream& get(char& c);
```

This version returns false when the end of file is detected, so it can conveniently be used to control an input loop like this: `while (cin.get(ch))`

EXAMPLE 12.16 Reading Characters with the `cin.get()` Function

This is the same as Example 12.14, except using this form of the `get()` function:

```
main()
{
    char c;
    while (cin.get(c))
        cout << c;
    cout << endl;
}
```

```
The woods are lovely, dark and deep.
The woods are lovely, dark and deep.
But I have promises to keep,
But I have promises to keep,
^D
```

A third form of the `get()` function is similar to the `getline()` function. Its prototype is

```
    istream& get(char* buffer, int n, char delim = '\n');
```

This reads characters into *buffer* until either *n*–1 characters are read or the *delim* character is encountered, whichever comes first. It does <u>not</u> extract *delim* from the input stream.

EXAMPLE 12.17 Reading Characters with the `cin.get()` Function

```
main()
{
    char buffer[80];
    cin.get(buffer, 8);          // reads next 7 characters into buffer
    cout << "[" << buffer << "]\n";
    cin.get(buffer, sizeof(buffer));
    cout << "[" << buffer << "]\n";
    cin.get(buffer, sizeof(buffer), '|');
    cout << "[" << buffer << "]\n";
}
```

```
ABCDE|FGHIJ|KLMNO|PQRST|UVWXY|Z
[ABCDE|F]
[GHIJ|KLMNO|PQRST|UVWXY|Z]
ABCDE|FGHIJ|KLMNO|PQRST|UVWXY|Z
[
ABCDE]
```

The first call `cin.get(buffer, 8)` reads the 7 characters `"ABCDE|F"` into `buffer` and then terminates the string with the null character `'\0'`. The second call `cin.get(buffer, 80)` reads the rest of the characters on the line, up to but not including the end-of-line character `'\n'`. These 24 characters which appended with the null character `'\0'` are read in to `buffer`. The third call `cin.get(buffer, 80, '|')` reads the end-of-line character from the first input line, followed by the 5 characters `"ABCDE"` that precede the `'|'` character on the second line; these 5 characters, appended with the null character `'\0'`, are read in to `buffer`.

The `getline()` function is almost the same as the third form of the `get()` function. The only difference is that it <u>does</u> extract the delimiter character from the input stream but does not store it in the *buffer*. Its prototype is

```
istream& getline(char* buffer, int n, char delim = '\n');
```

EXAMPLE 12.18 Reading Characters with the `cin.getline()` Function

```
main()
{
    char buffer[80];
    cin.getline(buffer, 8);
    cout << "[" << buffer << "]\n";
    cin.getline(buffer, sizeof(buffer));
    cout << "[" << buffer << "]\n";
    cin.getline(buffer, sizeof(buffer), '|');
    cout << "[" << buffer << "]\n";
}
```

```
ABCDE|FGHIJ|KLMNO|PQRST|UVWXY|Z
[ABCDE|F]
[GHIJ|KLMNO|PQRST|UVWXY|Z]
ABCDE|FGHIJ|KLMNO|PQRST|UVWXY|Z
[ABCDE]
```

Note that the second call `cin.getline(buffer, sizeof(buffer))` reads to the end of the input line, storing `GHIJ|KLMNO|PQRST|UVWXY|Z` in `buffer`. Unlike the `get()` function, the `getline()` function then extracts the newline character from the input stream, so that the next character to be read is the `A` on the next input line.

The `ignore()` function is used to "eat" characters in the input stream. It simply extracts characters, without copying them into any variable. Its prototype is

```
istream& ignore(int n = 1, int delim = EOF);
```

Called in its simplest form, `cin.ignore()` will simply extract one character from `cin`. More generally, `cin.ignore(n)` will simply extract `n` character from `cin`, and `cin.ignore(n,'$')` would extract all the characters up to the next occurrence of the `'$'` character (or to the end of the file).

EXAMPLE 12.19 Eating Characters with the `cin.ignore()` Function

```
main()
{
    int month, year;
    cout << "Enter date (mm/dd/yy): ";
    cin >> month;
    cin.ignore();                      // eats "/"
    cin.ignore(80, '/');               // eats "dd/" or "d/" or "/"
    cin >> year;
    cout << "Month = " << month << ", Year = 19" << year << endl;
}
```

```
Enter date (mm/dd/yy): 2/28/95
Month = 2, Year = 1995
```

This little input routine asks the user for a date in the standard `mm/dd/yy` form and then reads from it the `month` and the `year`, ignoring the day `dd`.

The `peek()` function is kind of an opposite of the `ignore()` function: it reads the next character in the input stream without extracting it. Its prototype is `int peek();`

EXAMPLE 12.20 Looking Ahead with the `cin.peek()` Function

```
main()
{
    char buffer[80], c;
    cout << cin.peek() << ", " << cin.peek() << ", ";
    c = cin.peek();
    cout << c << ", ";
    cin.get(buffer, 5);       // read the next 4 characters into buffer
    c = cin.peek();
    cout << c << ", " << cin.peek() << ", " << cin.peek() << endl;
}
```

ABCDEFG
65, 65, A, E, 69, 69

The first three calls to `cin.peek()` return the `'A'` in the input stream. Note that it is output directly as the integer 65 (the ASCII code for `'A'`). Then after reading "ABCD" into `buffer`, the next three calls to `cin.peek()` return the `'E'` in the input stream, output directly as the integer 69. Note that the calls to the `peek()` function have no effect upon the input stream.

The `putback()` function reverses the `get()` function by putting a character back into the input stream. Its prototype is

```
istream& putback(char c);
```

EXAMPLE 12.21 Using the `cin.putback()` Function

```
main()
{
    cin.putback('Z');
    cin.putback('Y');
    cin.putback('X');
    char buffer[80];
    cin.get(buffer, 9);       // read the next 8 characters into buffer
    cout << "[" << buffer << "], ";
    cin.putback('R');
    cin.putback('Q');
    cin.putback('P');
    cin.get(buffer, 9);       // read the next 8 characters into buffer
    cout << "[" << buffer << "]\n";
}
```

ABCDEFGHIJKLMN
[XYZABCDE], [PQRFGHIJ]

The first three calls to cin.putback() insert "XYZ" in front of the 'A' in the input stream. So the input stream actually contains "XYZABCDEFGHIJKLMN" before the first call to cin.get(). And after the second series of cin.putback() calls, the input stream contains "PQRFGHIJKLMN".

The istream class includes several versions of the read() function. This is an unformatted input function designed for the direct transfer of raw bytes. It works the same way as the get() function except that it does not append the null character to the bytes read. It is typically used with the gcount() function which simply returns the number of bytes read:

```
istream& read(char* buffer, int n);

istream& read(unsigned char* buffer, int n);

int gcount();
```

The second version of read() is used to transfer bit strings.

EXAMPLE 12.22 Transferring Bytes with the cin.read() Function

```
main()
{
    char buffer[] = "????????????????????";               // 20 '?'s
    cin.read(buffer, 8);                          // transfer 8 bytes buffer
    cout << "[" << buffer << "]; read: " << cin.gcount() << endl;
    cin.read(buffer, 4);                          // transfer 4 bytes buffer
    cout << "[" << buffer << "]; read: " << cin.gcount() << endl;
}
```

```
ABCDEFGHIJKLMN
[ABCDEFGH????????????]; read: 8
[IJKLEFGH????????????]; read: 4
```

This example illustrates use of the read() function and the gcount() function. First it initializes buffer with 20 '?'s. Then we use cin.read(buffer, 8) to transfer the first 8 bytes from cin to buffer. The output then shows that only the first 8 bytes of buffer have been changed. Note that no null character '\0' has been appended to those 8 bytes. The second read() repeats the process with the next 4 bytes, leaving the other 16 bytes unchanged.

12.7 UNFORMATTED OUTPUT FUNCTIONS

The istream class defines functions for unformatted output that are analogous to unformatted input functions.

The two versions of the put() function are the inverses of the corresponding get() functions:

```
int put(char c);

ostream& put(char c);
```

They both insert the character c into the output stream.

EXAMPLE 12.23 Using the `cout.put()` Function

This example shows the parallel nature of the `put(c)` and `get(c)` functions:

```
#include <iostream.h>

main()
{
    char c;
    while (cin.get(c))
        cout.put(c);
    cout << endl;
}
```

```
The woods are lovely, dark and deep.
The woods are lovely, dark and deep.
But I have promises to keep,
But I have promises to keep,
^D
```

Example 7.7 is similar.

EXAMPLE 12.24 Chaining the `cout.put()` Function

This example shows how the second version of the `put(c)` function can be concatenated into a chain of calls:

```
#include <iostream.h>

main()
{
    cout.put('H').put('e').put('l').put('l').put('o').put('\n');
}
```

```
Hello
```

This works because `cout.put()` returns the `cout` object itself.

The `write()` function has versions that are the inverses of the corresponding `read()` functions:

```
ostream& write(const char* buffer, int n);
ostream& write(const unsigned char* buffer, int n);
```

They both transfer n bytes from *buffer* to the output stream.

EXAMPLE 12.25 Using the `cout.write()` Function

```
#include <iostream.h>

main()
{
    cout.write("ABCDEFGHIJKLMNOPQRSTUVWXYZ", 8);
    cout << endl;
    cout.write("0123456789", 4);
    cout << endl;
}
```

Here is the output:

```
ABCDEFGH
0123
```

Like the corresponding `read()` function, the second version of the `write()` function is used to transfer bit strings.

When bytes are sent to an output stream they are *buffered*. This means that they are first accumulated in a region of memory called a "buffer," so that they can be sent later in "batch mode" to the output stream. The step that empties the output buffer and sends the string of bytes to the output stream is called *flushing the output buffer*. The `ostream` function `flush()` performs this essential task. It is usually used indirectly by using the stream manipulator `endl`.

12.8 STREAM MANIPULATORS

A *stream manipulator* is a special kind of stream class member function. When used with the insertion and extraction operators, they look like objects. But they really are function calls. For example, `cout << endl;` is actually a call to the stream manipulator function `endl()`. Here's how it works.

The `ostream` class includes the following overloaded insertion operator:

```
ostream& operator<<(ostream& (*p)(ostream&))
    { return (*p)(*this); }
```

The parameter `(*p)(ostream&)` is a pointer to a function (see Section 6.14) that has a single `ostream` parameter. When the statement

```
cout << endl;
```

is executed, `operator<<` is invoked, passing the `endl()` function to is as the parameter. But since this is a function parameter, the function pointer `p` is used to point to that function. So when `operator<<` is invoked, `p` points to the `endl()` function. This function is defined as

```
ostream& endl(ostream& ostr)
{
    ostr.put('\n');
    ostr.flush();
}
```

So when the statement `cout << endl;` is executed, `operator<<` is invoked with `p` pointing to the `cout.endl()` function, so that the statement

```
return (*p)(*this);
```

becomes

```
return cout.endl(*this);
```

which prints a newline, flushes `cout`, and then returns `cout`.

The next example shows how you can write your own stream manipulator.

EXAMPLE 12.26 A Home-Grown Stream Manipulator

```
ostream& beep(ostream& ostr)
{
    return ostr << "\a";
}

main()
{
    cout << beep;
}
```

When used as shown here, the stream manipulator sends the *alert character* `'\a'` to the output stream, which sounds the *system beep*.

All stream manipulators work this way. They are defined with prototypes like this:

```
ios& f(ios& ostr)
ostream& f(ostream& ostr)
istream& f(ostream& istr)
```

or, in the case of manipulators with parameters, like this:

```
ios& f(ios& ostr, int n)
ostream& f(ostream& ostr, int n)
istream& f(ostream& istr, int n)
```

Table 12.3 lists of some of the more common stream manipulators:

Table 12.3 Stream Manipulators

Manipulator	Stream	Action
binary	ios	Set stream mode to binary
dec	ios	Read or write integers base 10 (default)
endl	ostream	End output line and flush output stream
ends	ostream	End output string
flush	ostream	Flush output stream
hex	ios	Read or write integers base 16 (*i.e.*, in hexadecimal)
oct	ios	Read or write integers base 8 (*i.e.*, in octal)
resetiosflags(long *u*)	ios	Clear format flags specified by *u*
setbase(int *n*)	ostream	Write integers base *n* (default: 10)
setfill(int *ch*)	ostream	Set fill character to *ch* (default: ' ')
setiosflags(long *u*)	ios	Set format flags specified by *u*
setprecision(int *n*)	ios	Set floating-point precision to *n* digits (default: 6)
setw(int *n*)	ios	Set field width to *n* columns (default: 0)
text	ios	Set stream to text. (default)
ws	istream	Skip white space

We have already seen how the `endl` manipulator works. It inserts the newline character `'\n'` into the output stream and then calls the flush manipulator which "flushes" the buffer.

The `ends` manipulator simply inserts the null character `'\0'` into the output stream. This is illustrated in the next example.

EXAMPLE 12.27 Using the `ends` Stream Manipulator to Terminate a String

```
main()
{
    char buffer[] = "???????????????????";
    cin >> ws;
    cin.read(buffer, 8);
    cout << "[" << buffer << "]\n";
}
```

```
                         ABC     DEF    GH
[ABC    DE????????????]
```

The input begins with several newlines, tabs, and blanks. These are all skipped before the 8 characters "ABC   DE" are into `buffer`. Note that only the initial white space is eaten.

The `oct`, `dec`, `hex`, and `setbase(n)` manipulators are used to change the number base of integers that are input or output.

EXAMPLE 12.28 Using the `oct`, `dec`, and `hex` Stream Manipulators

```
main()
{
    int n = 510;
    cout << "  \tHexadecimal:\t " << hex << n << "\t " << n
        << "\n\t    Decimal:\t " << dec << n << "\t " << n
        << "\n\t      Octal:\t " << oct << n << "\t " << n << endl;
    cout << "Enter integer in octal: ";
    cin >> oct >> n;              // read integer base 8
    cout << "  \tHexadecimal:\t " << hex << n << "\t " << n
        << "\n\t    Decimal:\t " << dec << n << "\t " << n
        << "\n\t      Octal:\t " << oct << n << "\t " << n << endl;
    cout << "Enter integer in hexadecimal: ";
    cin >> hex >> n;             // read integer base 16
    cout << "  \tHexadecimal:\t " << hex << n << "\t " << n
        << "\n\t    Decimal:\t " << dec << n << "\t " << n
        << "\n\t      Octal:\t " << oct << n << "\t " << n << endl;
}
```

Here is the output:

```
       Hexadecimal:        1fe        1fe
          Decimal:         510        510
            Octal:         776        776
ter integer in octal: 775
       Hexadecimal:        1fd        1fd
          Decimal:         509        509
            Octal:         775        775
ter integer in hexadecimal: 1fc
       Hexadecimal:        1fc        1fc
          Decimal:         508        508
            Octal:         774        774
```

Printing each number twice shows that the manipulator resets the number base for all subsequent input or output until another manipulator is used.

The `ws` manipulator simply eats the next string of white space (blanks, tabs, newlines).

EXAMPLE 12.29 Using the `ws` Stream Manipulator to Eat white space

```
main()
{
    char buffer[] = "????????????????????";
    cin >> ws;
    cin.read(buffer, 8);
    cout << "[" << buffer << "]\n";
}
```

```
                    ABC     DEF    GH
[ABC    DE????????????]
```

The input begins with several newlines, tabs, and blanks. These are all skipped before the 8 characters "ABC   DE" are into `buffer`. Note that only the initial white space is eaten.

Review Questions

12.1   Why is the default constructor for the `ios` class declared `private`?

12.2   Why aren't the `width`, `fill`, and `precision` parameters of a stream packed into a bit string the way all the other parameters are?

12.3   If a stream's `_format` data member is `04035`, what format flags are set?

12.4   If a stream's `_format` data member is `047623`, what format flags are set?

12.5   Why is the `ios` class made to be a `virtual` base class for the `istream` and `ostream` classes?

12.6 Why is the use of the `<<` and `>>` operators called "formatted" I/O, and the use of the functions `put()`, `get()`, `write()`, `read()`, *etc.*, call "unformatted" I/O?

12.7 What is the difference between the `get()` function and the `getline()` function?

12.8 What is the difference between the `get()` function and the `read()` function?

Solved Problems

12.9 What should the function prototype for the `ws()` manipulator look like?

Every stream manipulator should have the general prototype
```
ios& f(ios&);
```
where `ios` is the stream class that `f` manipulates. Since the `ws` manipulator is used with `istreams` its prototype should be
```
istream& ws(istream&);
```

12.10 Write code that formats `cout` so that integers are printed in octal in a right-justified field of 12 columns.

```
cout.setf( ios::oct | ios::ios );
cout.width(12);
```

Solved Programming Problems

12.11 Write a program that uses the `setf()`, `fill()`, and `width()` functions to produce the following formatted output:

```
Chapter 10  A String Class...............................222
Chapter 11  Inheritance..................................244
Chapter 12  Streams......................................273
```

The idea here is to use left-justify the titles in a field width of 60 columns, with `'.'` as the fill character padding the field on the right, so that the page numbers align at the end of the field:

```
#include <iostream.h>

main()
{
    cout.setf(ios::left);
    cout.fill('.');
    const int w = 60;
    cout.width(w);
    cout << "\tChapter 10  A String Class" << "222\n";
    cout.width(w);
    cout << "\tChapter 11  Inheritance" << "244\n";
    cout.width(w);
    cout << "\tChapter 12  Streams" << "273\n";
}
```

12.12 Write a function to reverse a string in place (*i.e.*, without duplicating all the characters).

```
void reverse(char* s)
{
    char temp;
    char* end = s + strlen(s) - 1;
    while (s < end) {
        temp = *s;
        *s++ = *end;
        *end-- = temp;
    }
}
```

Supplementary Problems

12.13 What should the function prototype for the ends stream manipulator look like?

12.14 Write code that formats cout so that floats are printed in scientific notation with 12-digit precision.

Supplementary Programming Problems

12.15 Write a program that uses the setf(), fill(), and width() functions to produce the following formatted output:

```
Chapter 4   Functions.......................................56
Chapter 5   Arrays..........................................85
Chapter 6   Pointers and References.........................113
```

The trick here is to left-justify the titles, as done in Problem 12.11, and to right-justify the page numbers in another fixed-length field.

12.16 Write a program that uses the setf(), fill(), and width() functions to produce the following formatted output:

```
Chapter 4   Functions.......................................56
Chapter 5   Arrays..........................................85
Chapter 6   Pointers and References.........................113
```

12.17 Write code for each of the following:
  a. Print the integer 12345 in a left-justified 12-digit field.
  b. Print the integer 1000 in hexadecimal with the 0x prefix.
  c. Print 3.14159 in a 12-digit field with preceding zeros.
  d. Print in a 40-column field, "Hello" left-justified and "World" right-justified, padding between them with the '!' character.
  e. Read an integer in decimal and print it in octal.
  f. Read an integer in hexadecimal and print it in decimal.

12.18 Write a program that uses the `setf()`, `fill()`, and `width()` functions to produce the following formatted output:

```
Base system:                                              $3099.
        Intel 120MHz Pentium processor
        Intel Triton PCI chip set
        16MB RAM
        1280 EIDE hard drive (10ms)
        3.5" 1.44MB floppy drive
        4X CD-ROM drive
        17" MAG monitor
        64-bit PCI graphics accelerator with 2MB VRAM
        28,800-baud fax/modem
Extra 16MB memory:                                          640.
420MB tape backup system:                                  149.
Panasonic KX-P6100 laser printer:                          399.

                                    Subtotal:    $4287.
                                    Shipping:        75.
                                    Total:       $4362.
```

12.19 Write a function `set_width(int w)` that sets the field width for `cout` to `w` columns.

12.20 Write a function `set_fill(char c)` that sets the fill character for `cout` to `c`.

12.21 Write a function `set_precision(int d)` that sets the floating-point precision for `cout` to `d` digits.

12.22 Write a function `eof()` that returns 1 if `cin` is at the end-of-file and 0 otherwise.

12.23 Write a function `clear_eof()` that clears `cin`'s end-of-file flag without changing any other aspect of its state.

12.24 Write a single function `print_status()` that prints all the information available (precision, fill character, end-of-file status, *etc.*) about both `cin` and `cout`.

12.25 The call `write(buffer, 20)` will transfer the first 20 bytes of the string `buffer` to the output stream, provided that `buffer` contains at least 20 characters. Find out what this call does if `buffer` contains fewer than 20 characters, and explain what happens.

Answers to Review Questions

12.1 The default constructor for the `ios` class is declared `private` so that no `ios` object can be declared.

12.2 The `width`, `fill`, and `precision` parameters of a stream cannot be packed into a bit string because they are not boolean variables. Each of these three parameters can have more than two values.

12.3 The `_format` data value `04035` decomposes as $04035 = 04000 + 020 + 010 + 04 + 01$, so five flags are set: `scientific`, `dec`, `internal`, `right`, and `skipws`.

12.4 The `_format` data value `047623` decomposes as $047623 = 040000 + 04000 + 02000 + 01000 + 0400 + 0200 + 020 + 02 + 01$, so nine flags are set: `stdio`, `scientific`, `showpos`, `uppercase`, `showpoint`, `showbase`, `dec`, `internal`, `left`, and `skipws`.

12.5 The `ios` class made to be a `virtual` base class for the `istream` and `ostream` classes so that when the `iostream` class inherits from both the `istream` and `ostream` classes (and therefore indirectly from the `ios` class), it will not get duplicate copies of the members of the `ios` class.

12.6 Use of the `<<` and `>>` operators is called "formatted" I/O because these operators recognize the type of objects passed to them and use that information to format the input and output. For example, if `n` is an `int`, then `cin >> n` will read the input 27 as the integer 27, whereas `get()` will only read its first digit as the character `'2'`. The functions `put()`, `get()`, `write()`, `read()`, *etc.*, process all input and output as character data, so use of these functions is called "unformatted" I/O.

12.7 The only difference between the three-parameter version of the `get()` function and the `getline()` function is that the `get()` function does not extract the delimiter character from the input stream.

12.8 The `read()` function does not append the null character to the bytes read.

Chapter 13

Templates and Iterators

13.1 INTRODUCTION

A *template* is an abstract recipe for producing concrete code. Templates can be used to produce functions and classes. The compiler uses the template to generate the code for various functions or classes, the way you would use a cookie cutter to generate cookies from various types of dough. The actual functions or classes generated by the template are called *instances* of that template.

The same template can be used to generate many different instances. This is done by means of *template parameters* which work much the same way for templates as ordinary parameters work for ordinary functions. But whereas ordinary parameters are placeholders for objects, template parameters are placeholders for types and classes.

The facility that C++ provides for instantiating templates is one of its major features and one that distinguishes it from most other programming languages. As a mechanism for automatic code generation, it allows for substantial improvements in programming efficiency.

13.2 FUNCTION TEMPLATES

In many sorting algorithms, we need to interchange a pair of elements. This simple task is often done by a separate function. For example, the following function swaps integers:

```
void swap(int& m, int& n)
{
    int temp = m;
    m = n;
    n = temp;
}
```

If however, we were sorting `String` objects, then we would need a different function:

```
void swap(String& s1, String& s2)
{
    String temp = s1;
    s1 = s2;
    s2 = temp;
}
```

These two functions do the same thing. Their only difference is the type of objects they swap. We can avoid this redundancy by replacing both functions with a *function template*:

355

EXAMPLE 13.1 The `swap` Function Template

```
template <class T>
void swap(T& x, T& y)
{
    T temp = x;
    x = y;
    y = temp;
}
```

The symbol `T` is called a *type parameter*. It is simply a placeholder that is replaced by an actual type or class when the function is invoked.

A function template is declared the same way as an ordinary function, except that it is preceded by the specification

```
template <class T>
```

and the type parameter `T` may be used in place of ordinary types within the function definition. The use of the word `class` here means "any type." More generally, a template may have several type parameters, specified like this:

```
template <class T, class U, class V>
```

Function templates are called the same way ordinary functions are called:

```
int m = 22, n = 66;
swap(m, n);
String s1 = "John Adams", s2 = "James Madison";
swap(s1, s2);
Rational x(22/7), y(-3);
swap(x, y);
```

For each call, the compiler generates the complete function, replacing the type parameter with the type or class to which the arguments belong. So the call `swap(m,n)` generates the integer `swap` function shown above, and the call `swap(s1, s2)` generates the `swap` function for `String` class.

Function templates are a direct generalization of function overloading. We could have written several overloaded versions of the `swap` function, one for each type that we thought we might need. The single `swap` function template serves the same purpose. But it is an improvement in two ways. It only has to be written once to cover all the different types that might be used with it. And we don't have to decide in advance which types we will use with it; any type or class can be substituted for the type parameter `T`. Function templates share source code among structurally similar families of functions.

Here is another example of a function template:

EXAMPLE 13.2 The Bubble Sort Template

This is the Bubble Sort and a print function for vectors of any base type. (The `String` class is defined in Chapter 10.)

```
#include "String.h"

template<class T>
void sort(T* v, int n)
{
    T temp;
    for (int i = 1; i < n; i++)
        for (int j = 0; j < n-i; j++)
            if (v[j] > v[j+1]) swap(v[j], v[j+1]);
}

template<class T>
void print(T* v, int n)
{
    for (int i = 0; i < n; i++)
        cout << " " << v[i];
    cout << endl;
}

main()
{
    short a[9] = {55, 33, 88, 11, 44, 99, 77, 22, 66};
    print(a,9);
    sort(a,9);
    print(a,9);
    String s[7] = {"Tom", "Hal", "Dan", "Bob", "Sue", "Ann", "Gus"};
    print(s,7);
    sort(s,7);
    print(s,7);
}
```

```
55 33 88 11 44 99 77 22 66
11 22 33 44 55 66 77 88 99
Tom Hal Dan Bob Sue Ann Gus
Ann Bob Dan Gus Hal Sue Tom
```

Here, both `sort()` and `print()` are function templates. The type parameter `T` is replaced by the type `short` in the first calls and by the class `String` in the second calls.

A function template works like a macro. The compiler uses the template to generate each version of the function that is needed. In the previous example, the compiler produces two versions of the `sort()` function and two versions of the `print()` function, one each for the type `short` and one each for the class `String`. The individual versions are called *instances* of the function template, and the process of producing them is called *instantiating* the template. A function that is an instance of a template is also called a *template function*. Using templates is a form of automatic code generation; it allows the programmer to defer more of the work to the compiler.

13.3 CLASS TEMPLATES

A *class template* works the same way as a function template except that it generates classes instead of functions. The general syntax is

```
template<class T,...> class X { ... };
```

As with function templates, a class template may have several template parameters. Moreover, some of them can be ordinary non-type parameters:

```
template<class T, int n, class U> class X { ... };
```

Of course, since templates are instantiated at compile time, values passed to non-type parameters must be constants:

```
template<class T, int n>
class X {};

main()
{
    X<float,22>  x1;      // o.k.
    const int n = 44;
    X<char, n> x2;        // o.k.
    int m = 66;
    X<short, m> x3;       // Error: m must be constant
}
```

Class templates are sometimes called *parameterized types*.

The member functions of a class template are themselves function templates with the same template header as the class template. For example, the function `f()` declared in the class template

```
template<class T>
class X {
    T square(T t) { return t*t; }
};
```

is handled the same way that the following template function would be handled:

```
template<class T>
T square(T t) { return t*t; }
```

It is instantiated by the compiler, replacing the template parameter T with the type passed to it. Thus, the declaration

```
X<short> x;
```

generates the class and object

```
class X_short {
    short square(short t) { return t*t; }
};
X_short x;
```

except that your compiler may use some name other than `X_short` for the class.

EXAMPLE 13.3 A `Stack` Class Template

A *stack* is a simple data structure that simulates an ordinary stack of objects of the same type (*e.g.*, a stack of dishes) with the restrictions that an object can be inserted into the stack only at the top and an object can removed from the stack only at the top. In other words, a stack is a linear data structure with access at only one end. A stack class abstracts this notion by hiding the implementation of the data structure, allowing access only by means of public functions that simulate the limited operations described above.

Here is a class template for generating `Stack` classes:

```
template<class T>
class Stack {
public:
    Stack(int s = 100) : size(s), top(-1) { data = new T[size]; }
    ~Stack() { delete [] data; }
    void push(const T& x) { data[++top] = x; }
    T pop() { return data[top--]; }
    int isEmpty() const { return top == -1; }
    int isFull() const { return top == size - 1; }
private:
    int size;
    int top;
    T* data;
};
```

This definition uses an array `data` to implement a stack. The constructor initializes the `size` of the array, allocates that many elements of type `T` to the array, and initializes its `top` pointer to –1. The value of `top` is always one less than the number of elements on the stack, and except when the stack is empty, `top` is the index in the array of the top element on the stack. The `push()` function inserts an object onto the stack, and the `pop()` function removes an object from the stack. A stack `isEmpty()` when its `top` has the value –1, and it `isFull()` when its `top` pointer has the value `size - 1`.

Here is a program to test the `Stack` template:

```
main()
{
    Stack<int> intStack1(5);
    Stack<int> intStack2(10);
    Stack<char> charStack(8);
    intStack1.push(77);
    charStack.push('A');
    intStack2.push(22);
    charStack.push('E');
    charStack.push('K');
    intStack2.push(44);
    cout << intStack2.pop() << endl;
    cout << intStack2.pop() << endl;
    if (intStack2.isEmpty()) cout << "intStack2 is empty.\n";
}
```

```
44
22
intStack2 is empty.
```

The template has one parameter `T` which will be used to specify the type of the objects stored on the stack. The first line declares `intStack1` to be a stack that can hold up to 5 `ints`. Similarly, `intStack2` is a stack that can hold up to 10 `ints`, and `charStack` is a stack that can hold up to 8 `chars`.

After pushing and popping objects on and off the stacks, the last line calls the `isEmpty()` function for `intStack2`. At that instant, the two `Stack` classes and three `Stack` objects look like this:

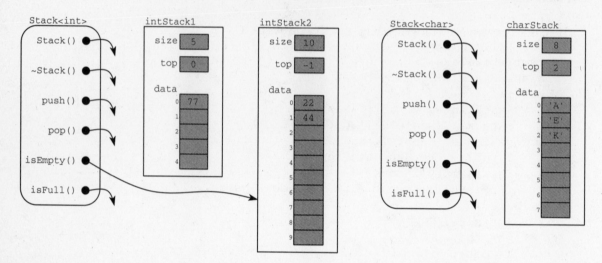

The call `intStack2.isEmpty()` returns 1 (*i.e.*, "true") because `intStack2.top` has the value –1 at that moment.

Note that there are two instances of the `Stack` class template: `Stack<int>` and `Stack<char>`. These are distinct classes, each generated by the compiler. Each class has its own six distinct member functions. For example, the two functions `Stack<int>::pop()` and `Stack<char>::pop()` are different: one returns an `int` and the other returns a `char`.

13.4 CONTAINER CLASSES

A *container* is simply an object that contains other objects. Ordinary arrays and stacks are containers. A *container class* is a class whose instances are containers. The `Stack<int>` and `Stack<char>` classes in Example 13.3 are container classes. Class templates are natural mechanisms for generating container classes because the contained objects' type can be specified using a template parameter.

A container is called *homogeneous* if all of its objects have the same type; otherwise it is called a *heterogeneous container*. Stacks, arrays, *etc.*, are homogeneous containers.

A *vector* is an indexed sequence of objects of the same type. The word is borrowed from mathematics where it originally referred to a three-dimensional point $\mathbf{x} = (x_1, x_2, x_3)$. Of course, that is just an array of 3 real numbers. The subscripts on the components are the same as the index values on the array, except that in C++ those values must begin with 0. Since subscripts cannot be written in source code, we use the bracket notation `[ ]` instead. So `x[0]` represents x_1, `x[1]` represents x_2, and `x[2]` represents x_3.

EXAMPLE 13.4 A `Vector` Class Template

```
template<class T>
class Vector {
public:
    Vector(unsigned n=8) : sz(n), data(new T[sz]) { }
    Vector(const Vector<T>& v) : sz(v.sz), data(new T[sz])
        { copy(v); }
    ~Vector() { delete [] data; }
    Vector<T>& operator=(const Vector<T>&);
    T& operator[](unsigned i) const { return data[i]; }
    unsigned size() { return sz; }
protected:
    T* data;
    unsigned sz;
    void copy(const Vector<T>&);
};

template<class T>
Vector<T>& Vector<T>::operator=(const Vector<T>& v)
{
    sz = v.sz;
    data = new T[sz];
    copy(v);
    return *this;
}

template<class T>
void Vector<T>::copy(const Vector<T>& v)
{
    unsigned min_size = (sz < v.sz ? sz : v.sz);
    for (int i = 0; i < min_size; i++)
        data[i] = v.data[i];
}
```

Note that each implementation of a member function must be preceded by the same template designator that precedes the class declaration: `template<class T>`.

This template would allow the following code:

```
Vector<short> v;
v[5] = 127;
Vector<short> w = v, x(3);
cout << w.size();
```

Here `v` and `w` are both `Vector` objects with 8 elements of type `short`, and `x` is a `Vector` object with 3 elements of type `short`. The class and its three objects can be visualized from the diagram shown below. It shows the situation at the moment when the member function `w.size()` is executing. The class `Vector<short>` has been instantiated from the template, and three objects `v`, `w`, and `x` have been instantiated from the class. Note that the `copy()` function is a `private` utility function, so it cannot be invoked by any of the class instances.

Note that the expression `v[5]` is used on the left side of an assignment, even though this expression is a function call. This is possible because the subscript operator returns a reference to a `Vector<T>`, making it an *lvalue*.

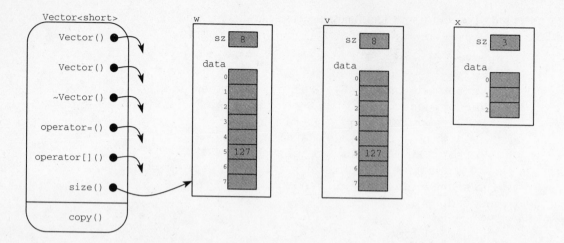

Class templates are also called *parametrized types* because they act like types to which parameters can be passed. For example, the object `b` above has type `Vector<double>`, so the element type `double` acts like a parameter to the template `Vector<T>`.

13.5 SUBCLASS TEMPLATES

Inheritance works with class templates the same way as with ordinary class inheritance. To illustrate this technique, we will define a subclass template of the `Vector` class template defined in Example 13.4.

EXAMPLE 13.5 A Subclass Template for Vectors

One problem with the `Vector` class as implemented by the template in Example 13.4 is that it requires *zero-based indexing*; *i.e.*, all subscripts must begin with 0. This is a requirement of the C++ language itself. Some other programming languages allow array indexes to begin with 1 or any other integer. We can add this useful feature to our `Vector` class template by declaring a subclass template:

```
template <class T>
class Array : public Vector<T> {
public:
    Array(int i, int j) : i0(i), Vector<T>(j-i+1) { }
    Array(const Array<T>& v) : i0(v.i0), Vector<T>(v) { }
    T& operator[](int i) const { return Vector<T>::operator[](i-i0);
}
    int firstSubscript() const { return i0; }
    int lastSubscript() const { return i0+sz-1; }
protected:
    int i0;
};
```

This `Array` class template inherits all the functionality of the `Vector` class template and also allows subscripts to begin with any integer. The first member function listed is a new constructor that allows the user to designate the first and last values of the subscript when the object is declared. The second function is the copy constructor for this subclass, and the third function is the overloaded subscript operator. The last two functions simply return the first and last values of the subscript range.

Note how the two `Array` constructors invoke the corresponding `Vector` constructors, and how the `Array` subscript operator invokes the `Vector` subscript operator.

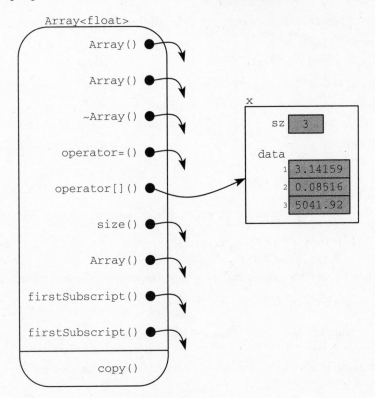

Here is a test driver and a sample run:

```
#include <iostream.h>
#include "Array.h"

main()
{
    Array<float> x(1,3);
    x[1] = 3.14159;
    x[2] = 0.08516;
    x[3] = 5041.92;
    cout << "x.size() = " << x.size() << endl;
    cout << "x.firstSubscript() = " << x.firstSubscript() << endl;
    cout << "x.lastSubscript() = " << x.lastSubscript() << endl;
    for (int i = 1; i <= 3; i++)
        cout << "x[" << i << "] = " << x[i] << endl;
}
```

```
x.size() = 3
x.firstSubscript() = 1
x.lastSubscript() = 3
x[1] = 3.14159
x[2] = 0.08516
x[3] = 5041.92
```

13.6 PASSING TEMPLATE CLASSES TO TEMPLATE PARAMETERS

We have already seen examples of passing a class to a template parameter:

```
Stack<Rational> s;     // a stack of Rational objects
Vector<String> a;      // a vector of String objects
```

Since template classes work like ordinary classes, we can also pass them to template parameters:

```
Stack<Vector<int>> s;       // a stack of Vector objects
Array<Stack<Rational>> a;   // an array of Stack objects
```

The next example shows how this "template nesting" can facilitate software reuse.

EXAMPLE 13.6 A `Matrix` Class Template

A *matrix* is essentially a two-dimensional vector. For example, a "2-by-3 matrix" is a table with 2 rows and 3 columns:

$$\begin{bmatrix} a & b & c \\ d & e & f \end{bmatrix}$$

We can think of this as a 2-element vector, each of whose elements is a 3-element vector:

$$\begin{bmatrix} \begin{bmatrix} a & b & c \end{bmatrix} & \begin{bmatrix} d & e & f \end{bmatrix} \end{bmatrix}$$

The advantage of this point of view is that it allows us to reuse our `Vector` class template to define a new `Matrix` class template.

To facilitate the dynamic allocation of memory, we define a matrix as a vector of pointers to vectors:

```
Vector<Vector<T>*>
```

We are passing a class template pointer to the template parameter indicated by the outside angle brackets. This really means that when the `Matrix` class template is instantiated, the instances of the resulting class will contain vectors of pointers to vectors.

```
template<class T>
class Matrix {
public:
    Matrix(unsigned r=1, unsigned c=1) : row(r)
        { for (int i=0; i<r; i++) row[i] = new Vector<T>(c); }
    ~Matrix() { for (int i=0; i<row.size(); i++) delete row[i]; }
    Vector<T>& operator[](unsigned i) const { return *row[i]; }
    unsigned rows() { return row.size(); }
    unsigned columns() { return row[0]->size(); }
protected:
    Vector<Vector<T>*> row;
};
```

Here the only data member is `row`, a vector of pointers to vectors. As a vector, `row` can be used with the subscript operator: `row[i]` which returns a pointer to the vector that represents the `i`th row of the matrix.

The default constructor assigns to each `row[i]` a `new` vector containing `c` elements of type T. The destructor has to `delete` each of these vectors separately. The `rows()` and `columns()` functions return the number of rows and columns in the matrix. The number of rows is the value that the member function `size()` returns for the `Vector<Vector<T>*>` object `row`. The number of columns is the value that the member function `size()` returns for the `Vector<T>` object `*row[0]`, which can be referenced either by `(*row[0]).size()` or by `row[0]->size()`.

Here is a test driver and a sample run:

```
main()
{
    Matrix<float> a(2,3);
    a[0][0] = 0.0;  a[0][1] = 0.1;  a[0][2] = 0.2;
    a[1][0] = 1.0;  a[1][1] = 1.1;  a[1][2] = 1.2;
    cout << "The matrix a has " << a.rows() << " rows and "
        << a.columns() << " columns:\n";
    for (int i=0; i<2; i++) {
        for (int j=0; j<3; j++) cout << a[i][j] << "   ";
        cout << endl;
    }
}
```

```
The matrix a has 2 rows and 3 columns:
0  0.1  0.2
1  1.1  1.2
```

The matrix `m` can be visualized like this:

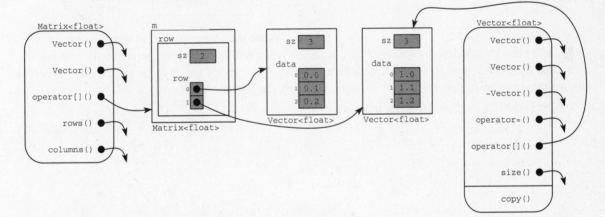

The diagram shows the situation during one of the subscript access calls `a[1][2]`.

Notice that the actual data values 0.2, 1.1, *etc.*, are stored in two separate `Vector<float>` objects. The `Matrix<float>` object `m` only contains pointers to those objects.

Note that our `Matrix` class template used *composition* with the `Vector` class template, while our `Array` class template used *inheritance* with the `Vector` class template.

13.7 A CLASS TEMPLATE FOR LINKED LISTS

Linked lists were introduced in Chapter 8. (See Example 8.2.) These data structures provide an alternative to vectors, with the advantage of dynamic storage. That is, unlike vectors, linked lists can grow and shrink dynamically according to how many data items are being stored. There is no wasted space for unused elements in the list.

EXAMPLE 13.7 A `List` Class Template

A list consists of a linked sequence of nodes. Each node contains one data item and a link to the next node. So we begin by defining a `ListNode` class template:

```cpp
template<class T>
class ListNode {
    friend class List<T>;
public:
    ListNode(T& t, ListNode<T>* p) : data(t), next(p) { }
protected:
    T data;                    // data field
    ListNode* next;            // points to next node in list
};
```

The constructor creates a new node, assigning the `T` value `t` to its `data` field and the pointer `p` to its `next` field:

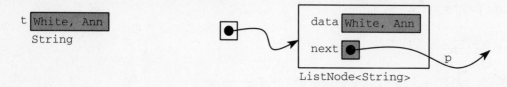

If `T` is a class (instead of an ordinary type), its constructor will be called by the declaration of `data`. Note that the class `List<T>` is declared here to be a `friend` of the `ListNode` class. This will allow the member functions of the `List` class to access the protected members of the `Node` class.

Here is the `List` class template interface:

```cpp
template<class T>
class List {
public:
    List() : first(0) { }
    ~List();
    void insert(T t);          // insert t at front of list
    int remove(T& t);          // remove first item t in list
    int isEmpty() { return (first == 0); }
    void print();
protected:
    ListNode<T>* first;
    ListNode<T>* newNode(T& t, ListNode<T>* p)
        { ListNode<T>* q = new ListNode<T>(t,p); return q; }
};
```

A `List` object contains only the pointer `first`:

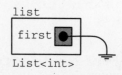

This points to a `ListNode` object. The default constructor initializes the pointer to `NULL`. After items have been inserted into the list, the `first` pointer will point to the first item in the list.

The `newNode` function invokes the `new` operator to obtain a new `ListNode` object by means of the `ListNode()` constructor. The new node will contain the `T` value `t` in its `data` field and the pointer `p` in its `next` field. The function returns a pointer to the new node. It is declared `protected` because it is a utility function that is used only by the other member functions.

The `List` destructor is responsible for deleting all the items in the list:

```
template<class T>
List<T>::~List()
{
    ListNode<T>* temp;
    for (ListNode<T>* p = first; p; ) {            // traverses list
        temp = p;
        p = p->next;
        delete temp;
    }
}
```

This has to be done in a loop that traverses the list. Each node is deleted by invoking the `delete` operator on a pointer to the node.

The `insert()` function creates a new node containing the `T` value `t` and then inserts this new node at the beginning of the list:

```
template<class T>
void List<T>::insert(T t)
{
    ListNode<T>* p = newNode(t,first);
    first = p;
}
```

Since the new node will be made the first node in the list, its `next` pointer should point to the node that is currently first in the list. Passing the `first` pointer to the `NewNode` constructor does that. Then the `first` pointer is reset to point to the new node.

The `remove()` function removes the first item from the list, returning its `data` value by reference in the parameter `t`. The function's return value is 1 or 0 according to whether the operation succeeded:

```
template<class T>
int List<T>::remove(T& t)
{
    if (isEmpty()) return 0; // flag to signal no removal
    t = first->data;          // data value returned by reference
    ListNode<T>* p = first;
    first = first->next;      // advance first pointer to remove node
    delete p;
    return 1;                 // flag to signal successful removal
}
```

The `print()` function simply traverses the list, printing each node's `data` value:

```
template<class T>
void List<T>::print()
{
    for (ListNode<T>* p=first; p; p=p->next)
        cout << p->data << " -> ";
    cout << "*\n";
}
```

Here is a test driver and a sample run:

```
#include <iostream.h>
#include "List.h"
#include "String.h"

main()
{
    List<String> friends;
    friends.insert("Bowen, Van");
    friends.insert("Dixon, Tom");
    friends.insert("Mason, Joe");
    friends.insert("White, Ann");
    friends.print();
    String name;
    friends.remove(name);
    cout << "Removed: " << name << endl;
    friends.print();
}
```

```
White, Ann -> Mason, Joe -> Dixon, Tom -> Bowen, Van -> *
Removed: White, Ann
Mason, Joe -> Dixon, Tom -> Bowen, Van -> *
```

Notice that, since each item is inserted at the beginning of the list, they end up in the opposite order from their insertion.

This `friends` list can be visualized like this:

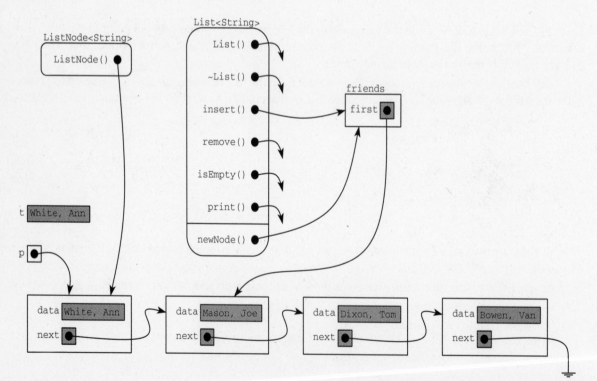

This shows the situation at the moment that the `insert()` function has invoked the `newNode()` function which has invoked the `ListNode()` constructor to create a new node for `"White, Ann"`.

13.8 ITERATOR CLASSES

A common activity performed on a container object is the *traversal* of the object. For example, to traverse a `List` object means to "travel" through the list, "visiting" each element. This was done by means of a `for` loop in both the destructor and the `print()` function in our `List` class template (Example 13.7).

An *iterator* is an object that has the ability to traverse through a container object. It acts like a pointer, locating one item in the container at a time. All iterators have the same basic functionality, regardless of the type of container to which they are attached. The five fundamental operations are:

- initialize the iterator at some initial position in the container;

- return the data value stored at the current position;

- change the data value stored at the current position;

- determine whether there actually is an item at the iterator's current position;

- advance to the next position in the container.

Since these five operations should be implemented by every iterator, it makes sense to declare an abstract base class with these functions. We actually need an abstract base class template because the container classes will be template instances:

```
template<class T>
class Iterator {
public:
    virtual int reset() =0;          // initialize the iterator
    virtual T operator()() =0;       // read current value
    virtual void operator=(T t) =0;  // write current value
    virtual int operator!() =0;      // determine whether item exists
    virtual int operator++() =0;     // advance to next item
};
```

Recall that every pure virtual function prototype begins with the keyword "virtual" and ends with the code "`() =0`". The parentheses are required because it is a function, and the initializer "`=0`" makes it a pure virtual function. Also recall that an *abstract base class* is any class that contains at least one pure virtual function. (See Section 11.9.)

Now we can use this abstract base class template to derive iterator templates for various container classes.

The `List` class template in Example 13.7 had an obvious shortcoming: it allowed insertions and deletions only at the front of the list. A list iterator will solve this problem:

EXAMPLE 13.8 An Iterator Class Template for the List Class Template

```
#include "List.h"
#include "Iterator.h"

template<class T>
class ListIter : public Iterator<T> {
public:
    ListIter(List<T>& l) : list(l) { reset(); }
    virtual void reset() { previous = NULL;  current = list.first; }
    virtual T operator()() { return current->data; }
    virtual void operator=(T t) { current->data = t; }
    virtual int operator!();      // determine whether current exists
    virtual int operator++();     // advance iterator to next item
    void insert(T t);             // insert t after current item
    void preInsert(T t);          // insert t before current item
    void remove();                // remove current item
protected:
    ListNode<T>* current;         // points to current node
    ListNode<T>* previous;        // points to previous node
    List<T>& list;                // this is the list being traversed
};
```

In addition to a constructor and the five fundamental operations, we have added three other functions that will make lists much more useful. They allow the insertion and deletion of items anywhere in the list.

The `operator!()` function serves two purposes. First it resets the `current` pointer if necessary, and then it reports back whether that pointer is NULL. The first purpose is to "clean up" after a call to the `remove()` function which deletes the node to which `current` points.

```
template<class T>
int ListIter<T>::operator!()
{
    if (current == NULL)                           // reset current pointer
        if (previous == NULL) current = list.first;
        else current = previous->next;
    return (current != NULL);      // returns TRUE if current exists
}
```

If the `current` and `previous` pointers are both NULL, then either the list is empty or it has only one item. So setting `current` equal to the list's `first` pointer will either make current NULL or leave it pointing to the first item in the list. If `current` is NULL but `previous` is pointing to a node, then we simply reset `current` to point to the item that follows that node. Finally, the function returns 0 or 1 according to whether `current` is NULL. This allows the function to be invoked in the form

```
    if (!it) . . .
```

where `it` is an iterator. The expression `(!it)` is read "a current item exists," because the function will return 1 (*i.e.,* "true") if `current` is not NULL. We use this function to check the status of the `current` pointer before invoking an insertion or deletion function that requires using the pointer.

The `operator++()` "increments" the iterator by advancing its `current` pointer to the next item in the list after advancing its `previous` pointer. It precedes this action with the same resetting procedure that the `operator!()` function performed if it finds the `current` pointer `NULL`:

```
template<class T>
int ListIter<T>::operator++()
{
    if (current == NULL)                        // reset current pointer
        if (previous == NULL) current = list.first;
        else current = previous->next;
    else {                                      // advance current pointer
        previous = current;
        current = current->next;
    }
    return (current != NULL);       // returns TRUE if current exists
}
```

This operator allows for easy traversal of the list:

```
    for (it.reset(); !it; it++) . . .
```

just like an ordinary `for` loop traversing an array. It resets the iterator to locate the first item in the list. Then after visiting that item, it increments the iterator to advance and visit the next item. The loop continues as long as `!it` returns "true", which means that there is still an item to be visited.

The `insert(t)` function creates a new node for `t` and then inserts that node immediately after the `current` node:

```
template<class T>
void ListIter<T>::insert(T t)
{
    ListNode<T>* p = list.newNode(t,0);
    if (list.isEmpty())
        list.first = p;
    else {
        p->next = current->next;
        current->next = p;
    }
}
```

The `insert` operation can be visualized like this:

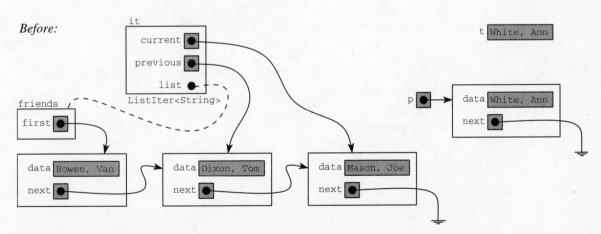

Note that the operation leaves the `current` and `previous` pointers unchanged.

After:

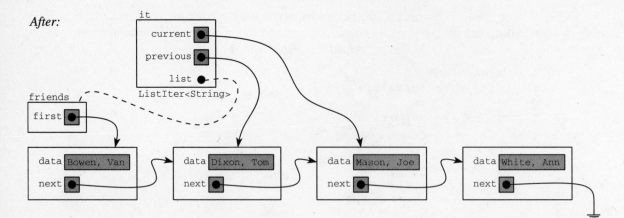

The `preInsert()` function is similar to the `insert()` function, except that it inserts the new node in front of the `current` node:

```
template<class T>
void ListIter<T>::preInsert(T t)
{
    ListNode<T>* p = list.newNode(t,current);
    if (current == list.first) list.first = previous = p;
    else previous->next = p;
}
```

The `preInsert` operation can be visualized like this:

Before:

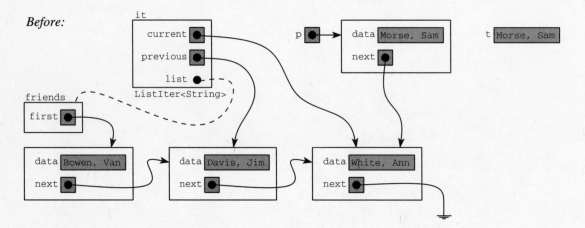

Note that like `insert`, this operation also leaves the `current` and `previous` pointers unchanged.

The `remove()` function deletes the `current` node:

```
template<class T>
void ListIter<T>::remove()
{
    if (current == list.first) list.first = current->next;
    else previous->next = current->next;
    delete current;
    current = 0;
}
```

It leaves the `previous` pointer unchanged and the current pointer NULL.

After:

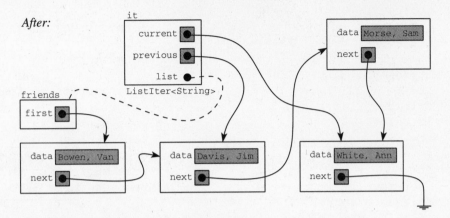

The `remove` operation can be visualized like this:

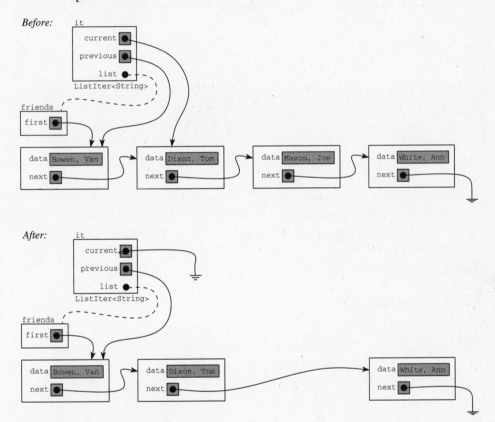

Here is a test driver for the list iterator:

```
#include <iostream.h>
#include "ListIter.h"
#include "String.h"
main()
{
    List<String> friends;
    ListIter<String> it(friends);
    it.insert("Bowen, Van");
    it++;                          // sets current to first item
```

```
    it.insert("Dixon, Tom");
    it++;                              // sets current to second item
    it.insert("Mason, Joe");
    it++;                              // sets current to third item
    it.insert("White, Ann");
    it++;                              // sets current to fourth item
    friends.print();
    it.reset();                        // sets current to first item
    it++;                              // sets current to second item
    it = "Davis, Jim";                 // replace with new name
    it++;                              // sets current to third item
    it.remove();                       // removes third item
    friends.print();
    if (!it) it.preInsert("Morse, Sam");
    friends.print();
    for (it.reset(); !it; it++)        // traverses entire list
        it = "[" + it() + "]";
    friends.print();
}
```

```
Bowen, Van -> Dixon, Tom -> Mason, Joe -> White, Ann -> *
Bowen, Van -> Davis, Jim -> White, Ann -> *
Bowen, Van -> Davis, Jim -> Morse, Sam -> White, Ann -> *
[Bowen, Van] -> [Davis, Jim] -> [Morse, Sam] -> [White, Ann] -> *
```

The `for` loop changes each `data` value in the list by prepending a left bracket and appending a right bracket to each string. Note that the assignment `it = "[" + it() + "]"` calls the `operator()()` and `operator=()` functions of the `ListIter<String>` class as well as the constructor `String(const char*)` and `operator+=()` function defined in the `String` class.

To give `ListIter` objects the access to the `protected` members of `List` objects that they need to do their job, we need to declare the `ListIter` class a `friend` of the `List` class:

```
template<class T>
class List {
    friend class ListIter<T>;
public:
    // other members
protected:
    ListNode<T>* first;
    // other members
};
```

`List` iterators also need the access to the `protected` members of `ListNode` objects:

```
template<class T>
class ListNode {
    friend class List<T>;
    friend class ListIter<T>;
public:
    ListNode(T& t, ListNode<T>* p) : data(t), next(p) { }
protected:
    T data;                 // data field
    ListNode* next;         // points to next node in list
};
```

An iterator acts like a window, allowing access to one item at a time in the container. Iterators are sometimes called *cursors* because they locate a specific element among the entire structure, the same way that a cursor on your computer screen locates one character location.

A structure may have more than one iterator. For example, one could declare three iterators on a list like this:

```
List<float> list;
ListIter<float> it1(list), it2(list), it3(list);
it1.insert(11.01);
it1++;
it1.insert(22.02);
it1++;
it1.insert(33.03);
for (it2.reset(); !it2; it2++)
    it2 = 10*it2;            // multiplies each stored number by 10
it3 = it1;                   // replaces 110.1 with 330.3 in first item
```

The iterators are independent of each other. While `it2` traverses the list, `it1` remains fixed on the third item.

Review Questions

13.1   What is the difference between a function template and a template function?

13.2   What is the difference between a class template and a template class?

13.3   What are the advantages and disadvantages of using a linked list instead of a vector?

13.4   How is an iterator like an array subscript?

Solved Programming Problems

13.5   Write and test a program that instantiates a function template that returns the minimum of two values.

A minimum function should compare two objects of the same type and return the object whose value is smaller. The type should be the template parameter `T`:

```
template <class T>
T min(T x, T y)
{
    return ( x < y ? x : y );
}
```

This implementation uses the conditional expression operator: `( x < y ? x : y )`. If `x` is less than `y`, the expression evaluates to `x`; otherwise it evaluates to `y`.

Here is the test driver and a sample run:

```
#include <iostream.h>
#include "Rational.h"

main()
{
    cout << "min(22, 44) = " << min(22, 44) << endl;
    cout << "min(66.66, 33.33) = " << min(66.66, 33.33) << endl;
    Rational x(22, 7), y(314, 100);
    cout << "min(x, y) = " << min(x, y) << endl;
}
```

```
min(22, 44) = 22
min(66.66, 33.33) = 33.33
min(x, y) = 314/100
```

13.6   Write and test a program that instantiates a function template that implements a binary search of a sorted array of objects.

A search function should be passed the array a, the object key to be found, and the bounds on the array index that define the scope of the search. If the object is found, its index in the array should be returned; otherwise, the function should return -1 to signal that the object was not found:

```
template<class T>
int search(T a[], T key, int first, int last)
{
    while (first <= last) {
        int mid = (first + last)/2;
        if (key < a[mid]) last = mid - 1;
        else if (key > a[mid]) first = mid + 1;
        else return mid;
    }
    return -1;  // not found
}
```

Within the while loop, the subarray from a[first] to a[last] is bisected by mid. If key < a[mid] then key cannot be in the second half of the array, so last is reset to mid-1 to reduce the scope of the search to the first half. Otherwise, if key > a[mid], then key cannot be in the first half of the array, so first is reset to mid+1 to reduce the scope of the search to the second half. If both conditions are false, then key == a[mid] and we can return.

Here is the test driver and a sample run:

```
template<class T> int search(T [], T, int, int);

String names[] = {"Adams","Black","Cohen","Davis","Evans","Frost",
                  "Green","Healy","Irwin","Jones","Kelly","Lewis"};

main()
{
    String name;
    while (cin >> name) {
        int location = search(names, name, 0, 9);
```

```
            if (location == -1) cout << name << " is not in list.\n";
            else cout << name << " is in position " << location << endl;
        }
}
```

```
Green
Green is in position 6
Black
Black is in position 1
White
White is not in list.
Adams
Adams is in position 0
Jones
Jones is in position 9
```

13.7 Implement and test a template for generating Queue classes. A *queue* works like a stack,
except that insertions are made at one end of the linear structure and removed from the other
end. It simulates an ordinary waiting line.

Like the implementation of the Stack template, this implementation uses an array data of size
elements of type T. The location in the array where the next object will be inserted is always given by
the value of (front % size), and the location in the array that holds the next object to be removed
is always given by the value of (rear % size):

```
template<class T>
class Queue {
public:
    Queue(int s = 100) : size(s+1), front(0), rear(0)
        { data = new T[size]; }
    ~Queue() { delete [] data; }
    void insert(const T& x) { data[rear++ % size] = x; }
    T remove() { return data[front++ % size]; }
    int isEmpty() const { return front == rear; }
    int isFull() const { return (rear + 1) % size == front; }
private:
    int size, front, rear;
    T* data;
};
```

The test driver uses a queue that can hold at most 3 chars:

```
#include <iostream.h>
#include "Queue.h"

main()
{
    Queue<char> q(3);
    q.insert('A');
    q.insert('B');
    q.insert('C');
    if (q.isFull()) cout << "Queue is full.\n";
    else cout << "Queue is not full.\n";
```

```
cout << q.remove() << endl;
cout << q.remove() << endl;
q.insert('D');
q.insert('E');
if (q.isFull()) cout << "Queue is full.\n";
else cout << "Queue is not full.\n";
cout << q.remove() << endl;
cout << q.remove() << endl;
cout << q.remove() << endl;
if (q.isEmpty()) cout << "Queue is empty.\n";
else cout << "Queue is not empty.\n";
}
```

```
Queue is full.
A
B
Queue is full.
C
D
E
Queue is empty.
```

13.8   Modify the `Vector` class template so that existing vectors can change their size.

We add two functions:

```
unsigned resize(unsigned n);
unsigned resize(unsigned n, T t);
```


Both function transform the vector into one of size n. If $n < sz$, then the last $sz - n$ elements are simply discarded. If $n == sz$, then the vector is left unchanged. If $n > sz$, then the first sz elements of the transformed vector will be the same as those of the prior version; the last $n - sz$ are assigned the value t by the second `resize()` function and are left uninitialized by the first. Both functions return the new size:

```
template<class T>
unsigned Vector<T>::resize(unsigned n, T t)
{
    T* new_data = new T[n];
    copy(v);
    for (i = sz; i < n; i++)
        new_data[i] = t;
    delete [] data;
    sz = n;
    data = new_data;
    return sz;
}
```

```
template<class T>
unsigned Vector<T>::resize(unsigned n)
{
    T* new_data = new T[n];
    copy(v);
    delete [] data;
    sz = n;
    data = new_data;
    return sz;
}
```

13.9 Add a constructor to the `Vector` class template that replicates an ordinary array as a vector.

The new constructor converts an array `a` whose elements have type `T`:

```
template<class T>
class Vector {
public:
    Vector(T* a) : sz(sizeof(a)), data(new T[sz])
        { for (int i = 0; i < sz; i++) data[i] = a[i]; }
    // other members
};
```

Here is a test driver for the new constructor:

```
main()
{
    int a[] = { 22, 44, 66, 88 };
    Vector<int> v(a);
    cout << v.size() << endl;
    for (int i = 0; i < 4; i++)
        cout << v[i] << "  ";
}
```

```
4
22  44  66  88
```

The advantage of this constructor is that we can initialize a vector now without having to assign each component separately.

13.10 Derive an `Array<T,E>` class template from the `Vector<T>` class template, where the second template parameter `E` holds an enumeration type to be used for the array index.

The derived template has three member functions: two constructors and a new subscript operator:

```
template <class T, class E>
class Array : public Vector<T> {
public:
    Array(E last) : Vector<T>(unsigned(last) + 1) { }
    Array(const Array<T,E>& a) : Vector<T>(a) { }
    T& operator[](E index) const
        { return Vector<T>::operator[](unsigned(index)); }
};
```

The first constructor calls the default constructor defined in the parent class `Vector<T>`, passing to it the number of `E` values that are to be used for the index. The new copy constructor and subscript operator also invoke their equivalent in the parent class.

Here is a test driver for the `Array<T,E>` template:

```
enum Days { SUN, MON, TUE, WED, THU, FRI, SAT };

main()
{
    Array<int,Days> customers(SAT);
    customers[MON] = 27;  customers[TUE] = 23;
    customers[WED] = 20;  customers[THU] = 23;
    customers[FRI] = 36;  customers[SAT] = customers[SUN] = 0;
    for (Days day = SUN; day <= SAT; day++)
        cout << customers[day] << "  ";
}
```

```
0  27  23  20  23  36  0
```

The enumeration type `Days` defines seven values for the type. Then the object `customers` is declared to be an array of `int`s indexed by these seven values. The rest of the program applies the subscript operator to initialize and then print the array.

Supplementary Programming Problems

13.11 Write and test a program that instantiates a function template that returns the maximum of two values.

13.12 Implement and test the following function template:
```
template <class T>
void printArray(T* array, const int count);
```

13.13 Write and test a program that instantiates the following function template:

```
template <class T>
T power(T base, int exp)
{
    T p = 1;
    for (int i = 1; i <= exp; i++)
        p *= base;
    for (int i = 1; i <= -exp; i++)
        p *= base;
    return p;
}
```

Instantiate the function template for several numerical types, including the `Rational` class defined in Chapter 8.

13.14 Write and test a program that instantiates a function template that implements a linear search of an array of objects.

13.15 Write and test a program that instantiates a function template that implements the Selection Sort on an array of objects.

13.16 Write and test a program that instantiates a function template that implements the Insertion Sort on an array of objects.

13.17 Write a program that simulates a waiting line at a bank. Instantiate the `Queue<short>` class to construct the waiting line, numbering the people who arrive 1, 2, 3, *etc.* Use a `Random` class to generate times in the range 0.0 to 8.0 minutes to be used both for the time between arrivals and for the service times. Compute and print the average waiting time and the average length of the line.

13.18 Implement and test a template for generating `Deque` classes. A *deque* (pronounced "deck") generalizes both a stack and a queue by allowing insertions and deletions at both ends of the linear structure. Use the following interface:

```
template<class T>
class Deque {
public:
    Deque(int = 100);
    ~Deque();
    void insertLeft(const T&);
    void insertRight(const T&);
    T removeLeft();
    T removeRight();
    int isEmpty() const;
    int isFull() const;
private:
    int size, left, right;
    T* data;
};
```

Hint: Let `left` and `right` always locate the next items on the left and right to be removed, so that they play the role of `Queue::front`.

13.19 Add the following constructor to the `Vector` class template:

```
Vector(const T a[], int n);
```

This function will duplicate an ordinary array as a `Vector`. For example, the code

```
String names[] = { "Ann", "Bob", "Cal", "Dan", "Eve" }
Vector<String> v(names);
```

would create the `String Vector v` with the same values that the `names` array has.

13.20 Add the following two member functions to the `Vector` class template:

```
T min();  // returns the minimum element in the vector
T max();  // returns the minimum element in the vector
```

Use of these functions, of course, presume that the order operators `<`, `>`, *etc.*, are defined for the type `T`. For example, they would not work on an instance of `Vector<Complex>`.

13.21 Add the following member function to the `Vector` class template:

```
int find(T t);
```

This function searches for the element `t` in the `Vector`. If found, it returns the index of the element; otherwise, it returns -1. Use the sequential search algorithm.

13.22 Add the following two I/O functions for the `Vector` class template:

```
friend ostream& operator<<(ostream&, const Vector<T>&);
friend istream& operator>>(istream&, Vector<T>&);
```

13.23 Add the following member function to the `Vector` class template:

```
void sort();
```

This function rearranges the elements of the `Vector` so that they are in increasing order. Use your favorite sorting algorithm. Use of this function, of course, requires that the order operators `<`, `>`, *etc.*, are defined for the type `T`.

13.24 Add the following member function to the `Vector` class template:

```
int find(T t);
```

This function searches for the element `t` in the `Vector`. If found, it returns the index of the element; otherwise, it returns -1. Use the binary search algorithm, assuming that the `Vector` has already been sorted.

13.25 Add a constructor to the `Vector` class template that replicates an ordinary array of elements of type `T`. This will allow the following simpler way to initialize a vector:

```
String a[] = { "Adams, Ned", "Blair, Tim", "Cooke, Sam" }
Vector<String> friends(a);
```

13.26 Replace the `Array` subclass template (Example 13.5) with an independent class template that replaces the `sz` data member with one that holds the last subscript value. Your new `Array` class template should have the same member functions as the `Array` subclass template.

13.27 Add a constructor to the `Matrix` class template that replicates an ordinary two-dimensional array as a matrix. (See Problem 13.8.) This will allow the following simpler way to initialize a matrix:

```
float a[] = { {2.2, 4.4, 6.6}, {3.3, 5.5, 7.7} }
Matrix<float> m(a);
```

13.28 Add the following two I/O functions for the `Matrix` class template:

```
friend ostream& operator<<(ostream&, const Matrix<T>&);
friend istream& operator>>(istream&, Matrix<T>&);
```

13.29 Add the following member function to the `Matrix` class template:

```
Matrix<T> transpose();
```

The *transpose* of a matrix is the matrix with the same elements except that the rows and columns have been interchanged. For example, the transpose of the 2-by-3 matrix on page 364 is the following 3-by-2 matrix:

$$\begin{bmatrix} a & d \\ b & e \\ c & f \end{bmatrix}$$

13.30 Add the following member function to the `Matrix` class template:

```
Vector<T> column(int j);
```

This function returns the `j`th column of the matrix.

13.31 Use the `Vector<String>` and `Matrix<short>` classes to process the following table of quiz scores for a student group:

Name	Q1	Q2	Q3	Q4	Q5
Adams, J.	78	91	88	83	80
Baker, P.	81	94	97	90	89
Cohen, A.	85	86	87	88	89
Davis, M.	82	56	75	81	88
Evans, C.	75	77	70	78	74
Flynn, R.	83	79	88	90	81
Gross, W.	86	87	88	89	90
Hayes, J.	91	94	99	87	92

Your program should do the following:

a. Declare the table and read in the test scores.

b. Print the scores in tabular form.

c. Compute and print each student's quiz average.

d. Compute and print the group average for each quiz.

13.32 Add a constructor to the `List` class template that replicates an ordinary array of elements of type `T`. This will allow the following simpler way to initialize a list:

```
String a[] = { "Adams, Ned", "Blair, Tim", "Cooke, Sam" }
List<String> friends(a);
```

13.33 Add the following two I/O functions for the `List` class template:

```
friend ostream& operator<<(ostream&, const List<T>&);
friend istream& operator>>(istream&, List<T>&);
```

13.34 Use composition to implement the `Stack` class template using the `List` class template. The only data member you need is `List<T> list`.

13.35 Use composition to implement the `Queue` class template using the `List` class template with the enhancements added in Problem 13.38.

13.36 Implement a copy constructor for the `List` class template:

```
List(const List<T>&);
```

13.37 Implement the assignment operator for the `List` class template:

```
List<T>& operator=(const List<T>&);
```

13.38 Add the following two member functions to the `List` class template:

```
void insertAtEnd(T t);       // insert t at the end of the list
int removeFromEnd(T& t);     // remove last item t from the list
```

13.39 Add the following member functions to the `List` class template:

```
void append(const List<T>&);
```

This function appends the list passed to it to the list that owns the function call. It does not create any new nodes.

13.40 Modify the `List` class template by adding a *dummy node* to the end of each list. The dummy node will act like a newline character in that it signals the end of the list. It is identified as the only node whose `next` pointer points to itself. Its `data` field is not used.

13.41 Add the following member functions to the `List` class template:

```
void reverse();
```

This function reverses the list, like this:

```
void reverse();
```

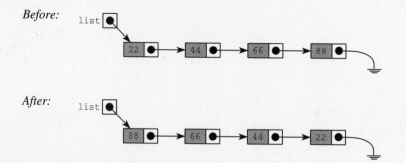

Do it two ways. First, do it by moving the actual data, using a stack. Then do it "in place" by changing pointers and not moving any data.

13.42 Add the following member functions to the `List` class template:

```
void merge(const List<T>&);
```

This function merges the list passed to it with the list that owns the function call. It assumes that both lists are sorted in increasing order, and thus requires that the order operators <, >, *etc.*, are defined for the type T. It does not create any new nodes.

13.43 Modify the `insert()` function in the `List` class template so that it maintains the list in increasing order. This presupposes that only types and classes that have implemented an order relation will be passed to the template parameter T.

13.44 Implement the `List` class template by using *circular lists*. This is done simply by having the `next` pointer of the last node point to the first node instead of being `NULL`.

13.45 Use the circularly linked implementation of Problem 13.44 to solve the *Josephus Problem*. This problem simulates the elimination of a group of *n* soldiers standing in a circle, using an increment *m*, where $1 \le m < n$. The soldiers are eliminated one at a time by counting up to *m*. For example, if there are *n*=8 soldiers and the increment is *m*=3, the order of elimination is 3, 6, 1, 5, 2, 8, 4, 7. That should be the output from the program with input 8 and 3.

Answers to Review Questions

13.1 A *function template* is a template that is used to generate functions. A *template function* is a function that is produced by a template. For example, `swap(T&, T&)` in Example 13.1 is a function template, but the call `swap(m, n)` generates the actual template function that is invoked by the call.

13.2 A *class template* is a template that is used to generate classes. A *template class* is a class that is produced by a template. For example, `Stack` in Example 13.3 is a class template, but the type `Stack<int>` used in the declarations is an actual template class.

13.3 Vectors have the advantage of *direct access* (also called "random access") to their components by means of the subscript operator. So if the elements are kept in order, we can locate them very quickly using the Binary Search Algorithm. Lists have the advantage of being dynamic, so that they never use more space than is currently needed, and they aren't restricted to a predetermined size (except for the size of the computer's memory). So vectors have a time advantage and lists have a space advantage.

13.4 Both iterators and array index act as locators into a data structure. The following code shows that they work the same way:

```
float a[100];              // an array of 100 floats
int i = 0;                 // an index for the array
a[i] = 3.14159;
for (i = 0; i < 100; i++) cout << a[i];
List<float> list;          // a list of floats
ListIter<float> it(list);  // an iterator for the list
it = 3.14159;
for (it.reset(); !it; it++) cout << it();
```

Chapter 14

Libraries

14.1 INTRODUCTION

A *software library* for a programming language is a collection of software components that can be used in any program written in that language. These components contain definitions of constants, classes, objects, and functions that can be used as if they were part of the definition of the language itself. For example, the `<iostream.h>` header file is a component of the Standard C++ Library. It defines the `cout` object that we use for output in C++ programs.

Libraries are usually included with C++ compilers. For example, Borland C++ provides several class libraries. These libraries typically include many I/O classes and container classes. Libraries can also be obtained independently. For example, as of 1995, the Standard Template Library is available by FTP and from some commercial vendors but has not yet been bundled with any C++ compilers.

14.2 THE STANDARD C++ LIBRARY

At this writing, C++ is now in its final stages of standardization. The ANSI/ISO Committee has approved a draft standard that will probably become the international standard definition of the C++ programming language before the end of 1996. Part of that standard includes what we shall refer to here as the *Standard C++ Library*. Since this standard is so new, it will be a while before most commercial compilers include all of its features. So we will focus here on those parts of the standard library that are already implemented.

The ANSI/ISO C++ Standard specifies 86 header files for the Standard C++ Library. Of these, 18 are the header files that comprise the Standard C Library, and the other 68 are the header files that are specific to the C++ language. The latter are divided into two groups: 20 header files that were specified in an earlier "draft standard," and 48 header files that make up the new *Standard Template Library*. To distinguish these two groups, we will refer to them as the "C++ Headers" and the "STL Headers." All 86 of these header files are listed in the table below.

The C++ Standard specifies that the 20 C++ header files be named without the traditional ".h" suffix. For example, the familiar `<iostream.h>` header is listed as `<iostream>`. Most vendors ignore this advice and retain the ".h" suffix, as we shall in this book. Moreover, to distinguish C headers from C++ headers, some vendors capitalize the names of their C++ headers. For example GNU C++ uses `<String.h>` for the Standard C++ `<string>` header to distinguish it from the Standard C `<string.h>` header. In contrast, Borland C++, which runs under case-insensitive DOS, uses `<cstring.h>` for the Standard C++ `<string>` header.

Since the C++ Standard is so new, the complete set of all 86 header files is not widely implemented yet. But most C++ compilers do come with a substantial subset, including all the C headers, the nine C++ stream headers (`<fstream>`, `<iomanip>`, `<ios>`, `<iostream>`,

Table 14.1 Standard C++ Library Header Files

C Headers	C++ Headers	STL Headers	
`<assert.h>`	`<bits>`	`<algo.h>`	`<lbvector.h>`
`<ctype.h>`	`<bitstring>`	`<algobase.h>`	`<ldeque.h>`
`<errno.h>`	`<complex>`	`<bool.h>`	`<list.h>`
`<float.h>`	`<defines>`	`<bvector.h>`	`<llist.h>`
`<iso646.h>`	`<dynarray>`	`<defalloc.h>`	`<lmap.h>`
`<limits.h>`	`<exception>`	`<deque.h>`	`<lmultmap.h>`
`<locale.h>`	`<fstream>`	`<faralloc.h>`	`<lmultset.h>`
`<math.h>`	`<iomanip>`	`<fdeque.h>`	`<lngalloc.h>`
`<setjmp.h>`	`<ios>`	`<flist.h>`	`<lset.h>`
`<signal.h>`	`<iostream>`	`<fmap.h>`	`<map.h>`
`<stdarg.h>`	`<istream>`	`<fmultmap.h>`	`<multimap.h>`
`<stddef.h>`	`<new>`	`<fmultset.h>`	`<multiset.h>`
`<stdio.h>`	`<ostream>`	`<fset.h>`	`<neralloc.h>`
`<stdlib.h>`	`<ptrdynarray>`	`<function.h>`	`<nmap.h>`
`<string.h>`	`<sstream>`	`<hdeque.h>`	`<nmultmap.h>`
`<time.h>`	`<streambuf>`	`<heap.h>`	`<nmultset.h>`
`<wchar.h>`	`<string>`	`<hlist.h>`	`<nset.h>`
`<wctype.h>`	`<strstream>`	`<hmap.h>`	`<pair.h>`
	`<typeinfo>`	`<hmultmap.h>`	`<projectn.h>`
	`<wstring>`	`<hmultset.h>`	`<set.h>`
		`<hset.h>`	`<stack.h>`
		`<hugalloc.g>`	`<tempbuf.h>`
		`<hvector.h>`	`<tree.h>`
		`<iterator.h>`	`<vector.h>`

`<istream>`, `<ostream>`, `<sstream>`, `<fstreambuf>`, and `<strstream>`), and some version of the C++ headers `<bitstring>`, `<complex>`, and `<string>`. Some container classes such as `List` and `Vector` may also be included, but these are not equivalent to those specified in the STL. The latter include built-in iterators and a large number of algorithms. Some of these header files have already been examined in earlier chapters. Chapter 10 describes most of the functions defined in the C header `<string.h>`. Chapter 12 reviews much of the contents of the C++ stream headers.

Appendix E lists many books on programming in C++. Some of these contain more thorough discussions of the Standard C++ Library. A complete treatment of the C headers is given in the book **[Plauger1]** (see Appendix E), while **[Plauger2]** similarly covers the C++ headers. The journal *The C++ Report* frequently includes information on the STL. Its contents are available on-line from the Hewlett Packard Corporation and from several independent vendors.

14.3 PROPRIETARY LIBRARIES

Typically, vendors of C++ compilers or more general C++ development environments will provide one or more libraries that include many of the Standard C++ headers as well as many other headers for I/O classes, container classes, and mathematical functions. For example, Borland C++ provides its Stream Class Library, its BIDS Library (Borland International Data Structures), and its OWL Library (Object Windows Library). These libraries are distributed over some 267 header files (in Borland C++ v.4.0), some of which are listed in Table 14.2.

Table 14.2 Some Borland C++ Header Files

C Headers	C++ Headers	BIDS Headers	OWL Headers
<assert.h>	<bcd.h>	<arrays.h>	<applicat.h>
<ctype.h>	<checks.h>	<assoc.h>	<button.h>
<errno.h>	<complex.h>	<bags.h>	<checkbox.h>
<float.h>	<constrea.h>	<binimp.h>	<clipboar.h>
<limits.h>	<cstring.h>	<date.h>	<control.h>
<locale.h>	<except.h>	<deques.h>	<dialog.h>
<math.h>	<fstream.h>	<dict.h>	<edit.h>
<setjmp.h>	<iomanip.h>	<dlistimp.h>	<gadget.h>
<signal.h>	<iostream.h>	<hashimp.h>	<menu.h>
<stdarg.h>	<new.h>	<heapsel.h>	<preview.h>
<stddef.h>	<ref.h>	<listimp.h>	<printer.h>
<stdio.h>	<regexp.h>	<queues.h>	<scroller.h>
<stdlib.h>	<stdiostr.h>	<seta.h>	<slider.h>
<string.h>	<strstrea.h>	<stacks.h>	<toolbox.h>
<time.h>	<typeinfo.h>	<vectimp.h>	<window.h>

Notice that Borland's BIDS Library includes some of the same container classes that are specified in the STL: <deques.h> defines a deque class template, <dict.h> defines a map class template, <listimp.h> defines a list class template, <seta.h> defines a set class template, and <vectimp.h> defines a vector class template. But these are not equivalent to those defined in the STL. As we shall see, the STL combines classes, iterators, and algorithms in a unique way.

Borland's OWL Library contains class definitions for writing graphical user interfaces using windows, menus, panels, clipboards, scrollers, *etc.* Such class libraries are typical of modern development environments. But they are highly proprietary and are not part of the C++ Standard.

Many C++ compilers use Microsoft's *Foundation Class Library.* This library defines a large number of classes, many of which are similar to those defined in Borland's BIDS and OWL libraries, including an application class, an array class template, a list class template, a map class template, various window classes, view classes, *etc.*

14.4 CONTENTS OF THE STANDARD C HEADERS

This section gives a brief summary of the contents of some of the Standard C header files. Since these are part of the C programming language, they do not contain any class definitions.

The `<assert.h>` header defines the `assert()` function:

```
void assert(int expr);
```

This function is used to check a condition within a block of code. If the condition is false, the program aborts; otherwise it continues normally.

EXAMPLE 14.1 Using the `<assert.h>` Header File

The `<assert.h>` header file contains the `assert()` function which is used to ensure that a condition that is needed is satisfied

```
#include <iostream.h>
#include <assert.h>
main()
{
    float x;
    cout << "Enter a non-zero number: ";
    cin >> x;
    assert( x != 0 );
    cout << "The reciprocal of " << x << " is " << 1.0/x;
}
```

```
Enter a non-zero number: 3
The reciprocal of 3 is 0.333333
```

```
Enter a non-zero number: 0
test_assert.c:9: failed assertion `x != 0'
```

The expression `1.0/x` will cause the program to crash if `x` is zero. The call `assert( x != 0 )` guarantees that that expression will not be evaluated if `x` is zero. As the second run shows, when `x` is zero, the execution of the program terminates during the call of the `assert()` function.

The `<ctype.h>` header defines several utility functions for testing characters:

```
int isalnum(int c);    // returns 1 if c is alphanumeric
int isalpha(int c);    // returns 1 if c is alphabetic
int iscntrl(int c);    // returns 1 if c is control
int isdigit(int c);    // returns 1 if c is a digit
int isgraph(int c);    // returns 1 if c is graphic
int islower(int c);    // returns 1 if c is lowercase
int isprint(int c);    // returns 1 if c is printable
int ispunct(int c);    // returns 1 if c is punctuation
int isspace(int c);    // returns 1 if c is whitespace
int isupper(int c);    // returns 1 if c is uppercase
int isxdigit(int c);   // returns 1 if c is a hexadecimal digit
```

It also defines the character conversion functions:

```
int tolower(int c);    // converts to lowercase
int toupper(int c);    // converts to uppercase
```

The `<float.h>` header file defines system dependent constants that describe the floating point types. Similarly the `<limits.h>` header defines system dependent characteristics for the integer types. Example 14.4 shows how to print these constants.

EXAMPLE 14.2 Using the `<float.h>` and `<limits.h>` Header Files

By printing the constants defined in these two header files, we can see how real and integer types are limited on this particular computer:

```
#include <iostream.h>
#include <limits.h>
#include <float.h>

main()
{
    cout << "\tBits used for one byte: " << CHAR_BIT << endl;
    cout << "\t        Smallest char: " << CHAR_MIN << endl;
    cout << "\t         Largest char: " << CHAR_MAX << endl;
    cout << "\t       Smallest short: " << SHRT_MIN << endl;
    cout << "\t        Largest short: " << SHRT_MAX << endl;
    cout << "\t         Smallest int: " << INT_MIN << endl;
    cout << "\t          Largest int: " << INT_MAX << endl;
    cout << "\t       Smallest float: " << FLT_MIN << endl;
    cout << "\t        Largest float: " << FLT_MAX << endl;
    cout << "\t      Digits for float: " << FLT_DIG << endl;
    cout << "\t      Smallest double: " << DBL_MIN << endl;
    cout << "\t       Largest double: " << DBL_MAX << endl;
    cout << "\t     Digits for double: " << DBL_DIG << endl;
}
```

```
        Bits used for one byte: 8
              Smallest char: -128
               Largest char: 127
             Smallest short: -32768
              Largest short: 32767
               Smallest int: -2147483648
                Largest int: 2147483647
             Smallest float: 1.17549e-38
              Largest float: 3.40282e+38
             Digits for float: 6
            Smallest double: 2.22507e-308
             Largest double: 1.79769e+308
           Digits for double: 15
```

This shows, for example, that on this machine the numerical range for a `char` is −128 to 127, and that values of type `double` contain 15 significant digits.

The `<time.h>` header defines functions that access the system clock. Example 14.4 shows how some of these work. Note that the calculation on x is only to kill time.

EXAMPLE 14.3 Using the `<time.h>` Header File

```
#include <iostream.h>
#include <time.h>

main()
{
    clock_t c;
    time_t t;
    char* s;
    double x = 3.14159265358979;
    cout << "CLOCKS_PER_SEC =  " << CLOCKS_PER_SEC << endl;
    for (long int i = 0; i < 1000000; i++)
        x = 1 + x/(1+x);
    c = clock();
    cout << "clock() =  " << c << endl;
    cout << "seconds =  " << c/CLOCKS_PER_SEC << endl;
    t = time(NULL);
    cout << "time(NULL) =  " << t << endl;
    s = ctime(&t);
    cout << "current time =  " << s << endl;
}
```

```
CLOCKS_PER_SEC =  1000000
clock() =  2956842
seconds =  2
time(NULL) =  805308632
current time =  Sun Jul  9 12:50:32 1995
```

The first line of output shows that this system increments its clock once per microsecond (*i.e.*, 1,000,000 times per second). Next the `for` loop causes a delay of 2.956842 seconds, as shown by the second line of output. So we see that the expression `c/CLOCKS_PER_SEC` shows how many CPU seconds have elapsed.

The call `time(NULL)` shows that 805,308,632 seconds have elapsed since January 1, 1970. The `ctime()` function converts this integer into the character string `s` that shows the current date and time.

The `<stdlib.h>` header file defines a diverse collection of constants and functions, including the following:

```
#define EXIT_SUCCESS 0            // for use with exit()
#define EXIT_FAILURE 1            // for use with exit()
#define NULL 0                    // null pointer
#define RAND_MAX 2147483646       // = INT_MAX - 1, for use with rand()
int rand();                       // returns random integers <= RAND_MAX
void srand(unsigned seed);        // seeds the random number generator
int abs(int i);                   // absolute value for integers
int atoi(const char* s)           // converts ASCII string to int
double atof(const char* s)        // converts ASCII string to double
void abort()                      // aborts program execution
void exit(int status)             // end program execution normally
```

The integers returned by `rand()` are uniformly distributed in the range 0 to `RAND_MAX`. However, the sequence of integers generated will be the same for the same seed. Use `srand()` first to initialize the seed. This is illustrated in the next example.

EXAMPLE 14.4 Using the `<stdlib.h>` and `<time.h>` Header Files

This shows how to use the system clock to set the seed for the random number generator:

```
#include <iostream.h>
#include <stdlib.h>
#include <time.h>

main()
{
    unsigned seed = time(NULL);
    srand(seed);
    for (int i = 0; i < 32; i++)
        cout << 1 + rand()%6 << " ";
    cout << endl;
}
```

```
2 5 2 5 2 3 4 5 2 1 4 3 2 5 4 3 4 3 4 5 4 3 2 5 4 5 6 5 6 1 6 1

6 5 6 5 2 1 2 3 6 5 4 3 2 1 4 3 2 3 2 5 6 5 2 3 4 1 6 3 4 5 4 5

4 5 4 5 4 3 2 3 4 3 6 3 2 3 4 1 6 1 2 3 6 1 2 3 4 5 6 3 2 5 2 3
```

The call `time(NULL)` returns the number of seconds that have elapsed in the twentieth century. By passing this integer to `srand()`, we ensure that each time the program is run it begins with a different seed. Thus each of the three runs produces a different sequence of 32 "random" numbers. The expression `1 + rand()%6` generates random integers in the range 1 to 6, simulating the toss of a die.

Note that some predefined `rand()` functions do not give very satisfactory results. For serious simulation, one should implement one's own random. See Problem 8.21.

The `<string.h>` header file defines a large number of very useful functions for manipulating null-terminated arrays of characters. These are described in Chapter 10.

The `<math.h>` header defines mathematical functions such as the following:

```
double sin(double x);              // sine
double atan(double x);             // arctangent
double cosh(double x);             // hyperbolic cosine
double pow(double x, double y);    // x to the power y
double exp(double x);              // e to the power x
double log(double x);              // natural logarithm (base e)
double log10(double x);            // common logarithm (base 10)
double sqrt(double x);             // square root of x
double ceil(double x);             // least integer >= x
double floor(double x);            // greatest integer <= x
double fabs(double x);             // absolute value for reals
```

The `<stddef.h>` header defines some special constants and types:

```
#define NULL ((void*) 0)           // null pointer
typedef char wchar_t;              // wide character type
typedef unsigned size_t;           // size type
```

Note the use of the preprocessor directive `#define`. This is the way constants are defined in C.

Different compilers may have different definitions for the wide character and size types. Wide characters are used to accommodate large character sets, such as the Chinese character set. The `size_t` type is used with certain library functions, such as the `strlen()` function defined in the `<string.h>` header file.

The `<stdio.h>` header file defines the non-stream I/O functions used by C programmers. For example, the `scanf()` and `printf()` functions are used for formatted input and output.

14.5 STRING STREAMS

We have named the second group of header files that comprise the Standard C++ Library the "C++ headers." These contain the C++ definitions that completed the "draft C++ Standard" before the Standard Template Library was included. Nine of these twenty headers are devoted to the stream processing that is described in Chapter 12. In this section we expand that study with a brief survey of string streams defined in `<strstream>`. The following section describes how file processing is managed using the file streams defined in `<fstream>`.

The `<strstream>` header file defines three classes that allow the use of string streams in C++. A *string stream* is a stream that exists only during the execution of the program in which it is defined. String streams are also called an *in-memory character sequences* and *internal files*. Stream buffers provide a convenient way to use a block of memory for formatting output and buffering input.

Here is the diagram shown on the first page of Chapter 12:

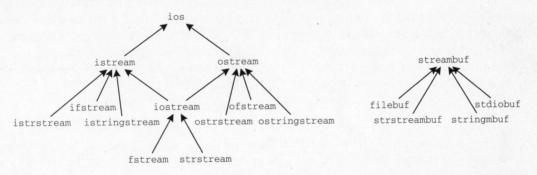

The three classes `istrstream`, `ostrstream`, and `strstreambuf` are defined in the `<strstream>` header.

An `istrstream` object is an input string stream that is attached to an ordinary `char*` string. The object works like an ordinary input stream (like `cin`) except that when the extraction operator `>>` is applied to it, data is read from its attached `char*` string instead of the keyboard. Similarly, an `ostrstream` object is an output string stream that is also attached to a `char*` string. It works like an ordinary output stream (like `cout`) except that when the insertion operator `<<` is applied to it, data is sent to its attached string instead of the display screen. The next example illustrates these classes.

String streams are useful for buffering input and output. Input from `cin` can be piped into an input string stream, and then examined and validated before processing the data that it receives. Similarly, output can be formatted in an output sting stream before it is sent to `cout`. This is sometimes called *incore formatting*.

EXAMPLE 14.5 Using `<strstream.h>` to Process String Streams

The `<strstream.h>` header file defines the `istrstream` and the `ostrstream` classes:

```
#include <strstream.h>

main()
{
    const int size = 80;
    char inbuf[size] = "Hello, world! 3.14159 65535 Q";
    char outbuf[size];
    istrstream istr(inbuf, size);    // input strstream for inbuf
    ostrstream ostr(outbuf, size);   // output strstream for outbuf
    char s1[size], s2[size];
    float x;
    long int n;
    char c, p = '|';
    istr >> s1 >> s2 >> x >> n >> c;
    cout << "\ts1 = [" << s1 << "]\n";
    cout << "\ts2 = [" << s2 << "]\n";
    cout << "\tx = " << x << endl;
    cout << "\tn = " << n << endl;
    cout << "\tc = " << c << endl;
    ostr << s1 << p << s2 << p << x << p << n << p << c << ends;
    cout << "[" << outbuf << "]\n";
}
```

```
        s1 = [Hello,]
        s2 = [world!]
        x = 3.14159
        n = 65535
        c = Q
[Hello,|world!|3.14159|65535|Q]
```

After declaring `inbuf` and `outbuf` as simple 80-character strings, the input string stream `istr` and the output string stream `ostr` are declared. These are tied to `inbuf` and `outbuf`, respectively. So `istr` acts like an input stream (like `cin`), except that the "input" comes from the `inbuf` string instead of the keyboard. Similarly, `ostr` acts like an output stream (like `cout`), except that the "output" goes to the `outbuf` string instead of the display screen.

The next example illustrates how string streams can be used as filters. It uses an output string stream to create form letters.

EXAMPLE 14.6 Using a String Streams as a Filter

This uses a function `form()` to create form letters:

```
#include <strstream.h>

char* form(char* name, int male)
{
    const size = 128;
    static char buffer[size];
```

```
        static ostrstream ostr(buffer, size);
        ostr.seekp(ios::beg);
        ostr << "Dear ";
        if (male) ostr << "Mr. ";
        else ostr << "Mrs. ";
        ostr << name
               << ",\n\tI have an exclusive offer for you and your ";
        if (male) ostr << "wife, Mrs.";
        else ostr << "husband, Mr.";
        ostr << name << "...\n" << ends;
        return buffer;
    }

    main()
    {
        cout << form("Baker", 1);
        cout << form("Green", 1);
        cout << form("North", 0);
        cout << form("Smith", 1);
    }
```

```
Dear Mr. Baker,
    I have an exclusive offer for you and your wife, Mrs.Baker...
Dear Mr. Green,
    I have an exclusive offer for you and your wife, Mrs.Green...
Dear Mrs. North,
    I have an exclusive offer for you and your husband, Mr.North...
Dear Mr. Smith,
    I have an exclusive offer for you and your wife, Mrs.Smith...
```

The `buffer` and `ostr` stream are declared to be `static` so that they are not recreated each time the function is called. Since the stream is reused this way, we have to call `ostr.seekp(ios::beg)` each time to reset the write pointer at the beginning of the stream to overwrite the previous string.

The `<sstream>` header file defines the three classes `istringstream`, `ostringstream`, and `stringbuf` for processing `string` streams. These are analogous to the `istrstream`, `ostrstream`, and `strstreambuf` classes, except that they are attached to instances of the `string` class that is defined in the `<string>` header instead of to ordinary C strings (`char*`).

14.6 FILE PROCESSING

A stream is a manager of a flow of bytes. An input stream manages bytes flowing into the program, and an output stream manages bytes flowing out of the program. Every stream is attached to some kind of origin or destination which the stream represents in the program. Instances of the `istream` class (like `cin`) represent the standard input device (*i.e.*, the keyboard). Instances of the `ostrstream` class represent `char*` strings that are being written to. Instances of the `istringstream` class represent `string` objects that are being read from. The beauty of the stream I/O class hierarchy is that it provides a simple uniform programming interface for all types of input and output.

The following diagram shows the relationships between streams and the things that they manage. As a manager of a data source or destination, we can imagine a stream as a pipe through which the data flows to or from the executing program:

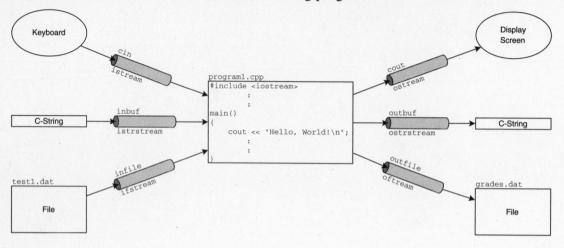

This shows 3 input streams and 3 output streams, each represented by a gray box. For example, `inbuf` is an input stream of type `istrstream` which manages the input of data from a C-string into the program, and `cout` is an output stream of type `ostream` which manages the output of data from the program to the display screen.

C++ uses streams to manage data flow, including flow to and from external files. A *file* is a sequence of bits stored on some external device such as a disk or magnetic tape. The bits are interpreted according to the protocol of some software system. If the bits are grouped into 8-bit bytes interpreted by the ASCII code, then the file is called a *text file* and can be processed by standard editors. If the bits are grouped into 32-bit words representing color pixels, then the file is a *graphics file* and is processed by specialized graphics software. If the file is an executable program, then its bits are interpreted as instructions to the computer's processor.

In C++, a file is simply an external stream: a sequence of bytes stored on disk. If the file is open for output, then it is an output file stream. If the file is open for input, then it is an input file stream. The `<fstream>` header defines the class `ofstream` of output file streams and the class `ifstream` of input file streams. Instances of these classes behave like other internal streams: the insertion and extraction operators apply the same way.

Example 14.4 shows how to write data to an external file. This requires instantiating the `ofstream` class which is defined in the `<fstream>` header. Analogously, Example 14.4 shows how to read data from external file.

EXAMPLE 14.7 Writing to an External Data File

The `<fstream.h>` header file defines the `ofstream` class which must be instantiated to write to an external file:

```
#include <iostream.h>   // defines cout stream
#include <fstream.h>    // defines ofstream class
#include <stdlib.h>     // defines exit() function

main()
{
    ofstream outfile("grades.dat", ios::out);
    if (!outfile) {
        cerr << "Error: output file could not be opened.\n";
        exit(1);
    }
    char id[9], name[16];
    int grade;
    cout << "\t1: ";
    int n = 1;
    while (cin >> id >> name >> grade) {
        outfile << name << " " << id << " " << grade << endl;
        cout << "\t" << ++n << ": ";
    }
    outfile.close();
}
```

```
1: Adams 209134662 83
2: Baker 552818829 77
3: Cohen 310051782 89
4: Davis 446112103 85
5: Evans 616336670 92
6: ^D:
```

The first line invokes the `ofstream` constructor which opens file `grades.dat` as an output file, constructs the stream `outfile`, and attaches that stream to the file. The second line invokes the overloaded negation operator `!` to ensure that the file is opened properly. If not, an error message is printed and the program is terminated. Otherwise, the program uses an input loop to read names, identification numbers, and grades from the standard input and writes them to the external file.

The resulting external file looks like this:

```
grades.dat
209134662 Adams 83
552818829 Baker 77
310051782 Cohen 89
446112103 Davis 85
616336670 Evans 92
```

EXAMPLE 14.8 Reading from an External Data File

The `<fstream.h>` header file defines the `ifstream` class which must be instantiated to read from an external file:

```
#include <iostream.h>   // defines cout stream
#include <fstream.h>    // defines ofstream class
#include <stdlib.h>     // defines exit() function

main()
{
    ifstream infile("grades.dat", ios::in);
    if (!infile) {
        cerr << "Error: input file could not be opened.\n";
        exit(1);
    }
    char id[9], name[16];
    int grade, sum = 0, count = 0;
    while (infile >> id >> name >> grade) {
        sum += grade;
        ++count;
    }
    infile.close();
    cout << "The grade average is " << float(sum)/count << endl;
}
```

```
The grade average is 85.2
```

This works like the previous example. Note how the `infile` stream is used to control the `while` loop the same way that the `cin` stream was used in the previous example.

A file can be opened for both input and output simultaneously in C++. This is illustrated in Example 14.9 which modifies an existing text file by capitalizing all of its lowercase characters.

EXAMPLE 14.9 Modifying a Text File

This program capitalizes all the characters in a text file. It gets the name of the text file from the command line argument `argv[1]` which passes it to the `fstream` constructor to open the file as `iofile`:

```
#include <fstream.h>    // defines ofstream class
#include <stdlib.h>     // defines exit() function
#include <ctype.h>      // defines islower(), toupper() functions

main(int argc, char** argv)
{
    fstream iofile(argv[1], ios::in | ios::out);
    if (!iofile) {
        cerr << "Error: file could not be opened.\n";
        exit(1);
    }
    char c;
    while ((c = iofile.get()) != EOF)
        if (islower(c)) {
            iofile.seekp(-1, ios::cur);
            iofile.put(toupper(c));
        }
    iofile.close();
}
```

Note that the logical expression `ios::in | ios::out` is used to open `iofile` for both input and output. This allows the file to be modified character-by-character.

The modification is done by applying the `seekp()` and `put()` functions to `iofile`. The call `iofile.seekp(-1, ios::cur)` uses the parameter –1 to backup over the character just read so that it could read or write it again. Then the call `iofile.put(toupper(c))` replaces that character with the capitalized version of the character `c`.

Suppose that the following file named `Gettysburg.txt` has been prepared:

Gettysburg.txt
```
Fourscore and seven years ago our fathers brought forth
upon this continent a new nation, conceived in liberty,
and dedicated to the proposition that all men are
created equal.
```

If the name of the executable program is `capitalize`, then the command

```
capitalize Gettysburg.txt
```

would transform that file into

Gettysburg.txt
```
FOURSCORE AND SEVEN YEARS AGO OUR FATHERS BROUGHT FORTH
UPON THIS CONTINENT A NEW NATION, CONCEIVED IN LIBERTY,
AND DEDICATED TO THE PROPOSITION THAT ALL MEN ARE
CREATED EQUAL.
```

In this case the command line parameter `argc` has the value 2, and the string array `argv` has the values `"capitalize"` for `argv[0]` and `"Gettysburg.txt"` for `argv[1]`.

14.7 THE STANDARD TEMPLATE LIBRARY

Table 14.1 shows the Standard C++ Library as three groups of header files. The third group is known as the *Standard Template Library*. This is a collection of 48 headers that define a large number of general-purpose container class templates together with iterator classes and generic algorithms for manipulating them. The library is remarkable for its efficiency, consistency, and elegance. It was developed at Hewlett-Packard by Alexander Stepanov and Meng Lee.

Example 14.10 shows how to use the Standard Template Library to merge two lists. Some implementations may require `<stl.h>` to be included instead of `<list.h>`.

EXAMPLE 14.10 Merging Two STL Lists

The `<list.h>` header file defines the `list` class template including its iterators and algorithms. This uses the `merge` algorithm to merge two integer lists:

```
#include <iostream.h>  // defines cout stream
#include <list.h>      // defines list and iterator classes

main()
{
    int a1[3] = { 22, 44, 88 };
    int a2[4] = { 33, 55, 77, 99 };
    list<int> l1(a1, a1 + 3);
    list<int> l2(a2, a2 + 4);
    l1.merge(l2);
    for (list<int>::iterator it = l1.begin(); it != l1.end(); it++)
        cout << *it << " ";
    cout << endl;
}
```

```
22 33 44 55 77 88 99
```

We first set up the two arrays `a1` and `a2` to be used to initialize the lists `l1` and `l2`. Notice how the name of the array is used as a pointer to locate the begining and ending of the array for the list constructor: `a1` is the address of the first element and `a1 + 3` is the address of the memory location immediately after the third element.

Notice how the `for` loop works the same way with an iterator as it would with an ordinary integer index: the iterator is initialized with `it = l1.begin()`, it is incremented with `it++`, and it controls the loop with the condition `it != l1.end()`.

The STL defines seven general container class templates: `deque`, `vector`, `list`, `set`, `map`, `multiset`, and `multimap`. A *deque* is a sequential structure that allows insertions and deletions at two ends. A *vector* is a direct generalization of an ordinary array, allowing indexed access. A *list* is a sequential structure that allows efficient insertions and deletions in the middle of the sequence. A *set* is an unstructured collection of unique elements. A *multiset* (also called a bag) is an unstructured collection of elements that need not be unique. A *map* (also called a dictionary or table) is a set whose elements have two parts: the *key* and the *data*. A *multimap* is the same as a map, except that the keys need not be unique. An ordinary telephone directory is a good example of a multimap, where the keys are the subscribers' names and the data are their addresses and telephone numbers. An "inverted directory" where the unique telephone numbers are the keys would be an example of a map. Maps and multimaps can be regarded as sets and multisets, respectively, except that the elements have two components: a key field and a data field. The key type must have an ordering, so `string` and `double` could be key types, but `complex` and `set` could not.

There are certain operations which one would like to apply to any container object: find the first element; find the last element; determine how many elements are in the container; insert an element; remove an element. The STL defines these operations as member functions that work the same way on all containers. They are summarized in Table 14.3. Here, `a` and `b` are container objects, `t` is a value of the container's template type, `n` is a nonnegative integer, and `p`, `i`, and `j` are iterators on the container.

The STL is a tightly woven system of classes, iterators, and algorithms. Its designers have been very successful in implementing the diverse behavior of container classes in a consistent and intuitive way. This is indicated by the functions listed in Table 14.3 and Table 14.4.

Table 14.3 Operations for All Container Classes

`a.insert(p, t)`	Inserts a copy of `t` before `p`
`a.insert(p, n, t)`	Inserts `n` copies of `t` before `p`
`a.insert(p, i, j)`	Copies `a[i]`...`a[j-1]` before `p`
`a.erase(i)`	Removes `a[i]`
`a.erase(i, j)`	Removes `a[i]`...`a[j-1]`
`i = a.begin()`	Sets `i` so that `a[i]` is the first element
`j = a.end()`	Sets `j` so that `a[j-1]` is the last element
`t = a.front()`	Assigns the first element of `a` to `t`
`t = a.back()`	Assigns the last element of `a` to `t`
`n = a.size()`	Assigns the number of element of `a` to `n`
`n = a.empty()`	Assigns 1 to `n` if `a` is empty; 0 otherwise
`a.swap(b)`	Swaps the contents of `a` and `b`

The STL is an algorithm-oriented library like the numerical libraries that FORTRAN programmers have been using since the 1960s. The 62 *generic algorithms* in the STL are categorized by the type of iterator they use. There are five types of iterators: *Random Access*, *Bidirectional*, *Forward*, *Input*, and *Output*. These are illustrated by the diagram below. It shows that the five iterator categories are nested. For example, every Input iterator is also a Forward iterator, and every Forward iterator is also a Bidirectional iterator. It also shows what kind of operations can be performed on each type of iterator. For example, all iterators can be incremented (`++i`), but only Bidirectional and Random Access iterators can be decremented (`--i`).

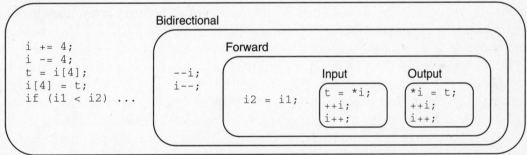

Table 14.4 lists some of the STL's generic algorithms. All seven of the container classes support Bidirectional iterators, so all containers can apply any of the algorithms in columns 2 through 5 of the table. But only `vector` and `deque` classes support Random Access iterators, so only instances of these classes can also apply the algorithms in the first column.

Example 14.11 shows how to use an STL `map` to maintain a personal telephone book. The elegance of the STL is apparent here. The code is self-documenting. The iterator `i` works like an ordinary integer index. But so do the key strings with the syntax:

```
m["Jones, Jenny"] = "379-0512";

m.erase("Baker, Sue");
```

Table 14.4 Algorithms Categorized by Iterator Type

Random Access	Bidirectional	Forward	Input	Output
sort()	copy_backward()	search()	find()	generate_n()
stable_sort()	reverse()	replace()	count()	fill_n()
partial_sort()	partition()	unique()	copy()	copy()
nth_element()	inplace_merge()	rotate()	equal()	
push_heap()		generate()	includes()	
pop_heap()		remove()	merge()	
make_heap()		fill()	max()	
sort_heap()			min()	
random_shuffle()			accumulate()	

EXAMPLE 14.11 Creating a Phone Book

This program uses a `map` to maintain a personal telephone directory. The class template takes three template parameters: the key type, the data type, and the comparison type. Here the person's name is the key and the telephone number is the data, so we use the `string` class for both the key type and the data type. The class `less<string>` provides for the ordinary lexicographical ordering on the keys:

```
#include <iostream.h>
#include <map.h>
#include <string.h>
int main ()
{
    typedef map< string, string, less<string> > mapType;
    mapType m;                              // the telephone book
    m["Jones, Jenny"] = "379-0512";
    m["Baker, Sue"] = "794-7935";
    m["Williams, Bill"] = "289-8085";
    m["Thomas, Tom"] = "379-1225";
    for (mapType::iterator i = m.begin(); i != m.end(); i++)
        cout << (*i).first << ": " << (*i).second << endl;
    m.erase("Baker, Sue");
    m.insert("Roberts, Bob", "289-0491");
    i = m.find("Thomas, Tom");
    cout << "Tom\'s number is " << (*i).second << endl;
    m.erase(i);
    for (i = m.begin(); i != m.end(); i++)
        cout << (*i).first << ": " << (*i).second << endl;
}
```

```
Baker, Sue: 794-7935
Jones, Jenny: 379-0512
Thomas, Tom: 379-1225
Williams, Bill: 289-8085
Tom's number is 379-1225
Jones, Jenny: 379-0512
Roberts, Bob: 289-0491
Williams, Bill: 289-8085
```

After inserting 4 records in our telephone book, we print the book and see that it is maintained in alphabetical order. Then we remove the listing for Sue Baker, insert a listing for Bob Roberts, find the listing for Tom Thomas, remove that listing, and then print the resulting updated book. Note that the `find()` function returns the location to the iterator `i`.

Review Questions

14.1   What is a *stream header*?

14.2   What is the difference between the C header `<string.h>` and the C++ header `<string>`?

14.3   How are the `List` and `Vector` classes defined in this book different from those defined in the STL?

14.4   What is the difference between the Standard C++ Library and proprietary libraries?

14.5   What is the purpose of the `assert()` function?

14.6   What is the purpose of the `#define` directive?

14.7   What is `wchar_t`?

14.8   What is a *string stream*?

14.9   What is *incore formatting*?

14.10 What is the difference between a set and a multiset?

14.11 What is the difference between a set and a map?

Supplementary Programming Problems

14.12 Write and test a program that counts the number of characters in an external text file.

14.13 Write and test a program that picks a card at random from an ordinary deck of 52 playing cards. Use the `time()`, `srand()`, and `rand()` functions as in Example 14.4.

14.14 Write and test a program that creates form letters like this:

> Dear Mr. Smith,
>   This is your lucky day! You have the unique opportunity to install aluminum siding on the Smith house at 1234 Main Street at an incredibly low price. This exclusive offer is available to you and the Smith family for only a limited time. So don't hesitate, Mr. Smith. Call today!

14.15 Write and test a program that counts the number of words in an external text file.

14.16 Write and test a program that counts the number of lines in an external text file.

14.17 Write and test a program that encodes an external text file by replacing each of its characters with the character that immediately follows it in the ASCII code.

Answers to Review Questions

14.1 A *stream header* is one of the nine header files that define stream classes in the Standard C++ Library: `<fstream>`, `<iomanip>`, `<ios>`, `<iostream>`, `<istream>`, `<ostream>`, `<sstream>`, `<fstreambuf>`, and `<strstream>`.

14.2 The C header `<string.h>` contains only functions for manipulating null-terminated arrays of characters (*i.e.*, C-strings). The C++ header `<string>` defines a `string` class similar to that in Chapter 12.

14.3 The `list` and `vector` classes defined in the STL include built-in iterator classes and algorithms such as `insert()` and `erase()`.

14.4 The Standard C++ Library is part of the ANSI/ISO standard specification of the C++ language. It specifies the 86 header files listed in Table 14.1. These define constants, functions, classes, and templates that should work with any C++ compiler in any software environment. Proprietary libraries such as those that Borland supplies with its C++ compiler work only with that compiler. They include many of the features of the Standard C++ Library. They also define special classes for creating I/O objects such as windows and menus.

14.5 The `assert()` function allows you to check certain conditions that should prevail at certain points in the program. The `assert()` function will terminate the program if the condition passed to it is not true.

14.6 The `#define` directive is used to define constants in the C programming language. (This is done with `const` in C++.) The directive is used in the C header files.

14.7 The `wchar_t` is a wide character type defined in the C header `<stddef.h>`. It is used for large alphabets, such as the Chinese and Japanese alphabets.

14.8 A *string stream* is an object that can access string of bytes in memory as if it were an external file. It works like an internal text file.

14.9 Incore formatting refers to the use of an output string stream for formatting the output before it is output. The name derives from the term "core" which referred to main memory in the 1950s.

14.10 The elements of a set must be unique. A multiset can have several copies of the same element.

14.11 A map can be regarded as a set whose elements have two components: a key and a data component.

Appendix A

The ASCII Code

Each character is stored as its ASCII[1] Code, which is an integer in the range 0 to 127. Note that the first 32 characters are *nonprinting characters*, so their symbols in the first column are indicated either with their control sequence or with their escape sequence. The *control sequence* of a nonprinting character is the combination of **Control** key and another key that is pressed on the keyboard to enter the character. For example, the *end-of-file character* (ASCII code 4) is entered with the `Ctrl-D` sequence. The *escape sequence* of a nonprinting character is the combination of the backslash character "\" (called the "control character") and a letter that is typed in C++ source code to indicate the character. For example, the *newline character* (ASCII code 10) is written "\n" in a C++ program.

Character	Description	Decimal	Octal	Hex	Binary
Ctrl-@	Null, end of string	0	0	0x0	0000 0000
Ctrl-A	Start of heading	1	01	0x1	0000 0001
Ctrl-B	Start of text	2	02	0x2	0000 0010
Ctrl-C	End of text	3	03	0x3	0000 0011
Ctrl-D	End of transmission, end of file	4	04	0x4	0000 0100
Ctrl-E	Enquiry	5	05	0x5	0000 0101
Ctrl-F	Acknowledge	6	06	0x6	0000 0110
\a	Bell, alert, system beep	7	07	0x7	0000 0111
\b	Backspace	8	010	0x8	0000 1000
\t	Horizontal tab	9	011	0x9	0000 1001
\n	Line feed, new line	10	012	0xa	0000 1010
\v	Vertical tab	11	013	0xb	0000 1011
\f	Form feed, new page	12	014	0xc	0000 1100
\r	Carriage return	13	015	0xd	0000 1101
Ctrl-N	Shift out	14	016	0xe	0000 1110
Ctrl-O	Shift in	15	017	0xf	0000 1111
Ctrl-P	Data link escape	16	020	0x10	0001 0000
Ctrl-Q	Device control 1, resume scroll	17	021	0x11	0001 0001
Ctrl-R	Device control 2	18	022	0x12	0001 0010
Ctrl-S	Device control 3, stop scroll	19	023	0x13	0001 0011
Ctrl-T	Device control 4	20	024	0x14	0001 0100
Ctrl-U	Negative acknowledgment	21	025	0x15	0001 0101
Ctrl-V	Synchronous idle	22	026	0x16	0001 0110

1. ASCII is an acronym for the American Standard Code for Information Interchange

Character	Description	Decimal	Octal	Hex	Binary
Ctrl-W	End transmission block	23	027	0x17	0001 0111
Ctrl-X	Cancel	24	030	0x18	0001 1000
Ctrl-Y	End of message, interrupt	25	031	0x19	0001 1001
Ctrl-Z	Substitute, exit	26	032	0x1a	0001 1010
Ctrl-[	Escape	27	033	0x1b	0001 1011
Ctrl-/	File separator	28	034	0x1c	0001 1100
Ctrl-]	Group separator	29	035	0x1d	0001 1101
Ctrl-^	Record separator	30	036	0x1e	0001 1110
Ctrl-_	Unit separator	31	037	0x1f	0001 1111
	Blank, space	32	040	0x20	0010 0000
!	Exclamation point	33	041	0x21	0010 0001
"	Quotation mark, double quote	34	042	0x22	0010 0010
#	Hash mark, number sign	35	043	0x23	0010 0011
$	Dollar sign	36	044	0x24	0010 0100
%	Percent sign	37	045	0x25	0010 0101
&	Ampersand	38	046	0x26	0010 0110
'	Apostrophe, single quote	39	047	0x27	0010 0111
(	Left parenthesis	40	050	0x28	0010 1000
)	Right parenthesis	41	051	0x29	0010 1001
*	Asterisk, star, times	42	052	0x2a	0010 1010
+	Plus	43	053	0x2b	0010 1011
,	Comma	44	054	0x2c	0010 1100
−	Dash, minus	45	055	0x2d	0010 1101
.	Dot, period, decimal point	46	056	0x2e	0010 1110
/	Slash	47	057	0x2f	0010 1111
0	Digit zero	48	060	0x30	0011 0000
1	Digit one	49	061	0x31	0011 0001
2	Digit two	50	062	0x32	0011 0010
3	Digit three	51	063	0x33	0011 0011
4	Digit four	52	064	0x34	0011 0100
5	Digit five	53	065	0x35	0011 0101
6	Digit six	54	066	0x36	0011 0110
7	Digit seven	55	067	0x37	0011 0111
8	Digit eight	56	070	0x38	0011 1000
9	Digit nine	57	071	0x39	0011 1001
:	Colon	58	072	0x3a	0011 1010
;	Semicolon	59	073	0x3s	0011 1011
<	Less than	60	074	0x3c	0011 1100
=	Equal to	61	075	0x3d	0011 1101
>	Greater than	62	076	0x3e	0011 1110

Character	Description	Decimal	Octal	Hex	Binary
?	Question mark	63	077	0x3f	0011 1111
@	Commercial at sign	64	0100	0x40	0100 0000
A	Letter capital A	65	0101	0x41	0100 0001
B	Letter capital B	66	0102	0x42	0100 0010
C	Letter capital C	67	0103	0x43	0100 0011
D	Letter capital D	68	0104	0x44	0100 0100
E	Letter capital E	69	0105	0x45	0100 0101
F	Letter capital F	70	0106	0x46	0100 0110
G	Letter capital G	71	0107	0x47	0100 0111
H	Letter capital H	72	0110	0x48	0100 1000
I	Letter capital I	73	0111	0x49	0100 1001
J	Letter capital J	74	0112	0x4a	0100 1010
K	Letter capital K	75	0113	0x4b	0100 1011
L	Letter capital L	76	0114	04xc	0100 1100
M	Letter capital M	77	0115	0x4d	0100 1101
N	Letter capital N	78	0116	0x4e	0100 1110
O	Letter capital O	79	0117	0x4f	0100 1111
P	Letter capital P	80	0120	0x50	0101 0000
Q	Letter capital Q	81	0121	0x51	0101 0001
R	Letter capital R	82	1022	0x52	0101 0010
S	Letter capital S	83	0123	0x53	0101 0011
T	Letter capital T	84	0124	0x54	0101 0100
U	Letter capital U	85	0125	0x55	0101 0101
V	Letter capital V	86	0126	0x56	0101 0110
W	Letter capital W	87	0127	0x57	0101 0111
X	Letter capital X	88	0130	0x58	0101 1000
Y	Letter capital Y	89	0131	0x59	0101 1001
Z	Letter capital Z	90	0132	0x5a	0101 1010
[	Left bracket	91	0133	0x5b	0101 1011
\	Backslash	92	0134	0x5c	0101 1100
]	Right bracket	93	0135	0x5d	0101 1101
^	Caret	94	0136	0x5e	0101 1110
_	Underscore	95	0137	0x5f	0101 1111
'	Accent grave	96	0140	0x60	0110 0000
a	Letter lowercase A	97	0141	0x61	0110 0001
b	Letter lowercase B	98	0142	0x62	0110 0010
c	Letter lowercase C	99	0143	0x63	0110 0011
d	Letter lowercase D	100	0144	0x64	0110 0100
e	Letter lowercase E	101	0145	0x65	0110 0101
f	Letter lowercase F	102	0146	0x66	0110 0110

Character	Description	Decimal	Octal	Hex	Binary
g	Letter lowercase G	103	0147	0x67	0110 0111
h	Letter lowercase H	104	0150	0x68	0110 1000
i	Letter lowercase I	105	0151	0x69	0110 1001
j	Letter lowercase J	106	0152	0x6A	0110 1010
k	Letter lowercase K	107	0153	0x6B	0110 1011
l	Letter lowercase L	108	0154	0x6C	0110 1100
m	Letter lowercase M	109	0155	0x6D	0110 1101
n	Letter lowercase N	110	0156	0x6	0110 1110
o	Letter lowercase O	111	0157	0x6F	0110 1111
p	Letter lowercase P	112	0160	0x70	0111 0000
q	Letter lowercase Q	113	0161	0x71	0111 0001
r	Letter lowercase R	114	0162	0x72	0111 0010
s	Letter lowercase S	115	0163	0x73	0111 0011
t	Letter lowercase T	116	0164	0x74	0111 0100
u	Letter lowercase U	117	0165	0x75	0111 0101
v	Letter lowercase V	118	0166	0x76	0111 0110
w	Letter lowercase W	119	0167	0x77	0111 0111
x	Letter lowercase X	120	0170	0x78	0111 1000
y	Letter lowercase Y	121	0171	0x79	0111 1001
z	Letter lowercase Z	122	0172	0x7a	0111 1010
{	Left brace	123	0173	0x7b	0111 1011
|	Pipe	124	0174	0x7c	0111 1100
}	Right brace	125	0175	0x7d	0111 1101
~	Tilde	126	0176	0x7e	0111 1110
Delete	Delete, rub out	127	0177	0x7f	0111 1111

Appendix B

C++ Keywords

C++ has 48 keywords. These special words are used to define the syntax of the language.

Keyword	Description	Example
asm	Allows information to be passed to the assembler directly	`asm ("check");`
auto	Storage class for objects that exist only within their own block	`auto int n;`
break	Terminates a loop or a `switch` statement	`break;`
case	Used in a `switch` statement to specify control expression	`switch (n/10)`
catch	Specifies actions to take when an exception occurs	`catch(error)`
char	An integer type	`char c;`
class	Specifies a class declaration	`class X { ... };`
const	Specifies a constant definition	`const int s = 32;`
continue	Jumps to beginning of next iteration in a loop	`continue;`
default	The "otherwise" case in a `switch` statement	`default: sum = 0;`
delete	Deallocates memory allocated by a `new` statement	`delete a;`
do	Specifies a `do..while` loop	`do {...} while ...`
double	A real number type	`double x;`
else	Specifies alternative in an `if` statement	`else n = 0;`
enum	Used to declare an enumeration type	`enum bool { ... };`
extern	Storage class for objects declared outside the local block	`extern int max;`
float	A real number type	`float x;`
for	Specifies a `for` loop	`for ( ; ; ) ...`
friend	Specifies a `friend` function in a class	`friend int f();`
goto	Causes execution to jump to a labeled statement	`goto error;`
if	Specifies an `if` statement	`if (n > 0) ...`
inline	Declares a function whose text is to be substituted for its call	`inline int f();`
int	An integer type	`int n;`
long	Used to define integer and real types	`long double x;`
new	Allocates memory	`int* p = new int;`
operator	Used to declare an operator overload	`X operator++();`
private	Specifies `private` declarations in a class	`private: int n;`
protected	Specifies `protected` declarations in a class	`protected: int n;`
public	Specifies `public` declarations in a class	`public: int n;`
register	Storage class specifier for objects stored in registers	`register int i;`
return	Statement that terminates a function and returns a value	`return 0;`

Keyword	Description	Example
short	An integer type	`short n;`
signed	Used to define integer types	`signed char c;`
sizeof	Operator that returns the number of bytes used to store an object	`n = sizeof(float);`
static	Storage class of objects that exist for the duration of the program	`static int n;`
struct	Specifies a structure definition	`struct X { ... };`
switch	Specifies a `switch` statement	`switch (n) { ... }`
template	Specifies a `template` class	`template <class T>`
this	Pointer that points to the current object	`return *this;`
throw	Used to generate an exception	`throw X();`
try	Specifies a block that contains exception handlers	`try { ... }`
typedef	Declares a synonym for an existing type	`typedef int Num;`
union	Specifies a structure whose elements occupy the same storage	`union z { ... };`
unsigned	Used to define integer types	`unsigned int b;`
virtual	Declares a member function that is defined in a subclass	`virtual int f();`
void	Designates the absence of a type	`void f();`
volatile	Declares objects that can be modified outside of program control	`int volatile n;`
while	Specifies a `while` loop	`while (n > 0) ...`

Appendix C

C++ Operators

This table lists all the operators in C++, grouping them by order of precedence. The higher-level precedence operators are evaluated before the lower-level precedence operators. For example, in the expression (a - b*c), the * operator will be evaluated first and the - operator second, because * has precedence level 13 which is higher than the level 12 precedence of -. The column labeled "Assoc." tells whether an operator is right associative or left associative. For example, the expression (a - b - c) is evaluated as ((a - b) - c) because - is left associative. The column labeled "Arity" tells whether an operator operates on one, two, or three operands (unary, binary, or ternary). The column labeled "Ovrldbl." tells whether an operator is overloadable. (See Chapter 8.)

Op	Description	Prec.	Assoc.	Arity	Ovrldbl.	Example
::	Global scope resolution	17	Right	Unary	No	::x
::	Class scope resolution	17	Left	Binary	No	X::x
.	Direct member selection	16	Left	Binary	No	s.len
->	Indirect member selection	16	Left	Binary	Yes	p->len
[]	Subscript	16	Left	Binary	Yes	a[i]
()	Function call	16	Left	n/a	Yes	Yes
()	Type construction	16	Left	n/a	Yes	int(ch)
++	Post-increment	16	Right	Unary	Yes	n++
--	Post-decrement	16	Right	Unary	Yes	n--
sizeof	Size of object or type	15	Right	Unary	No	sizeof(a)
++	Pre-increment	15	Right	Unary	Yes	++n
--	Pre-decrement	15	Right	Unary	Yes	--n
~	Bitwise NOT	15	Right	Unary	Yes	~s
!	Logical NOT	15	Right	Unary	Yes	!p
+	Positive	15	Right	Unary	Yes	+n
-	Negative	15	Right	Unary	Yes	-n
*	Dereference	15	Right	Unary	Yes	*p
&	Address	15	Right	Unary	Yes	&x
new	Allocation	15	Right	Unary	Yes	new p
delete	Deallocation	15	Right	Unary	Yes	delete p
()	Type conversion	15	Right	Binary	Yes	(int)ch
.*	Direct member selection	14	Left	Binary	No	x.*q
->*	Indirect member selection	14	Left	Binary	Yes	p->q
*	Multiplication	13	Left	Binary	Yes	m*n
/	Division	13	Left	Binary	Yes	m/n

Op	Description	Prec.	Assoc.	Arity	Ovrldbl.	Example
%	Remainder	13	Left	Binary	Yes	`m%n`
+	Addition	12	Left	Binary	Yes	`m + n`
–	Subtraction	12	Left	Binary	Yes	`m - n`
<<	Bit shift left	11	Left	Binary	Yes	`cout << n`
>>	Bit shift right	11	Left	Binary	Yes	`cin >> n`
<	Less than	10	Left	Binary	Yes	`x < y`
<=	Less than or equal to	10	Left	Binary	Yes	`x <= y`
>	Greater than	10	Left	Binary	Yes	`x > y`
>=	Greater than or equal to	10	Left	Binary	Yes	`x >= y`
==	Equal to	9	Left	Binary	Yes	`x == y`
!=	Not equal to	9	Left	Binary	Yes	`x != y`
&	Bitwise AND	8	Left	Binary	Yes	`s&t`
^	Bitwise XOR	7	Left	Binary	Yes	`s^t`
|	Bitwise OR	6	Left	Binary	Yes	`s|t`
&&	Logical AND	5	Left	Binary	Yes	`u && v`
||	Logical OR	4	Left	Binary	Yes	`u || v`
?:	Conditional expression	3	Left	Ternary	No	`u ? x : y`
=	Assignment	2	Right	Binary	Yes	`n = 22`
+=	Addition assignment	2	Right	Binary	Yes	`n += 8`
–=	Subtraction assignment	2	Right	Binary	Yes	`n -= 4`
*=	Multiplication assignment	2	Right	Binary	Yes	`n *= -1`
/=	Division assignment	2	Right	Binary	Yes	`n /= 10`
%=	Remainder assignment	2	Right	Binary	Yes	`n %= 10`
&=	Bitwise AND assignment	2	Right	Binary	Yes	`s &= mask`
^=	Bitwise XOR assignment	2	Right	Binary	Yes	`s ^= mask`
|=	Bitwise OR assignment	2	Right	Binary	Yes	`s |= mask`
<<=	Bit shift left assignment	2	Right	Binary	Yes	`s <<= 1`
>>=	Bit shift right assignment	2	Right	Binary	Yes	`s >>= 1`
`throw`	Throw exception	1	Right	Unary	Yes	`throw(22)`
,	Comma	0	Left	Binary	Yes	`++m,--n`

Appendix D

C++ Types

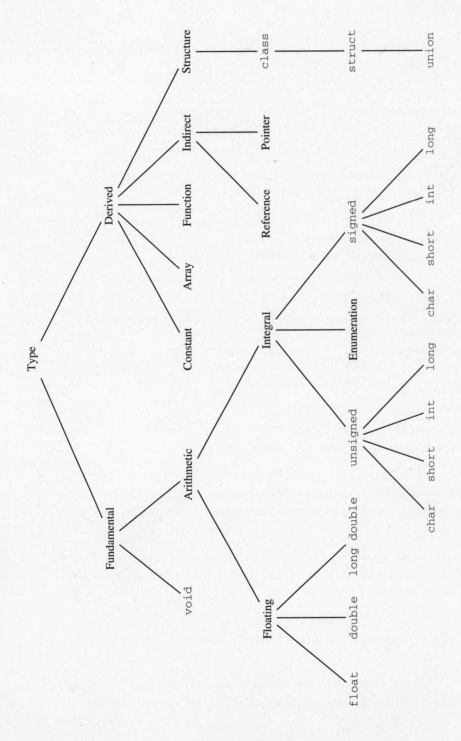

413

Appendix E

References

[Adams]

C++ An Introduction to Computing, by Joel Adams, Sanford Leestma, and Larry Nyhoff.
Prentice Hall, Englewood Cliffs, NJ (1995) 0-02-369402-5.

[Barton]

Scientific and Engineering C++, by John J. Barton and Lee R. Nackman.
Addison-Wesley Publishing Company, Reading, MA (1994) 0-201-53393-6.

[Bergin]

Data Abstraction, the Object-Oriented Approach Using C++, by Joseph Bergin.
McGraw-Hill, Inc., New York, NY (1994) 0-07-911691-4.

[Bronson]

A First Book of C++, by Gary J. Bronson.
West Publishing Company, St. Paul, MN (1995) 0-314-04236-9.

[Budd]

Classic Data Structures in C++, by Timothy A. Budd.
Addison-Wesley Publishing Company, Reading, MA (1994) 0-201-50889-3.

[Capper]

Introducing C++ for Scientists, Engineers and Mathematicians, by D. M. Capper.
Springer-Verlag, London (1994) 3-540-19847-4.

[Cargill]

C++ Programming Style, by Tom Cargill.
Addison-Wesley Publishing Company, Reading, MA (1992) 0-201-56365-7.

[Carrano]

Data Abstraction and Problem Solving with C++, by Frank M. Carrano.
Benjamin/Cummings Publishing Company, Redwood City, CA (1993) 0-8053-1226-9.

[Carroll]

Designing and Coding Reusable C++, by Martin D. Carroll and Margaret A. Ellis.
Addison-Wesley Publishing Company, Reading, MA (1995) 0-201-51284-X.

[Cline]

C++ FAQs, by Marshall P. Cline and Greg A. Lomow.
Addison-Wesley Publishing Company, Reading, MA (1995) 0-201-58958-3.

[Coplien]

Advanced C++, Programming Styles and Idioms, by James O. Coplien.
Addison-Wesley Publishing Company, Reading, MA (1992) 0-201-54855-0.

[Deitel]

C++ How to Program, by H. M. Deitel and P. J. Deitel.
Prentice Hall, Englewood Cliffs, NJ (1994) 0-13-117334-0.

[Dewhurst]

Programming in C++, Second Edition, by Stephen C. Dewhurst and Kathy T. Stark.
Prentice Hall, Englewood Cliffs, NJ (1995) 0-13-182718-9.

[Ellis]

The Annotated C++ Reference Manual, by Margaret A. Ellis and Bjarne Stroustrup.
Addison-Wesley Publishing Company, Reading, MA (1992) 0-201-51459-1.

[Friedman]

Problem Solving, Abstraction, and Design Using C++, by F. L. Friedman and E. B. Koffman.
Addison-Wesley Publishing Company, Reading, MA (1994) 0-201-52649-2.

[Graham]

Learning C++, by Neill Graham.
McGraw-Hill, Inc, New York, NY (1991) 0-07-023983-5.

[Hansen]

The C++ Answer Book, by Tony L. Hansen.
Addison-Wesley Publishing Company, Reading, MA (1990) 0-201-11497-6.

[Headington]

Data Abstraction and Structures Using C++, by Mark R. Headington and David D. Riley.
D. C. Heath and Company, Lexington, MA (1994) 0-669-29220-6.

[Horowitz]

Fundamentals of Data Structures in C++, by Ellis Horowitz, Sartaj Sahni, and Dinesh Mehta.
W. H. Freeman and Company, New York, NY (1995) 0-7167-8292-8.

[Johnsonbaugh]

Object-Oriented Programming in C++, by Richard Johnsonbaugh and Martin Kalin.
Prentice Hall, Englewood Cliffs, NJ (1995) 0-02-360682-7.

[Knuth1]

The Art of Computer Programming, Volume 1: Fundamental Algorithms, Second Edition,
by Donald E. Knuth.
Addison-Wesley Publishing Company, Reading, MA (1973) 0-201-03809-9.

[Knuth2]

The Art of Computer Programming, Volume 2: Seminumerical Algorithms, Second Edition,
by Donald E. Knuth.
Addison-Wesley Publishing Company, Reading, MA (1981) 0-201-03822-6.

[Knuth3]

The Art of Computer Programming, Volume 3: Sorting and Searching, by Donald E. Knuth.
Addison-Wesley Publishing Company, Reading, MA (1973) 0-201-03803-X.

[Ladd]

C++ Templates and Tools, by Scott Robert Ladd.
M&T Books, New York, NY (1995) 0-55851-437-6.

[Lippman]

The C++ Primer, Second Edition, by Stanley B. Lippman.
Addison-Wesley Publishing Company, Reading, MA (1991) 0-201-54848-8.

[Meyers]

Effective C++, by Scott Meyers.
Addison-Wesley Publishing Company, Reading, MA (1992).

[Model]

Data Structures, Data Abstraction: A Contemporary Introduction Using C++, by M. L. Model.
Prentice Hall, Englewood Cliffs, NJ (1994) 0-13-088782-X.

[Murray]

C++ Strategies and Tactics, by Robert B. Murray.
Addison-Wesley Publishing Company, Reading, MA (1993) 0-201-56382-7.

[Nagler]

Learning C++, by Eric Nagler.
West Publishing Company, St. Paul, MN (1993) 0-314-02464-6.

[Nelson]

C++ Programmers Guide to the Standard Template Library, by Mark Nelson.
IDG Books Worldwide, Inc., Foster City, CA (1995) 0-56884-314-3.

[Oualline]

Practical C++ Programming, by Steve Oualline.
O'Reilly & Associates, Sebastopol, CA (1995) 1-56592-139-9.

[Perry]

An Introduction to Object-Oriented Design in C++, by Jo Ellen Perry and Harold D. Levin.
Addison-Wesley Publishing Company, Reading, MA (1996) 0-201-76564-0.

[Plauger1]

The Standard C Library, by P. J. Plauger.
Prentice Hall, Englewood Cliffs, NJ (1992) 0-13-131509-9.

[Plauger2]

The Draft Standard C++ Library, by P. J. Plauger.
Prentice Hall, Englewood Cliffs, NJ (1995) 0-13-117003-1.

[Pohl.1]

Object-Oriented Programming Using C++, by Ira Pohl.
The Benjamin/Cummings Publishing Company, Inc, Redwood City, CA (1993) 0-8053-5384-4.

[Pohl.2]

C++ for Pascal Programmers, Second Edition, by Ira Pohl.
The Benjamin/Cummings Publishing Company, Inc, Redwood City, CA (1994) 0-8053-3158-1.

[Prata]

C++ Primer Plus, by Stephen Prata.
Waite Group Press, Corte Madera, CS (1991) 0-878739-02-6.

[Ranade & Zamir]

C++ Primer for C Programmers, by Jay Ranade and Saba Zamir.
McGraw-Hill, Inc., New York, NY (1994) 0-07-051487-9.

[Rudd]

    C++ Complete, by Anthony Rudd.

    John Wiley & Sons, Inc, New York, NY (1994) 0-471-06565-X.

[Satir]

    C++: The Core Language, by Gregory Satir and Doug Brown.

    O'Reilly & Associates, Sebastopol, CA (1995) 0-56592-116-X.

[Savitch]

    Problem Solving with C++, by Walter Savitch.

    Addison-Wesley Publishing Company, Reading, MA (1996) 0-8053-7440-X.

[Sedgewick]

    Algorithms in C++, by Robert Sedgewick.

    Addison-Wesley Publishing Company, Reading, MA (1992) 0-201-51059-6.

[Sengupta]

    C++ Object-Oriented Data Structures, by Saumyendra Sengupta and Carl Phillip Korobkin.

    Springer-Verlag, New York, NY (1994) 0-387-94194-0

[Sessions]

    Class Construction in C and C++, by Roger Sessions.

    PTR Prentice Hall, Englewood Cliffs, NJ (1992) 0-13-630104-5.

[Shammas]

    Advanced C++, by Namir Clement Shammas.

    SAMS Publishing, Carmel, IN (1992) 0-672-30158-X.

[Stepanov]

    "The Standard Template Library," *Technical Report HPL-94-34*, by A. A. Stepanov and M. Lee.

    Hewlett-Packard Laboratories, April 1994.

[Stroustrup1]

    The C++ Programming Language, Second Edition, by Bjarne Stroustrup.

    Addison-Wesley Publishing Company, Reading, MA (1991) 0-201-53992-6.

[Stroustrup2]

    The Design and Evolution of C++, by Bjarne Stroustrup.

    Addison-Wesley Publishing Company, Reading, MA (1994) 0-201-54330-3.

[Teale]

    C++ IOStreams, by Steve Teale.

    Addison-Wesley Publishing Company, Reading, MA (1993) 0-201-59641-5.

[Wang]

    C++ with Object-Oriented Programming, by Paul S. Wang.

    PWS Publishing Company, Boston, MA (1994) 0-534-19644-6.

[Weiss]

    Data Structures and Algorithm Analysis in C++, by Mark Allen Weiss.

    Benjamin/Cummings Publishing Company, Redwood City, CA (1994) 0-8053-5443-3.

[Winston]

    On to C++, by Patrick Henry Winston.

    Addison-Wesley Publishing Company, Reading, MA (1994) 0-201-58043-8.

Appendix F

Pre-Defined Functions

This appendix describes the pre-defined functions provided in the C++ libraries. Each entry lists the function name, its prototype, a brief description of what it does, and the header file where it is declared.

Function	Prototype and Description	Header File
abort()	`void abort();` Aborts the program.	`<stdlib.h>`
abs()	`int abs(int n);` Returns the absolute value of `n`.	`<stdlib.h>`
acos()	`double acos(double x);` Returns the inverse cosine (arccosine) of `x`.	`<math.h>`
asin()	`double asin(double x);` Returns the inverse sine (arcsine) of `x`.	`<math.h>`
atan()	`double atan(double x);` Returns the inverse tangent (arctangent) of `x`.	`<math.h>`
atof()	`double atof(const char* s);` `Returns the floating-point number represented literally in the string s.`	`<stdlib.h>`
atoi()	`int atoi(const char* s);` Returns the integer represented literally in the string `s`.	`<stdlib.h>`
atol()	`long atol(const char* s);` Returns the integer represented literally in the string `s`.	`<stdlib.h>`
bad()	`int ios::bad();` Returns nonzero if `badbit` is set; returns 0 otherwise.	`<iostream.h>`

bsearch()	`void* bsearch(const void* x, void* a,`
	`                size_t n,`
	`                size_t s,`
	`                int (*cmp)`
	`                    (const void*, const void*));`
	`Implements the Binary Search Algorithm to search for x in the sorted array a of n elements each of size s using the function *cmp to compare any two such elements. If found, a pointer to the element is returned; otherwise, the NULL pointer is returned.`
		`<stdlib.h>`

ceil()	`double ceil(double x);` Returns `x` rounded up to the next whole number.	`<math.h>`

`clear()`	`void ios::clear(int n=0);` Changes stream state to `n`.	`<iostream.h>`
`clearerr()`	`void clearerr(FILE* p);` Clears the end-of-file and error flags for the file `*p`.	`<stdio.h>`
`close()`	`void fstreambase::close();` Closes the file attached to the owner object.	`<fstream.h>`
`cos()`	`double cos(double x);` Returns the inverse cosine of `x`.	`<math.h>`
`cosh()`	`double cosh(double x);` Returns the hyperbolic cosine of `x`: $(e^x + e^{-x})/2$.	`<math.h>`
`difftime()`	`double difftime(time_t t1, time_t t0);` Returns time elapsed (in seconds) from time `t0` to time `t1`.	`<math.h>`
`eof()`	`int ios::eof();` Returns nonzero if `eofbit` is set; returns 0 otherwise.	`<iostream.h>`
`exit()`	`void exit(int n);` Terminates the program and returns `n` to the invoking process.	`<stdlib.h>`
`exp()`	`double exp(double x);` Returns the exponential of `x`: e^x.	`<math.h>`
`fabs()`	`double fabs(double x);` Returns the absolute value of `x` .	`<math.h>`
`fail()`	`int ios::fail();` Returns nonzero if `failbit` is set; returns 0 otherwise.	`<iostream.h>`
`fclose()`	`int fclose(FILE* p);` Closes the file `*p` and flushes all buffers. Returns 0 if successful; returns `EOF` otherwise.	`<stdio.h>`
`fgetc()`	`int fgetc(FILE* p);` Reads and returns the next character from the file `*p` if possible; returns `EOF` otherwise.	`<stdio.h>`
`fgets()`	`char* fgets(char* s, int n, FILE* p);` Reads the next line from the file `*p` and stores it in `*s`. The "next line" means either the next `n-1` characters or all the characters up to the next endline character, whichever comes first. The `NUL` character is appended to the characters stored in `s`. Returns s if successful; returns `NULL` otherwise.	`<stdio.h>`

`fill()`	`char ios::fill();`
	Returns the current fill character.
	`char ios::fill(char c);`
	Changes the current fill character to `c` and returns the previous fill character.
		`<iostream.h>`

`flags()`	`long ios::flags();`
	Returns the current format flags.
	`long ios::flags(long n);`
	Changes the current format flags to `n`; returns previous flags.
		`<iostream.h>`

`floor()`	`double floor(double x);` Returns `x` rounded down to the next whole number.	`<math.h>`
`flush()`	`ostream& ostream::flush();` Flushes the output buffer and returns the updates stream.	`<iostream.h>`

fopen()	`FILE* fopen(const char* p, const char* s);` Opens the file `*p` and returns the address of the structure that represents the file if successful; returns `NULL` otherwise. The string `s` determines the file's *mode*: `"r"` for *read*, `"w"` for *write*, `"a"` for *append*, `"r+"` for reading and writing an existing file, `"w+"` for reading and writing an existing file, and `"a+"` for reading and appending an existing file.	`<stdio.h>`
fprintf()	`int fprintf(FILE* p, const char* s, ... );` Writes formatted output to the file `*p`. Returns the number of characters printed if successful; otherwise it returns a negative number.	`<stdio.h>`
fputc()	`int fputc(int c, FILE* p);` Writes character `c` to the file `*p`. Returns the character written or `EOF` if unsuccessful.	`<stdio.h>`
fputs()	`int fputs(const char* s, FILE* p);` Writes string `s` to the file `*p`. Returns a nonnegative integer if successful; otherwise it returns `EOF`.	`<stdio.h>`

fread()	`size_t fread(void* s, size_t k, size_t n,`
	`            FILE* p);`
	Reads up to `n` items each of size `k` from the file `*p` and stores them at location `s` in memory. Returns the number of items read.
		`<stdio.h>`

fscanf()	`int fscanf(FILE* p, const char* s, ... );` Reads formatted input from the file `*p` and stores them at location `s` in memory. Returns `EOF` if end of file is reached; otherwise it returns the number of items read into memory.	`<stdio.h>`
fseek()	`int fseek(FILE* p, long k, int base);` Repositions the position marker of the file `*p` `k` bytes from its base, where `base` should be `SEEK_SET` for the beginning of the file, `SEEK_CUR` for the current position of the file marker, or `SEEK_END` for the end of the file. Returns 0 if successful.	`<stdio.h>`
ftell()	`long ftell(FILE* p);` Returns the location of the position marker in file `*p` or returns -1.	`<stdio.h>`

fwrite()	`size_t fwrite(void* s, size_t k, size_t n,`
	`             FILE* p);`
	Writes `n` items each of size `k` to the file `*p` and returns the number written.
		`<stdio.h>`

gcount()	`int istream::gcount();` Returns the number of characters most recently read.	`<iostream.h>`

get()	`int istream::get();`
	`istream& istream::get(signed char& c);`
	`istream& istream::get(unsigned char& c);`
	`istream& istream::get(signed char* b, int n,`
	`                      char e='\n');`
	`istream& istream::get(unsigned char* b, int n,`
	`                      char e='\n');`
	Reads the next character `c` from the `istream`. The first version returns `c` or `EOF`. The last two versions read up to `n` characters into `b`, stopping when `e` is encountered.
		`<iostream.h>`

getc()	`int getc(FILE* p);` Same as `fgetc()` except implemented as a macro.	`<stdio.h>`
getchar()	`int getchar();` Returns the next character from standard input or returns `EOF`.	`<stdio.h>`
gets()	`char* gets(char* s);` Reads next line from standard input and stores it in s. Returns `s` or `NULL` if no characters are read.	`<stdio.h>`
good()	`int ios::good();` Returns nonzero if stream `state` is zero; returns zero otherwise.	`<iostream.h>`
ignore()	`istream& ignore(int n=1, int e=EOF);` Extracts up to `n` characters from stream, or up to character `e`, whichever comes first. Returns the stream.	`<iostream.h>`
isalnum()	`int isalnum(int c);` Returns nonzero if `c` is an alphabetic or numeric character; returns 0 otherwise.	`<ctype.h>`
isalpha()	`int isalpha(int c);` Returns nonzero if `c` is an alphabetic character; otherwise returns 0.	`<ctype.h>`
iscntrl()	`int iscntrl(int c);` Returns nonzero if `c` is a control character; otherwise returns 0.	`<ctype.h>`
isdigit()	`int isdigit(int c);` Returns nonzero if `c` is a digit character; otherwise returns 0.	`<ctype.h>`
isgraph()	`int isgraph(int c);` Returns nonzero if `c` is any non-blank printing character; otherwise returns 0.	`<ctype.h>`
islower()	`int islower(int c);` Returns nonzero if `c` is a lowercase alphabetic character; otherwise returns 0.	`<ctype.h>`
isprint()	`int isprint(int c);` Returns nonzero if `c` is any printing character; otherwise returns 0.	`<ctype.h>`
ispunct()	`int ispunct(int c);` Returns nonzero if `c` is any punctuation mark, except the alphabetic characters, the numeric characters, and the blank; otherwise returns 0.	`<ctype.h>`
isspace()	`int isspace(int c);` Returns nonzero if `c` is any white-space character, including the blank `' '`, the form feed `'\f'`, the newline `'\n'`, the carriage return `'\r'`, the horizontal tab `'\t'`, and the vertical tab `'\v'`; otherwise returns 0.	`<ctype.h>`
isupper()	`int isupper(int c);` Returns nonzero if `c` is an uppercase alphabetic character; otherwise returns 0.	`<ctype.h>`
isxdigit()	`int isxdigit(int c);` Returns nonzero if `c` is one of the 10 digit characters or one of the 12 hexadecimal digit letters: `'a'`, `'b'`, `'c'`, `'d'`, `'e'`, `'f'`, `'A'`, `'B'`, `'C'`, `'D'`, `'E'`, or `'F'`; otherwise returns 0.	`<ctype.h>`

`labs()`	`long labs(long n);` Returns absolute value of `n`.	`<stdlib.h>`
`log()`	`double log(double x);` Returns the natural logarithm (base e) of `x`.	`<math.h>`
`log10()`	`double log10(double x);` Returns the common logarithm (base 10) of `x`.	`<math.h>`
`memchr()`	`void* memchr(const void* s, int c, size_t k);` Searches the `k` bytes of memory beginning at `s` for character `c`. If found, the address of its first occurrence is returned. Returns `NULL` otherwise.	`<string.h>`

`memcmp()`	`int memcmp(const void* s1, const void* s2,`
	`        size_t k);`
	`Compares  the k bytes of memory beginning at`
	`s1 with the k bytes of memory beginning at s2`
	`and returns a negative, zero, or a positive`
	`integer according to whether the first string`
	`is lexicographically less than, equal to, or`
	`greater than the second string.`
		`<string.h>`

`memcpy()`	`void* memcpy(const void* s1, const void* s2,`
	`        size_t k);`
	`Copies  the k bytes of memory beginning at s2`
	`into memory location s1 and returns s1.`
		`<string.h>`

`memmove()`	`int memmove(const void* s1, const void* s2,`
	`        size_t k);`
	`Same as memcpy() except strings may overlap.`
		`<string.h>`

`open()`	`void fstream::open(const char* f, int m,`
	`                int p=filebuf::openprot);`
	`void ifstream::open(const char* f,`
	`                int m=ios::in,`
	`                int p=filebuf::openprot);`
	`void ofstream::open(const char* f,`
	`                int m=ios::out,`
	`                int p=filebuf::openprot);`
	Opens the file `f` in mode `m` with protection `p`.
		`<fstream.h>`

`peek()`	`int istream:: peek();` Returns next character (or `EOF`) from stream without extracting it.	`<iostream.h>`
`pow()`	`double pow(double x, double y);` Returns `x` raised to the power `y` (x^y).	`<math.h>`

`precision()`	`int ios::precision();`
	`int ios::precision(int k);`
	Returns the current precision for the stream. The second version changes the current precision to `k` and returns the old precision.
		`<iostream.h>`

`tolower()`	`int tolower(int c);` Returns the lowercase version of `c` if `c` is an uppercase alphabetic character; otherwise returns `c`.	`<ctype.h>`
`toupper()`	`int toupper(int c);` Returns the uppercase version of `c` if `c` is a lowercase alphabetic character; otherwise returns `c`.	`<ctype.h>`

AppendixG

Hexadecimal Numbers

Humans normally use the base 10 numbering system. This is called the *decimal* system for the Greek word *deka* for "ten." Our ancient ancestors learned it by counting with their 10 fingers.

Computers have only 2 fingers (*i.e.*, there are only 2 possible values for each bit), so the *binary* system works well for computers. But the trouble with binary numbers is that their representations require long strings of bits. For example, 1996 is represented as 11111001100 in binary. Most humans find long strings like that difficult to process.

Binary numbers are easy to convert to other bases if the base is a power of 2. For example, conversion between binary and octal (base $8 = 2^3$) merely requires grouping the binary bits into groups of 3 and interpreting each triplet as an octal digit. For example, to convert the binary numeral 11111001100 write 11,111,001,100 = 3714. Here, 11 converts to 3, 111 converts to 7, 001 converts to 1, and 100 converts to 4. Conversion from octal back to binary is just as simple. For example, 2650 converts to 10110101000, which is 1448 in decimal. Note that octal numerals use only the first 8 decimal digits: 0, 1, 2, 3, 4, 5, 6, 7.

After 8, the next power of 2 is 16. Using that base makes the numerals even shorter. This is called the *hexadecimal* system (from the Greek *hex* + *deka* for "six" + "ten"). Conversion between binary and hexadecimal is just as simple as it is between binary and octal. For example, to convert the binary numeral 10111010100 to hexadecimal, group the bits into groups of 4 (from right to left) and then translate each group into the corresponding hexadecimal digit: 101,1101,0100 = 5d4. Here, 101 converts to 5, 1101 converts to 11, and 0100 converts to 4. The hexadecimal digits 10, 11, 12, 13, 14, and 15 are denoted by the first six letters of the alphabet: a, b, c, d, e, f.

The *output manipulators* dec, hex, and oct are used for converting different bases:

EXAMPLE G.1

This shows how both the value and the address of a variable can be printed:

```
#include <iostream.h>
main()
{
    int n = 1492;  //  base 10
    cout << "Base  8: n = " << oct << n << endl;
    cout << "Base 10: n = " << n << endl;
    cout << "Base 16: n = " << hex << n << endl;
}
```

```
Base  8: n = 2724
Base 10: n = 1492
Base 16: n = 5d4
```

Here the manipulator `oct` is used to convert the next output to octal form. Note that the output reverts back to decimal until the `hex` manipulator is used.

The next example shows how to input integers in octal and hexadecimal. Octal numerals are denoted with a `0` prefix, and hexadecimal numerals are denoted with a `0x` prefix:

EXAMPLE G.2

This shows how both the value and the address of a variable can be printed:

```
#include <iostream.h>
main()
{
    int n;
    cout << "Enter an octal numeral (use 0 prefix): ";
    cin >> n;
    cout << "Base  8: n = " << oct << n << endl;
    cout << "Base 10: n = " << dec << n << endl;
    cout << "Base 16: n = " << hex << n << endl;
    cout << "Enter a decimal numeral: ";
    cin >> n;
    cout << "Base  8: n = " << oct << n << endl;
    cout << "Base 10: n = " << dec << n << endl;
    cout << "Base 16: n = " << hex << n << endl;
    cout << "Enter a hexadecimal numeral (use 0x prefix): ";
    cin >> n;
    cout << "Base  8: n = " << oct << n << endl;
    cout << "Base 10: n = " << dec << n << endl;
    cout << "Base 16: n = " << hex << n << endl;
}
```

```
Enter an octal numeral (use 0 prefix): 0777
Base  8: n = 777
Base 10: n = 511
Base 16: n = 1ff
Enter a decimal numeral: 511
Base  8: n = 777
Base 10: n = 511
Base 16: n = 1ff
Enter a hexadecimal numeral (use 0x prefix): 0x1ff
Base  8: n = 777
Base 10: n = 511
Base 16: n = 1ff
```

Index